How to
Airbrush Pin-Ups

Frank Season

Published by:
ArtKulture
An Imprint of Wolfgang Publications

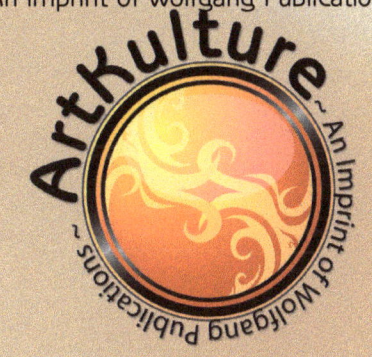

PO Box 223 • Stillwater, MN 55082
www.wolfpub.com

Legals

Published in 2009 by Wolfgang Publications Inc.,
PO Box 223, Stillwater MN 55082

© Wolfgang Publications, 2009

All rights reserved. With the exception of quoting brief passages for the purposes of review no part of this publication may be reproduced without prior written permission from the publisher.

The information in this book is true and complete to the best of our knowledge. All recommendations are made without any guarantee on the part of the author or publisher, who also disclaim any liability incurred in connection with the use of this data or specific details.

We recognize that some words, model names and designations, for example, mentioned herein are the property of the trademark holder. We use them for identification purposes only. This is not an official publication.

ISBN-13: 978-1-929133-80-2
ISBN-10: 1-929133-80-4

Printed and bound in U.S.A.

How-to Airbrush Pin-Ups

One - Steve Driscoll
　　Transparent Paint for a real-life Glow 6

Two - Edward Reed
　　Working in the Best Vargas Tradition 30

Three - Steve Nunez
　　Versatility is the Key 44

Four - Tom Nguyen
　　A Pencil Drawing with Color 58

Five - Steve Leahy
　　Working on a Small Scale 80

Six - Susan Heidi
　　Quality Takes Time 94

Seven - Elizabeth Austin
　　Beautiful Eyes and Great Color 118

Sources/Catalog 142

Acknowledgements

At ArtKulture and Wolfgang (ArtKulture's parent company), we've produced plenty of how-to books. Books like *Airbrush 101* and *Advanced Airbrush Art* use a format similar to that seen here. There is one huge difference, however, between those books and this one. The sequences in those books took only one day, or possibly one full day and part of a second, to shoot. Most of the sequences seen here required that the artist put up with the photographer for three and four days. This means working together in small studios, often not much bigger than a very small bedroom, for the better part of a week.

For their patience, and for sharing the many secrets learned over years and years of painting, we are eternally grateful to the seven artists seen in this book. Two of the artists, Edward Reed and Steve Nunez, went so far as to send in their own images. All the artists wrote the captions, so the words are their own, with only minimal editing.

At Wolfgang Publications we are grateful to our seven guest artists: Liz Austin, Steve Driscoll, Susan Heidi, Steve Leahy, Tom Nguyen, Steve Nunez and Edward Reed. More information on these talented individuals can be found on the Sources page at the back of the book.

Introduction

Interest in both airbrushes and pin-ups are at an all time high. Yet, no one (we know of) has tried to produce a book that explains how to use an airbrush to create a perfect pin-up.

Rather than using a more conventional how-to format, we've chosen to give you a look at how seven different artists create their pin-ups. Some of the artists are well known, while others toil away in relative obscurity. Each approaches the topic in a unique fashion. Some use transparent paint, while others use opaque pigments. Most use acrylics, though at least one creates with true watercolors. None of them, at least in the sequences illustrated in this book, use urethanes (aka: automotive paints) with all their disposal and toxicity issues.

The word pin-up is rather vague. The definition is at best murky. Does the word pin-up mean erotic and overtly sexual, or does it mean an image that is more subtle. Something more along the lines of what Alberto Vargas created more than forty years ago - a painting that creates sexual tension with subtle suggestion, the right pose, and pure beauty.

In this case, we've tried to stay in the later camp. Most of the work seen in *How to Airbrush Pin-Ups* contains what Edward Reed calls "a certain innocence." The images are sexy partly for what they don't show. The artists who created the images understand that sometimes it's what you can't see that makes an image, or a woman, sexy.

Each chapter contains a Q&A with the artist, a chance for the reader to learn first hand how each artist started their career, how they achieve the correct skin tones, and which paints and airbrushes they prefer.

Though the interviews are important, the majority of each chapter is made up by a series of sequential photos that show the pin-up as it develops. From the first sketch to the final eyelash, we've tried to leave out none of the steps. Captions for the chapters are provided by the artist themselves, so they can explain in their own words why they added violet to the skin tone to create a shadow, or prefer frisket for masking instead of paper cutouts.

In the end, the book is only another tool meant to help in your quest to create beautiful pin-ups. All the tools in the world don't make great art. Good art comes from people who practice, practice, practice.

Chapter One

Steve Driscoll

Transparent Paint for a real-life Glow

Though he might be best known for his pin-up images, many of which grace motorcycle tanks and the panels of hot rods, Steve Driscoll is a very versatile artist. And though the sequence seen here was done in his home-studio, he is also the airbrush artist at a sizable body and paint shop, TJ Design, in Shakopee, Minnesota. The image seen here was created over a number of days. Each painting session started about 10:00 AM and ran to roughly 3:00 PM. The schedule was dictated by the fact that Steve had to be in the shop both early in the morning and later in the afternoon. Work

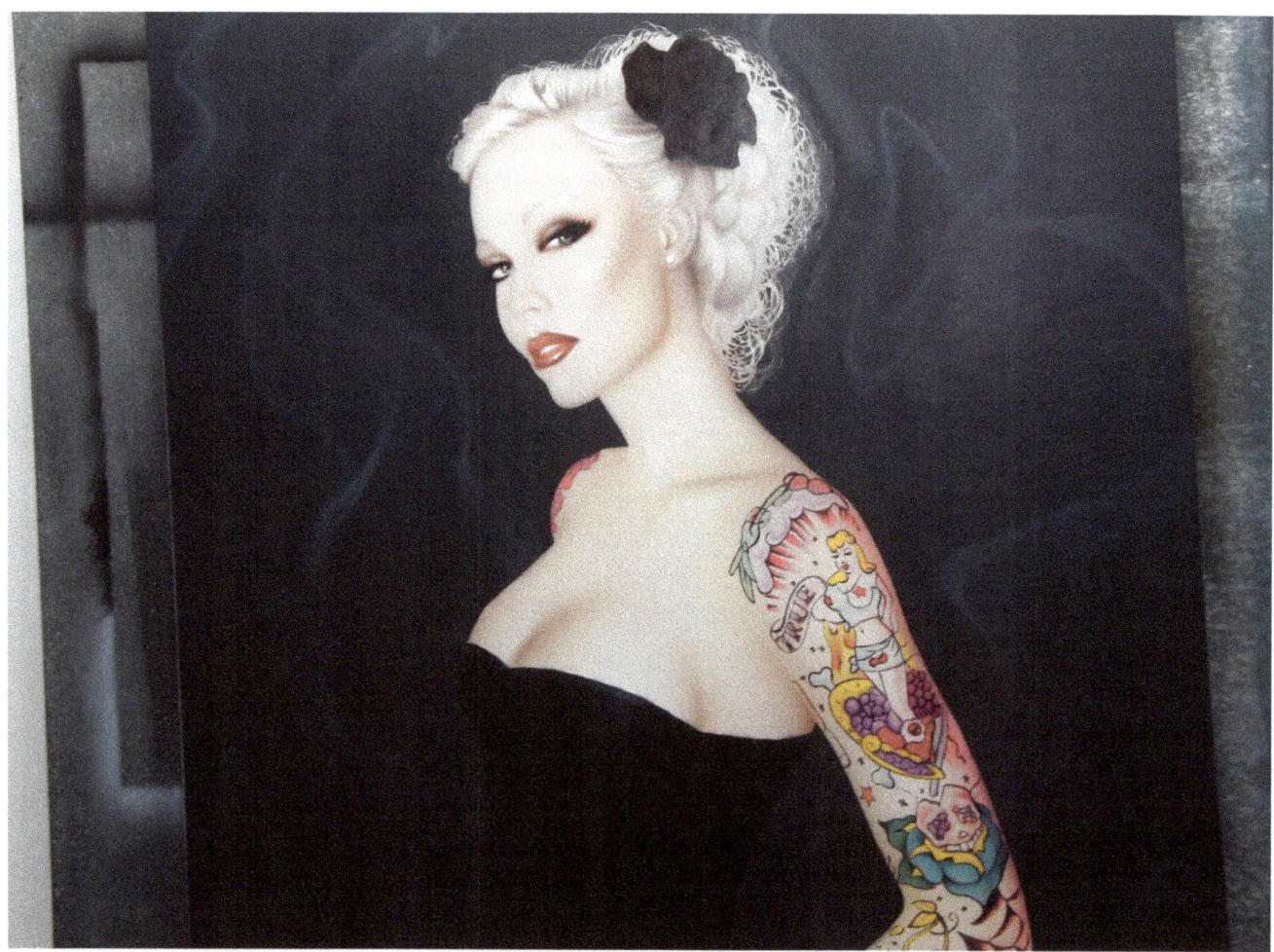

Creating a pin-up portrait of the beautiful Sabina Kelly gives me the opportunity to paint her platinum blonde hair, light-toned skin, and stunning tattoo work. A big challenge.

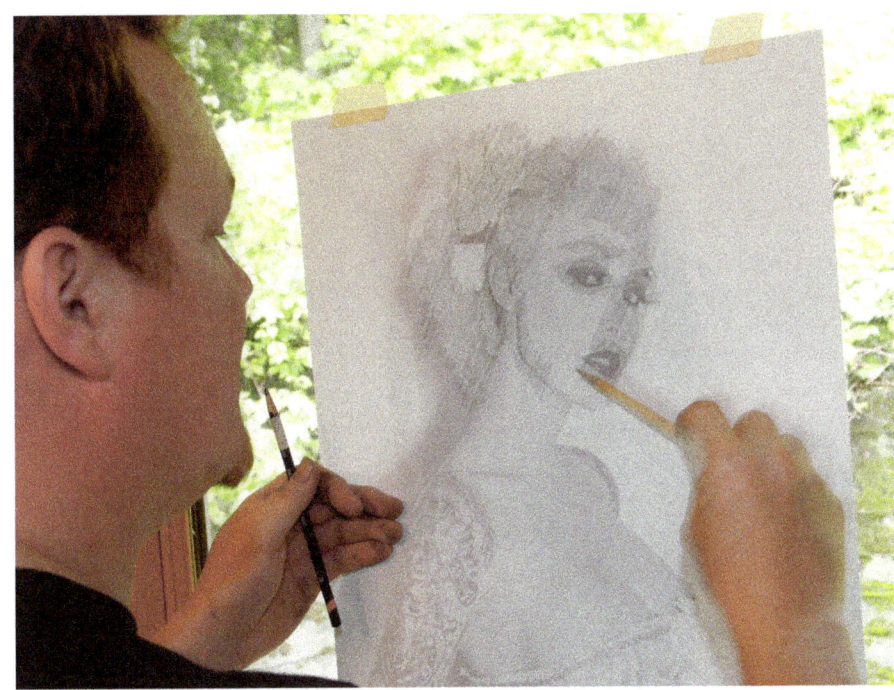

Steve is extremely comfortable with the airbrush, to the point where he prefers to use nothing else, "If I could, I wouldn't use anything except an airbrush," explains Steve. "There are times though when I use a hand brush, like for eyelashes and, in this case, outlining the tattoos. For these tasks Steve prefers Windsor Newton brushes. When he's all done the image won't be converted to a limited run of prints, because Steve doesn't typically sell prints. In most cases, his art goes to the person who commissioned the painting.

My first step is to transfer the image to the illustration board. I hold a copy of the picture up to a window as if it's a light box so I can see the image...

on the panel seen here was sandwiched into a normal workday.

Like a number of artists seen in this book, Steve did this painting with transparent acrylic paint. Unlike some other artists, Steve likes to use big paper cutouts as masks, in lieu of frisket.

The most detailed and difficult part of this particular image isn't the eyes or the face, but rather the tattoo on Sabina's left arm. Creating the tattoo required multiple masks, numerous color changes, detail work done with a hand brush, and enormous amounts of patience.

Steve reports that doing detail work like the tattoo or the eyes, isn't necessarily hard, in the conventional sense, but that it does require concentration.

Speaking of time, the creation of this particular panel required five separate four to five hour sessions. And while you might think that starting and stopping (in one case for over a week) on a big project like this would be hard, Steve says it's almost the opposite. "Sometimes it's good to step away from the painting for a few days. That way when you come back you're fresh and don't fee like this is just work."

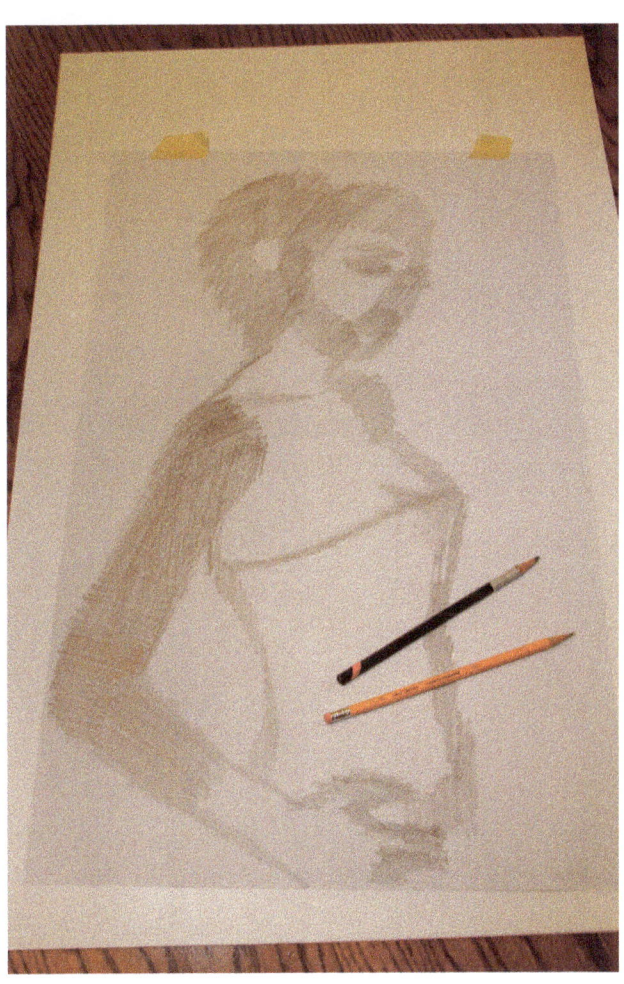

...and don't miss any detail. I go over the edges of the image with a pencil as shown, you can see how the graphite is transferred to the back of the image.

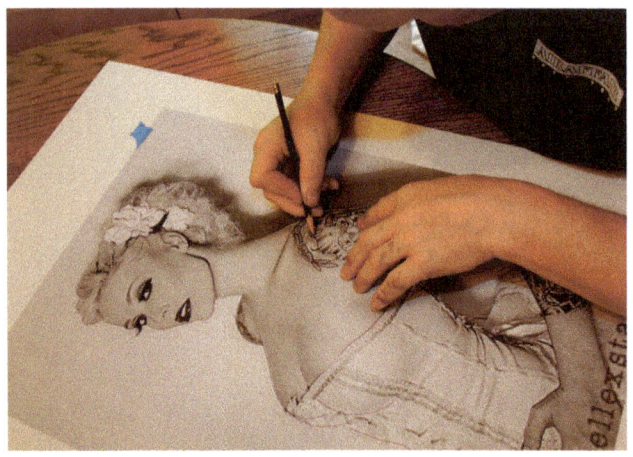

1. I now trace Sabina's outline onto the board with a hard pencil. Make sure to tape down the image so it can't move while you work.

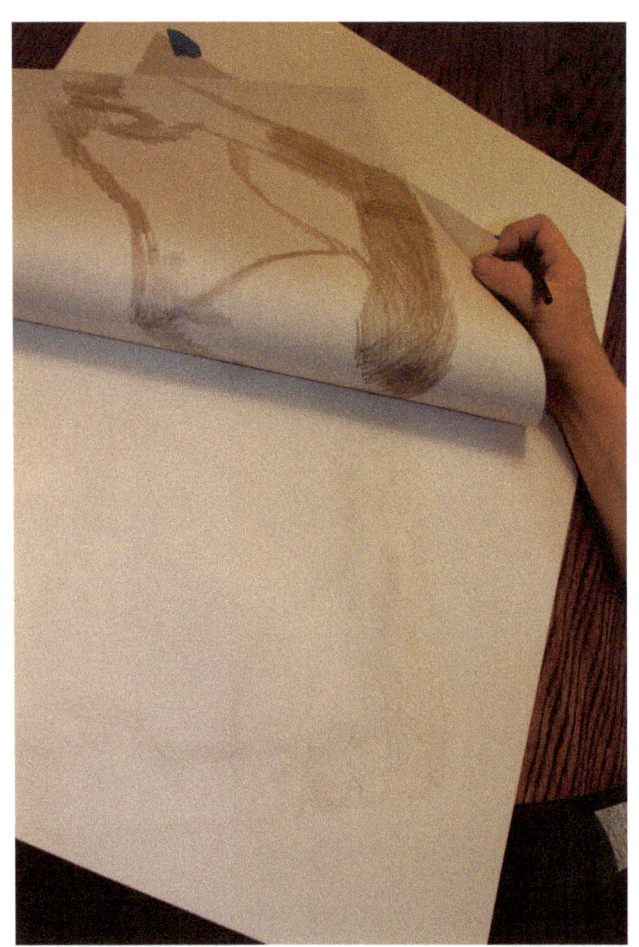

2. Look close and you can see how the details of the image are transferred to the board.

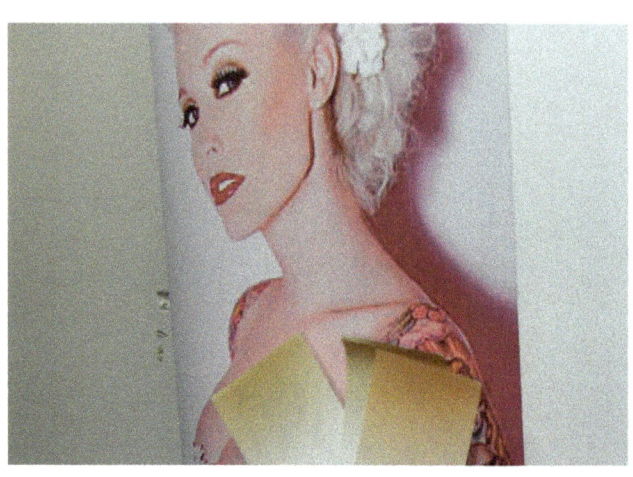

3. I spray some samples of my flesh tones to find one that best suits the tones in the reference photo.

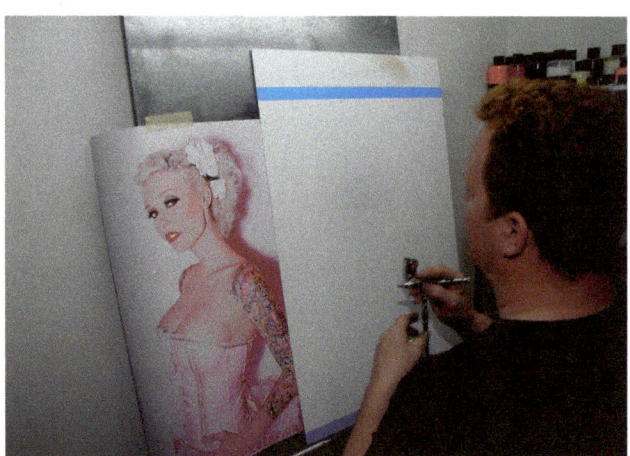

4. I start airbrushing like this is the only color I have. I'll build all the structure and detail I can with this first transparent color.

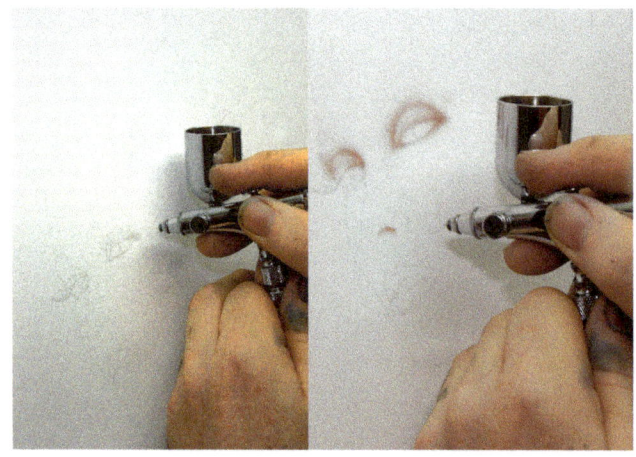

5. Now I'm using the airbrush to contour and shade the structure.

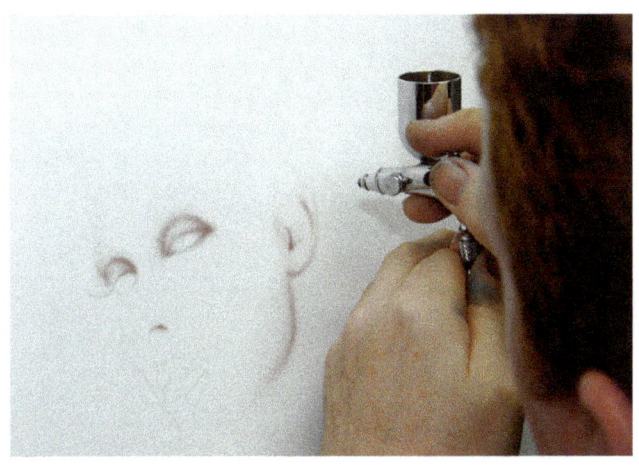

1. My philosophy is, "you use the shadows to push things away..."

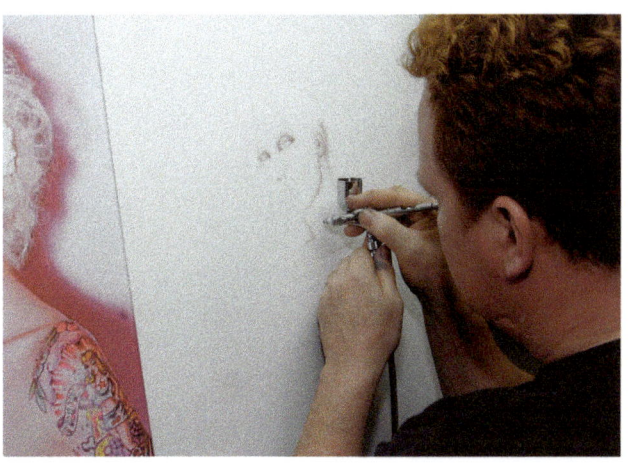

2. "...and the highlights to pull things forward."

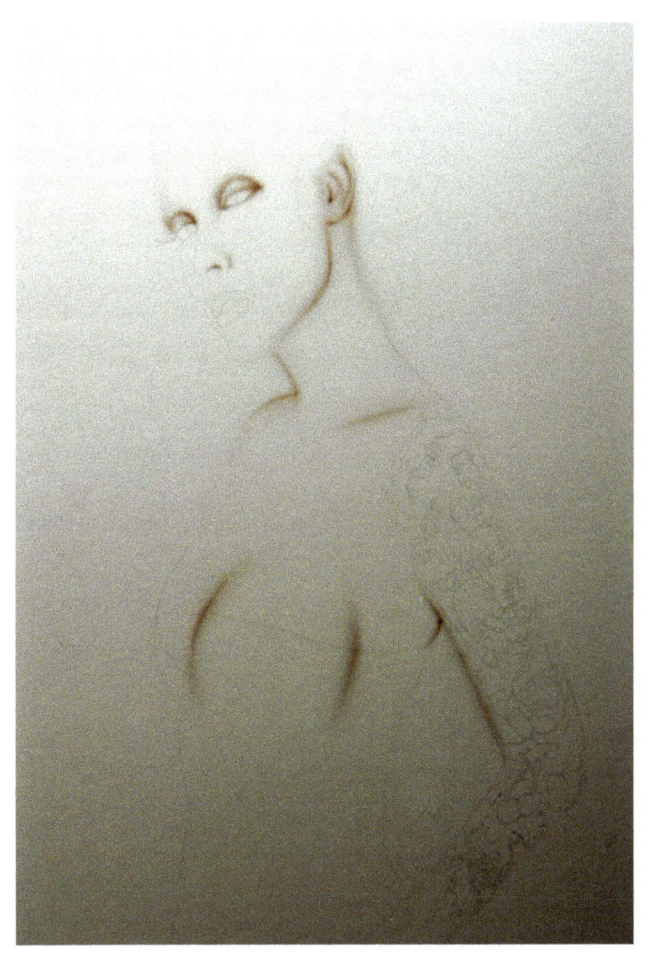

3. At this point I'm mostly creating shadows...

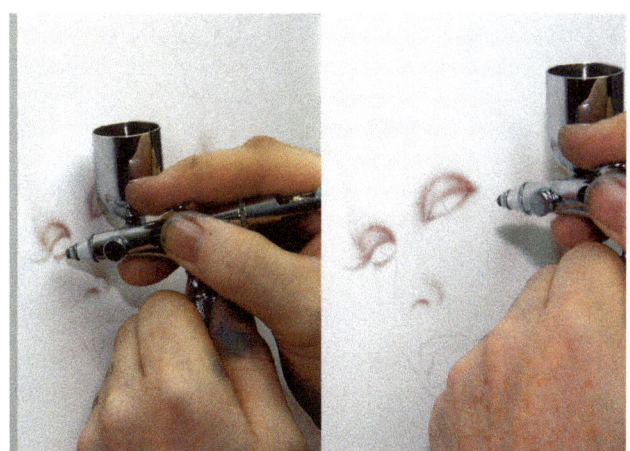

4. ...and the outlines of body parts.

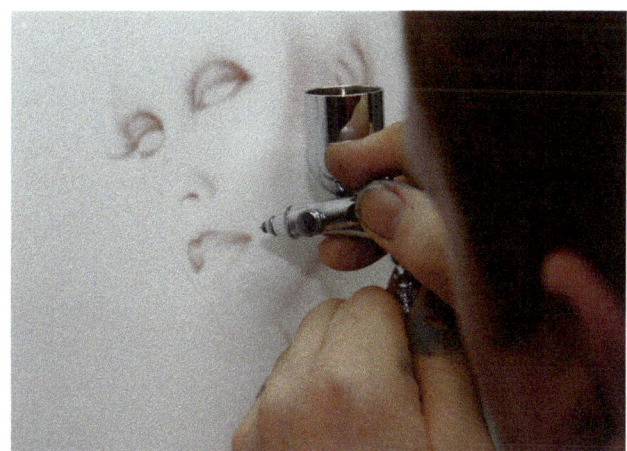

5. Here you can see the eyes are partly formed, and I'm working on the lips.

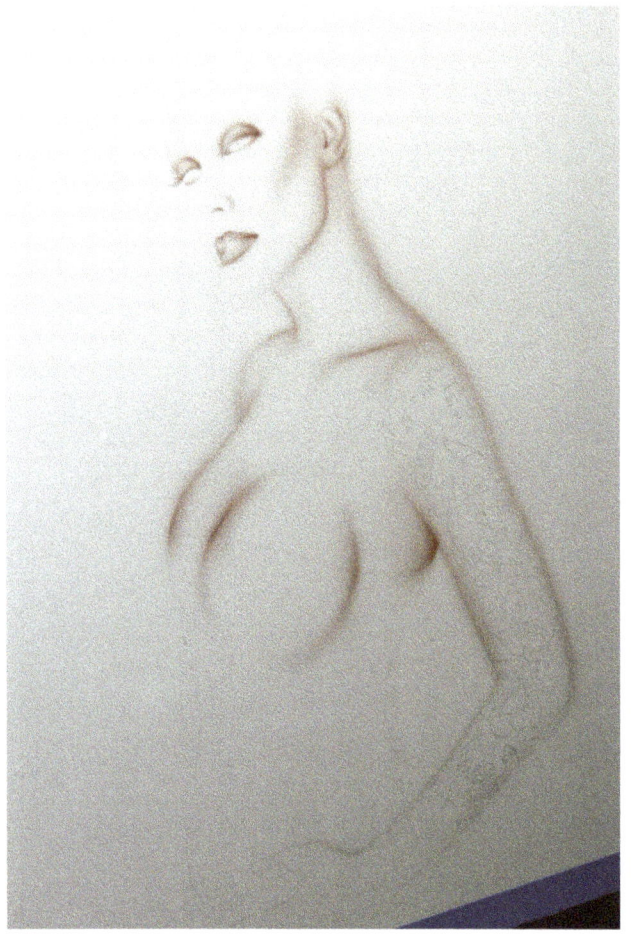

1. I continue to build the skin tones, even over the tattoos.

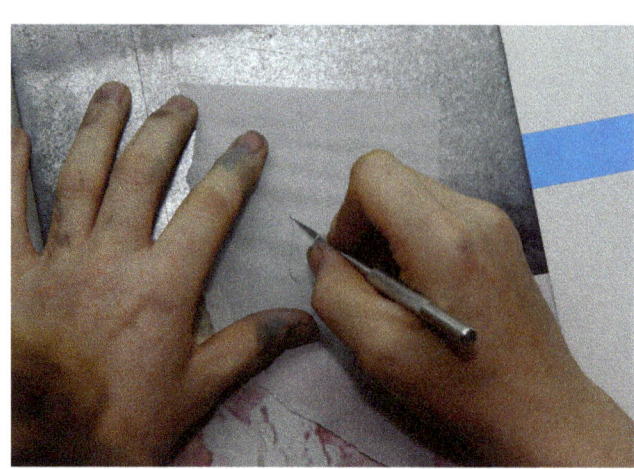

2. With a piece of tracing paper, I draw out the bridge of the nose.

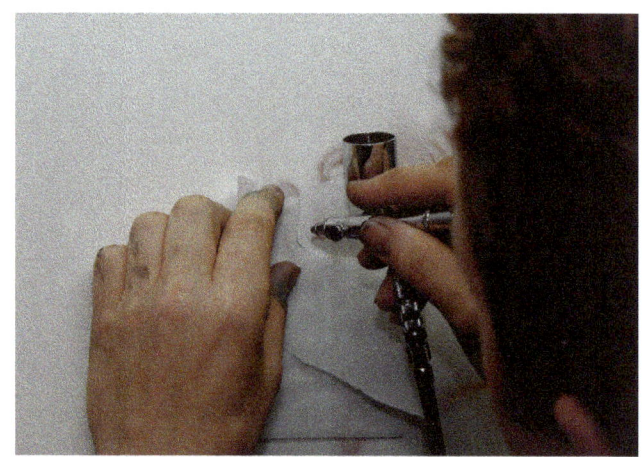

3. This gives me a hand-held shield to create a sharp shadow.

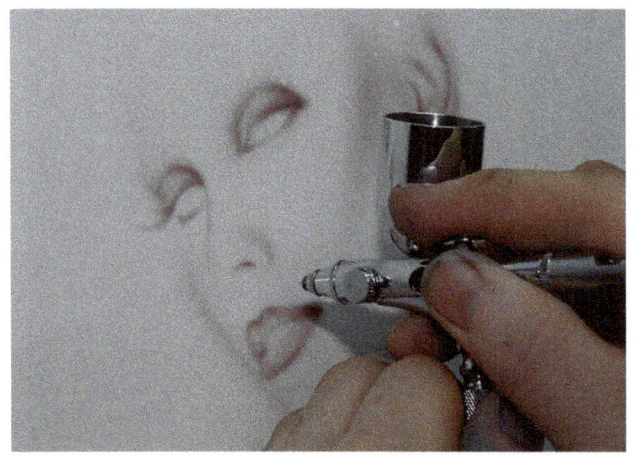

4. When trying to achieve a soft natural portrait, never outline anything...

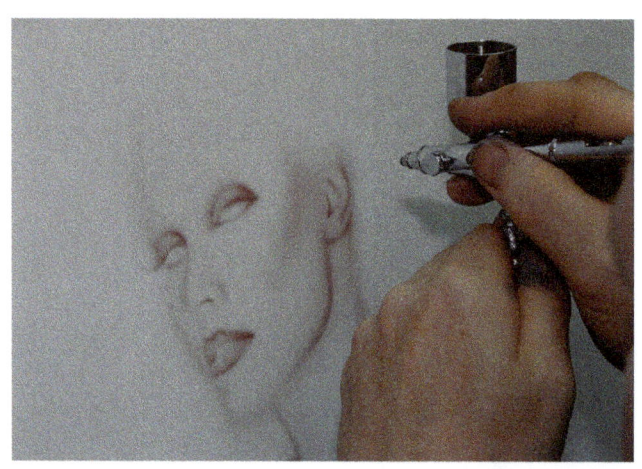

5. ...always soften any sharp strokes by doing a soft fade next to the edge.

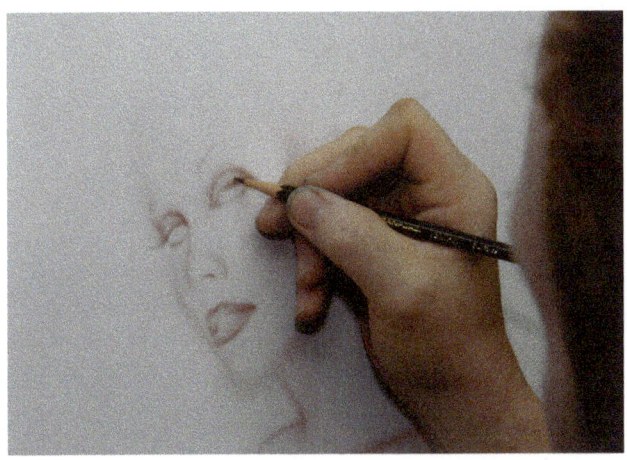

1. I redraw any facial details that are beginning to get faint from the painting.

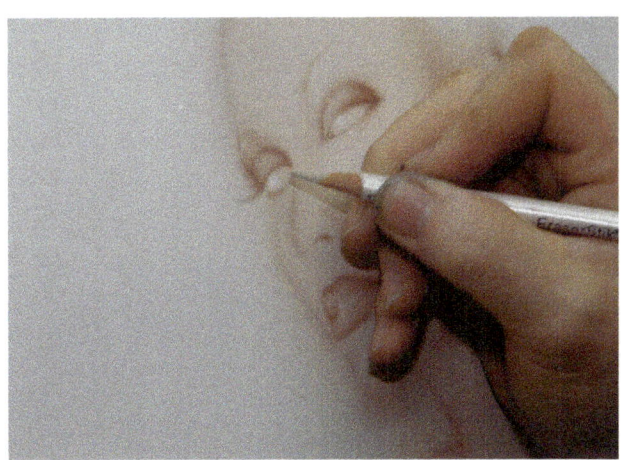

4. With a stick eraser I start to develop my highlights, starting in the eyes I work my way out.

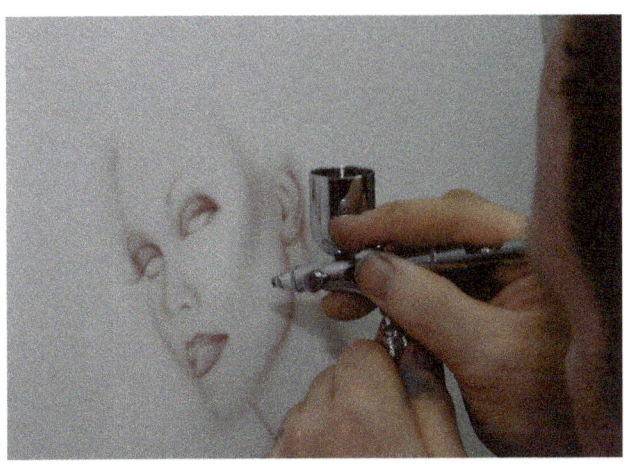

2. I continue to define the features by laying down more of my flesh tone.

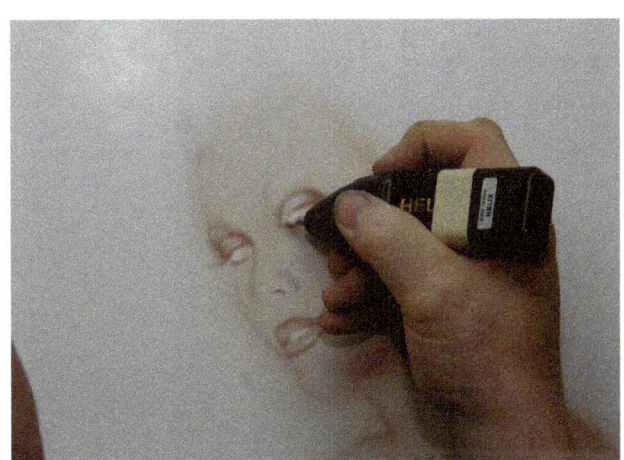

5. For the sharper more stark highlights I use an electric eraser.

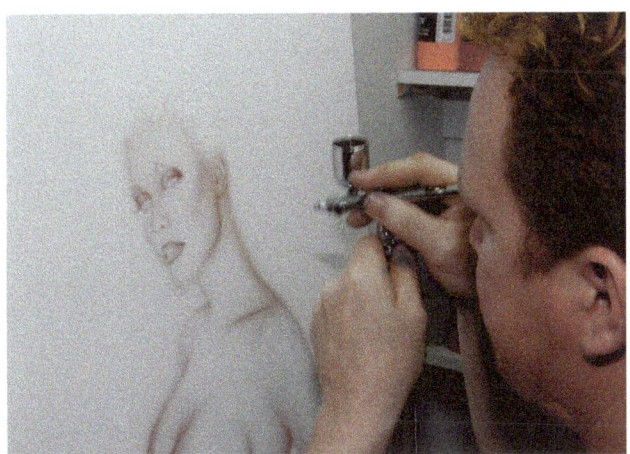

3. After finishing the contour of the face and figure I back away from the surface and mist paint over the entire figure.

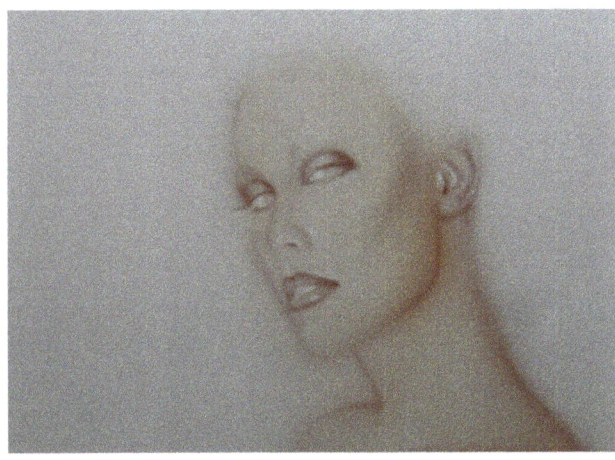

6. Now the fullness of the face starts to show.

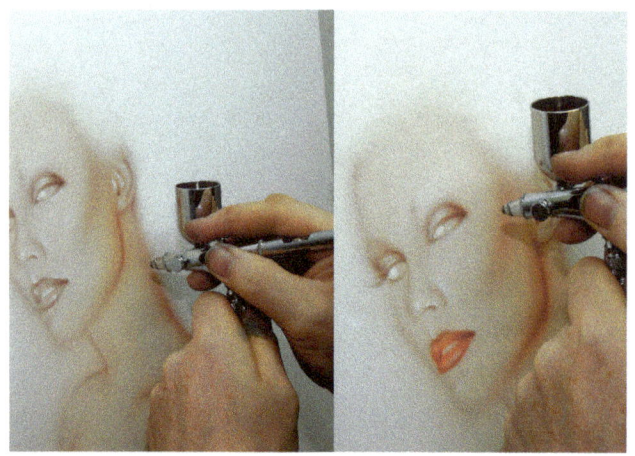

1. Now I add bright red to my flesh tone to start brightening the skin.

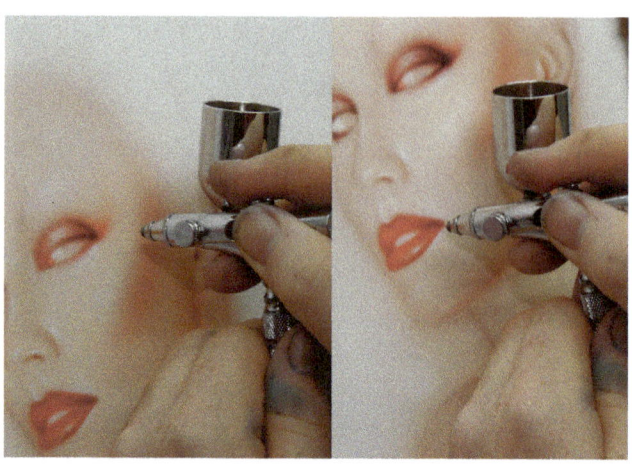

4. Notice how the darker colors push that area back, setting the eyes deeper in the face.

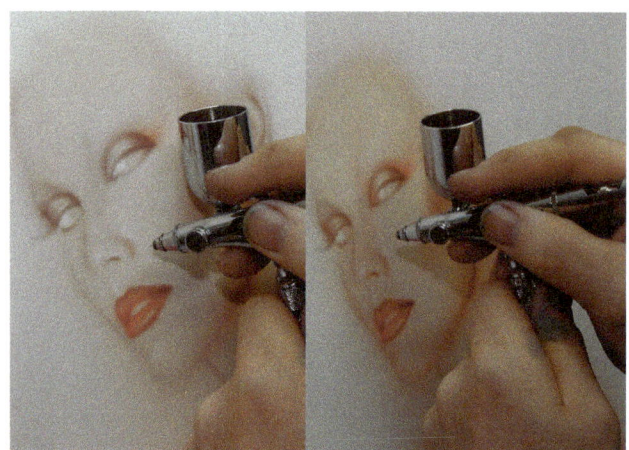

2. Adding reds to the shadows helps to develop richer, darker shadows.

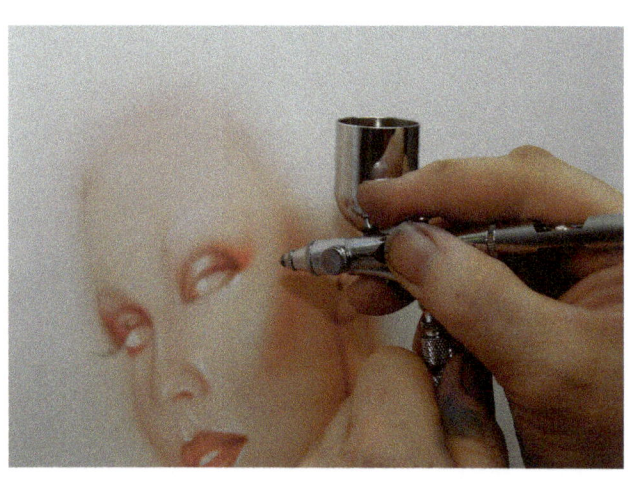

3. I continue to add red to the facial features as needed.

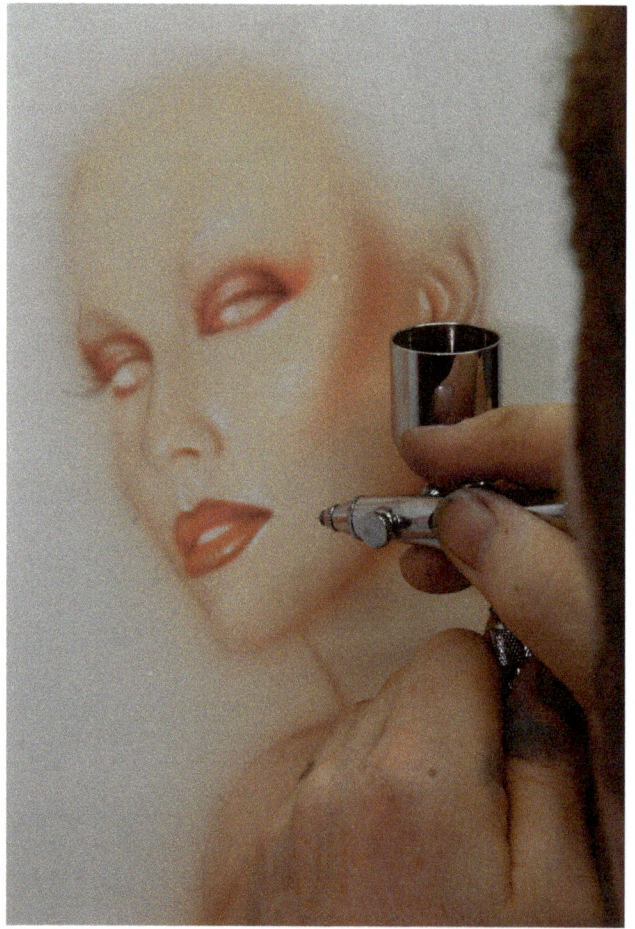

5. Adding a few drops of violet and smoke I can further develop and darken the shadows.

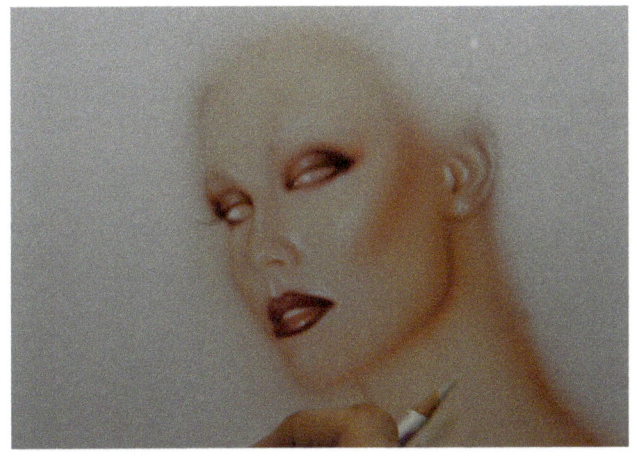

After darkening the shadows I redo the highlights.

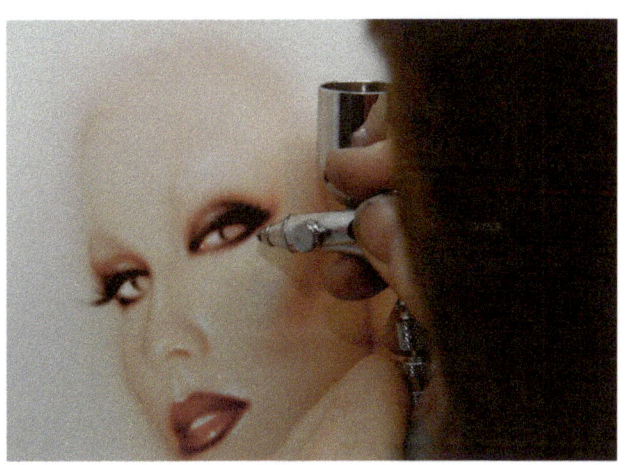

Now I define the iris of the eyes...

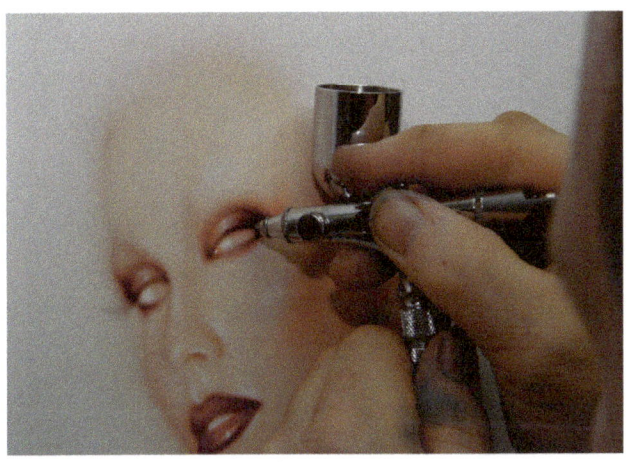

Adding black to the paint mix I develop the darkest parts around the eyes.

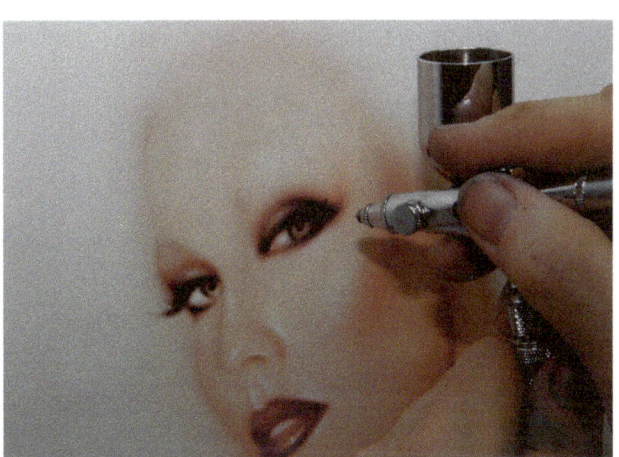

...and the pupils.

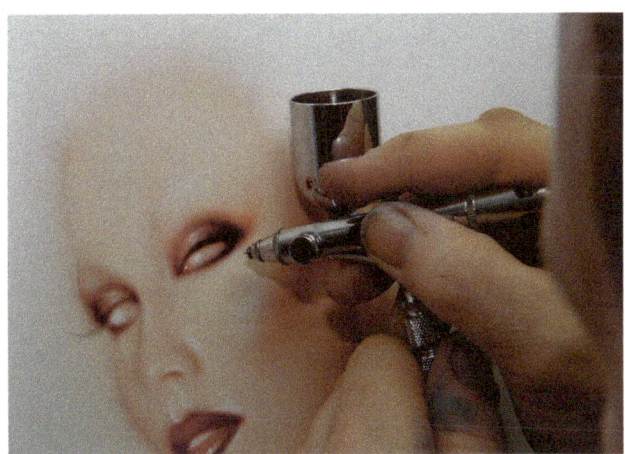

I try to keep the lower lid pretty tight, but soft enough to be subtle.

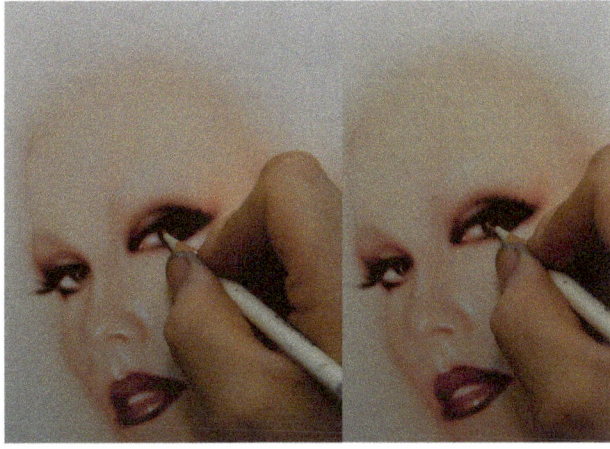

Using the stick eraser I soften the iris so later I can add color to the eyes.

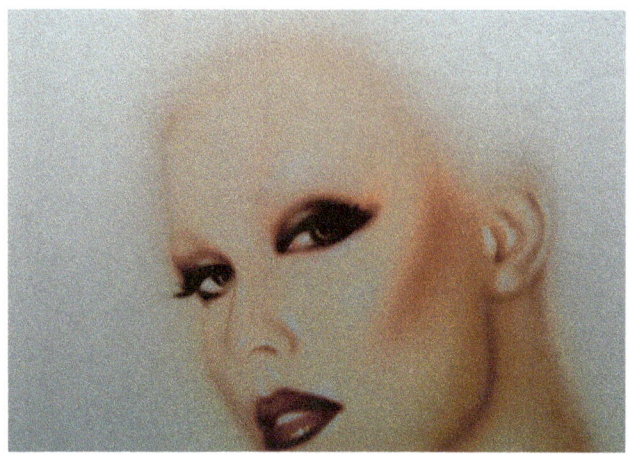

1. This progress show shows development of the facial features so far.

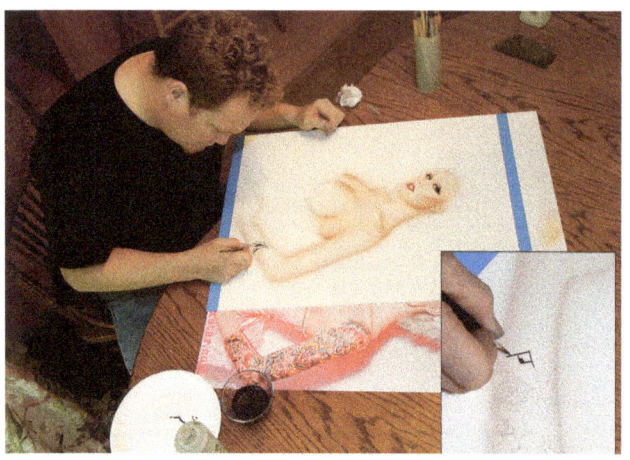

2. After mixing black, violet and white I start to paint the outlines of the tattoos.

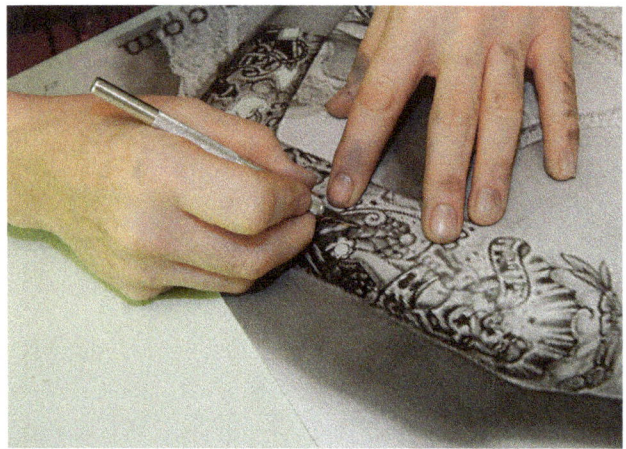

3. Using one of the copies of the reference picture, I start to cut out the colored parts of the tattoo.

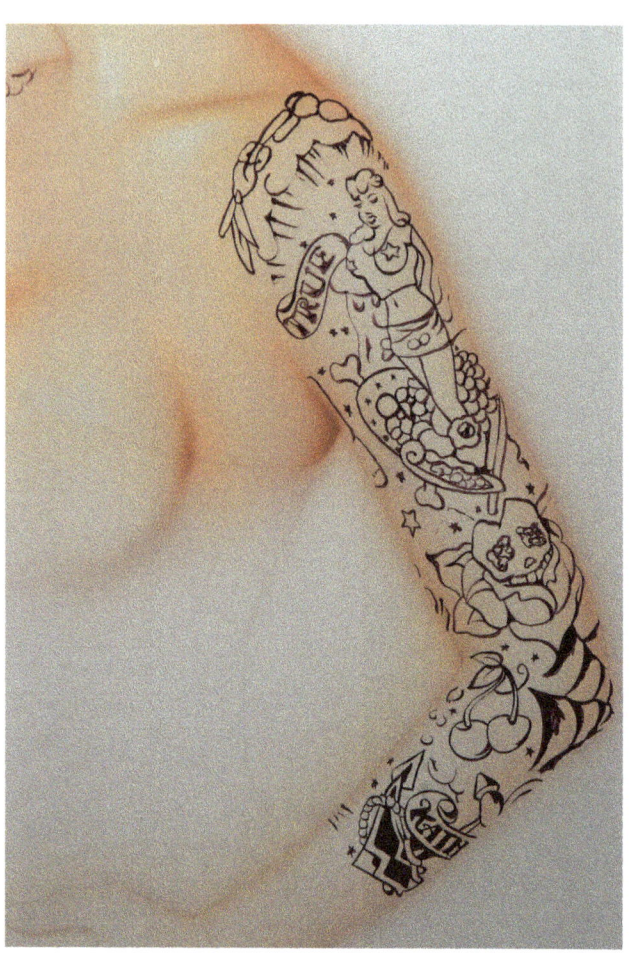

4. I use a #2 Windsor Newton series 7 brush for all the outlining work.

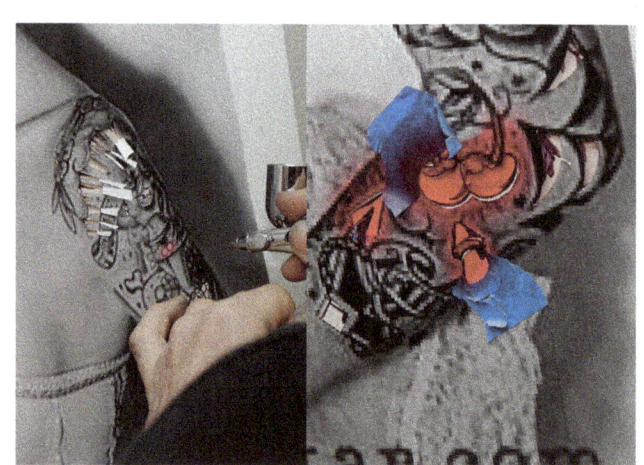

5. Since the colors are so close, you will need several copies to use as masks. I start with the red and lay down the color.

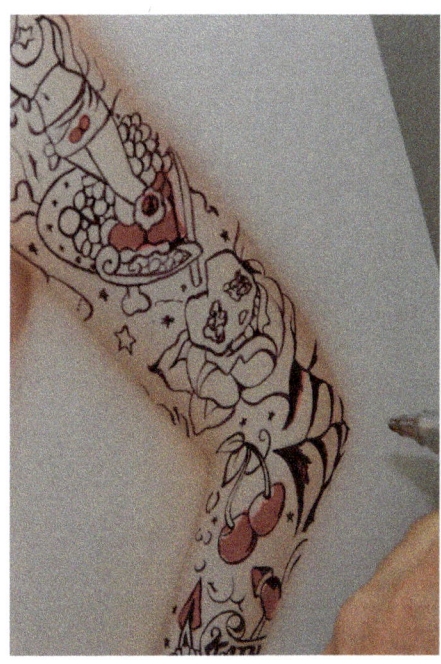

Here I'm adding red to the tattoo, at her elbow, working free hand.

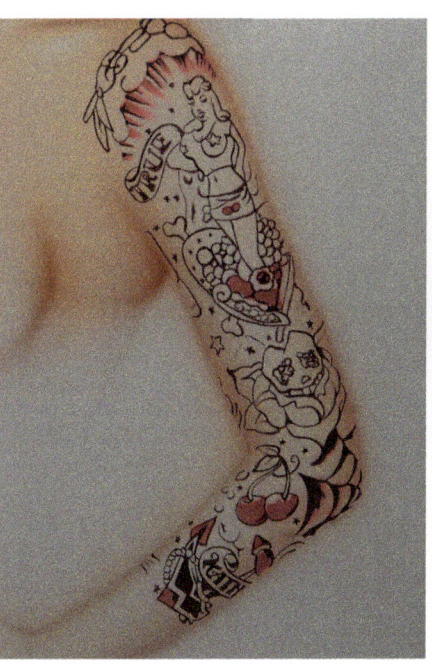

And here's a progress shot.

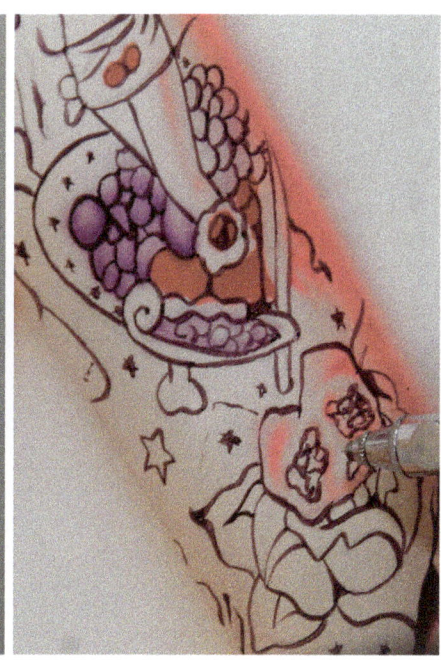

Some of the more subtle areas, like that shown, are airbrushed free hand without masks.

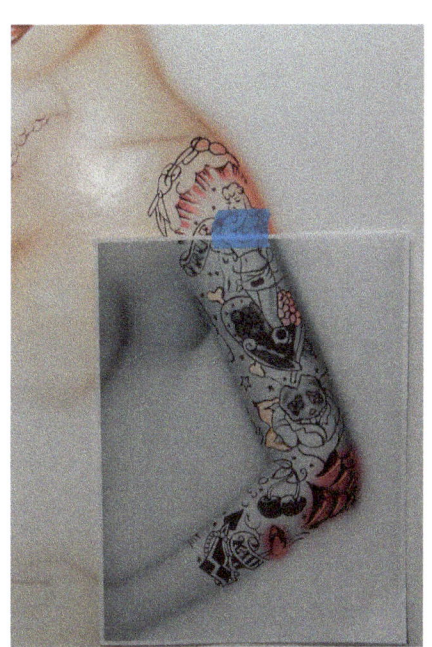

Other areas, however, require the use of carefully cut stencils.

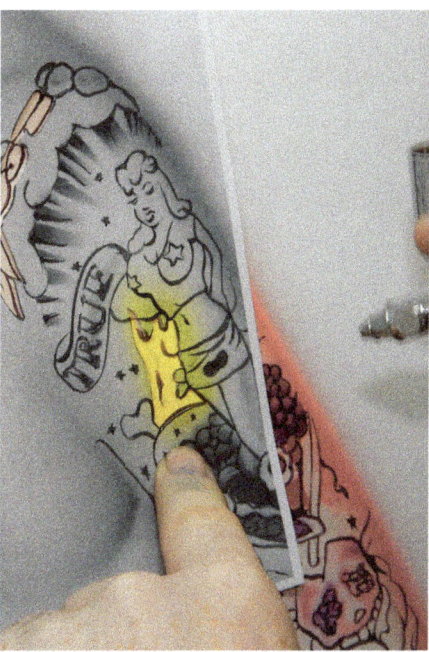

Next I do the yellow of the flame...

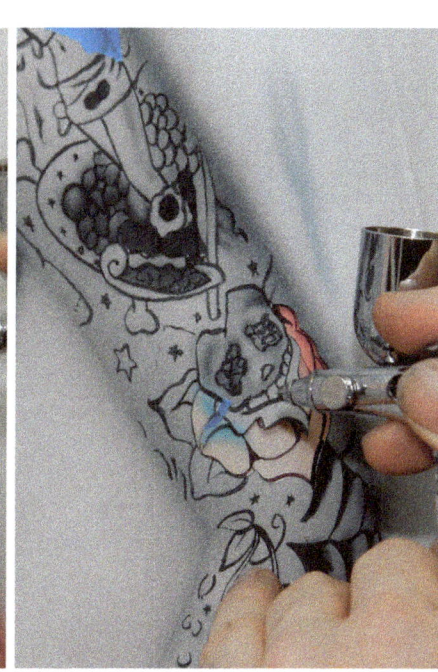

...and the blue of the flower petals.

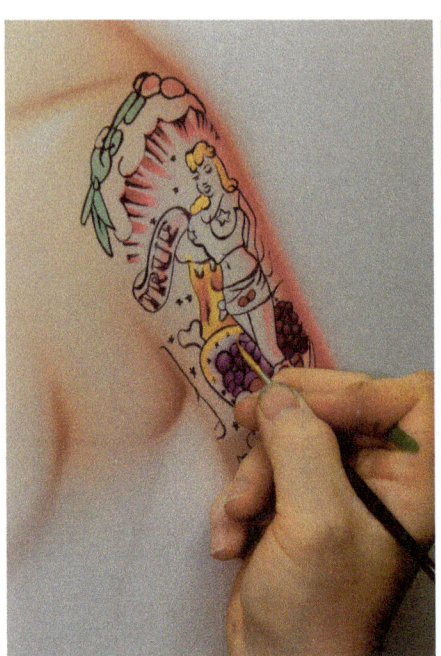 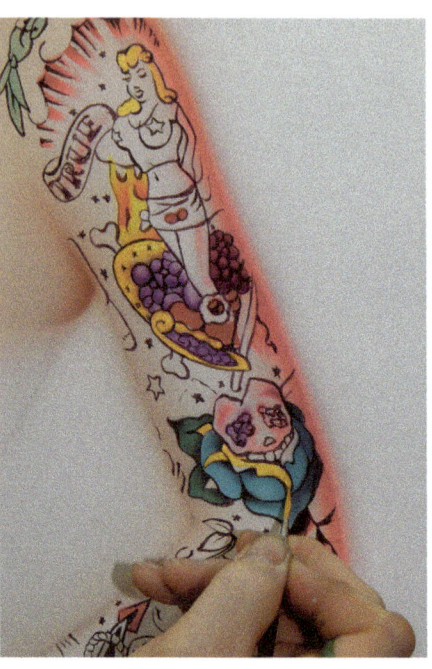 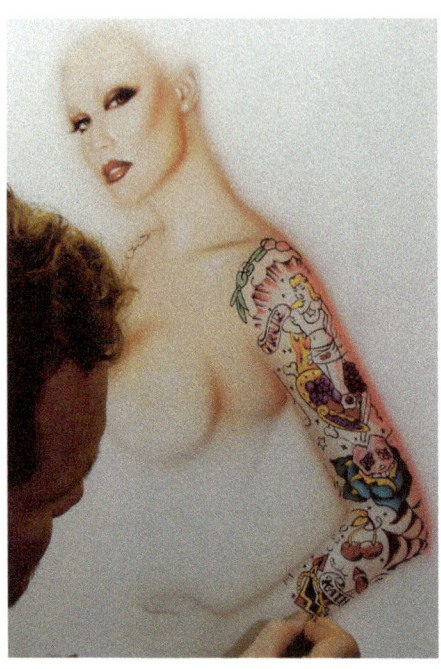

Mixing up a golden yellow, I brush in all the areas that use that same hue.

The yellow works well with the brush because it's a strong color...

...gradually I work my way down the arm.

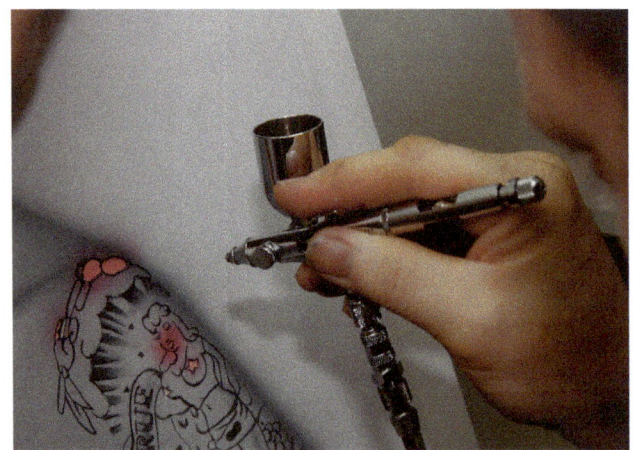 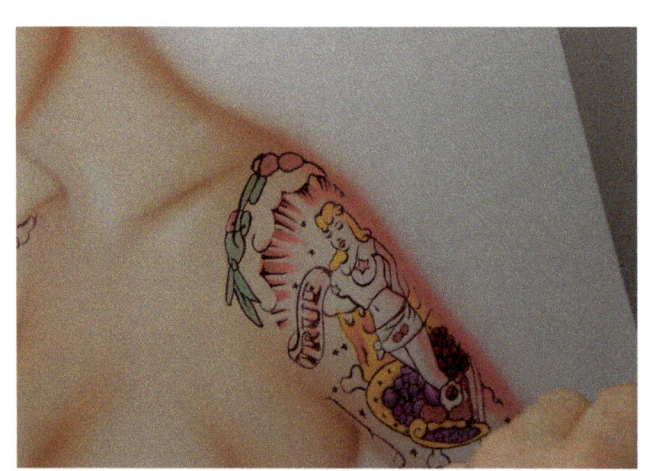

On her upper shoulder the color is a very bright red, applied with the help of a mask...

...and here's the area after I pull the mask.

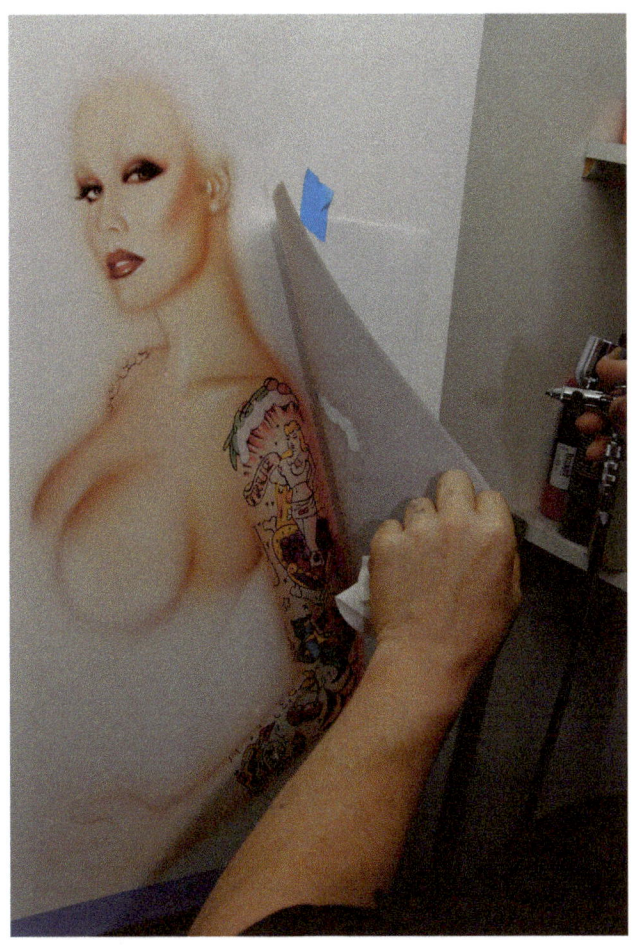

1. With the introduction of opaque white on the tattoo...

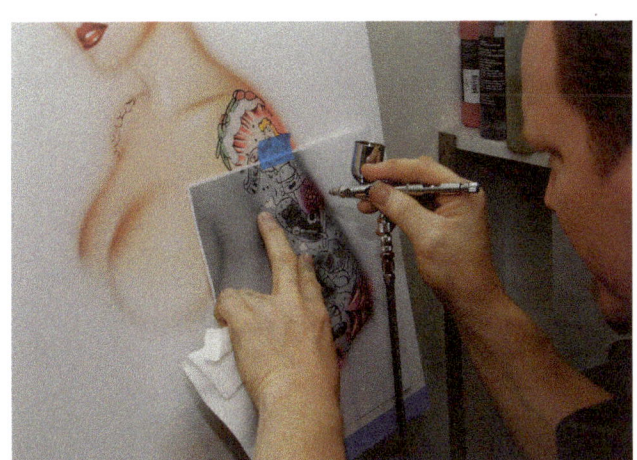

2. ...I can see the piece coming together for the first time.

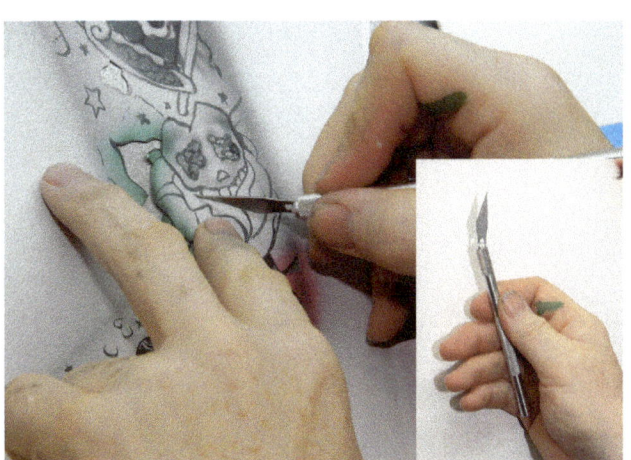

3. This is a little trick I learned years ago. Put the blade in the Xacto knife as shown - it makes doing cutouts super easy, the blade follows like a caster.

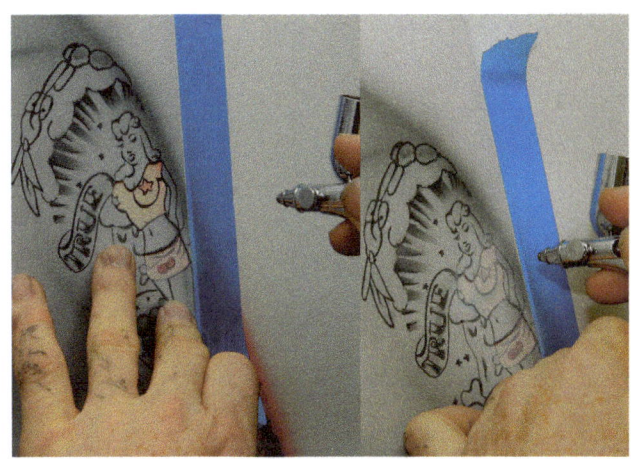

4. After doing the cutout I apply white, then blue to the girl's clothes.

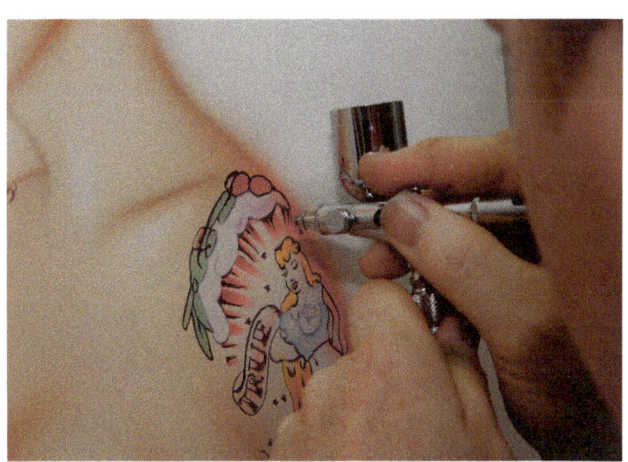

5. I'm softening up the edges of the sunburst with a little red applied free hand.

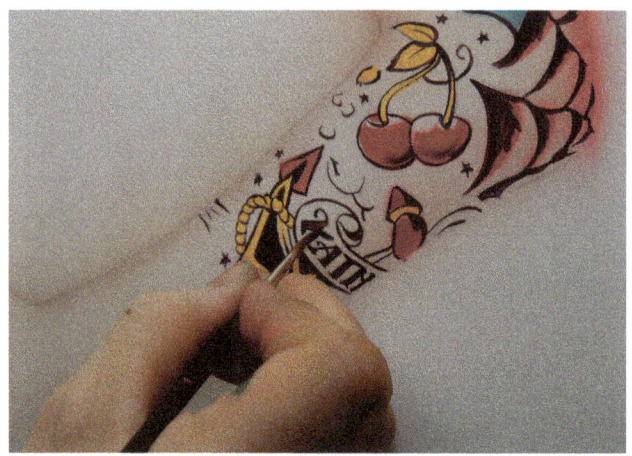

1. More hand brushing of the red details.

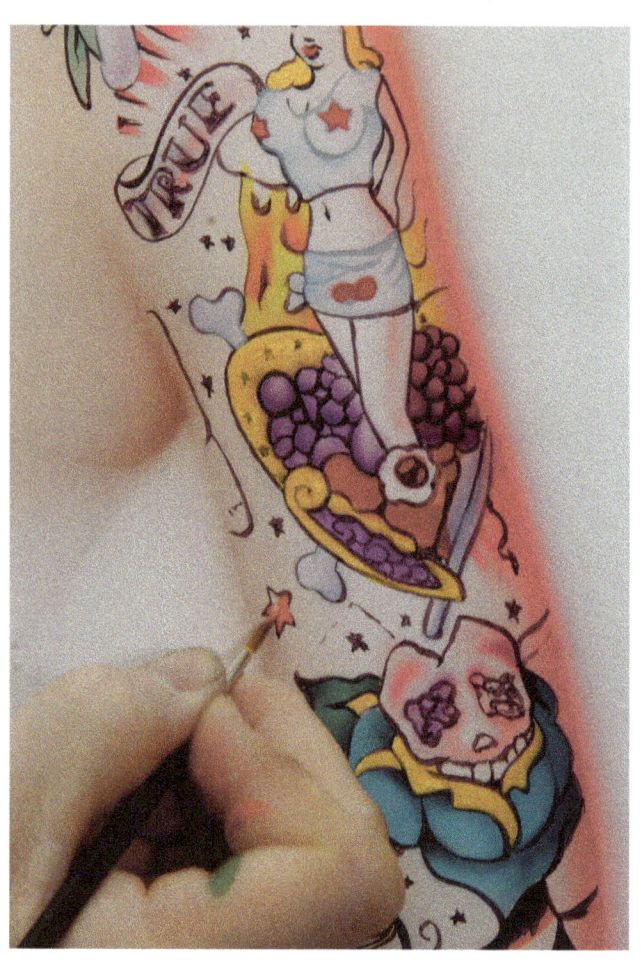

2. I'm finishing up the first layer of tattoo color.

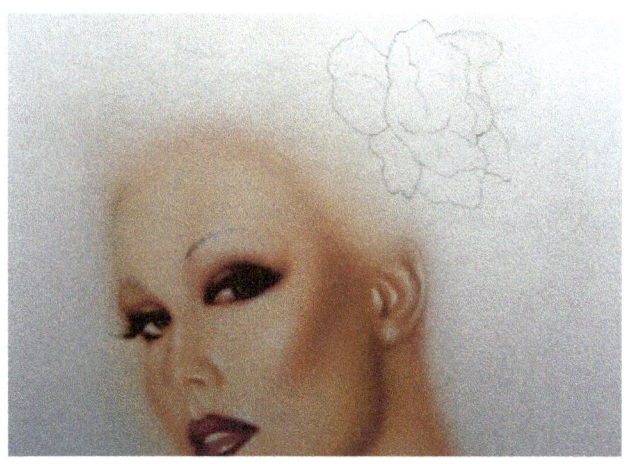

3. Progress shot shows the face well developed, and the outline of the flower in her hair.

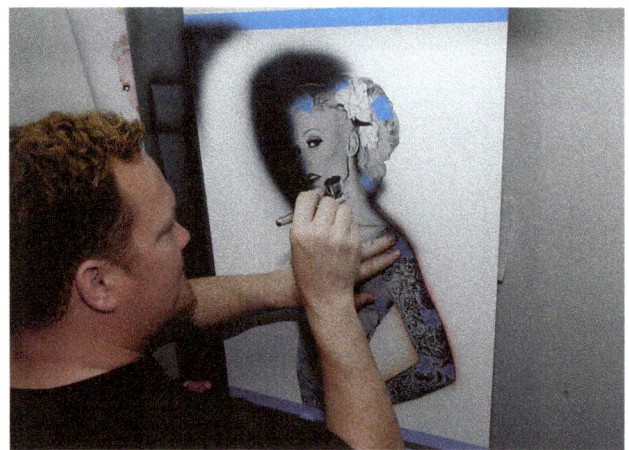

4. I cut another mask and begin to spray in the background color.

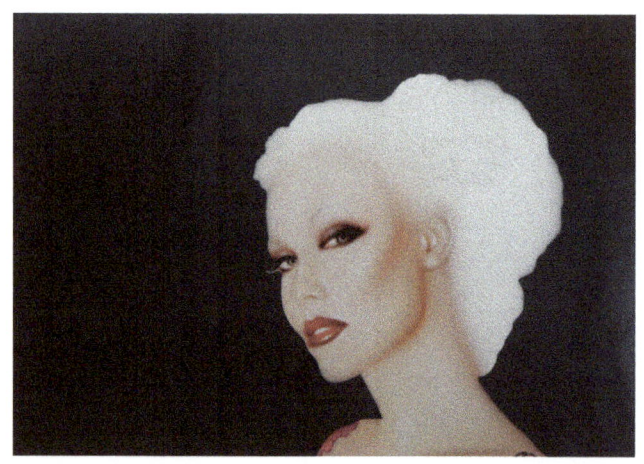

5. The color is mostly black with some blue and a little white, using opaque colors.

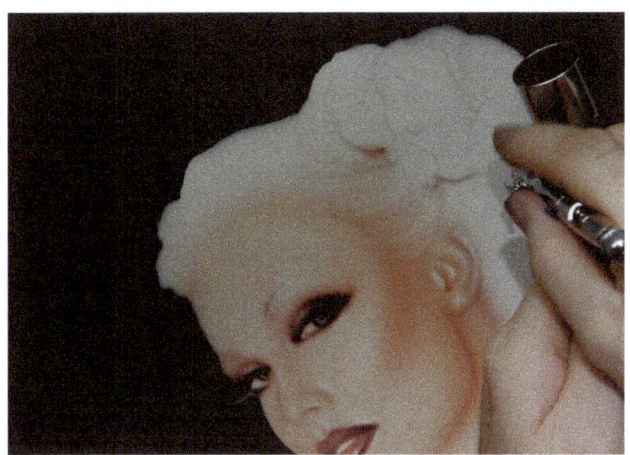

I add violet and white to the sunwashed flesh tone and start to develop the hair.

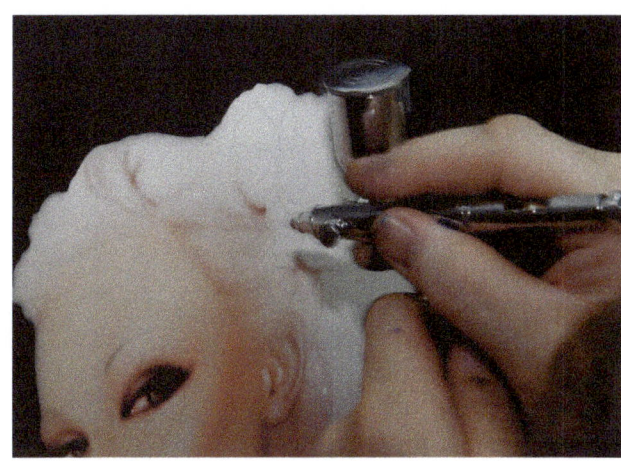

Using soft dagger strokes...

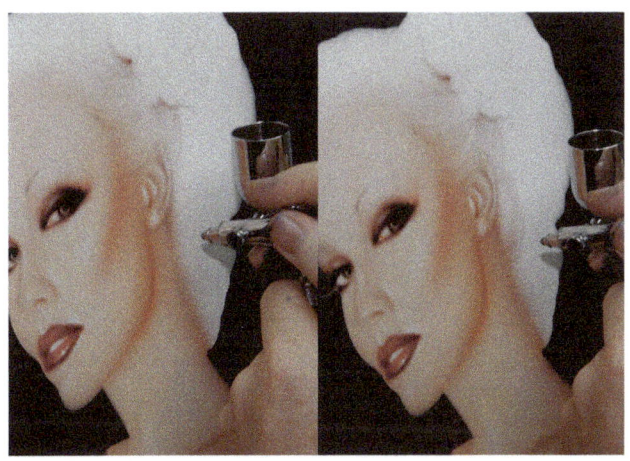

Try to think of the hair as a wave or a sculpture...

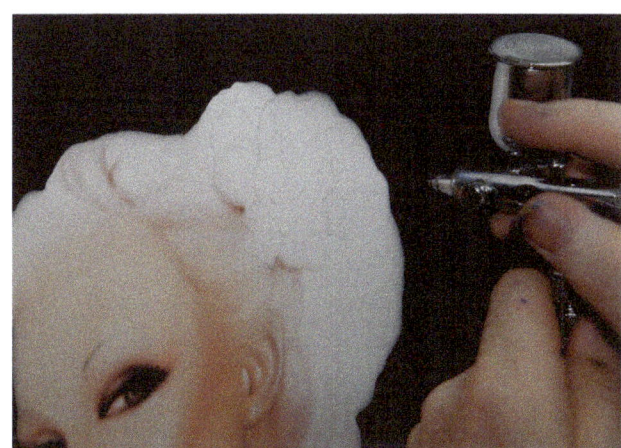

...I create the flow of the hair.

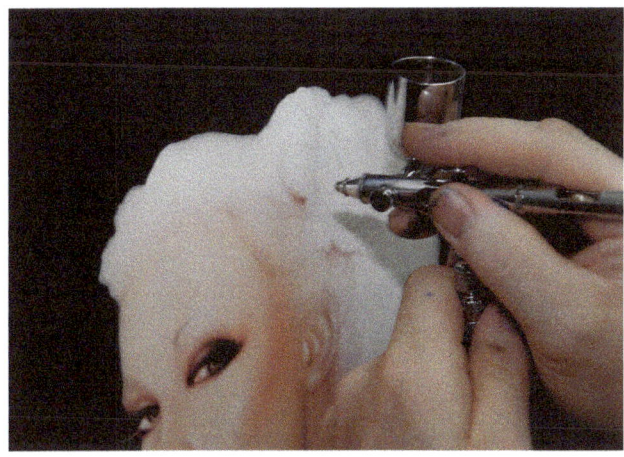

...not as single strands of hair.

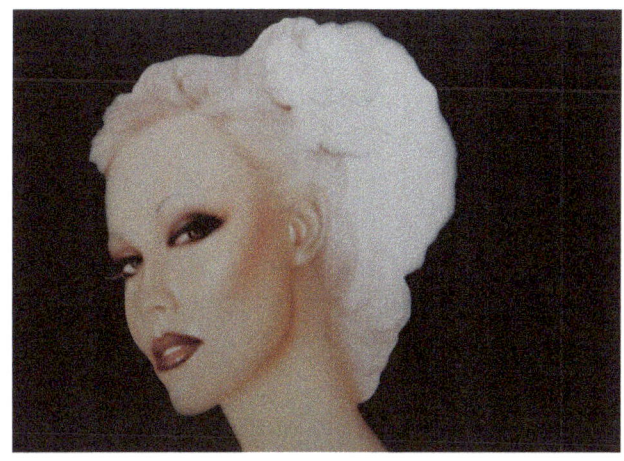

Notice the soft flow, there aren't any real tight lines.

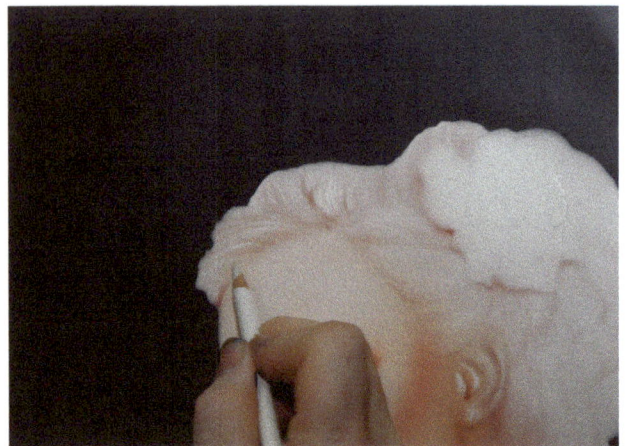

Using the stick eraser...

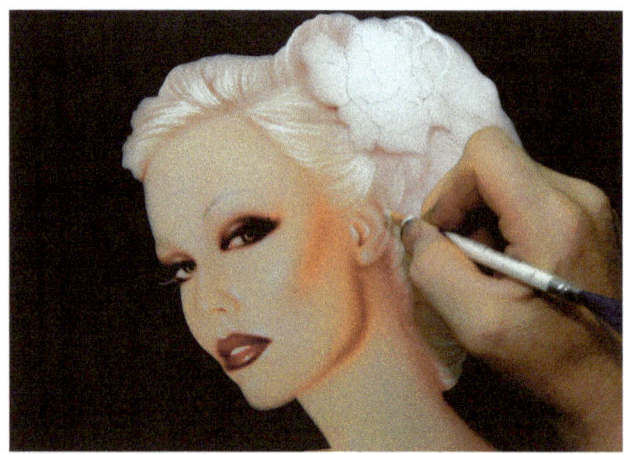

When you do this be sure to follow the flow of the hair so the shape isn't unnatural.

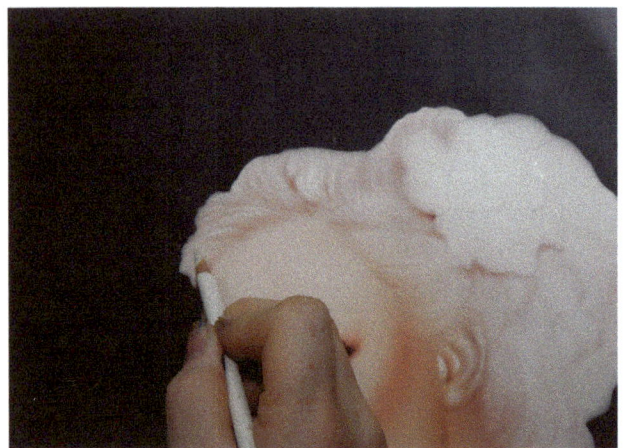

I create highlights in the hair.

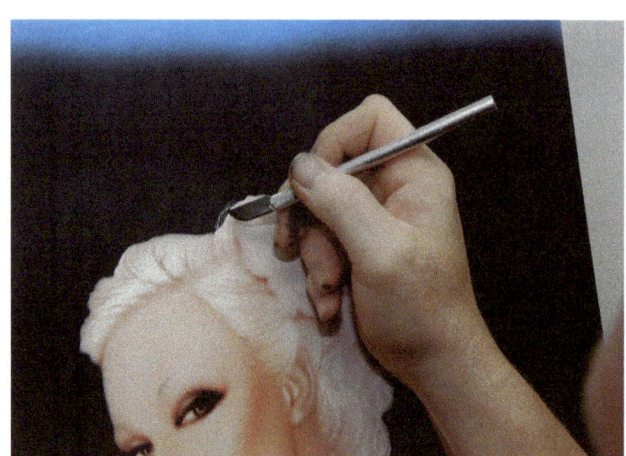

With a #10 Xacto knife I start to put in the outer, loose hair.

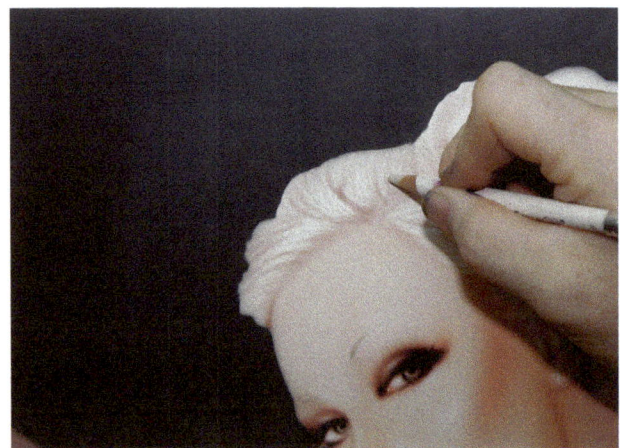

I don't do them all at one time, so they are more random and have a more layered appearance.

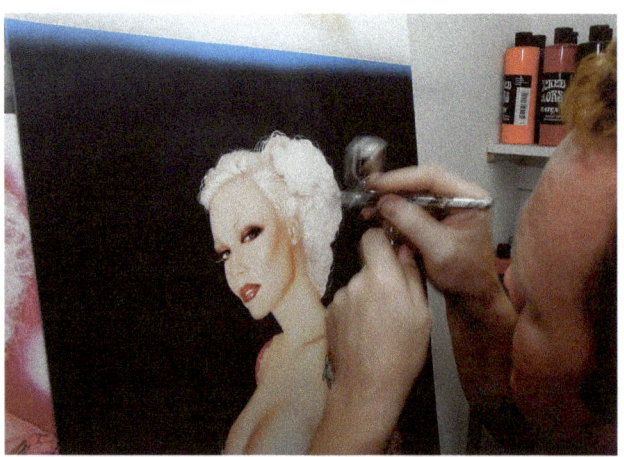

Next I spray a light layer of color to push back the highlights and get more depth.

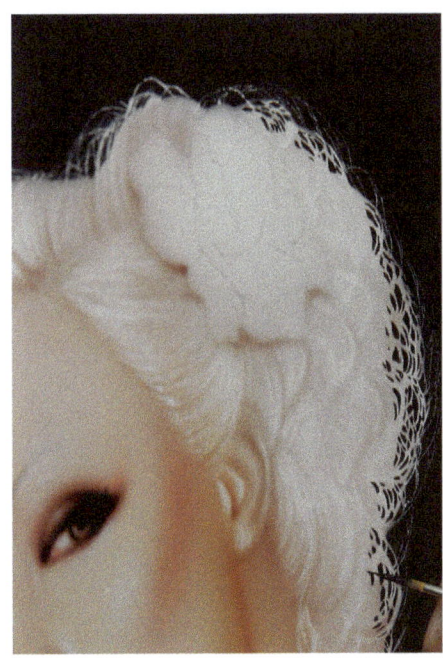 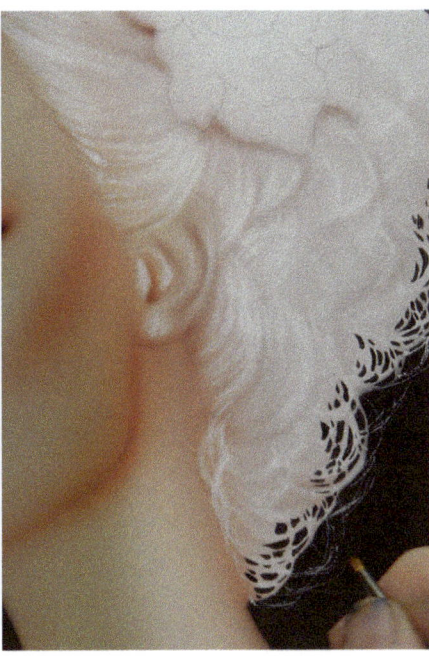 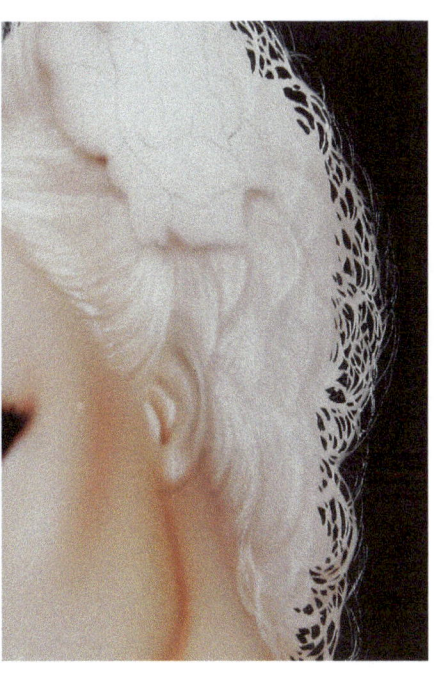

Using a brush and my background color I paint in the areas...

...of background that show through the hair.

Try and use your reference as a guide when doing areas like this.

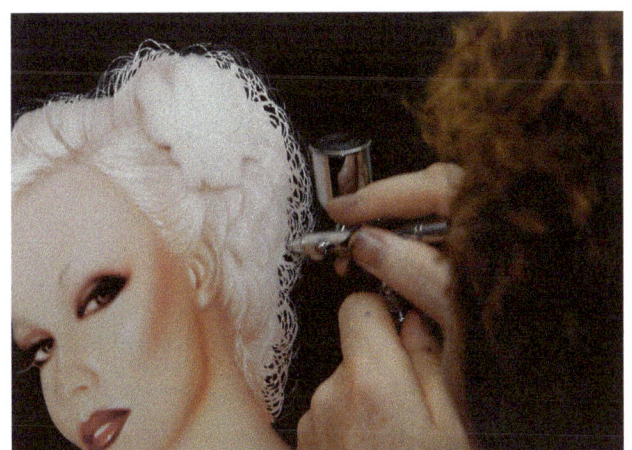 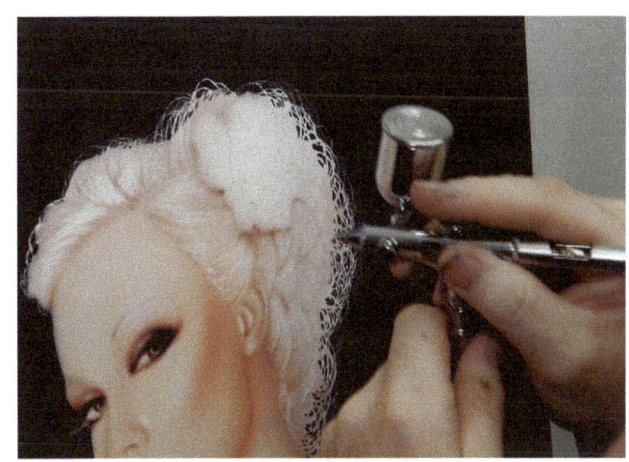

I add another layer of paint...

...to deepen the texture of the hair.

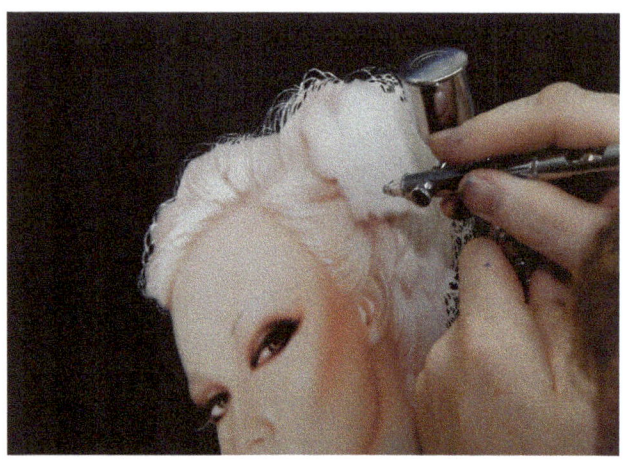

After doing another lighter layer of highlights I add another layer of hair color.

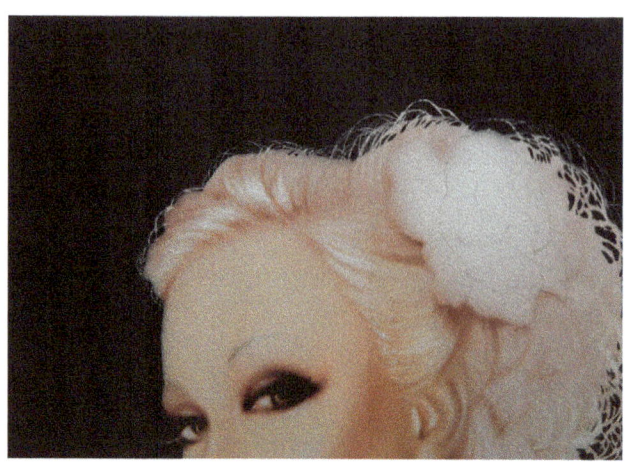

I add some violet to the mix to create the darkest areas.

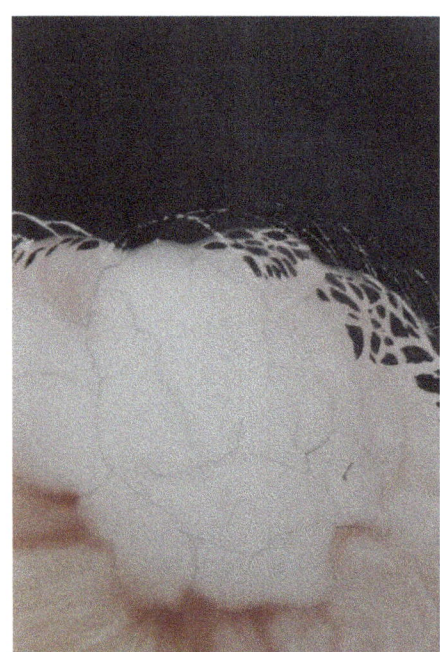

Highlights or starbursts in the hair (at the edge) really make it come to life.

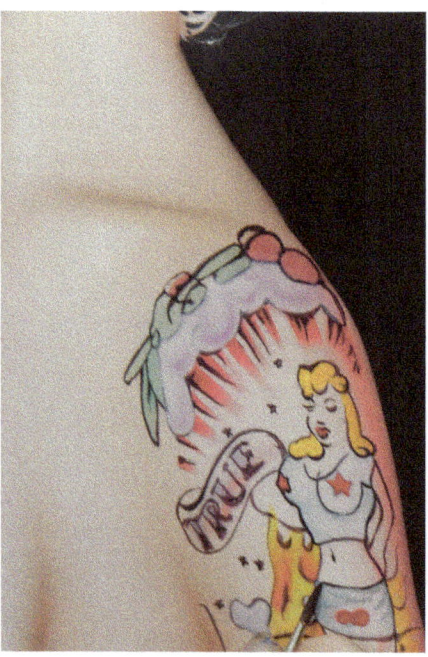

Here's the tattoo area as I work to re-apply the outline color.

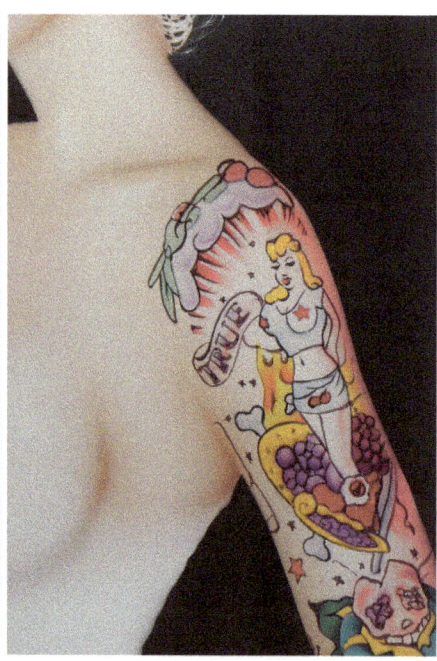

And the same area after the outlines are finished.

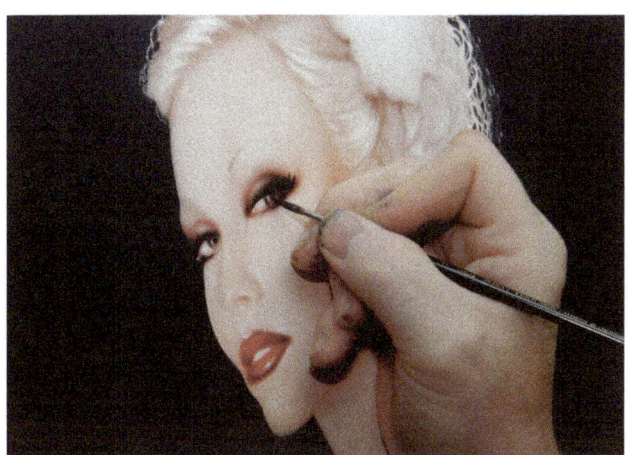

1. With a brush I add some very dark brown to the eyelashes.

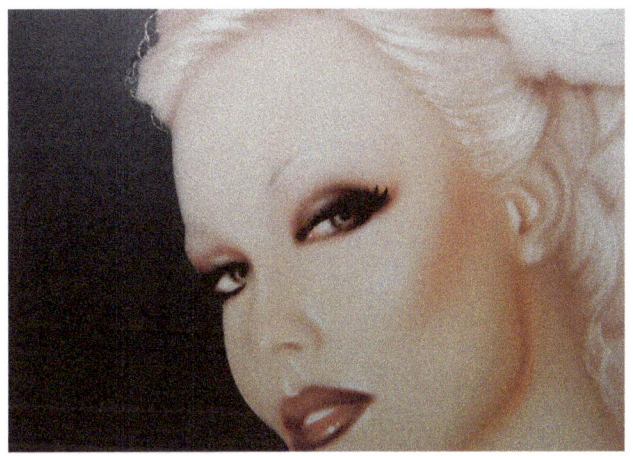

2. Here you get a close up look at the results.

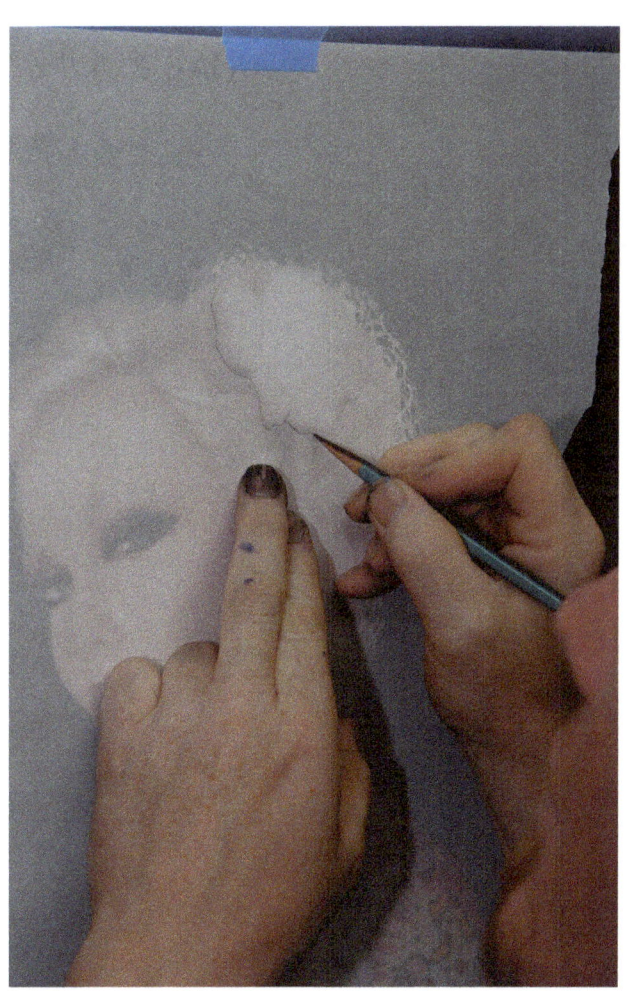

3. I cut the flower out of the tracing paper as shown.

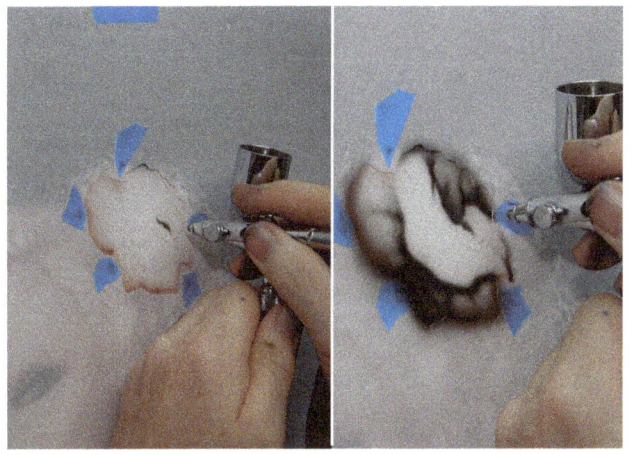

4. Using transparent black I start to develop the shape of the flower.

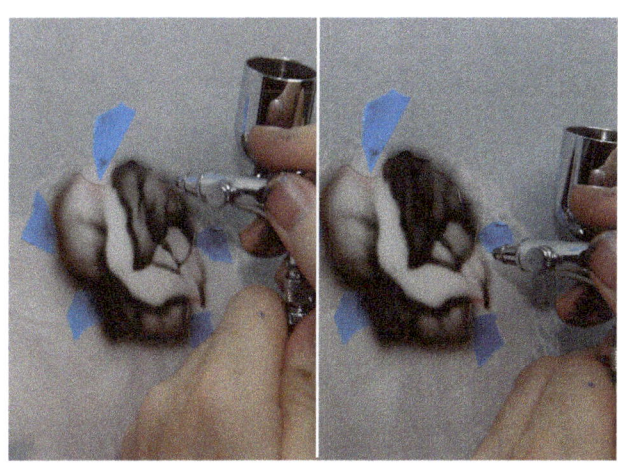

5. You can see how I've cut small holes in the mask to hold it in place.

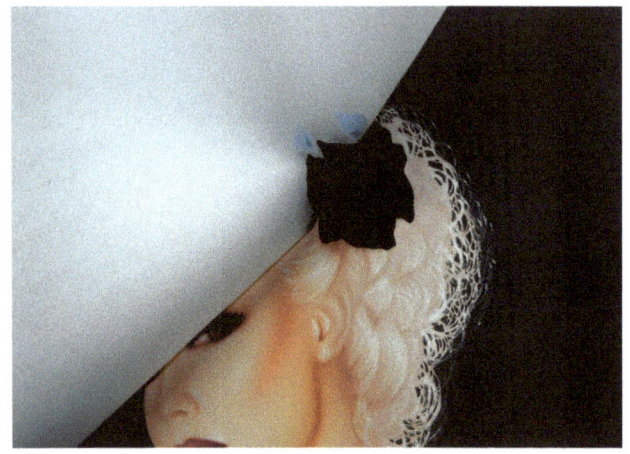

Now I pull the mask off the flower.

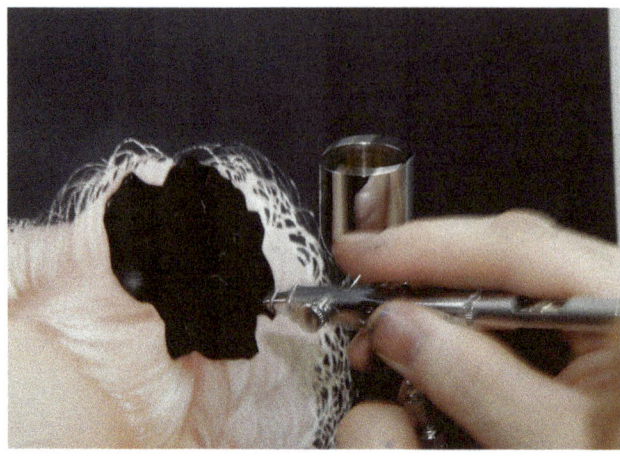

Spraying a light mist of black helps the flow and pushes the highlights back.

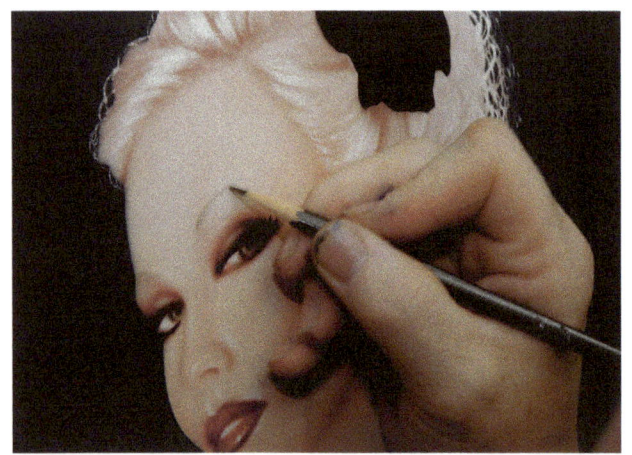

Her eyebrows are drawn with a brown pencil.

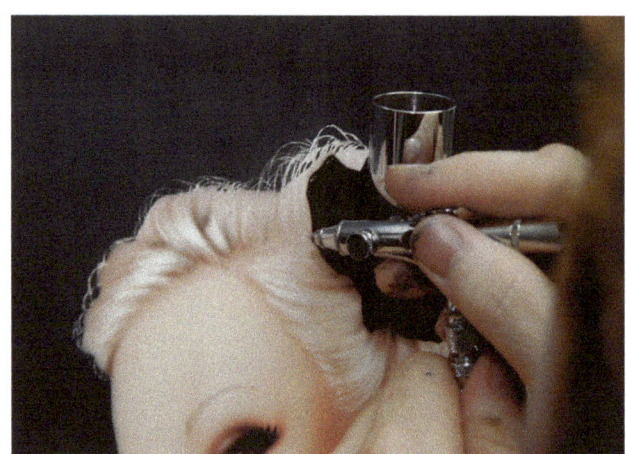

Now that the flower is done I know how dark to make the shadows in the hair.

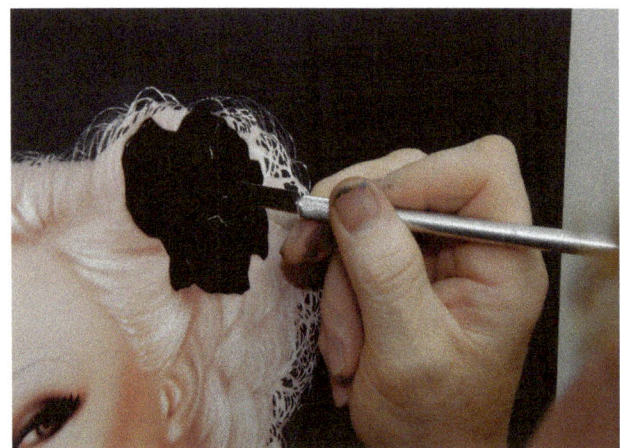

Using the #10 blade again, I add highlights to the flower.

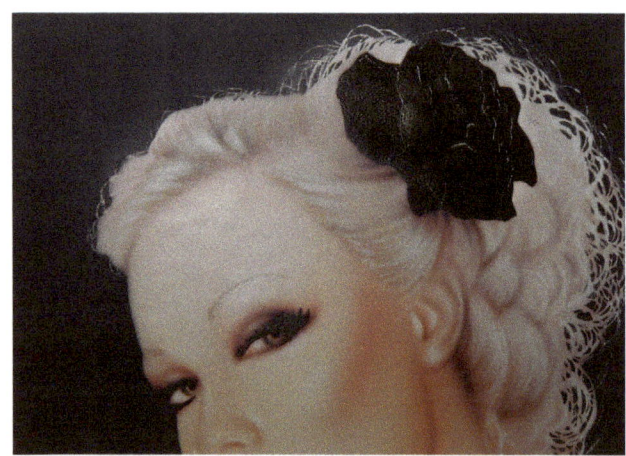

Sunburst flesh with violet and green is my mix for the darkest shadows in her hair.

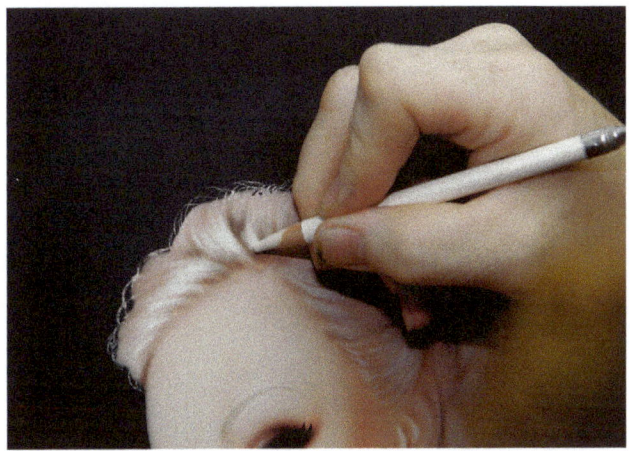

1. Next I create another layer of highlights in her hair.

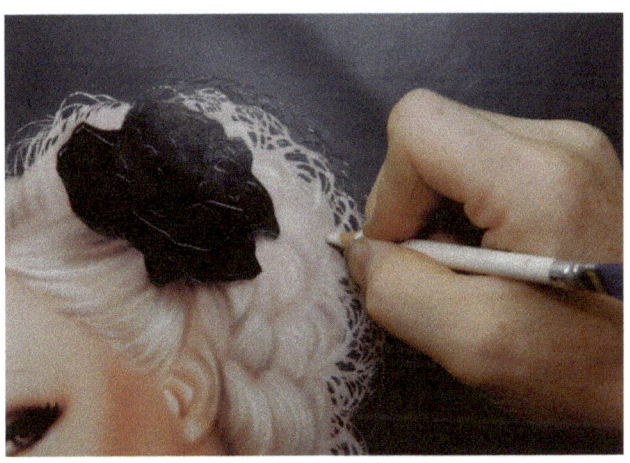

2. Using the stick eraser I bring the loose hair into the body of the hair.

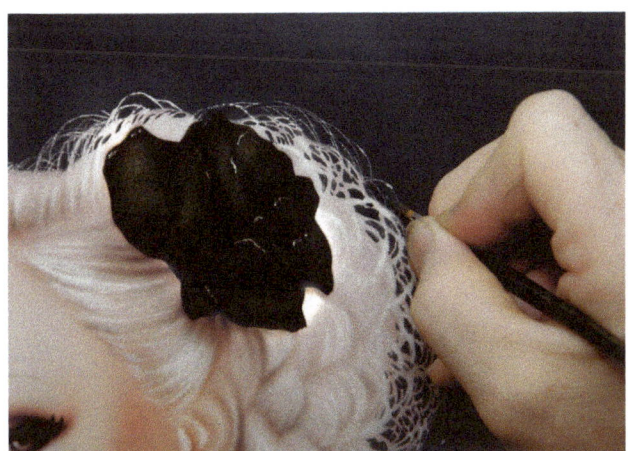

3. Next I tighten up the loose hair by painting the back ground color in tightly.

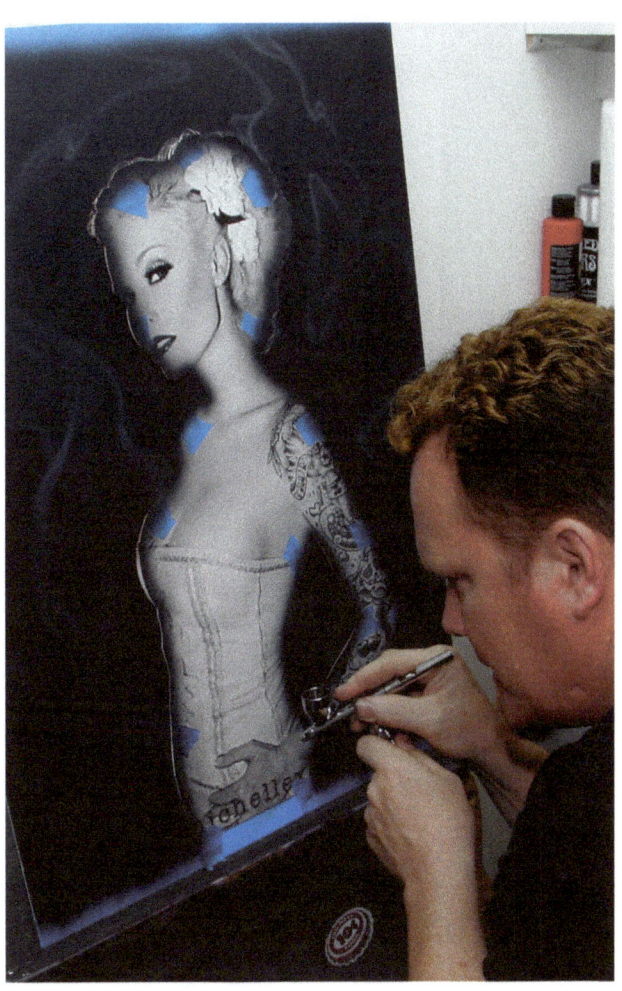

4. After coloring the image again, I start adding the smoke to the background.

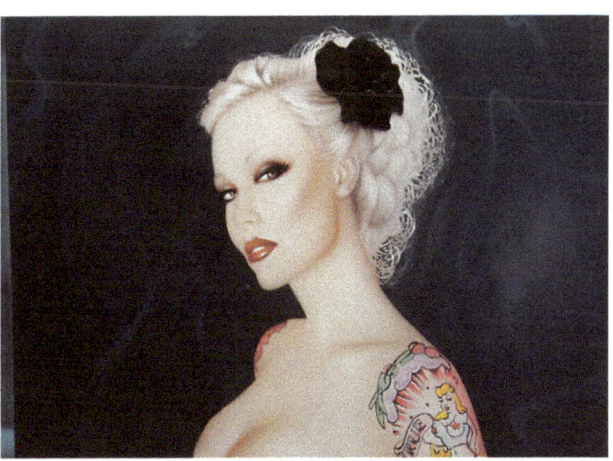

5. This is the smoke after washing over it with some royal blue.

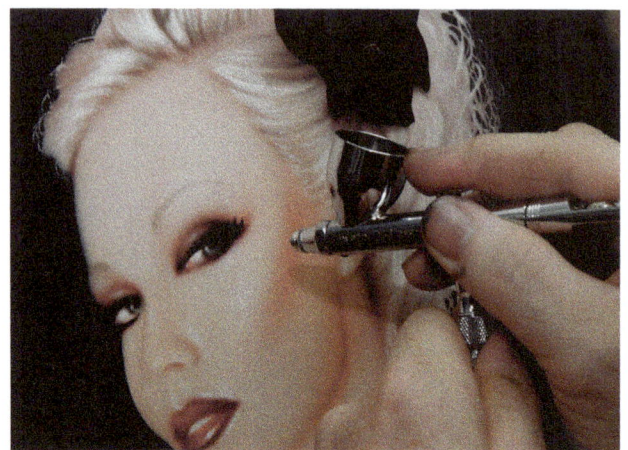
Details, details - adding blue to the eye color.

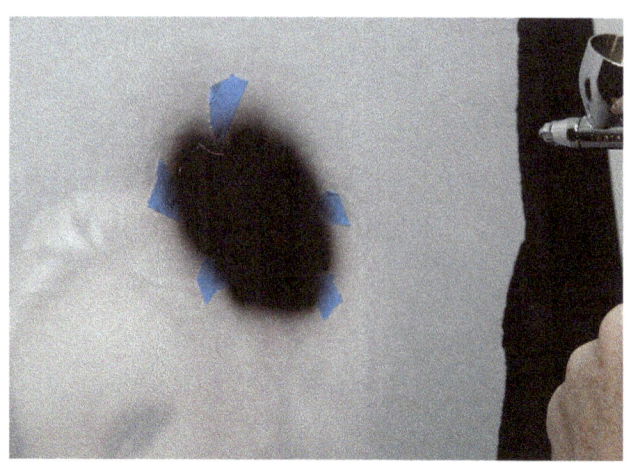
I add a bit of bright red over the flower to deepen the color.

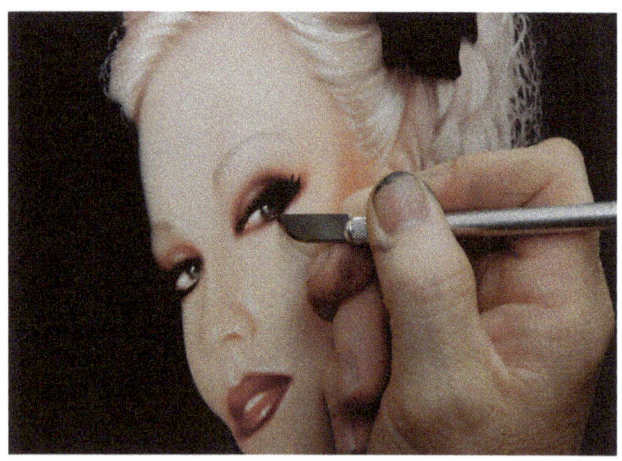
With the #10 blade I'm adding the smaller highlights to the eyes.

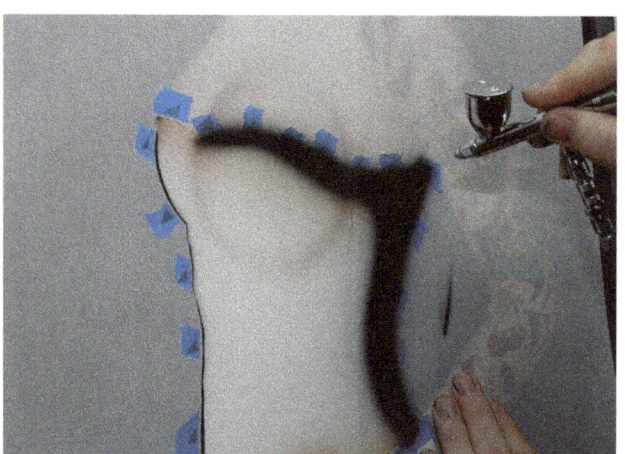
After tracing and cutting out the dress I start to layer the black.

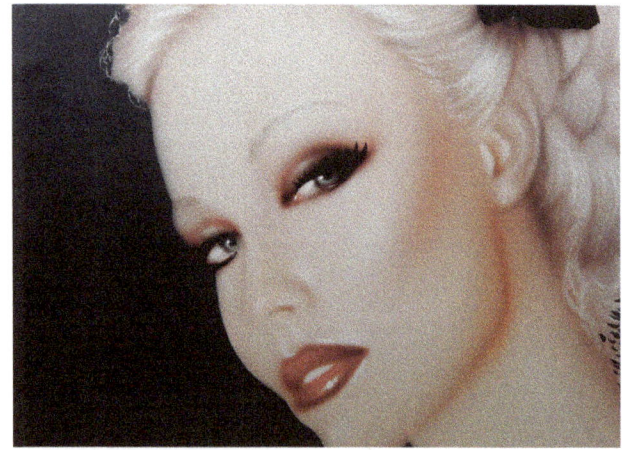
And here's the final effect.

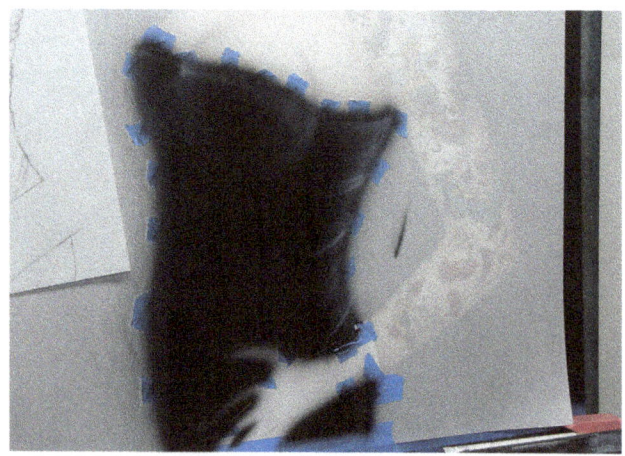
Here is the first layer of highlights. These are soft dagger strokes to get movement in the materials.

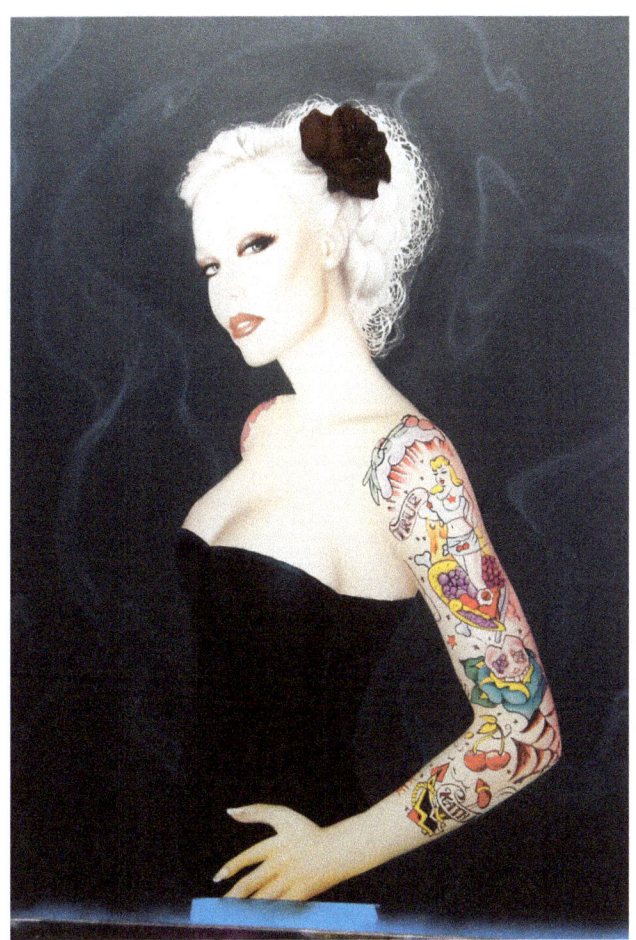

With just a few details to finish, the image is essentially finished. Note how the royal blue applied over the black gives the dress the look of velvet.

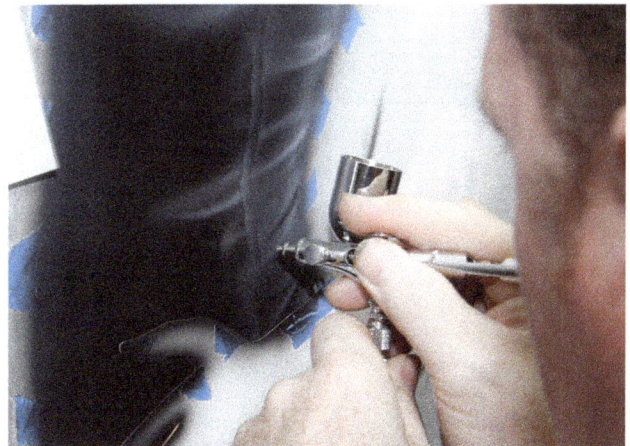

After creating the highlights I tighten the folds in the material with a little black.

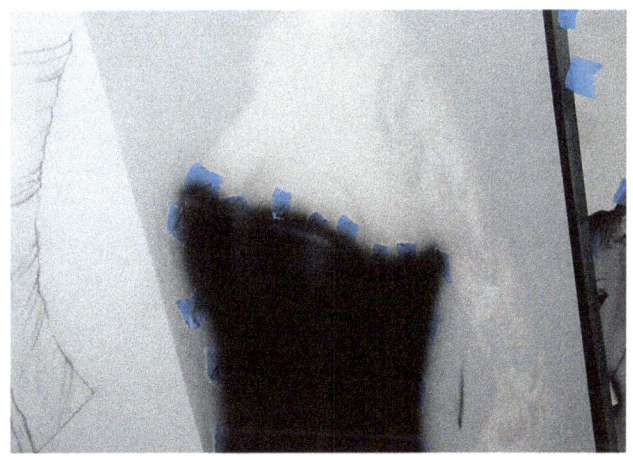

Near the end I apply a wash of royal blue over the entire dress.

Now I can pull my masking to reveal the finished painting.

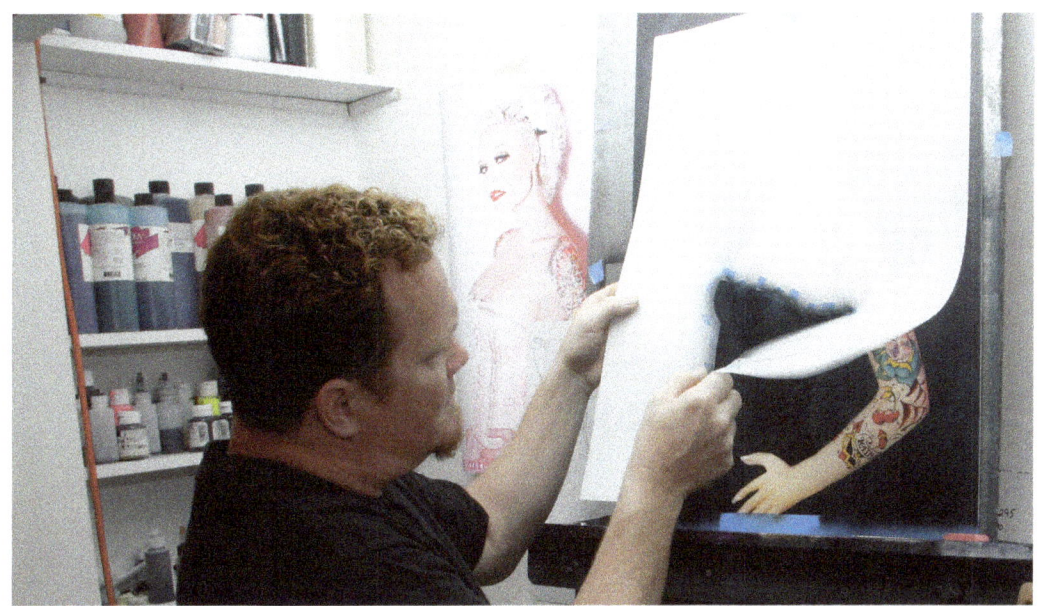

Steve Driscoll Q&A

Give us a little background on you, how did you get started in art, and are pin-ups the main focus of the work you do?

I've always been interested in art. Since I was five years old I wanted to be an artist. At first I wanted to do animation, because of Disney of course.

I can't remember not drawing, ever since I was really little. I was always drawing pictures of people and portraits. In 1992 I was living in 'Vegas, working a night shift at a warehouse. One night I slipped and tore up my knee. I couldn't work for nine weeks, so I started spending my days at a friend's body shop. Pretty soon I was playing with the airbrush in his shop, I had tried one in high school and always liked it. Then one day a customer asked me to do a mural on a lowrider, and I did, and that was it, I never did go back to working at the warehouse.

Today, I think pin-ups are 20% of what I do, but it fluctuates.

Even with the automotive and motorcycle work I do, a lot of that is pin-ups. And when I teach classes, some of those are pin-up oriented as well.

Did you take art classes? How did you learn to sketch and airbrush?

Mainly just in high school. I did take a couple of art classes in college, but they weren't very good. My high school teacher was way better than the university teachers, Myke Knutson, he's still a good friend. He was not your typical art teacher, he was more in-depth. My senior year he created two new art classes just for me because I had already taken all the other classes they had to offer. What I know about color I learned from him, or on my own.

Who inspires you, who are some of the artists you look up to?

There are three: First is Normal Rockwell, I consider him my all time favorite. He doesn't get the recognition he deserves. He was a very good storyteller with his paintings, and the paintings themselves are exceptional.

Chuck Close would be number two. In 1968 he was using an airbrush to do photo realistic portraits that are seven feet by nine feet. His technique is the same as mine. He achieved his highlights by erasing, only he used a big roll of rubber on an electric drill to erase. It's a subtractive process. They have one of his paintings at the Walker Art Center here in Minneapolis.

Number three is Maxfield Parish, his stuff is kind of similar to Rockwell, it's realistic, and the colors are unbelievable. His images have an older look to them. He didn't get much recognition as an artist, which is too bad, he was considered an illustrator.

Novice artists sometimes have trouble rendering believable skin tones, how do you achieve life-like skin tones?

Layers, lots of layers of transparent color. And I don't use white for highlights, I erase to create the highlight. That way you still get some of the skin tone showing through from the deeper layers, you get more vibrant colors than if you use opaque colors.

Another area where people have trouble is with faces, are there tricks or particular methods you use to create a good portrait?

I think I succeed by paying careful attention to the minute details that make a person look a certain way. You have to be careful with portraits; the smallest change will alter how the painting looks. It's hit and miss in the beginning, then you learn what's important.

How about the equipment you use, which airbrush do you typically use and why? And what do you use for a compressor?

Iwata is the only one I use, I've tried others and always come back to Iwata. The durability and ability

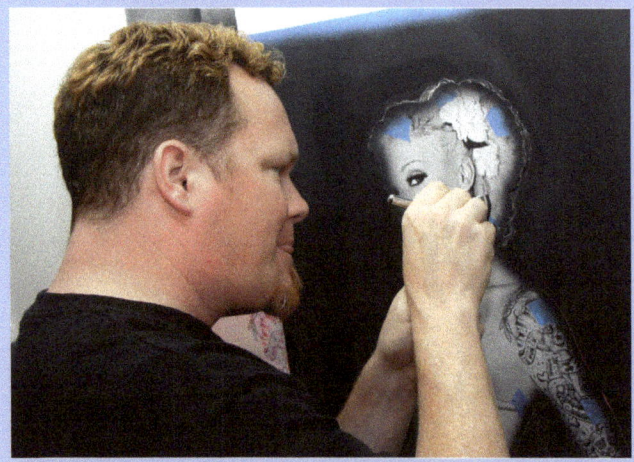

Comfortable painting on canvas, press-board or steel, Steve Driscoll splits his time between studio and shop.

Steve Driscoll Q&A

to do detail work is unsurpassed. It's a great all around airbrush. The compressor I use is from Medea.

Paint, which brand of paint do you use and why?

For canvas I use Medea ComArt, and some Liquitex. I like ComArt, it dries fast, and you can erase it right away without waiting long for it to dry. For automotive work I use House of Kolor paints, they are very user-friendly and the colors are super vibrant, you can also manipulate them to do what you want, you can make them transparent or opaque. There are so many different ways to use their paint.

How did you learn to mix paint to create unique colors, and tell us a little about your paint kits?

I'm pretty much self-taught. When I teach, and students are trying to mix a color, I tell them it's not, "what do I have to add to it to make a color, but what do I have to add to the paint to kill a color." It's a complimentary thing, the color opposite on the color wheel will kill that color. If it's too violet you can add green, which will kill the violet. I tell them to keep notes and formulas on everything they do, every time they mix paints.

My own kit is a Com-Art product from Medea. It has five different flesh tones, they are all transparent paints. The kit comes with everything you need to mix up flesh tones. In addition to the five flesh tones there's a shading additive to darken the flesh tones, and four other colors you might need if you're painting a whole portrait.

Do you use other media, like hand brushes, to add detail or achieve effects that are hard to do with an airbrush?

Yes, because there are times when you need better control or a tighter line. There are situations, like a painting of an athlete, where the jersey has hard edges at the intersection of two colors. Then I use a brush or I mask off one color from another.

How do you find the models, typically who does the photographs that you use for reference?

A lot of times the models approach me. Sometimes they have the photos with them or else they have them shot. If the model is local, then I might pick a photographer, but I don't do much photography.

What makes a good pin-up?

I think a lot of times it's the innocence of the model. There's a sexual component, but there's innocence as well. If they are visually engaging, looking at you, it's OK to look back. But when they aren't looking at you there's almost a voyeuristic quality to the image, like you aren't supposed to look. There's a difference between pin-up and erotic art, when you get into erotic art there isn't any of that innocence.

If you were going to give ten words of advice to someone just starting out to do pin-ups, what would that advice be?

Paint what you want, not what you think someone wants. Be true to yourself. I read somewhere that you should paint for your peers, so you feel like someone is always looking over your shoulder. That's good advice and it does make you do your best. But it's also a double-edged sword, because it can cause you to second-guess yourself too often.

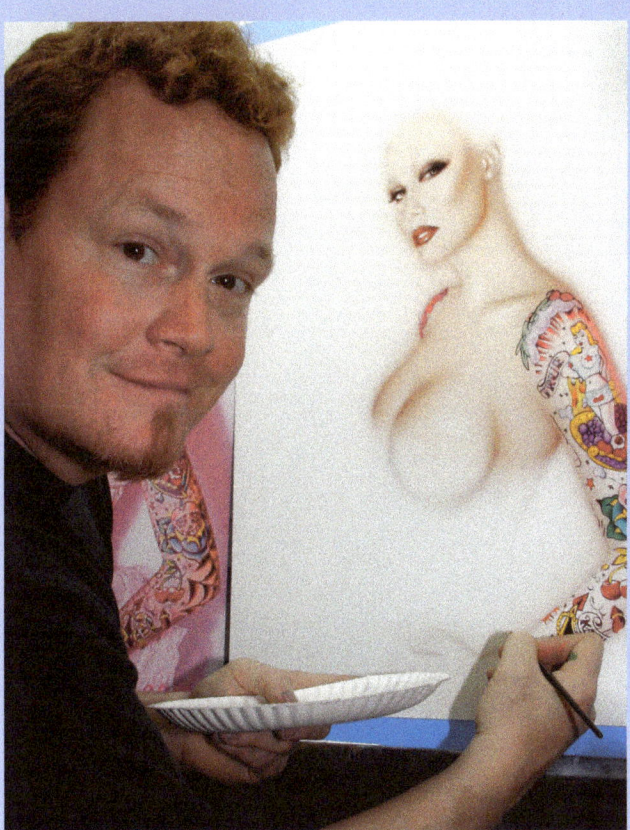

Always smiling, Steve keeps his good humor no matter how tight the deadline.

Chapter Two

Edward Reed

Working in the best Vargas Tradition

Edward Reed's bathing beauty captures the best of what we think is best in a Vargas painting from years gone by. Created with airbrush and hand brush, Edward shows us that simple images work well, and that the pose is as important as any other part of this unique art. In this particular sequence, we learn as much about color and the use of water-color paint, as we do about airbrushing. A member of the staff at The Art League School in Alexandria, Virginia, Edward's comfort with the position of teacher comes through in his well written and concise captions.

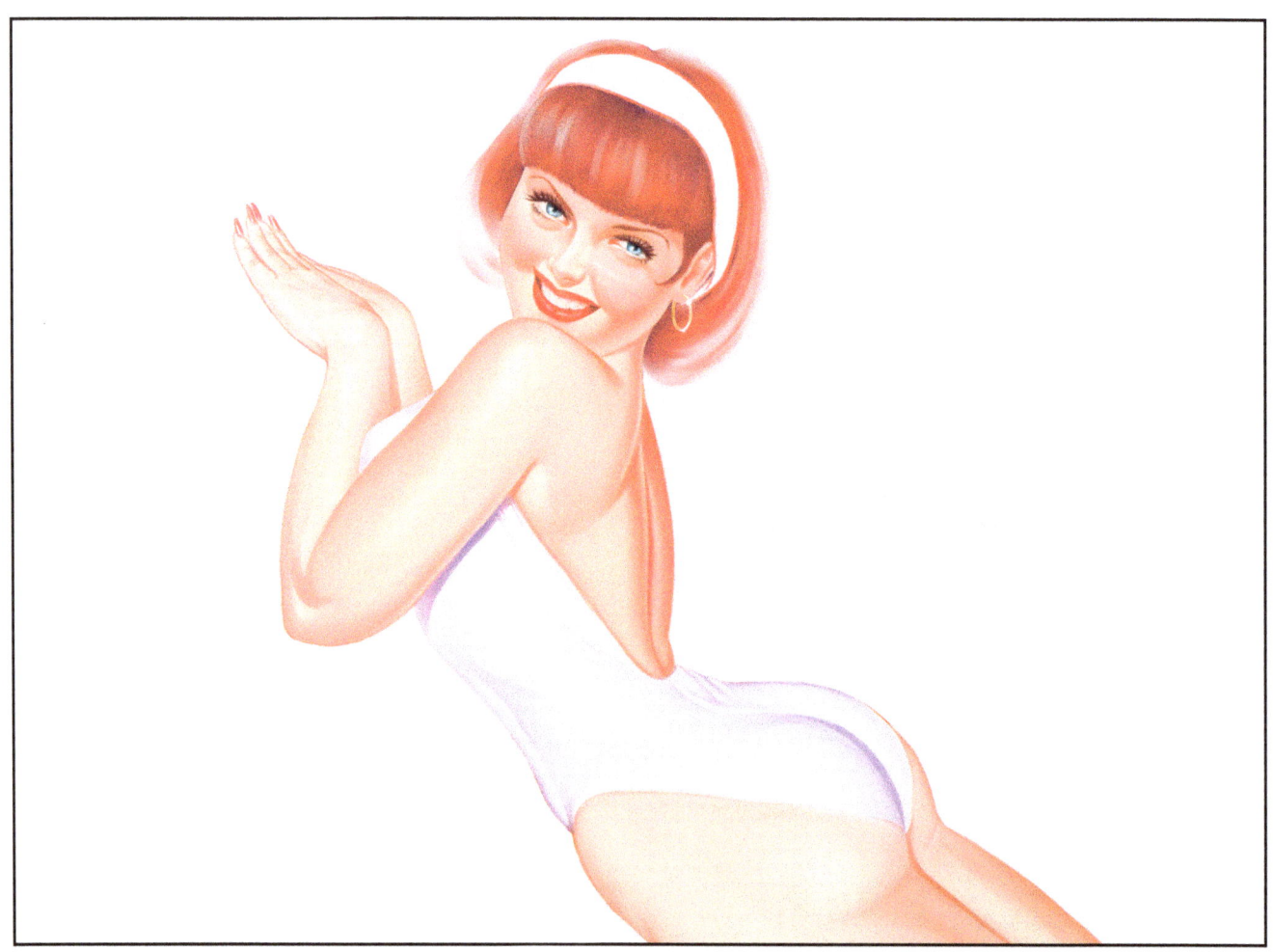

Beach Blanket Bingo is an old school style pin-up designed with an aerodynamic shape reminiscent of a sexy automobile hood ornament! This pose accentuates her curves in all the right places and gave me the opportunity to execute streamlined muscle contours while making her look as if she could fly through the air!

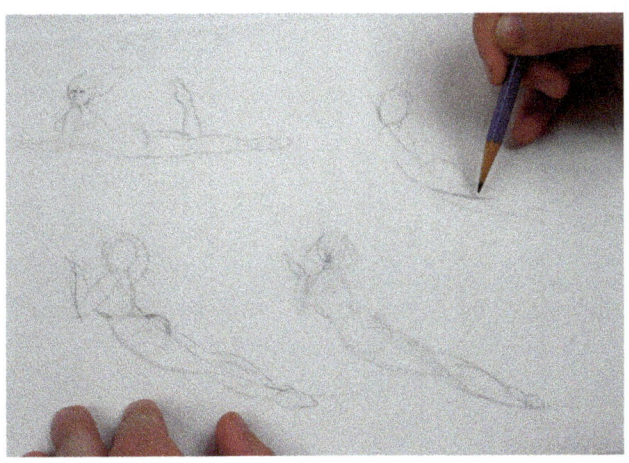

I draw thumbnails of the basic pose, creating a streamlined and curvy shape. I use translucent vellum so I can trace previous sketches and flip the image to refine my composition.

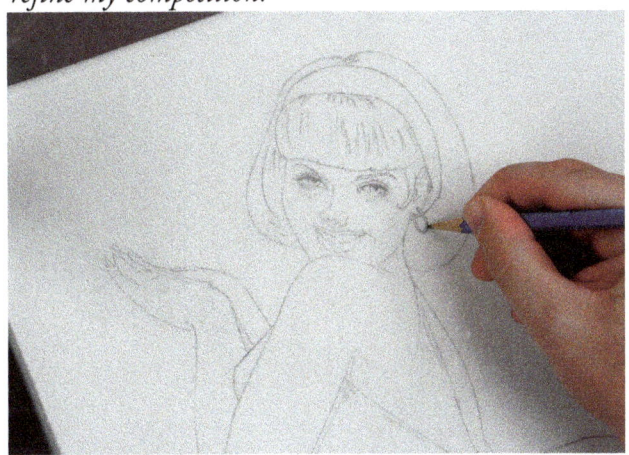

I enlarge my sketch on a photocopier and trace the drawing, refining the details. I transfer the image to watercolor paper using a transfer sheet, and trace over every line with a 5H pencil.

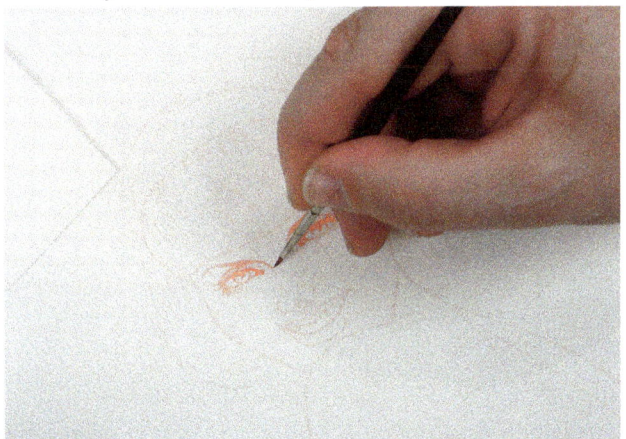

Using vermilion and a 00 watercolor brush, I hand paint over all the transferred lines, and render the details starting with the facial features.

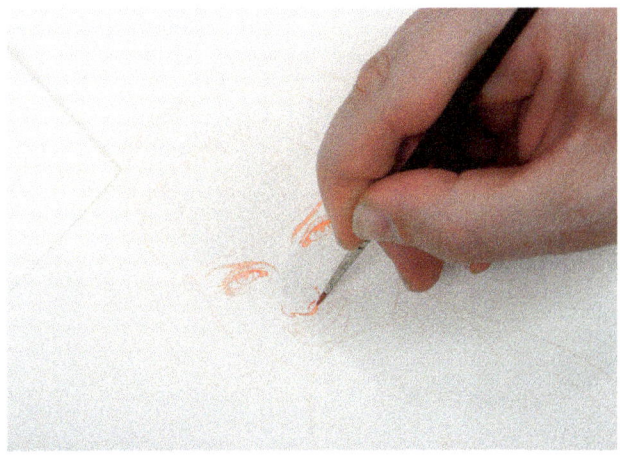

Lines are tapered to a fine point by pulling up and away with the watercolor brush to achieve very fine detail. Some of the hard cast shadow elements are also hand painted.

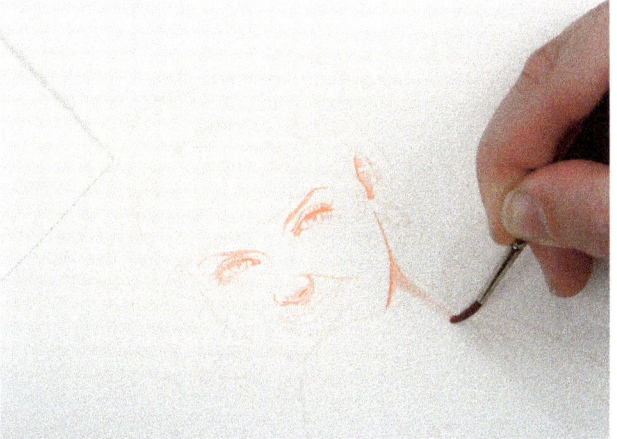

Cast and form shadows are faded in by adding clean water to the area, then adding pigment by dragging the brush through the wet area. This will bleed away creating a soft cast shadow.

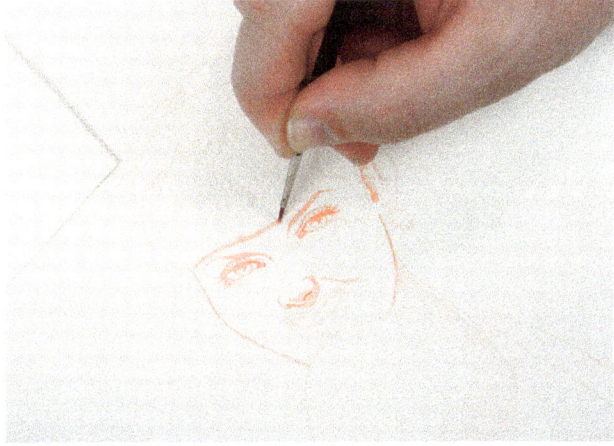

A cast shadow is added under the hairline, and details of the inner ear are painted.

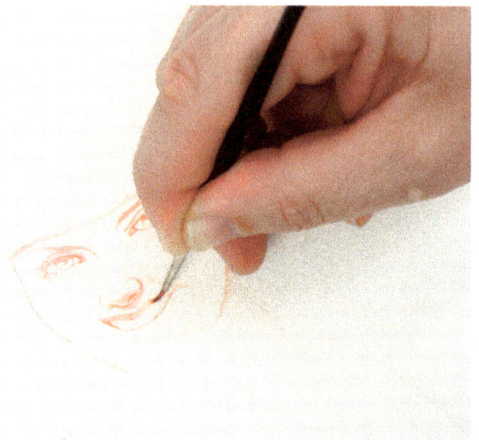
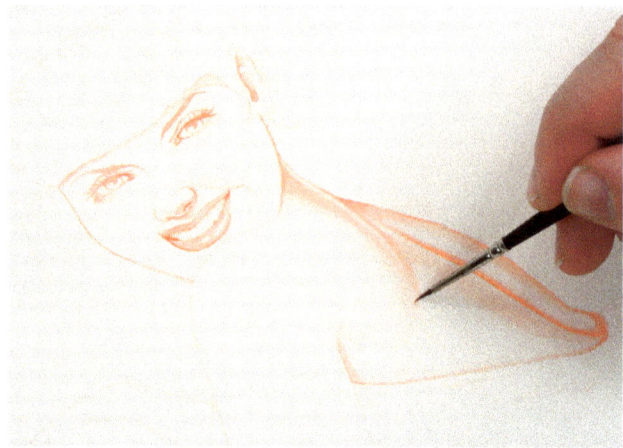

The upper lip is painted just enough to define its shape. The lower lip is hand painted, and I leave some areas unpainted to depict highlights.

A moist brush can be dragged through the area to pick up paint, if any pigment bleeds into an area you want to remain lighter.

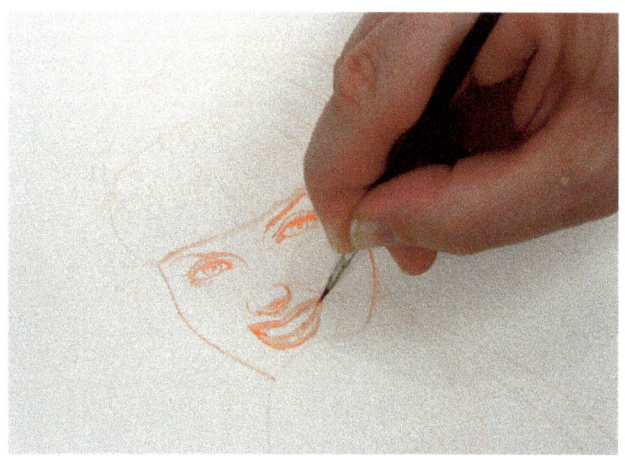
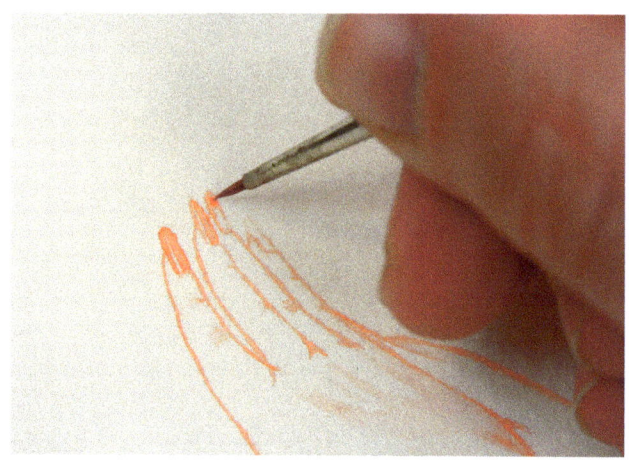

The corners of the mouth are painted with a small amount of vermilion mixed with burnt sienna. I drag it across the teeth, under the upper lip, to create a shadow adding depth.

I paint the fingernails leaving a thin strip unpainted to create the shiny highlight of her nail polish.

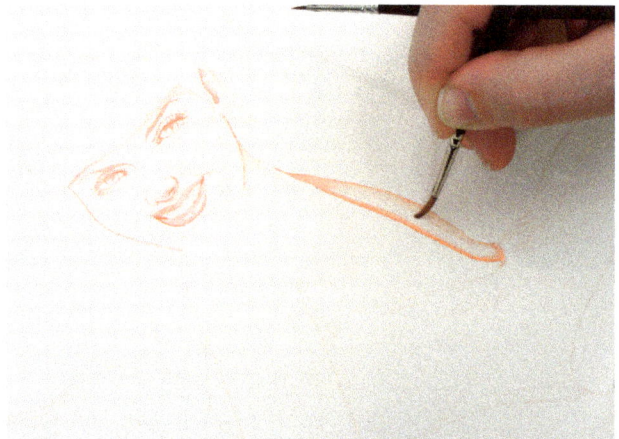
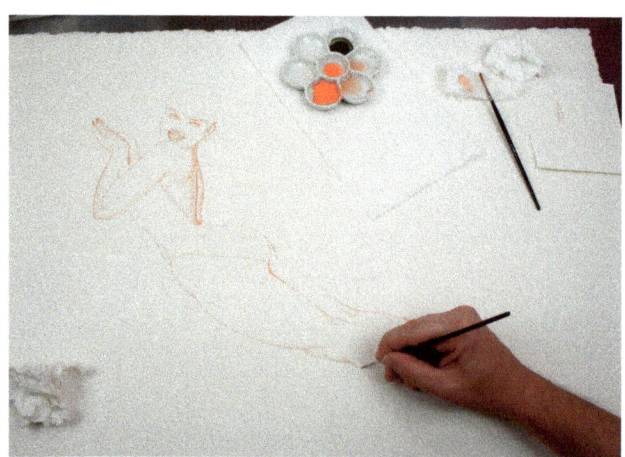

I apply clean water on her back and add vermilion to the edges, then using a clean moist brush, drag along the edge of the pigment to fade it out for a soft airbrush-like edge.

The leg is "painted" with clear water. This makes manipulating the pigment easier and lessens the chance of the paint drying too quickly and creating unwanted hard edges.

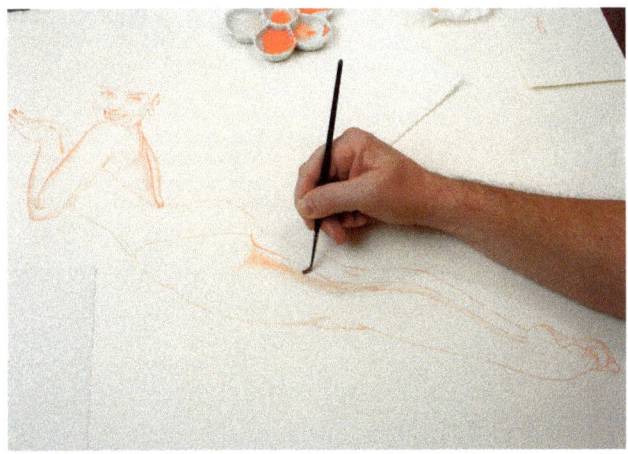

The pigment is added with a watercolor brush along the leg area, and a clean moist brush is dragged along the edge of the paint to soften the edge for a nice fading blend.

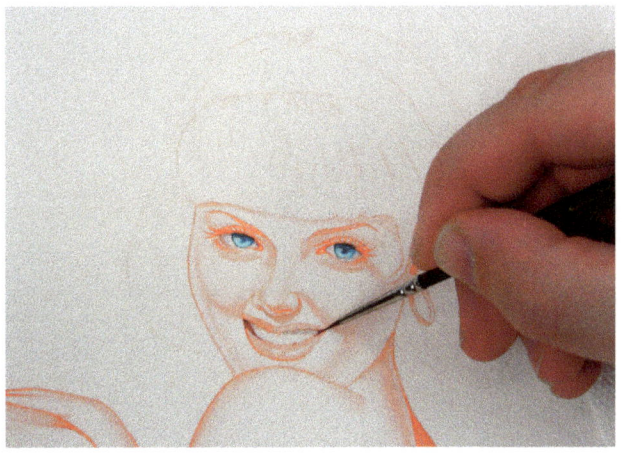

A touch of violet is added to my burnt sienna mix, and the recesses of the corners of her mouth are further defined for added contrast.

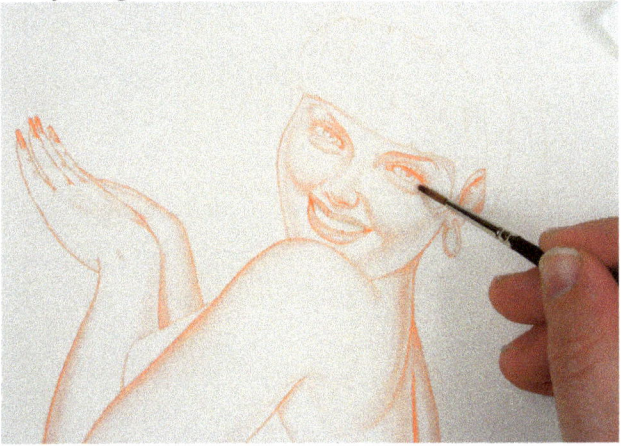

I work on the tiny facial features with the same blending techniques, by first making the area water bearing. Shape defining shadows are carefully applied and blended.

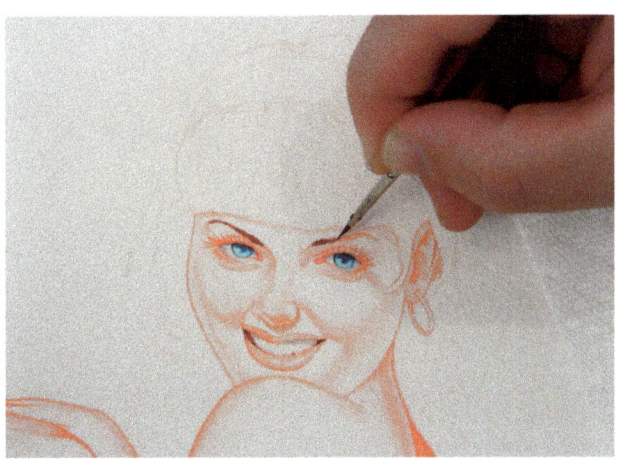

The same burnt sienna with violet is used to paint the eyebrows. Just a flat basic shape here, no individual hairs needed.

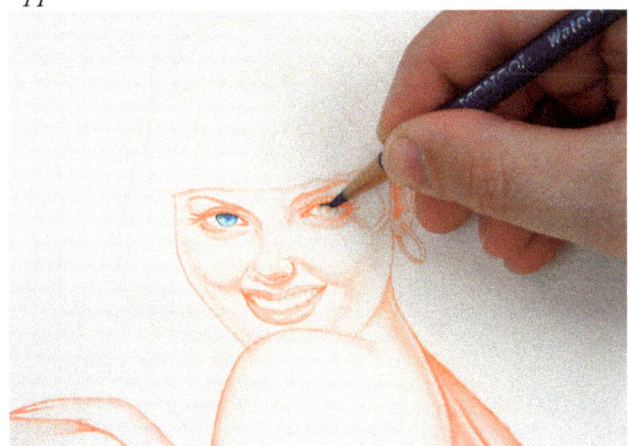

I use a Mongol waxless watercolor pencil to color the eyes. Add water to make the iris wet, then draw around the iris and pupil with blue. A damp brush is used to spread the pigment.

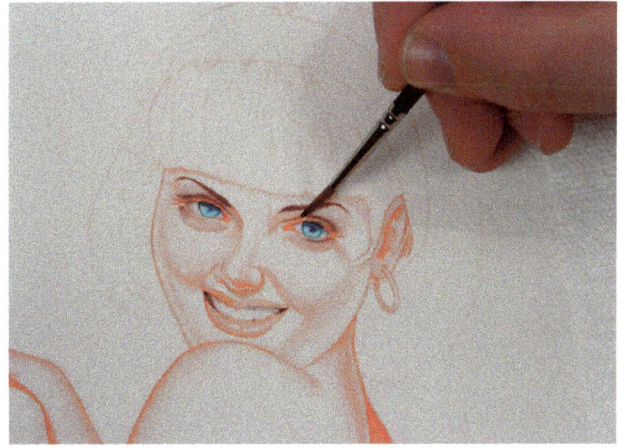

The crease in the eyelid is defined with the same violet/burnt sienna mix, and dragging a moist brush along the edge softens the hard line.

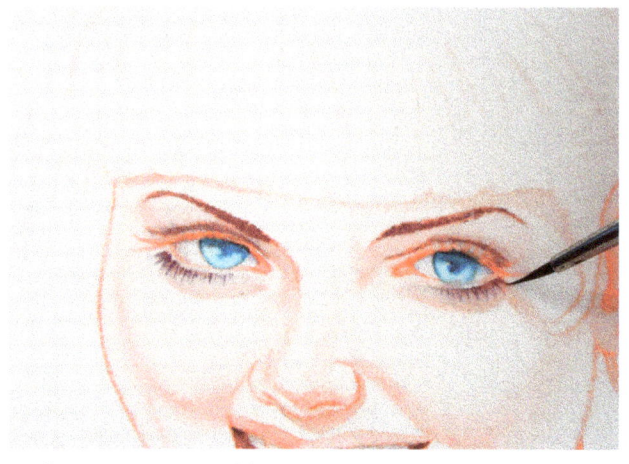

I drag a mixture of burnt sienna along the lower edge of the eye to create eyeliner. Violet is used for the lower eyelashes with a 000 brush, as I hold my breath!

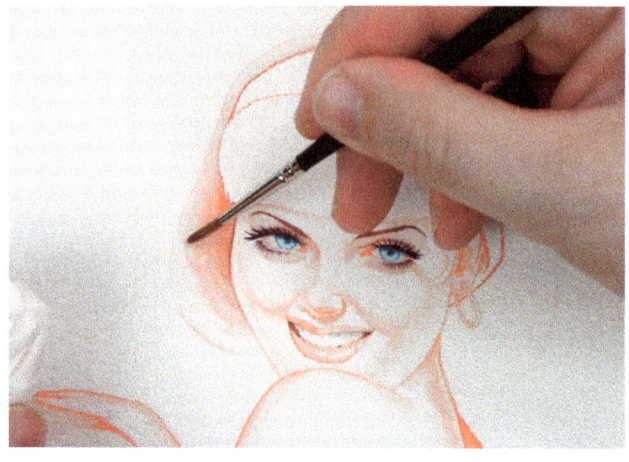

I add clean water to the hair before adding paint. A diluted mixture of english red light is applied. Drag the brush in the direction of the flow of the hair.

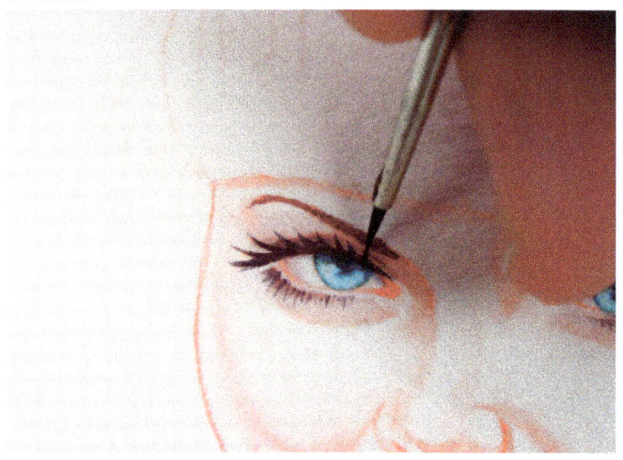

A bit of burnt sienna is added to a more concentrated mixture of violet, and then the upper eyelashes are painted using the drag and lift technique to create the taper.

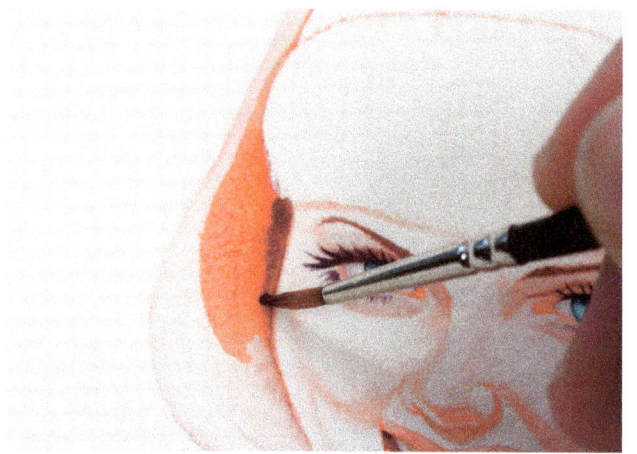

Violet is added to the burnt sienna close to the face for depth, and to create shadow areas in the hair.

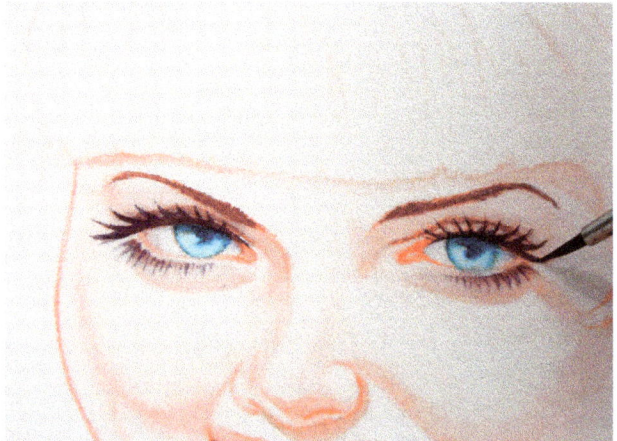

I recommend practicing eyelashes, and to test your brush on another scrap sheet first! You don't want too much pigment on your brush, or too wet of a mixture.

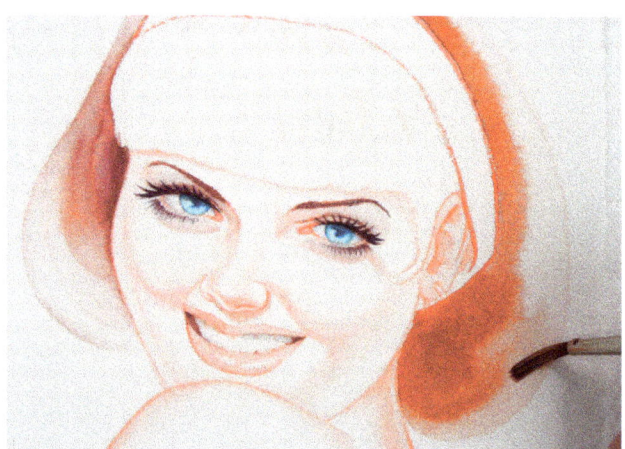

Think of the hair as a cloud. Apply color and blend it softly, keeping highlights and shadows in mind. Creating individual strand of hair would make it look like straw.

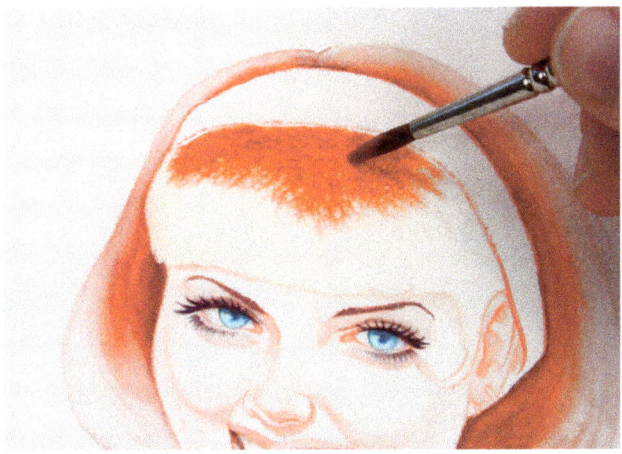

Paint is added to the top of her bangs and at the bottom, leaving an unpainted area in the middle to create a highlight.

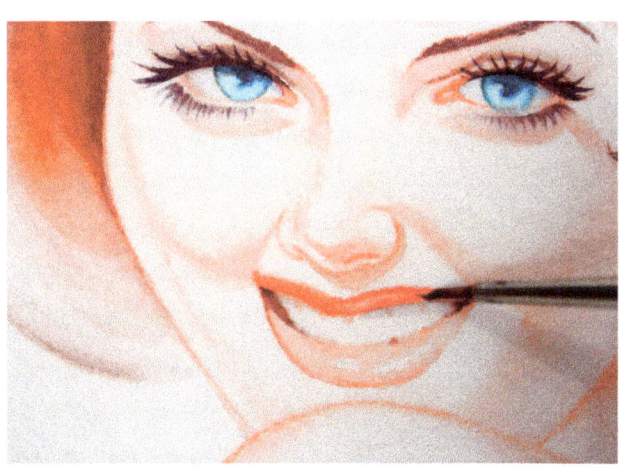

Back to the lips! rose madder and vermilion are mixed to create a nice lipstick color. This is carefully painted on the upper lip first and allowed to dry.

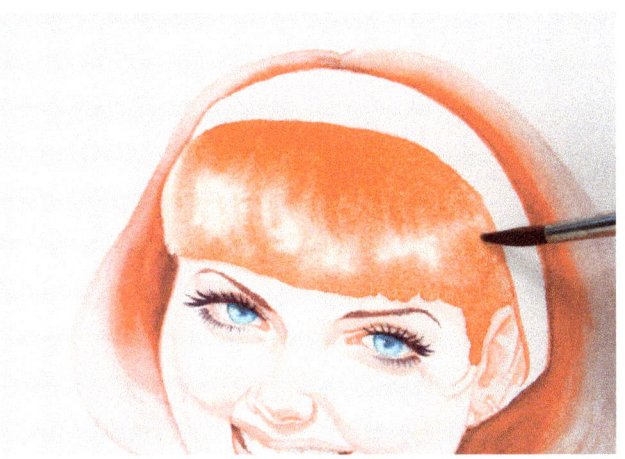

A clean damp brush is used to coax the pigment into the area.

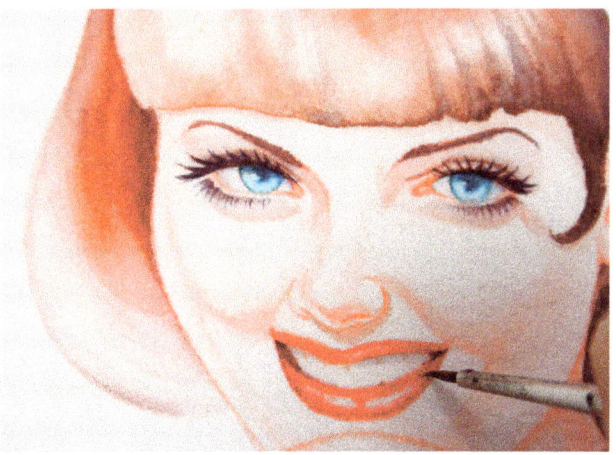

Rose madder is painted on the lower lip - and the corners of her mouth - for color continuity. I avoid adding too much where the lip highlights are allowing white paper to show through.

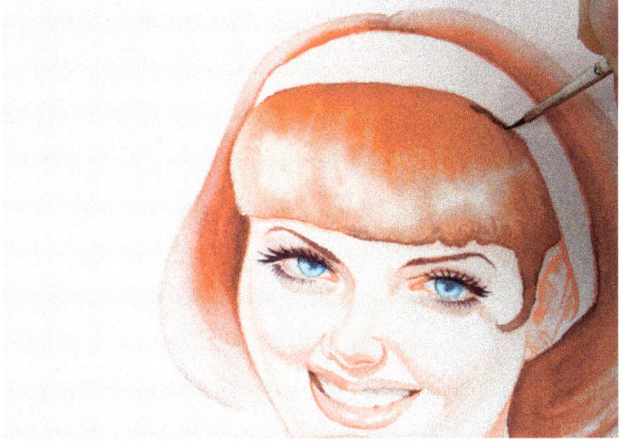

While the english red light is still a bit wet, I add some violet to the edge near the hair band.

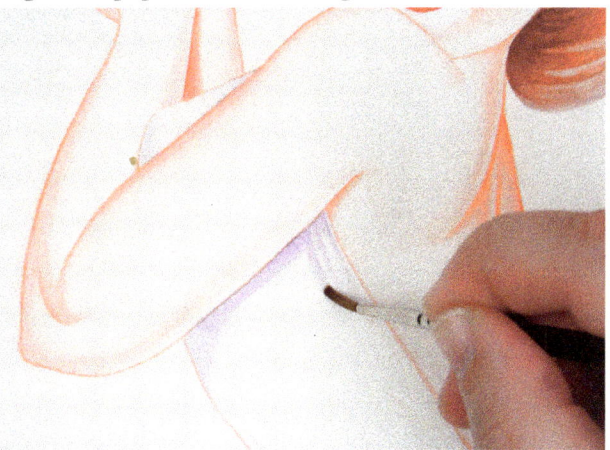

Wrinkles and shadows are created on her white swimsuit using a thin application of violet. Just like with the skin, I first add water to the area I wish to paint.

Edward Reed Q&A

Give us a little background on you, how did you get started in art, and are pin-ups the main focus of the work you do?

I have been drawing science fiction and fantasy art for as long as I can remember, but I started taking my talent more seriously when I became an assistant for an airbrush artist in Panama City Beach, Florida in 1987. I think I was about 19 years old at the time. It took a couple of summers before I had the skill and nerve to go out on my own, but it was the best education in art I could get - and not have to pay for!

During the off season I had a lot of time on my hands, but I was usually too burned out from airbrushing 80 to 90 hours a week to want to do any personal airbrush work. Instead I opted for a different medium and that was watercolors on cotton rag paper. It was art therapy really. I could still be creative, but in a refreshing way.

I had quite an interest in all things World War II - and liked the girlie nose art on the warplanes, but at the time I wasn't fully aware of the sources for the pin-ups, which of course were the Varga Girl, and Petty Girl of Esquire and True magazine. I fell in love with the work - and tried my hand at recreating some of their art - since they used watercolors and an airbrush. It was a natural fit for what I had already trained myself to do.

Who inspires you, who are some of the artists you look up to?

Oh the list is very long! Of course Olivia is probably the artist who inspired me the most to get into pin-up art. I like all of the pin-up artists of the golden age, including Alberto Vargas and George Petty, but its today's artists that inspire me the most. Artists like Michael Parkes, Casey Baugh, Luis Royo, Drew Struzan and Brom, to name only a few. Today I am more interested in the digital artists like Linda Bergkvist, Marta Dahlig, Robert Chang, and Steven Stahlberg.

Novice artists sometimes have trouble rendering believable skin tones, how do you achieve life-like skin tones?

I still struggle with this myself, but mostly because I am impatient. It is particularly challenging with transparent watercolors because they tend to shift to red. You have to test mixes and see what they look like once they dry because you don't have a real accurate color when they are still wet. I like to use a light wash of burnt sienna as a base for building my flesh tones, otherwise I tend to mix my own using vermilion and Hooker's green light. You can create your own values of burnt sienna with those two colors. Sometimes I will add a touch of thalo blue to cool it down, and I add a touch of violet as a colorcast to darken the hue for shadow areas and details like eyelashes.

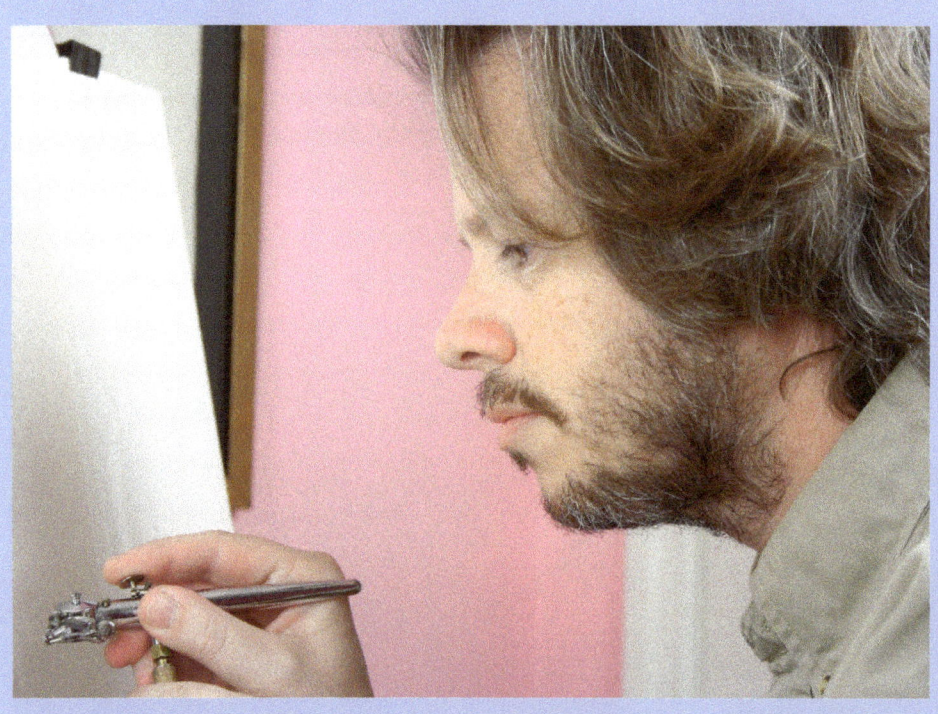

Edward Reed using the Paasche AB Turbo in his studio in Summerville, South Carolina.

Edward Reed Q&A

If I use opaque mediums I tend to use more greens and blue in my base flesh color to grey it down some, so it doesn't appear too shiny or look like plastic. If you look at your own skin you will be surprised at how many colors are really there - some coming from within, and others coming from various light sources that cast down upon us. I think the trick is to build your colors up slowly and stay away from dark greys and black, as that will just make the flesh look dirty. I save highlights for last and rarely use straight white. Usually it's a very light version of the fleshtone. For backfill light to highlight contours and add a three-dimensional feel, I use a cool bright turquoise. This tends to give strength and contrast to the overall warm reds in the skin tones and it really pops!

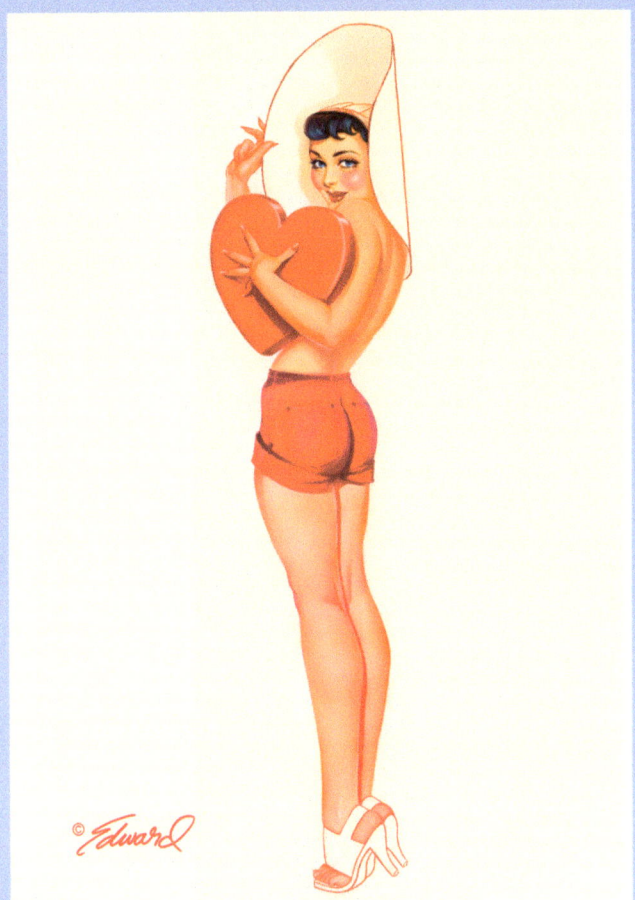

"Be Mine" Watercolor and Gouache on watercolor board 12 x18 inches.

Another area where people have trouble is with faces, are there tricks or particular methods you use to create a good portrait?

Sometimes less is more. I see some artists try to put every wrinkle and pore onto the face and it ages the portrait considerably. As for pin-up type artwork I tend to make features a bit rounder and perhaps smoother. The eyes are everything, so I take special care there. Sometimes you need to make them ever so slightly larger to make the piece more appealing and cuter. When we draw facial features in two-dimensional form certain details tend to look too small, even if anatomically correct. With pin-up the technique is to idealize the features, and that might mean leaving out certain details that will detract from the overall look of the face. Those are things like spaces between the teeth, wrinkles at the edges of the eyes or smile lines. And sometimes it means exaggerating or caricaturizing some features slightly - like pouty fuller lips. You have to edit some features to make a pleasing portrait. I find that a three quarter angle is a more flattering pose for the head as well.

How about the equipment you use, which airbrush do you typically use and why?

I prefer to use the Paasche AB Turbo for my watercolors as it delivers the most subtle and finest spray - with the utmost control - and it forces me to build the colors slowly. It's almost impossible to overwork an airbrush painting with the Turbo. I also use an Iwata Micron as it atomizes as finely, but I use it for slightly broader and larger chunks of the anatomy - such as the legs or arms.

Paint, which brand of paint do you use and why?

I don't use student grade or cheap watercolors because you want a very finely ground pigment that is colorfast. I tend to buy Winsor & Newton watercolors and Gouache. But Holbein, Old Holland and Schmincke Horadam are in my collection as well.

How did you learn to mix paint to create unique colors?

Edward Reed Q&A

Color theory is best learned by trial and error! Most people understand primary and secondary colors, but it's the tertiary colors that can get you in trouble. You don't need to fully understand what color contaminations are in a particular color you are using when mixing it with another. When I airbrushed t-shirts you had to be careful about allowing the opposites on the color wheel to blend together, because you could end up with a brown or grey band of color in the faded blends - and that would muddy an otherwise brightly colored beach scene. So you worked mostly with analogous blending techniques. If you wanted contrasting complimentary colors, then you had to be sure your colors didn't overspray and mix on the surface much, but rather just butted up against each other in solid fields. After a while you could see the effects of cool colors against warmer opposites and color mixing whether directly on the surface, or in a color cup - just became intuition.

If you work around color every day for years you can pick up any single tube of paint, look at the pigment and see if and how much secondary color is in the pigment and if it is a warm or cool hue. You can then match your other analogous, or complementary color to have the same cool or warm secondary relationship and not end up creating a neutral tone if one isn't intended. Tertiary colors have less distinctive color contrasts and often create a more earthy or dull tone.

Do you use other media like hand brushes to add detail or achieve effects that are hard to do with an airbrush?

Yes. When I hand paint details I use the finest Kolinsky sable watercolor brushes, like Winsor & Newton Series 7 brushes, for the best control and detail. Never use cheap watercolor brushes! For special textures and effects I might use sponges to apply pigment, or paper towels to dab and lift color. Salt creates very interesting effects when watercolors start to dry! Experimentation can lead to interesting results - that you can then use to create unique looks for your painting. Screens, a paper doily, and lace can create nice effects for clothing.

Do you work with live models or do you work from a printed image or photograph.

I am not much of a photographer but I sometimes photograph my own models. Mostly I work with other photographers who allow me to use their work for reference material. That can be a bit limiting though, as you have to settle for the poses or costumes they used. But I tend to change them up and not just recreate the photograph they shot.

When I photograph my own models I like to do high energy one hour shoots, with maybe 3 or 4 costumes changes. Anything longer and you tend to lose the energy and the freshness of the model. I usually end up with about 300 shots and out of that I will have about a dozen or so that work great for a painting. If I have a planned pose in mind then I might take my time and make sure the shot is composed and lit per-

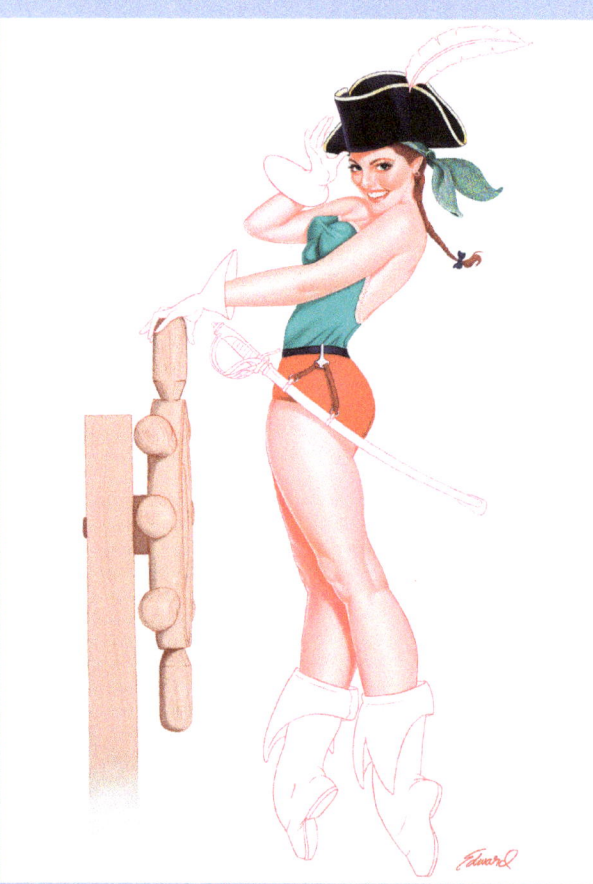

"Ahoy There!" Watercolor and Gouache on watercolor board 12 x 18 inches.

Edward Reed Q&A

fectly, but so far I am lucky in that the two models I work with just move around and strike lots of different poses and facial expressions, so all I have to do is push the shutter button and try to keep up!

If you do work with models, how do you pick them and where do you find them?

There are a number of model/photographer network websites, and I found both of my current models through ModelMayhem.com. Both are local girls who live rather close by so travel is easy. I have plenty of local models to choose from, but I look, for girls with that cute "girl next-door" look, with perhaps resemblance to a "Petty Girl" or a "Varga Girl." I got lucky and found both! What I think is cute or beautiful may not be what another artists agrees with, but I like to think I have good taste and can find a girl who is both cute and pretty, with an all around appealing charm that works in a pin-up painting.

What makes a good pin-up?

A cute smile and bright eyes! This is going to be the first thing most people will notice. I like full lips too! Of course long legs and nice curves are ideal for a pin-up. I also look for elegant hands. When it comes to a drawing or painting of a person, the face is noticed and critiqued first, then they will see the hands. If you make the hands overly detailed, or don't take care to taper the fingers just right, then the whole pin-up fails (without the right taper they look too masculine). Everything about the hands has to be feminine, soft and delicate. Hands can be just as expressive as the eyes. Here I also see artists putting in way too much detail. They want to put in the veins and the bone structure and it ages the hands. There is so much that can be left out and this will actually aid in creating youthful, soft hands.

Otherwise, a themed costume and a simple pose are all that's required. There are only so many poses the human body can assume, so to add visual interest and create an appealing image you should think about what she is wearing, or what props might be introduced to create some kind of relationship or story to give each pin-up an identity and personality.

Most importantly though, a pin-up girl is cute and flirty and not overtly sexual. Pin-up art should be fun and lighthearted otherwise you are creating erotica or a nude portrait, which isn't "pin-up" at all. She should be the cute girl next door caught giggling. That is what the Petty Girl was and that is what I call a "pin-up." When I look at a Petty girl I feel her giddiness and I want to giggle too!

If you look at the golden age of pin-up, the most successful paintings were the girls glancing your way with a cute smile. After all, it's quite uplifting to a guy's self-esteem when a pretty girl looks at you and smiles. It doesn't take much to make our day!

If you were going to give ten words of advice to someone just starting out, what would that advice be?

Perseverance, dedication, commitment, determination, tenacity, passion, research, evaluate, refine, PRODUCE!

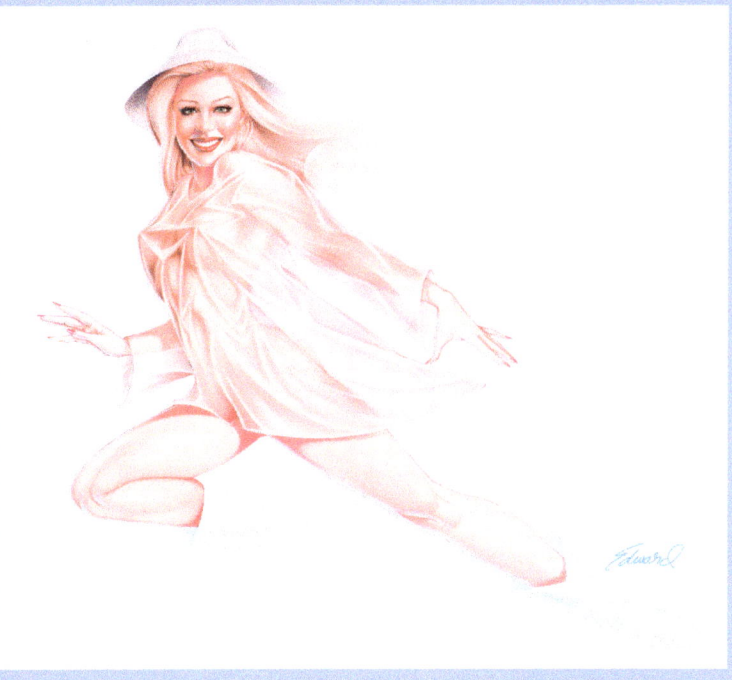

"Slickers" Watercolor and Gouache on watercolor board 20 x 23 inches.

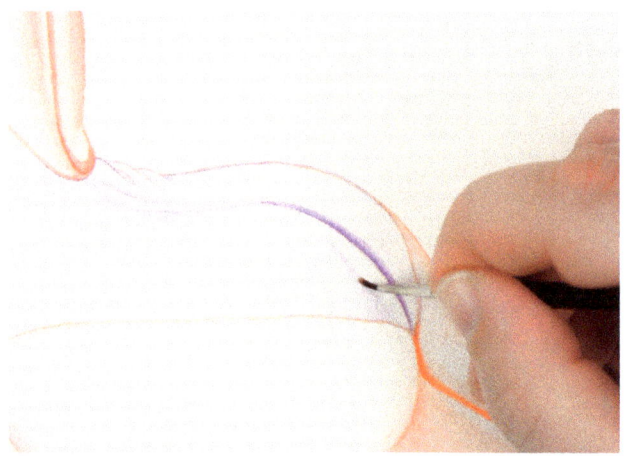

Add the pigment to the wet area and coax the pigment with a damp brush to blend it and fade it out.

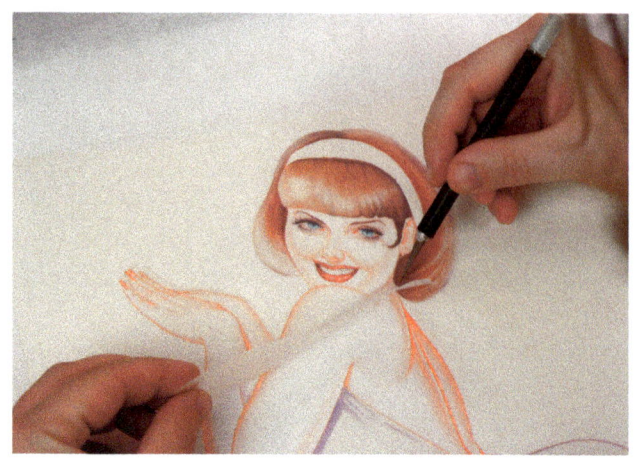

The sign maker's tape is a bit thicker than regular airbrusher's frisket so it takes a slightly heavier hand to cut it. Only the flesh areas are exposed now for airbrushing.

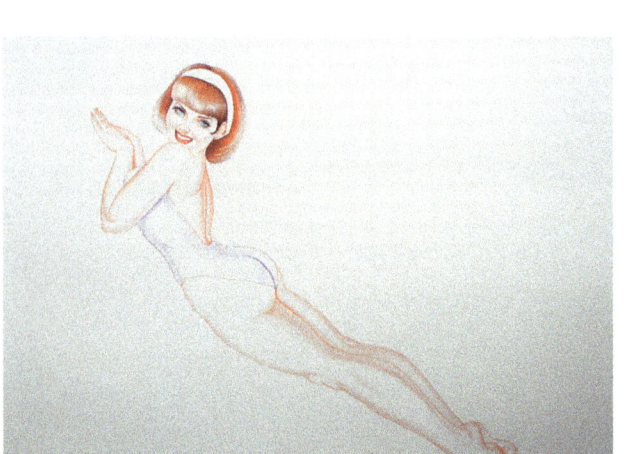

The hand painted pinup so far. This "modeling in" of the form and shape will be a great guide when we start airbrushing to further define the form and enhance the tonal values.

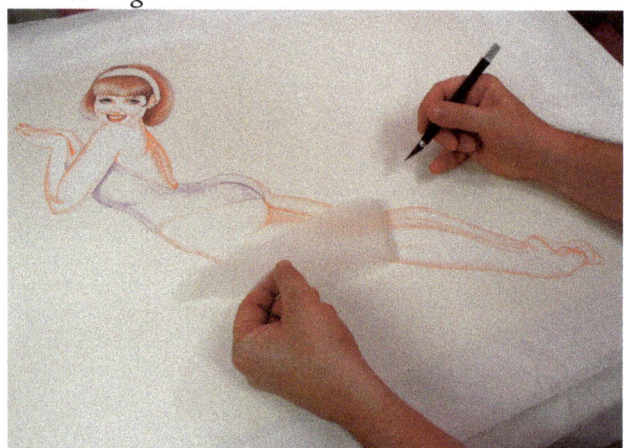

I only use the masking in large sections to keep overspray from appearing on the background or landing on the white swimsuit.

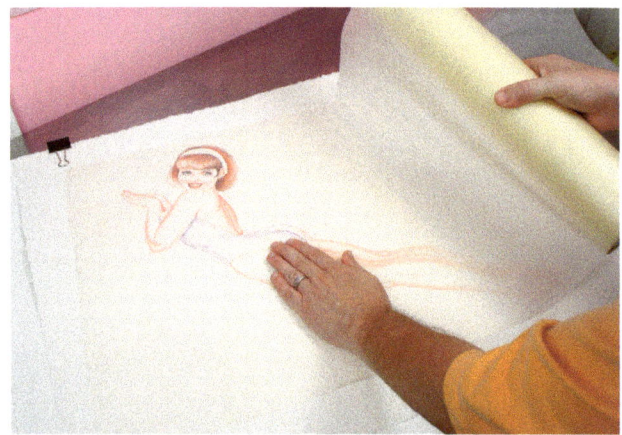

Frisket doesn't adhere to watercolor paper. I use low tack TransferRite® sign makers tape as it adheres, but doesn't tear the fibers of the paper or lift any of the pigment.

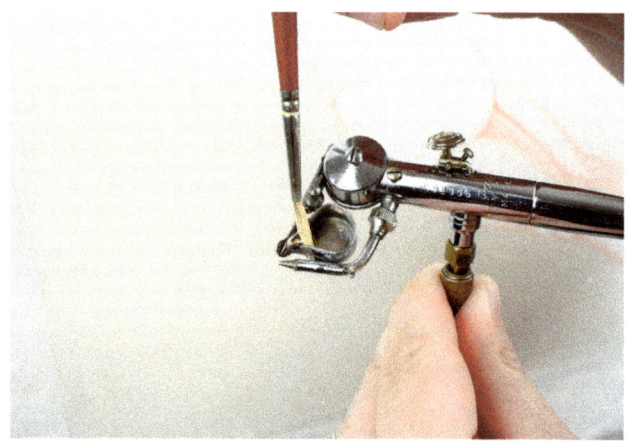

I load the Paasche AB Turbo with a thin mixture of naples yellow for the initial flesh tone, and spray the entire exposed area with the naples yellow.

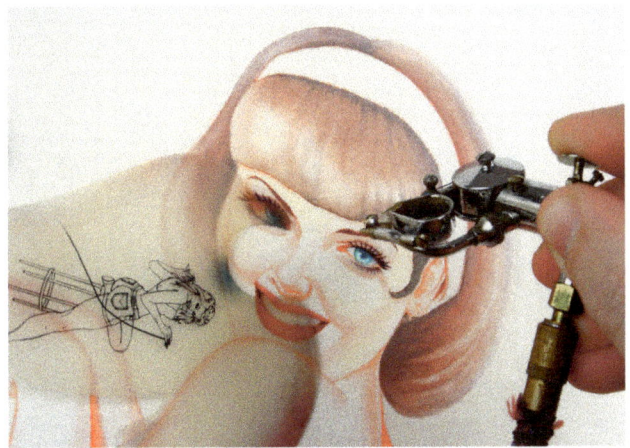

I use freehand shields to block areas that I don't want to receive the color - such as the eyes here.

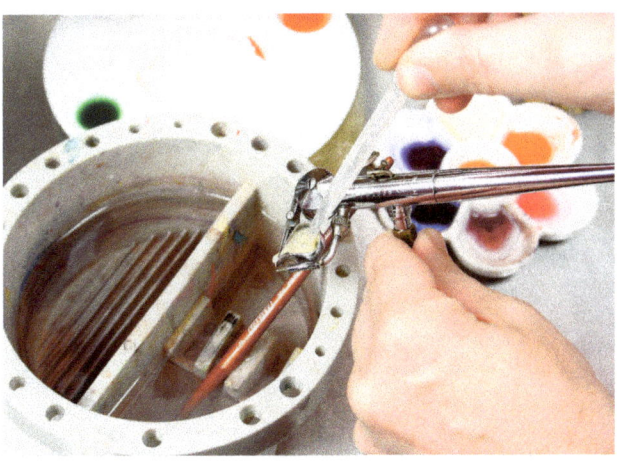

A plastic pipette is used to add water to the color cup. Then the water is sucked out to clean the airbrush for the next color.

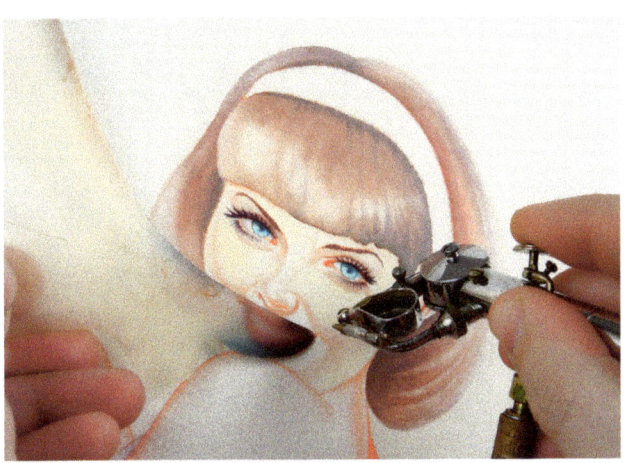

I block the lips and teeth as I spray around the face.

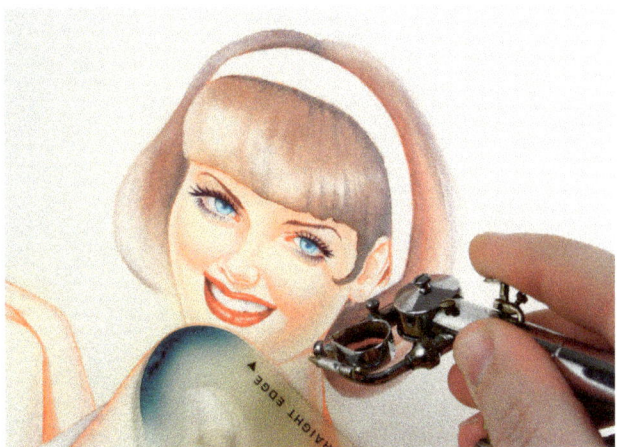

I block the shoulder and spray vermilion slowly, moving back and forth in the direction of the contours to define the shape of the face.

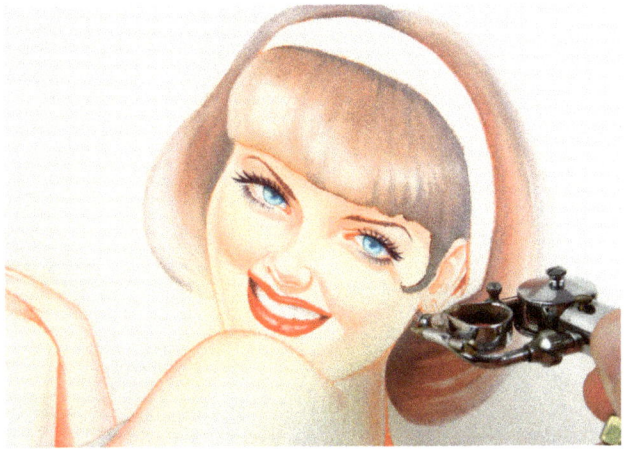

The Turbo is quite subtle and has a very controlled spray, so I feel confident enough to airbrush freehand without the shields on other areas of the body.

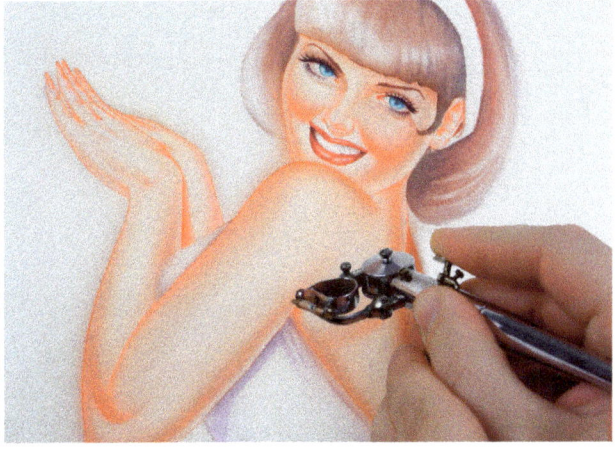

Muscle contours are enhanced and smoothed out using a straight vermilion hue.

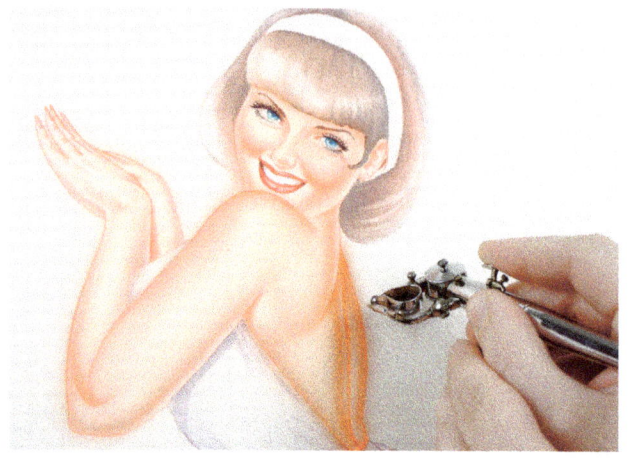

A mixture of burnt sienna, or violet and vermilion mixed together in the color cup are used to deepen the shadows from here on out.

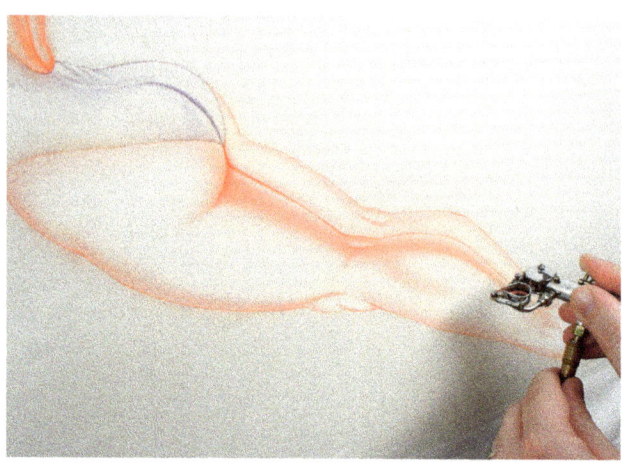

Keeping in mind a general light source, I think of the muscle contours as hills and valleys where light hits the peaks, and shadows are created in the valleys.

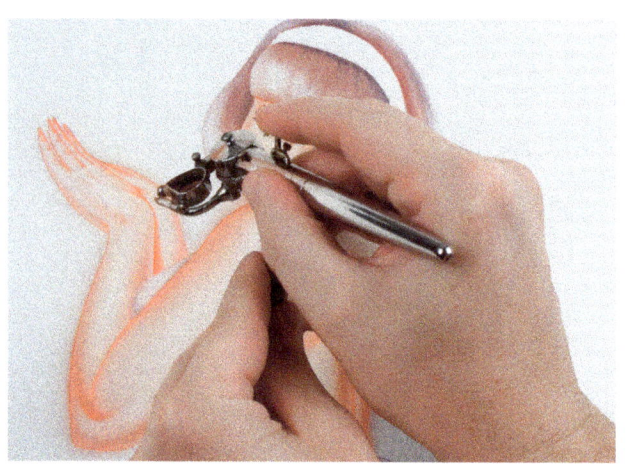

I can get extremely close to the surface with the AB. Turbo to enhance the features of her hands and fingers.

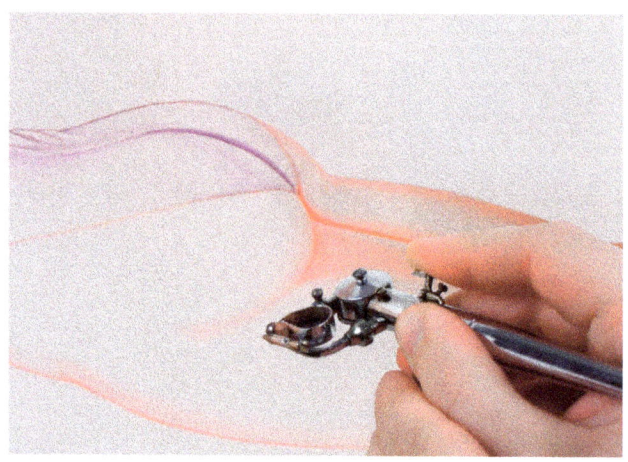

A form shadow is created at the bottom curve of her buttock to give it more form and plumpness! It is best to keep some muscle definition subtle and soft.

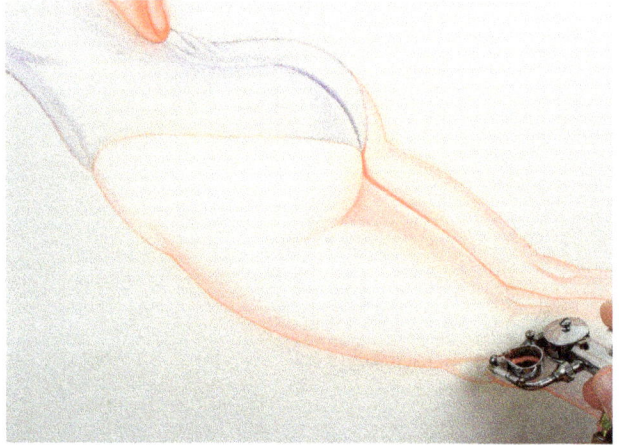

All the previous hand painted edge work is now smoothed out and the values beefed up by airbrushing over the pre-painted muscle definition.

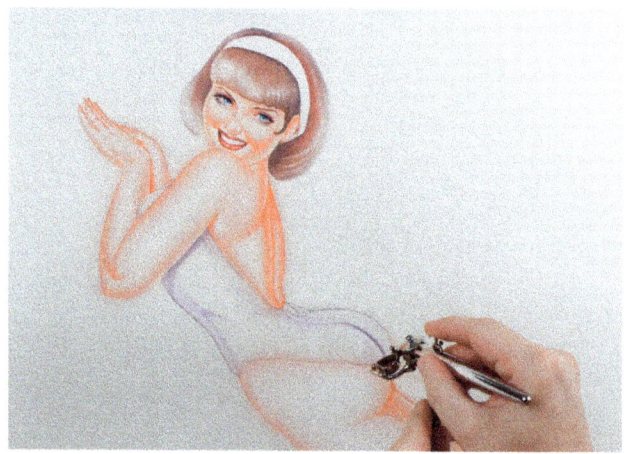

The tight, form fitting bathing suit would pinch and squeeze the soft skin, so a subtle spray of our flesh color is applied along the edge of the swimsuit.

Below: A light mist of vermilion is applied evenly over the entire body to balance the values for overall uniformity.

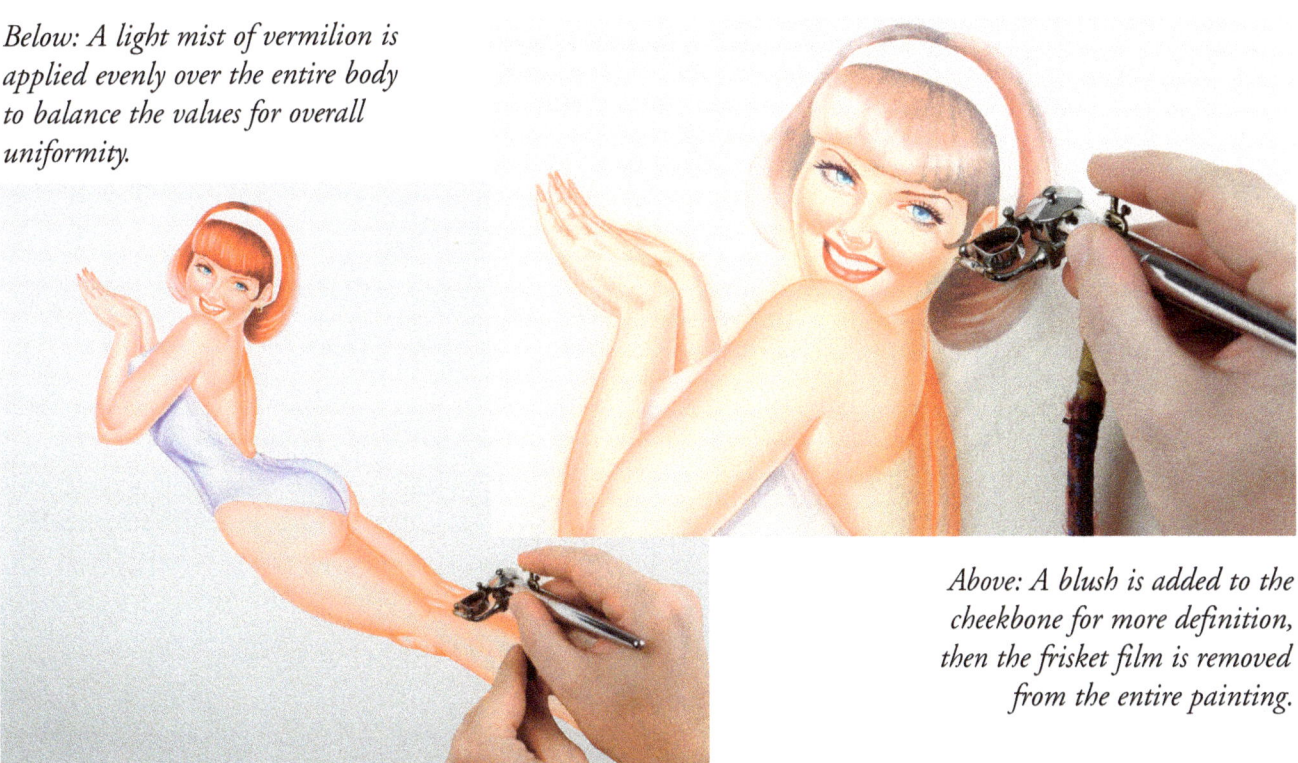

Above: A blush is added to the cheekbone for more definition, then the frisket film is removed from the entire painting.

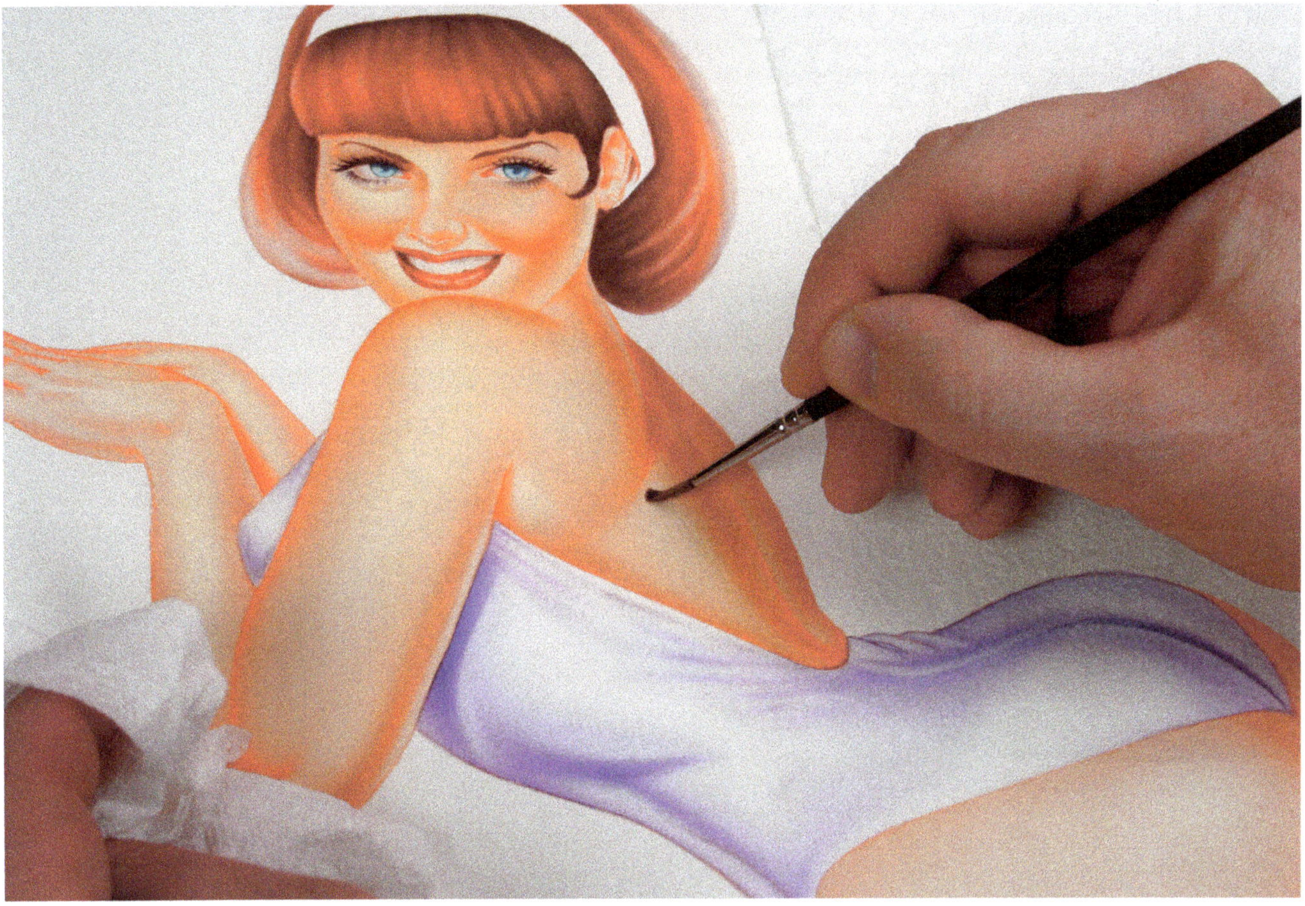

Watercolor can be removed to bring out highlights by using a damp brush. Use a paper towel to dab the area that was brushed with clear water. Lifting out the pigment will enhance the highlights.

Chapter Three
Steve Nunez
Versatility is the Key

Working mostly without masks or frisket, Steve Nunez creates pin-ups, portraits and nudes that are simply stunning both for their visual impact and their tight detail. That Steve can achieve the detail he does, with very little masking, is testimony to his considerable skills.

Like a number of artists in this book, Steve did a lot of T-shirt painting early in his career. In his case, the T-shirt booth not only gave him an opportunity to learn airbrushing, it gave a chance to practice free hand airbrushing. And though those youthful T-shirt days are long

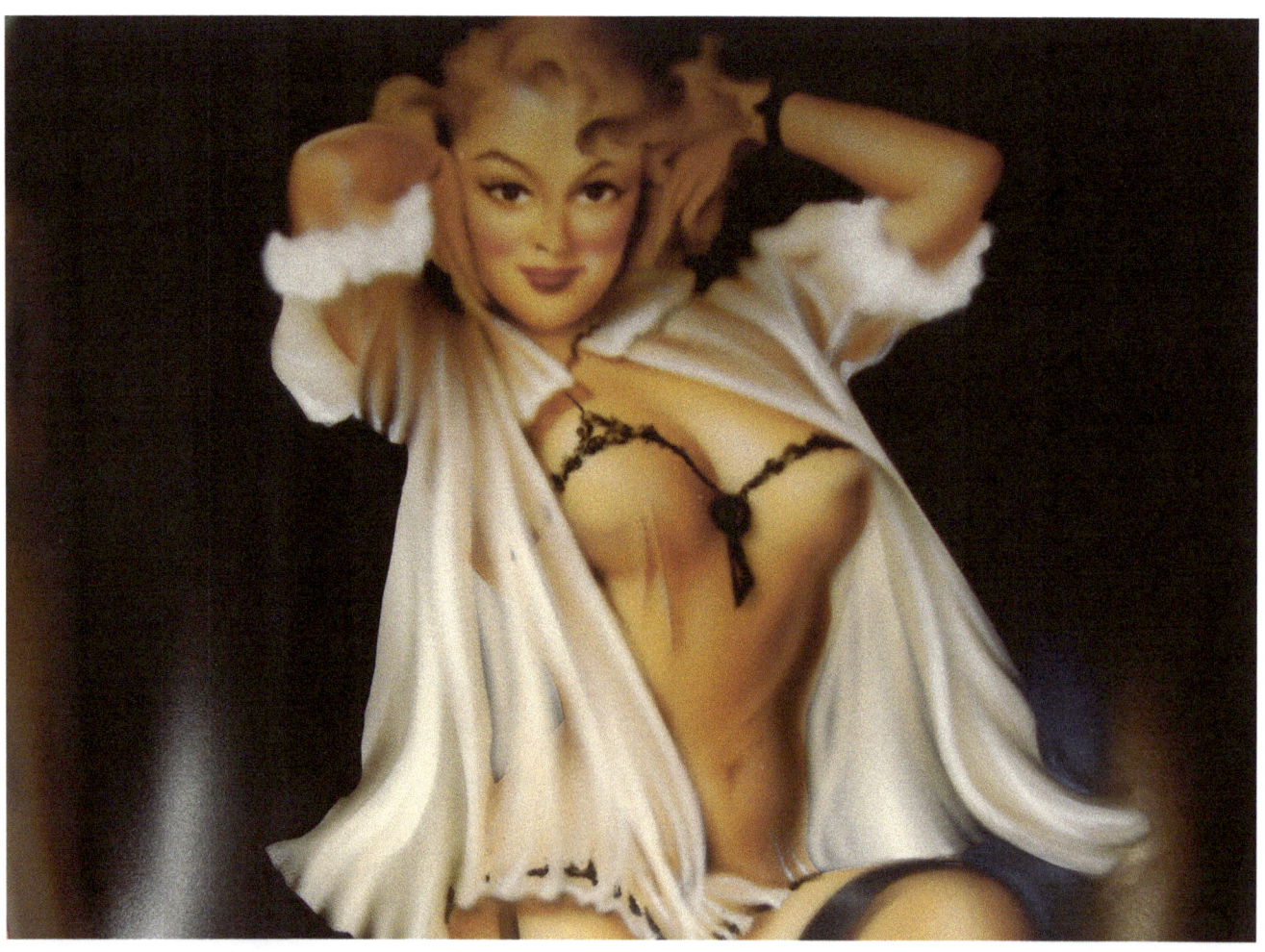

Custom airbrushed "Retro-style" pin-up girl using Alsa Corp airbrush paints.

gone, Steve's abilities to work without masks remains.

Watching Steve work, you will see that he often uses the airbrush like a pencil or a pen – in the sense that the lines he creates are very tight and well defined. His thin lines are so tight they might have been painted with a pinstripe brush.

Even Steve's portraits are built, pass-by-pass, with minimal use of masks or templates. Airbrushing images of famous and beautiful women is one of Steve's specialties. As you watch the image develop, you soon realize this is a man with total control of the airbrush. Steve can create a set of eyelashes, or a perfectly round iris, working free hand without a hand brush or a mask cut from frisket.

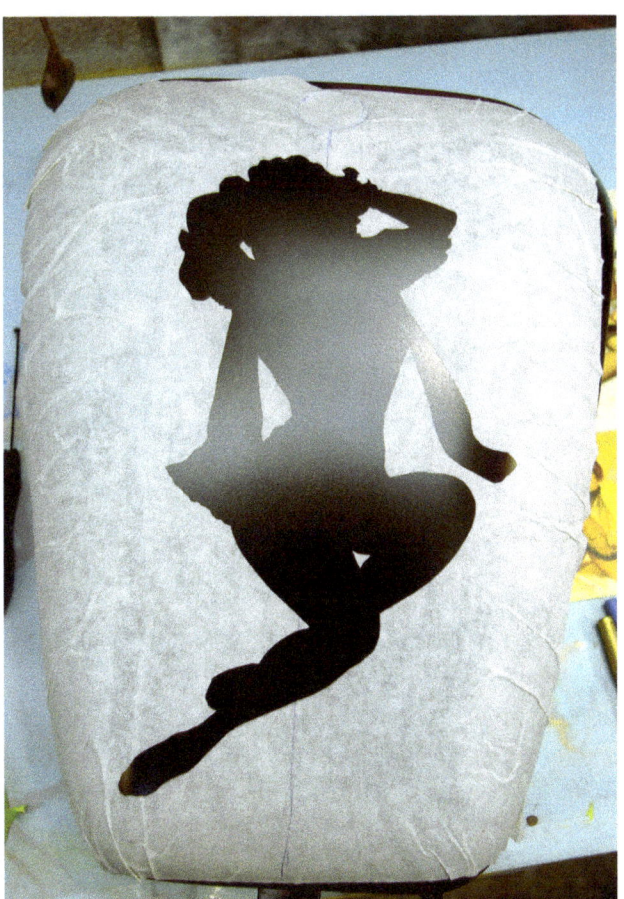

Here the female figure is cut out with an "Xacto" knife, leaving the paintable area ready for paint application.

Many of Steve's images grace the tanks and panels of motorcycles. Most of these images are created with his favorite Alsa paints, then clearcoated with automotive urethane paint. Working on panels that are anything but flat seems to bother Steve not a bit. The photo realistic quality of those images is off the scale. Take a look at Steve's "Theme" bikes on his web site and you will soon become a believer (Steve's web address can be found in the Sources section at the back of the book).

Though he reports being introduced to airbrushing in high school, Steve also reports a complete lack of formal art training. His considerable skills are apparently the result of study, practice and innate ability.

Rather than present one lengthy sequence, we include two, both photographed by Steve.

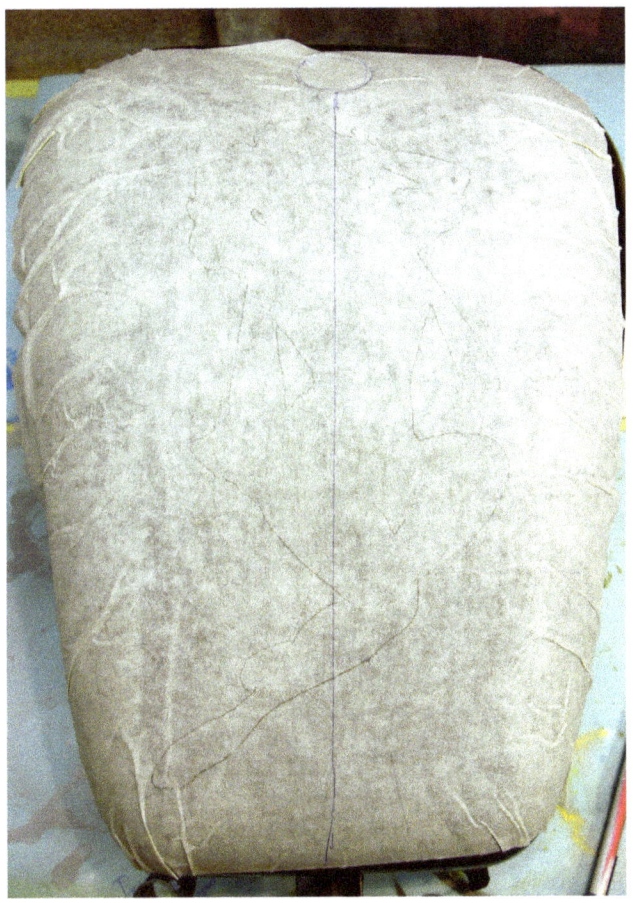

The tank has been sanded and painted with Alsa Corp "Jet Black." The tank is then covered with low-tack application tape. The design is then drawn right onto the tape surface.

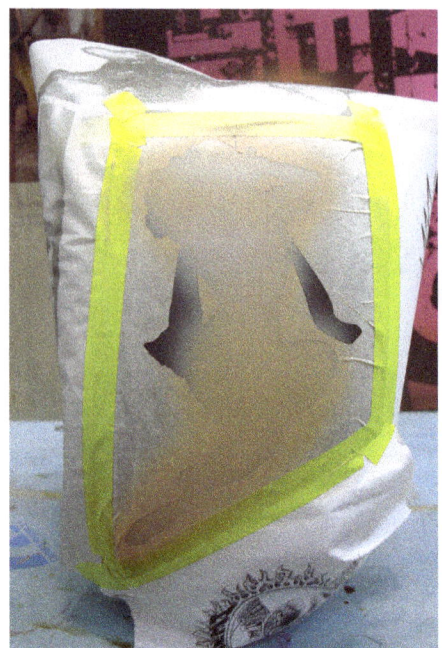
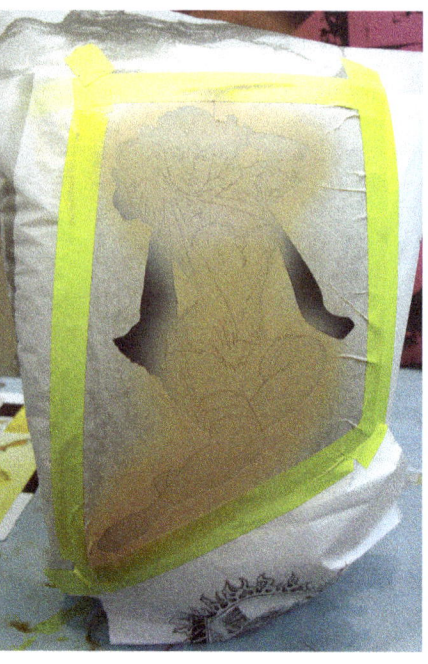
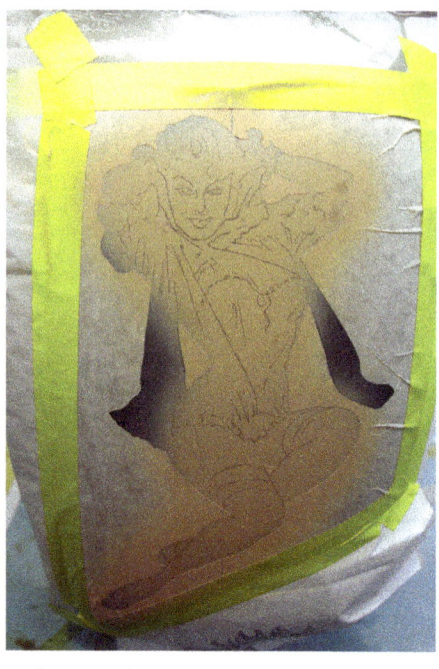

The flesh color is then sprayed onto the general skin areas.

The drawing is then sketched over the flesh areas - with a soft 3B pencil.

The caped area is left bare as I will add touches of light white to denote a transparent lacy look.

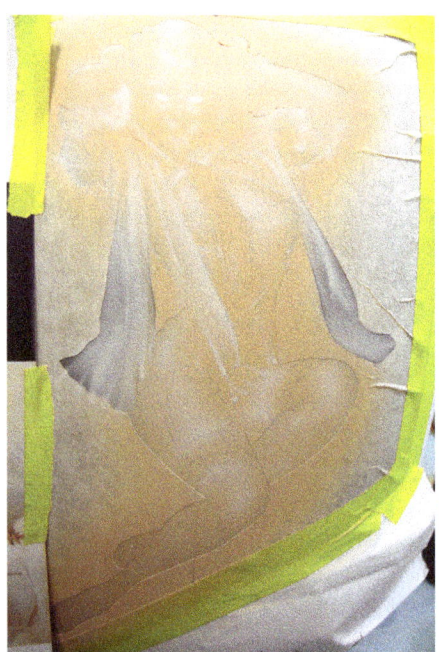
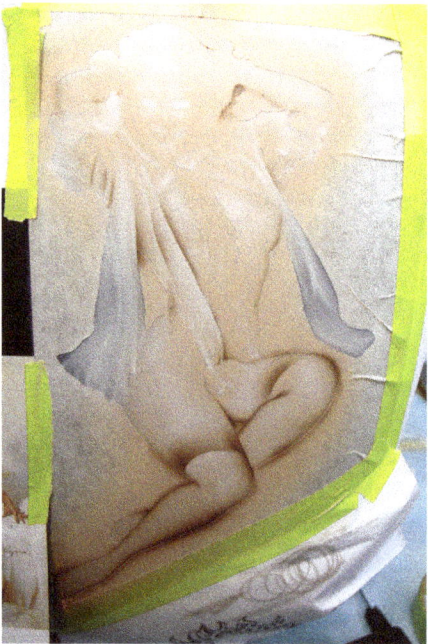
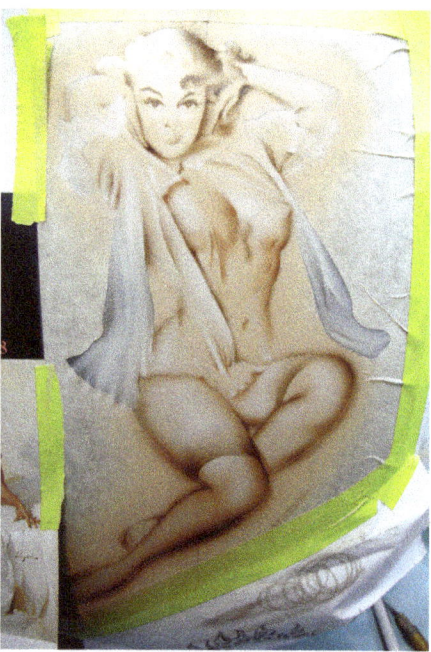

The white highlights are now added and begin to define the figure.

A light brownish flesh tone is added to give the figure some dimension.

More refined airbrushed highlighted areas begin to dictate the figures tonalities.

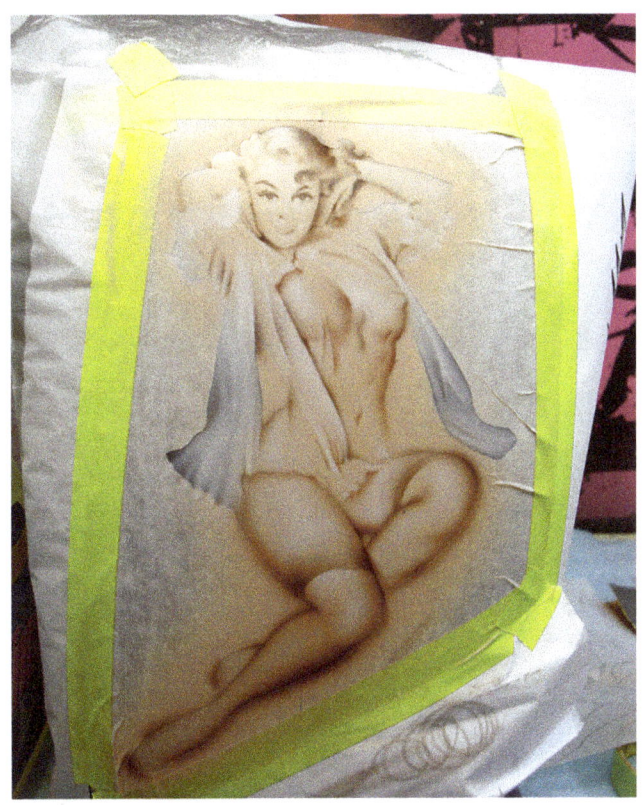
Gradually I begin to add shade and lighter values...

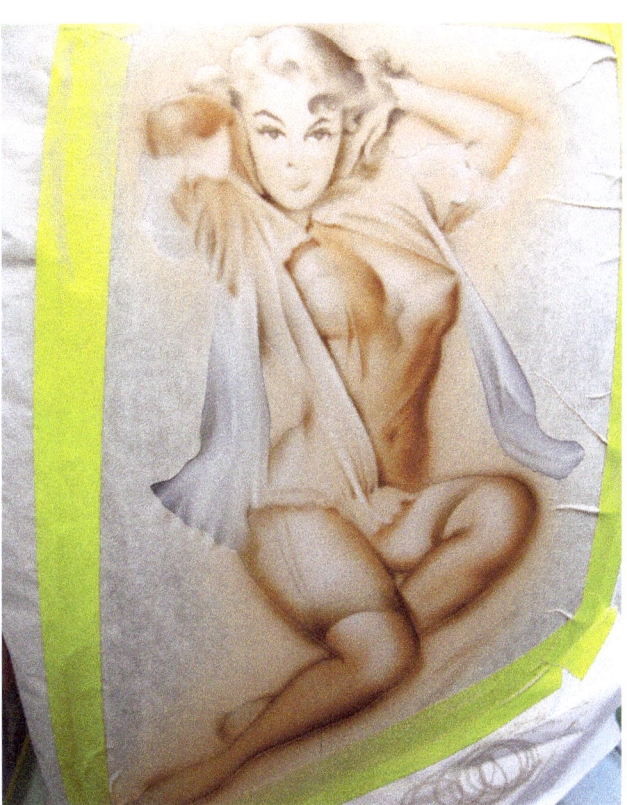
...to increase depth using Alsa Corp candy brown.

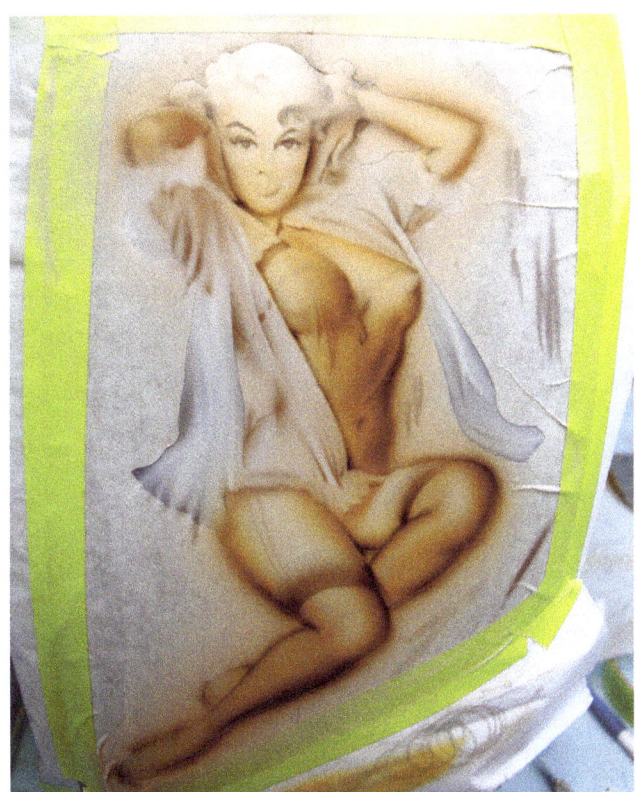
These photos show the progression of tone accomplished by simply using Alsa Corp candies...

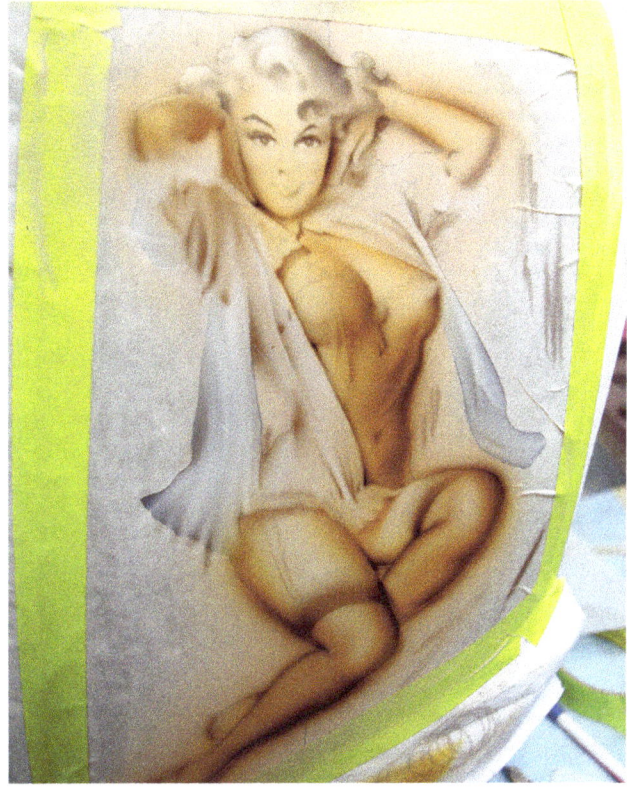
...with Blender to add a sense of depth.

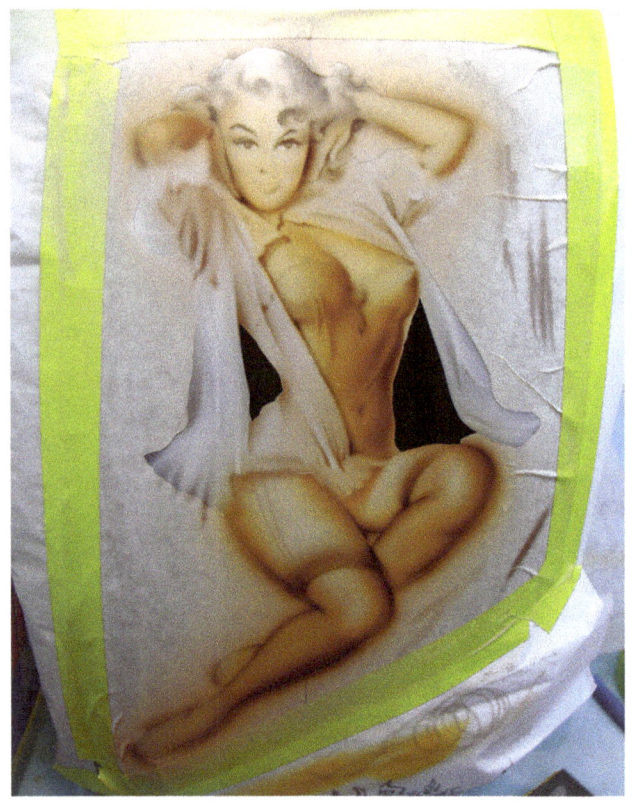

This series of panels shows how even after the basic image is created...

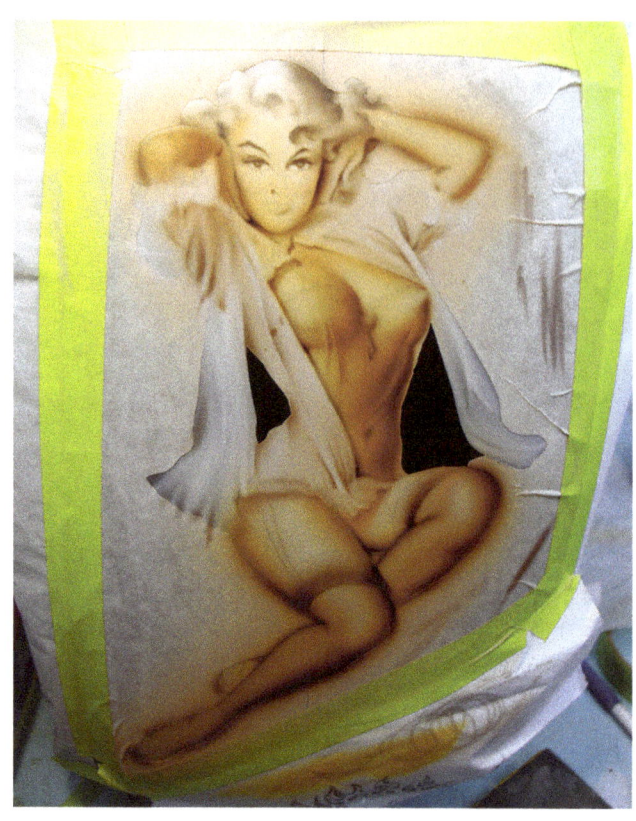

...there is still plenty of work to do. In this case...

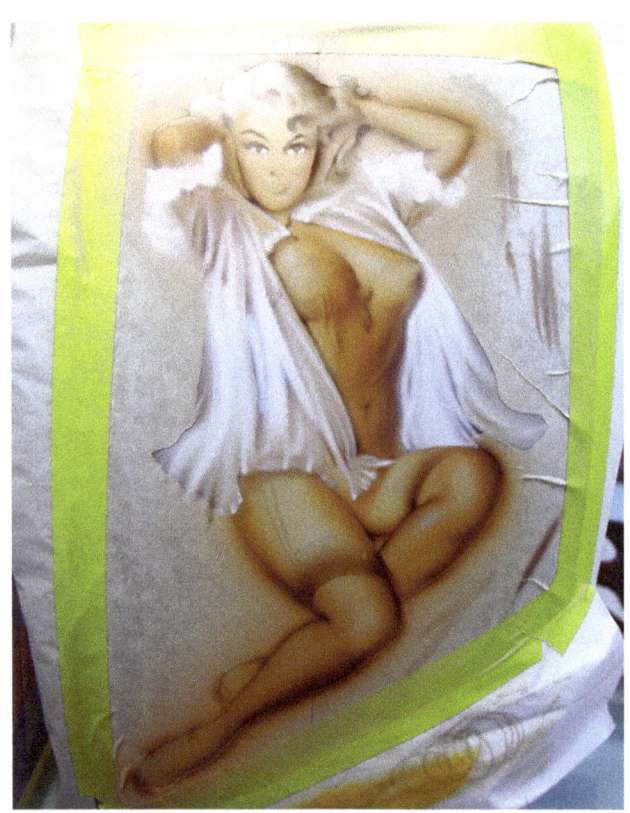

...much of that work involves her negligee...

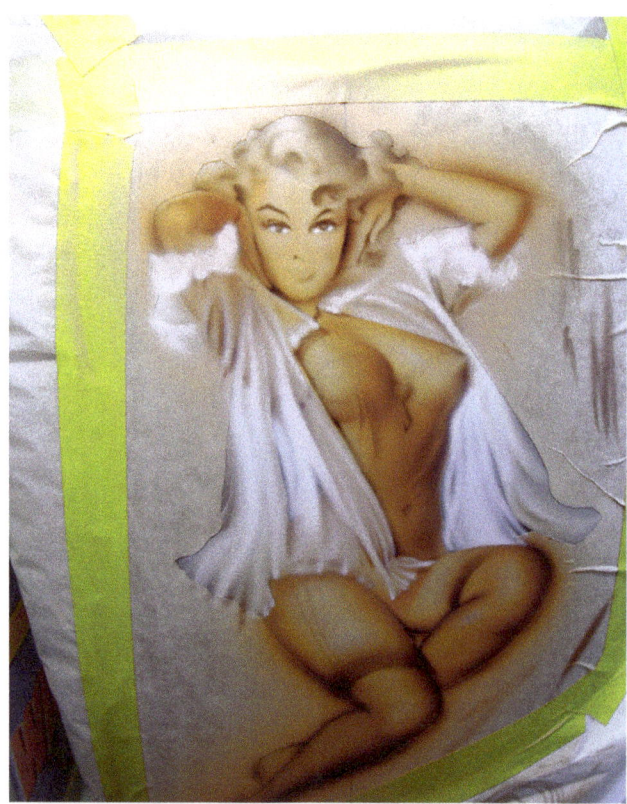

...which is developed and enhanced, step by step.

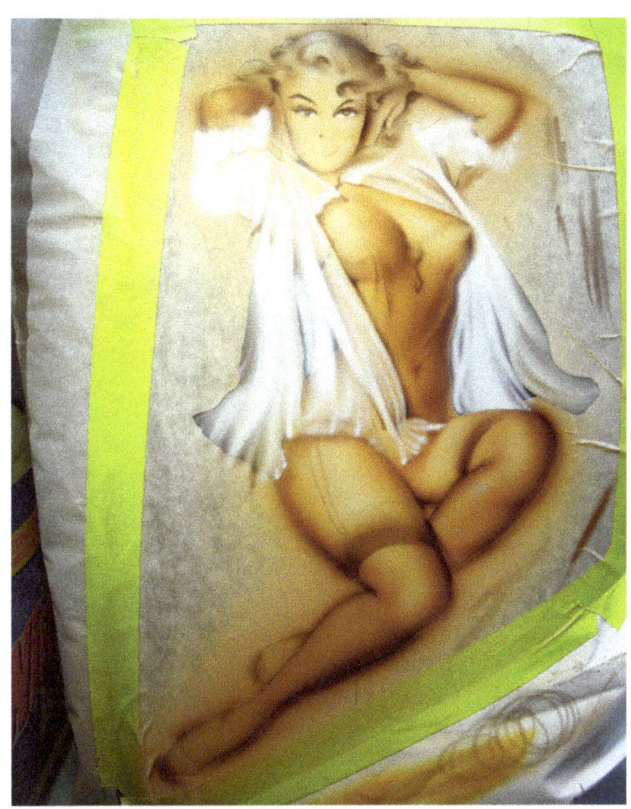

Final touches of brownish shading are added to finalize the flesh tones.

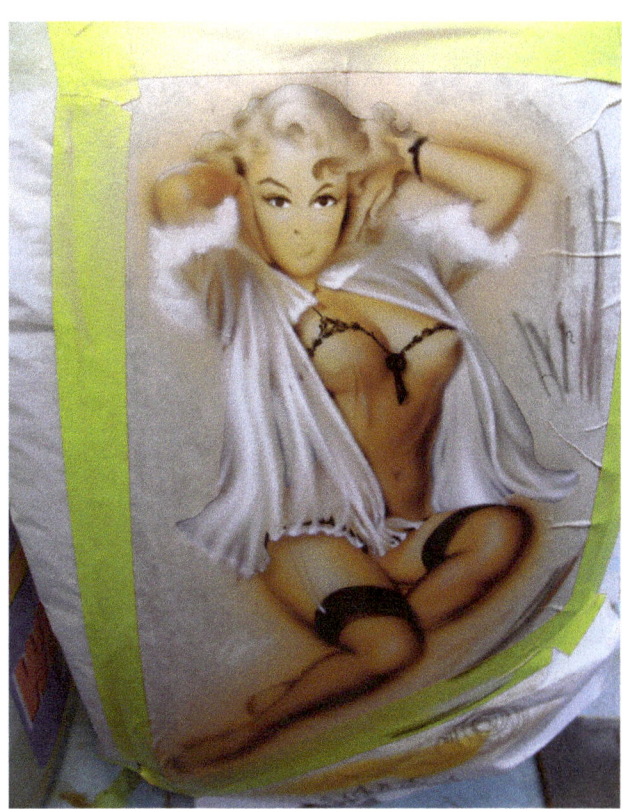

I begin adding black to the darkest areas.

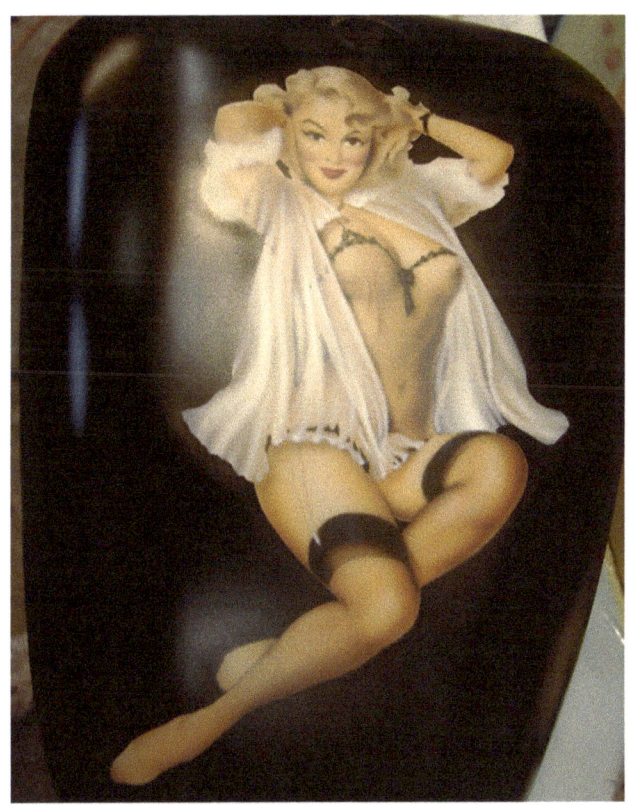

The edges of the design have been slightly wet-sanded with 1500 grit sandpaper to ensure a glass-like finish when clear-coated.

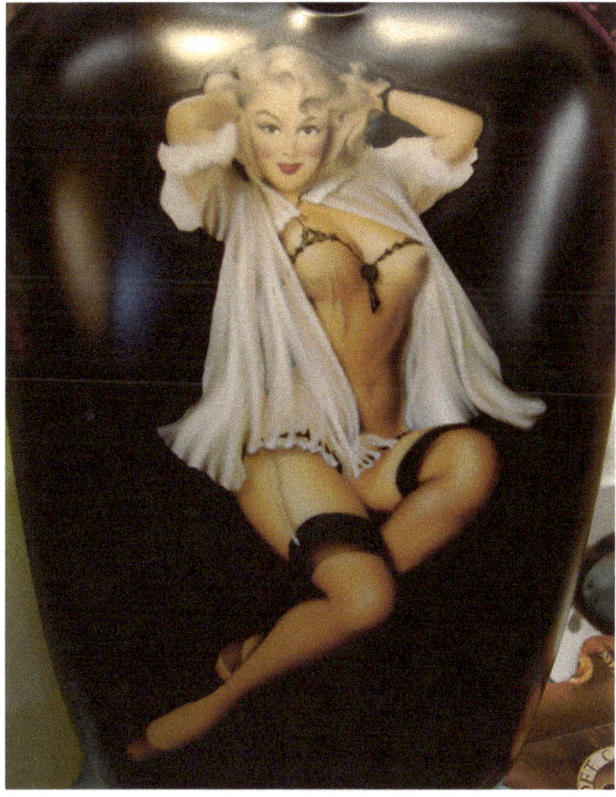

The edges of the figure have been feathered with Alsa Jet Black to keep the design from looking like a decal.

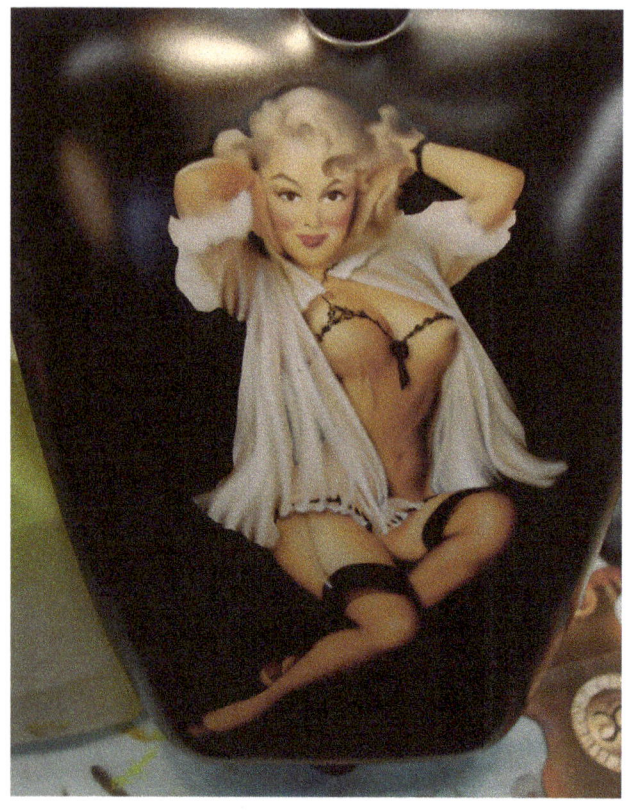

The changes seen here are subtle, but if you look close......

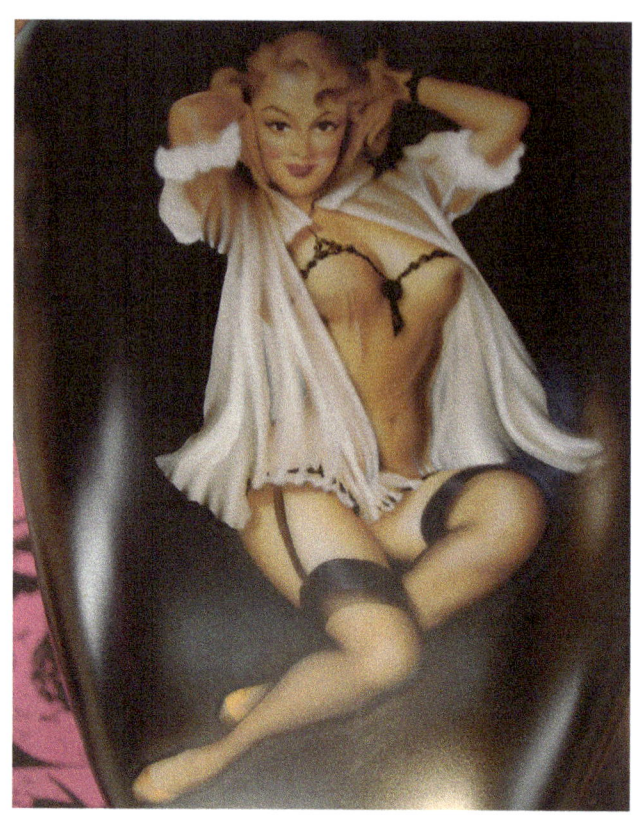

...you can see the progression in tonality...

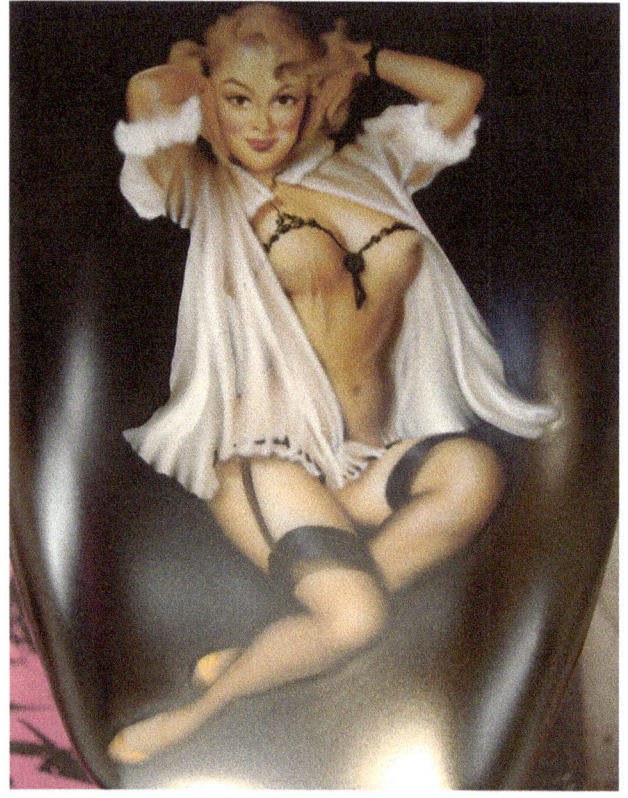

...and details change...

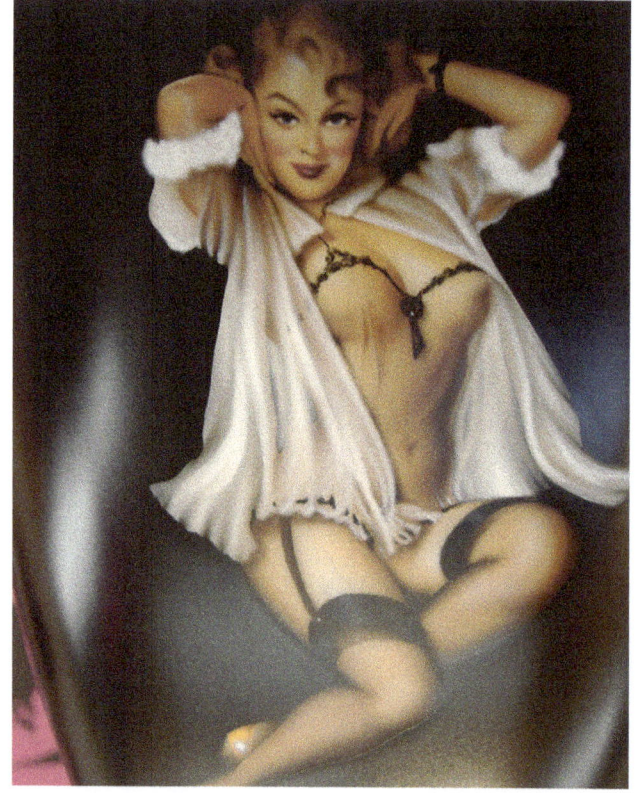

...as more and more airbrushing is completed.

A reverse mask has been positioned to paint the outside areas with a metal-flake copper color. The photo shows the nearly finished figure completely masked out to protect it from the metallic flakes used in the copper tribal designs.

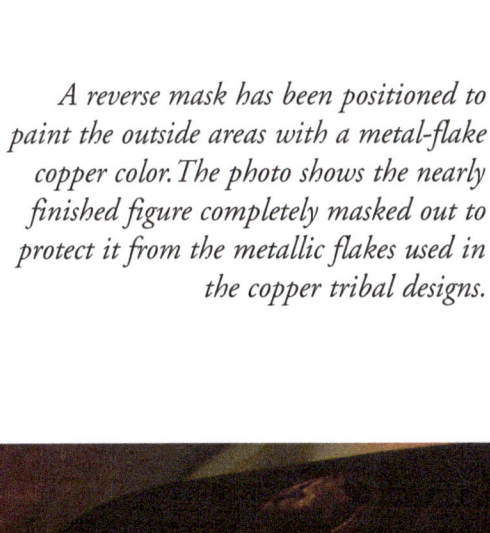

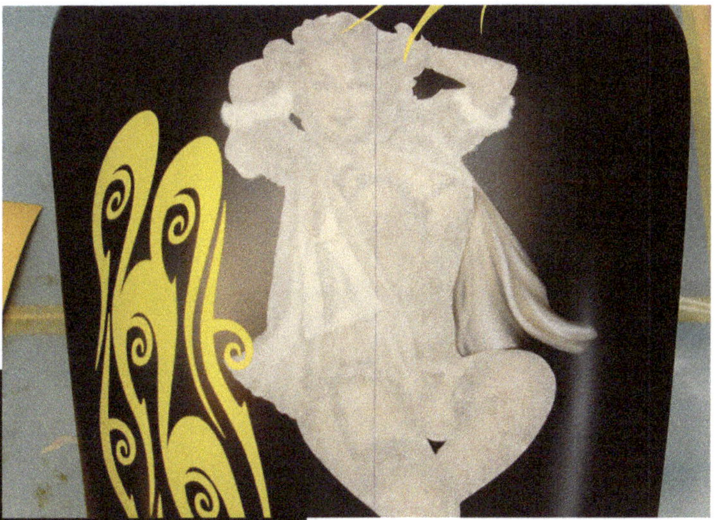

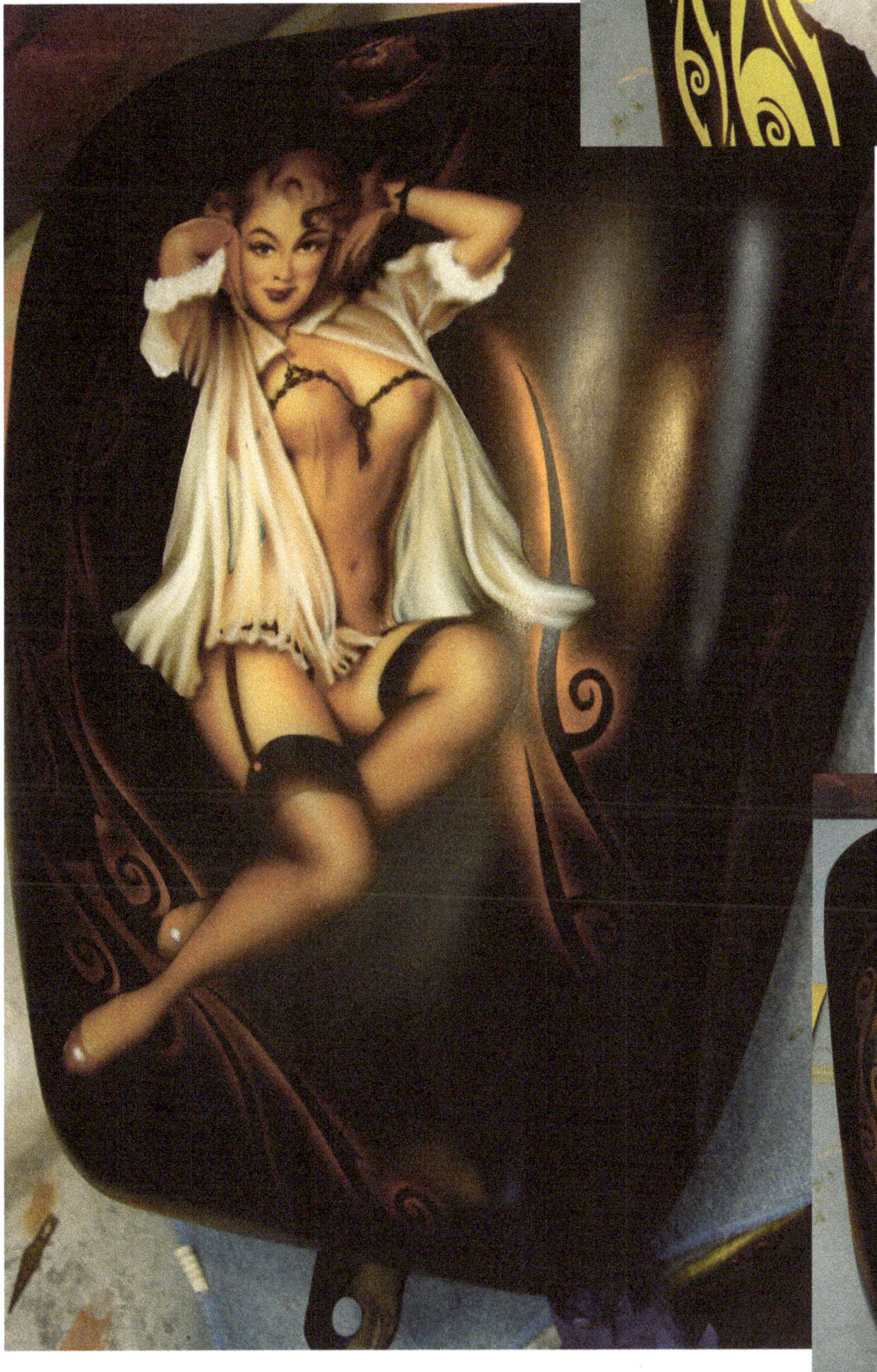

At the end of the project, there were just a few details to deal with and the image is finished.

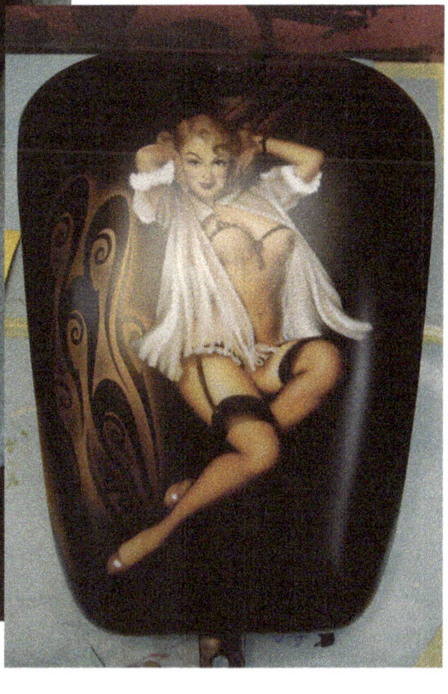

Steve Nunez Q&A

Give us a little background on you, how did you get started in art, and are pin-ups the main focus of the work you do?

I was introduced to airbrushing in high school while attending Brooklyn Technical High School back in the mid 80's. I saw airbrushing done by graffiti artists - thus the interest and introduction to airbrushing.

Did you take art classes? How did you learn to sketch and airbrush?

Being self-taught, I don't have any formal training in airbrushing or art of any kind. I began airbrushing T-shirts in the 1980's while in high school and that quickly taught me the essentials of free hand airbrushing (without masks).

Who inspires you, who are some of the artists you look up to?

I enjoy many forms of visual art, I don't have any one particular artist who inspires me, but the entire range of artists who's work I've seen and admired all inspire me.

Novice artists sometimes have trouble rendering believable skin tones, how do you achieve life-like skin tones?

Well my sponsor, Alsa Corp., makes a set of flesh tones ready to spray, so that might help many artists get a decent pallet of available skin tones. I just mix colors visually to get the tones I'm looking for. I pretty much make it up as I go along. A nice collection of browns, oranges, pinks and whites should be enough to get most artists by.

Another area where people have trouble is with faces, are there tricks or particular methods you use to create a good portrait?

Well an opaque projector is the best tool for achieving photo-realistic sketches, unless you're blessed with the talent to sketch out a portrait with near photo-like accuracy. Another technique that suits me is flipping the artwork upside down, as it can reveal small details missed when painting in a conventional right-side-up form.

How about the equipment you use, which airbrush do you typically use and why? And what do you use for a compressor?

I have a ton of airbrushes and don't really have a favorite to be honest. I basically use a Peak C3 or Iwata HP-C as my

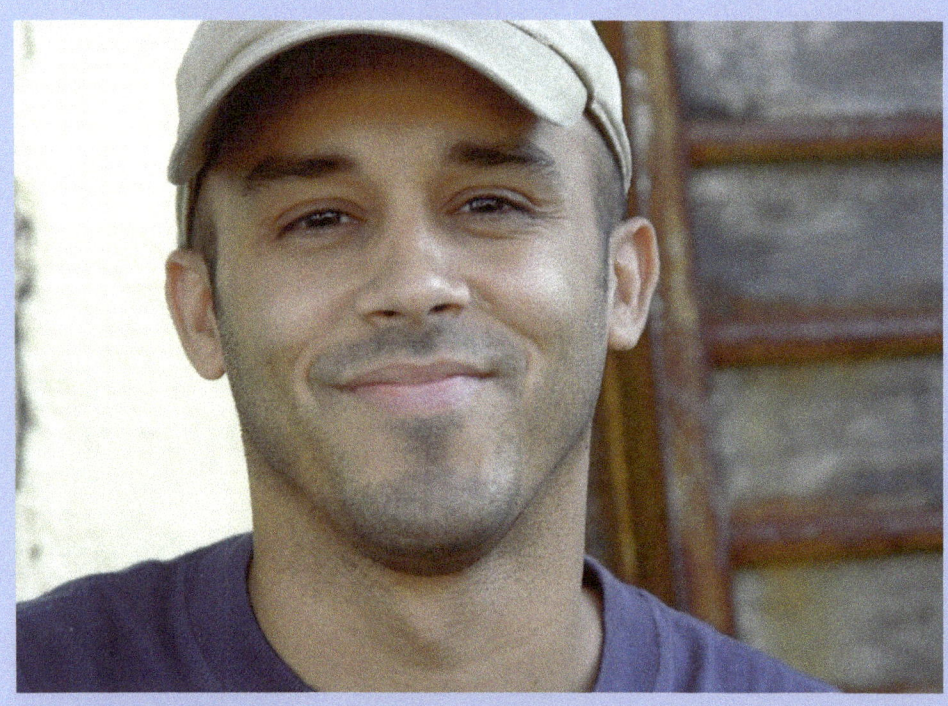

A resident of NY City, Steve Nunez is a self taught airbrush artist with a knack for creating life-like images of beautiful women.

Steve Nunez Q&A

main workhorses, as they're versatile and inexpensive. As for compressors I have a few as well, I use a Sears industrial compressor as well as a Super Silent 30, which I have as a backup should it become necessary.

Paint, which brand of paint do you use and why?

I use and endorse Alsa Corp. paint, as it's simply the best paint I've used and they've decided to sponsor me. I know there are many good paints out there, but I personally use Alsa Corp. paint and I've never been limited in terms of my creativity. Their paint simply allows me to do anything I can think up!

How did you learn to mix paint to create unique colors?

Lots of trial and error, I'm pretty much a "mix as you go" kind of guy, just eye-balling my colors seems to work well for me.

Do you use other media like hand brushes to add detail or achieve effects that are hard to do with an airbrush?

I do use hand brushes when painting canvas, but not with automotive paints, just acrylic paints on canvas. I do not like the look that hand painting has when it's used with automotive type paint. Good, tight, free-handing with the airbrush usually suffices when done well.

How do you find the models, typically who does the photographs that you use for reference?

I've been fortunate enough to find a few local girls who will pose nude in exchange for the original photos or artwork. So finding live models isn't too hard here in NYC. I'm an avid photo-enthusiast and shoot the models myself, usually with a Canon EOS Mark II N. You can't however, rule out magazine references as well, you do have to be mindful of copyright issues.

What makes a good pin-up?

Well a beautiful reference is a good start, but imagination and style all come into play. I think sexy and playful without being pornographic, strikes the best balance. You want to leave something up to the viewer.

If you were going to give ten words of advice to someone just starting out, what would that advice be?

Practice freehand techniques as much as possible, that's a great base.

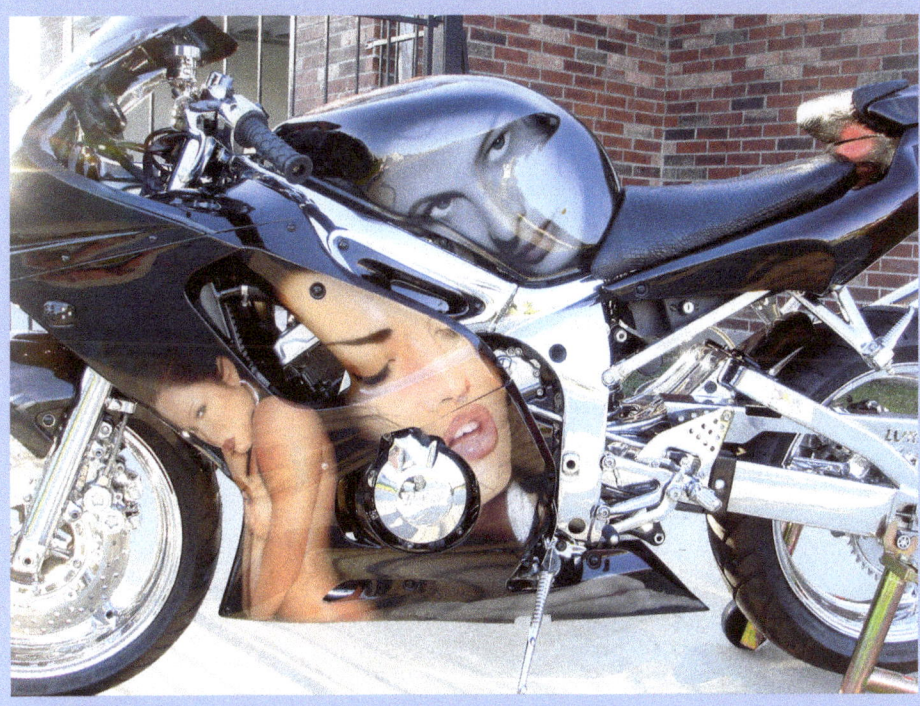
Convert your motorcycle into a rolling tribute to your favorite movie star or model with a little help from Steve Nunez.

Brenda I

The entire metal panel has been sanded and primed in a skin tone color. The initial stages of shoulder formation are visible.

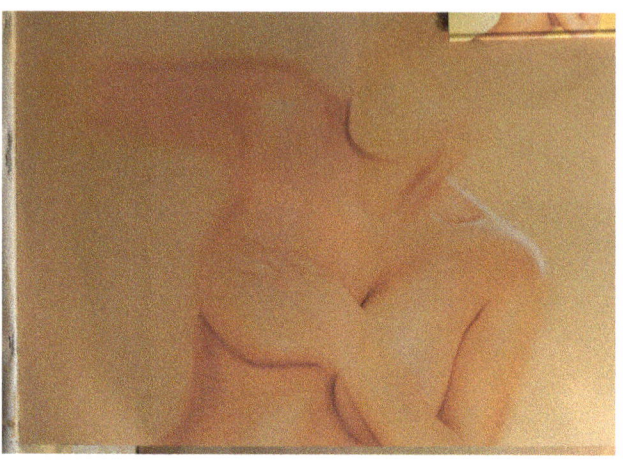

Continuation of shading and sketching using the airbrush.

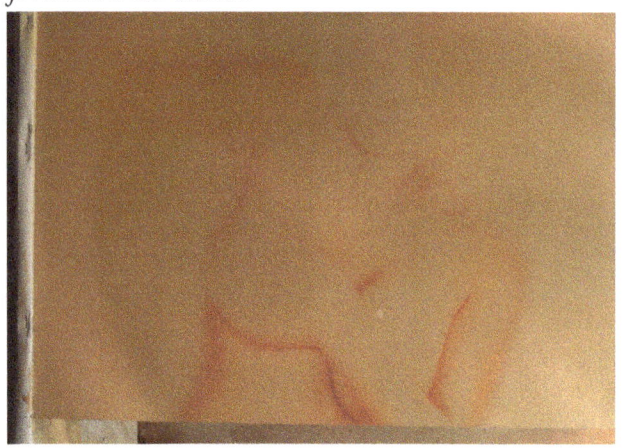

Slightly more tone has been added as well as Alsa Corp candy brown/true gold mix.

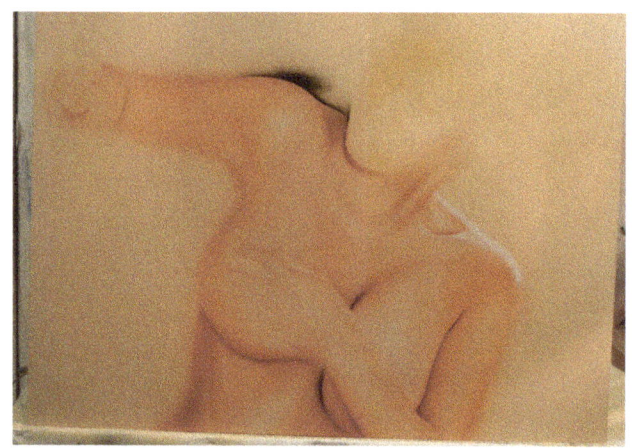

Alsa Corp. black is being added to define fore and aft areas.

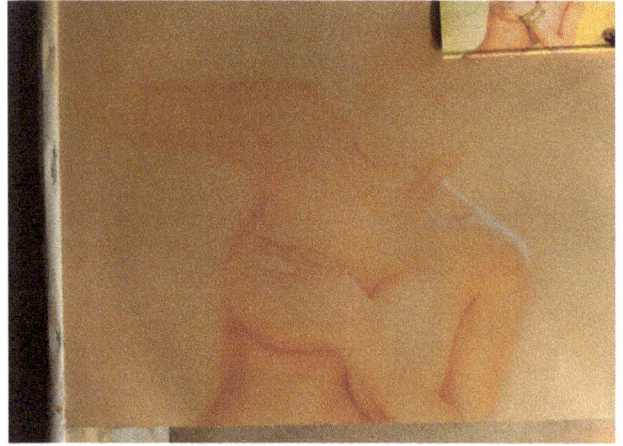

Following the photo reference - the shading is continued.

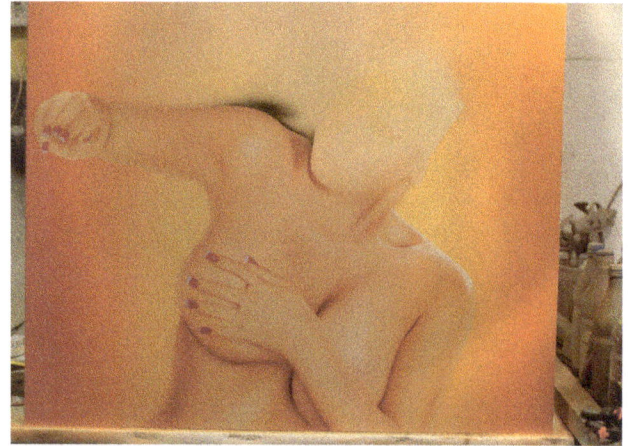

At this stage the background is blended with a gradation of orange and yellow.

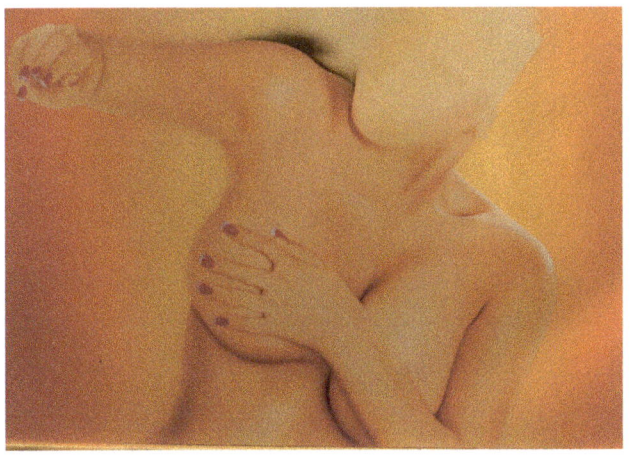

Some skin reflections and defining is performed and enhanced for preparation to the next step.

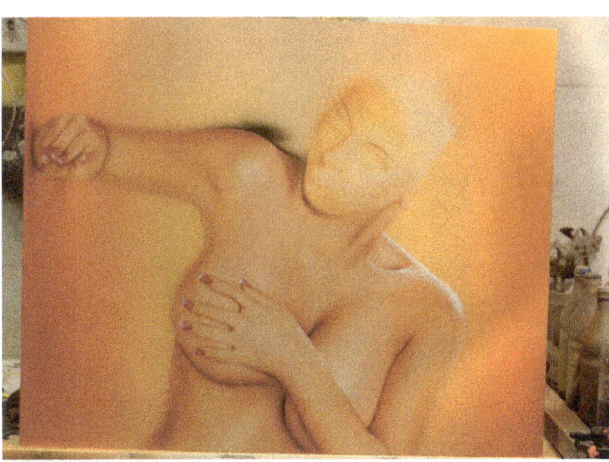

I begin airbrushing facial features to define the look she will have.

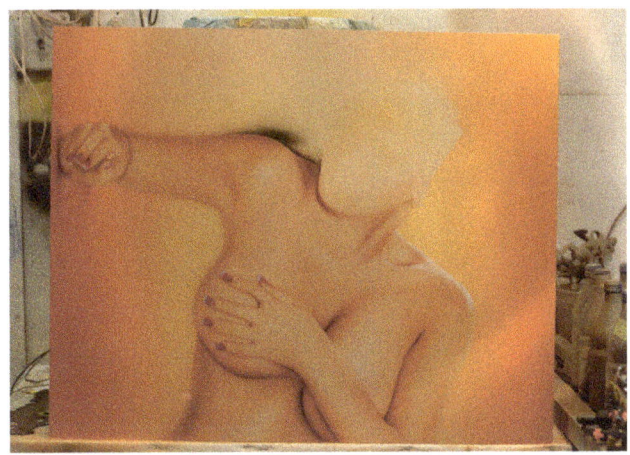

Medium yellow tones are graded...

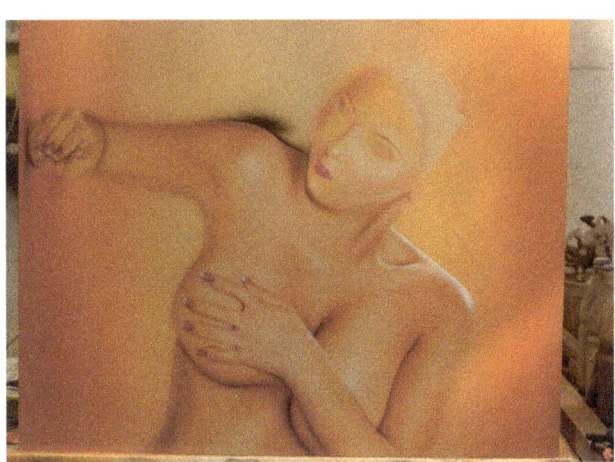

Facial skin toning is just about completed.

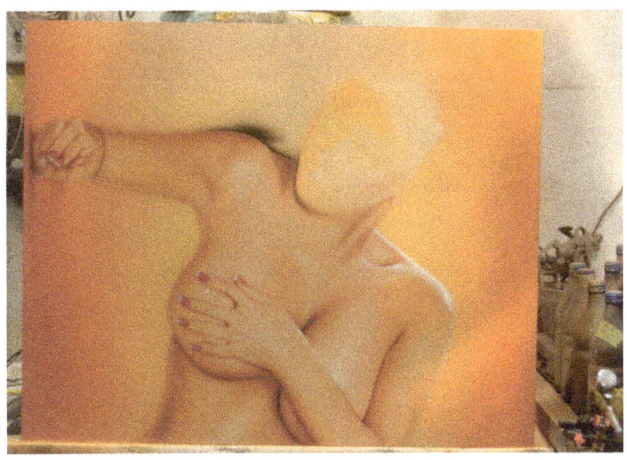

... in the facial areas to define the features.

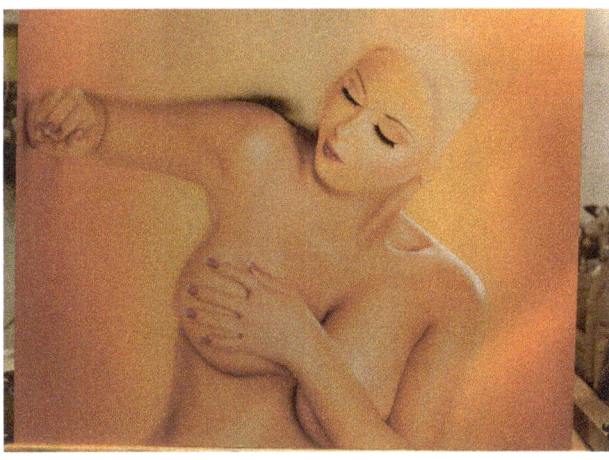

Lips and eyelashes are put in and will be further defined at a later stage.

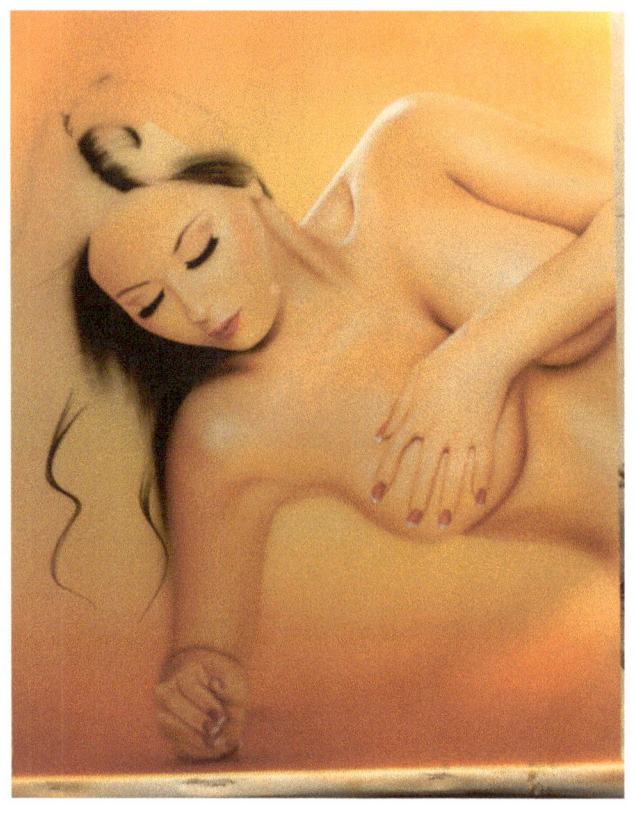

I put the painting right side up, and begin some definition with dark tones.

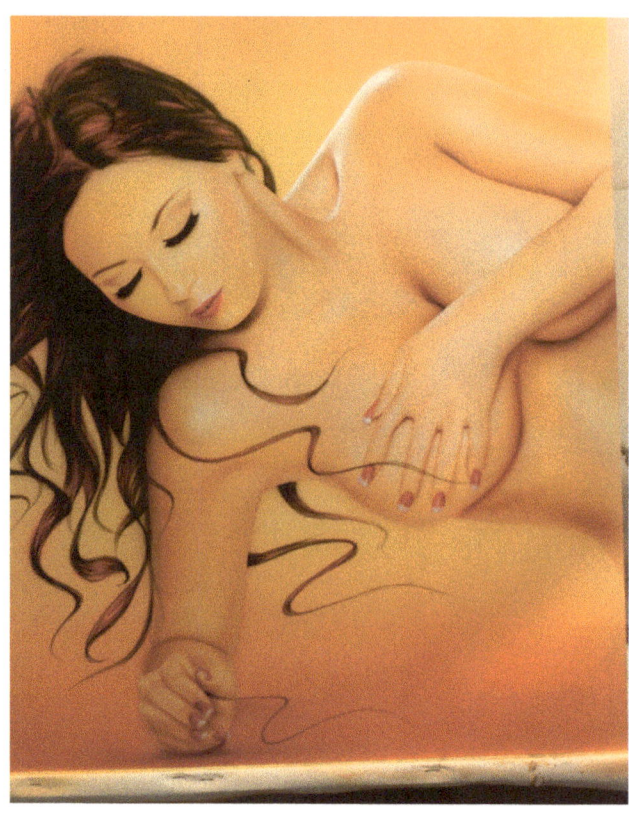

At this stage the hair is beginning to take form and will dictate the feel of the painting.

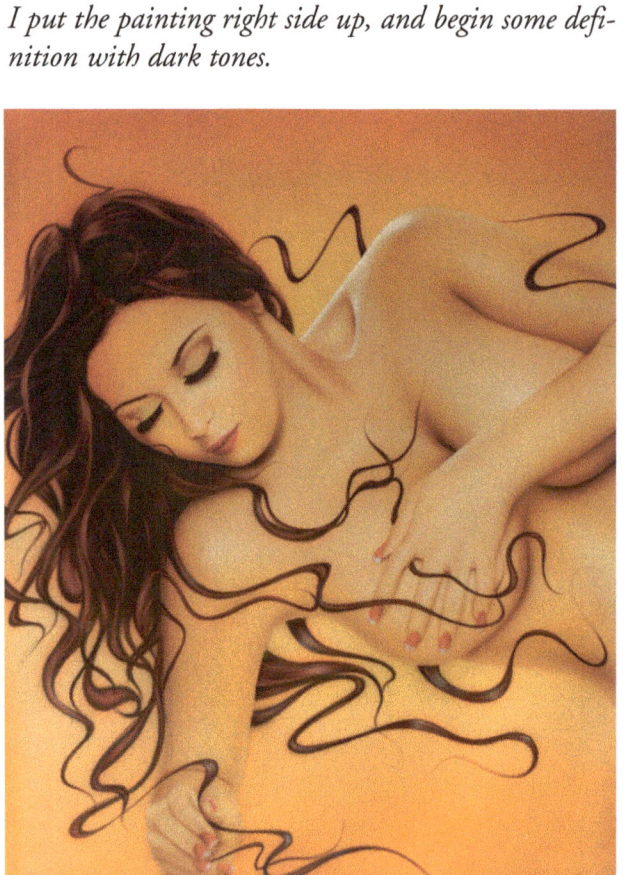

The loose hair strands gives a sense of "fun" and add a nice flair.

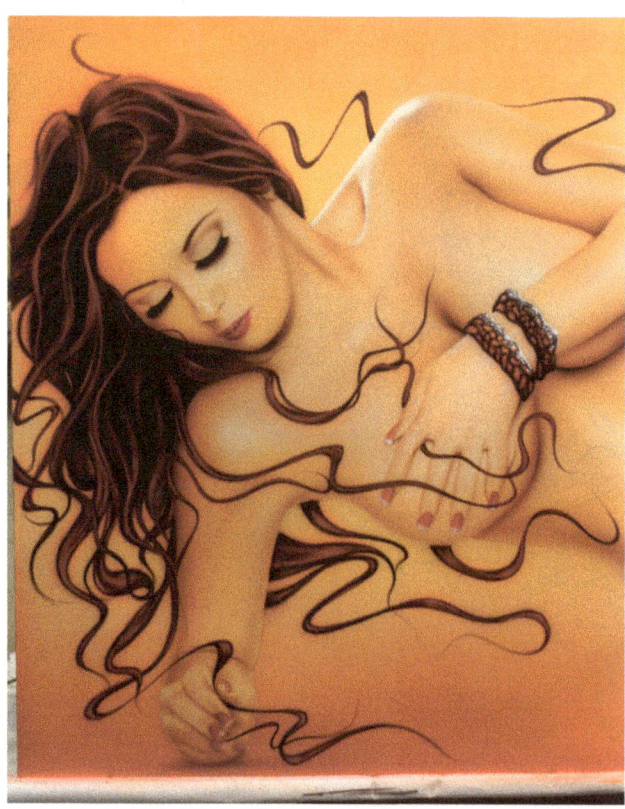

Finally, I go over all the elements and look for areas that might need retouching or refining.

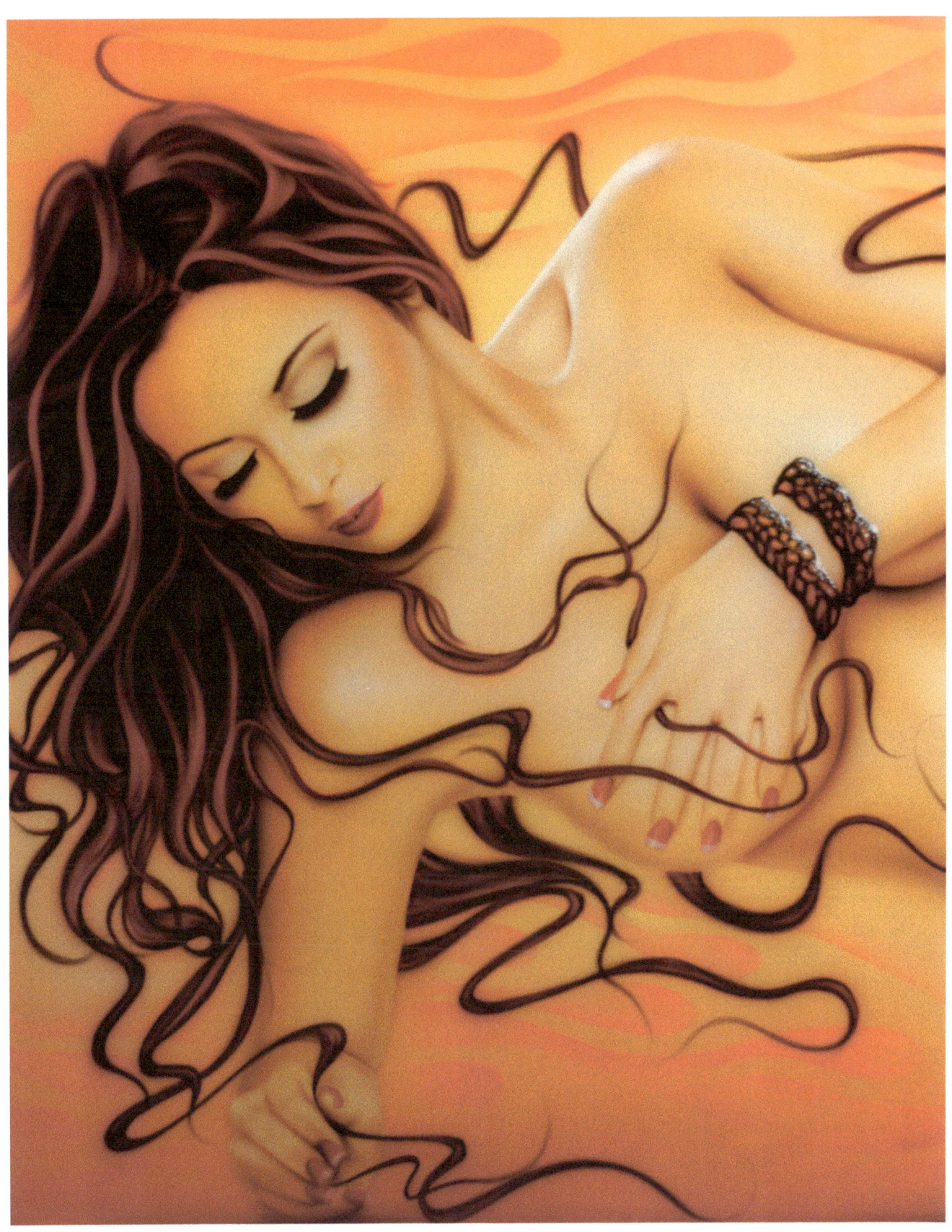

Here's the finished piece with soft scalloped flames in the background and Alsa Corps. metallic flakes....a fun project completed in about 3 hours. This project was entirely created with Alsa Corp. paints and reducers. 95% of the airbrushing was performed free hand without stencils.

Chapter Four
Tom Nguyen
A Pencil Drawing with Color

Until a few years ago, the closest Tom Nguyen came to doing pin-up work was drawing Wonder Woman panels for DC Comics. Creating comics requires great drawing skills, and it is these drawing sills that underlie Tom's pin-up images. Less than ten years ago, Tom decided to combine his drawing skills with his airbrushing skills to create a unique pin-up style.

While some pin-up artists do only a cursory outline of the image, Tom's images are fully

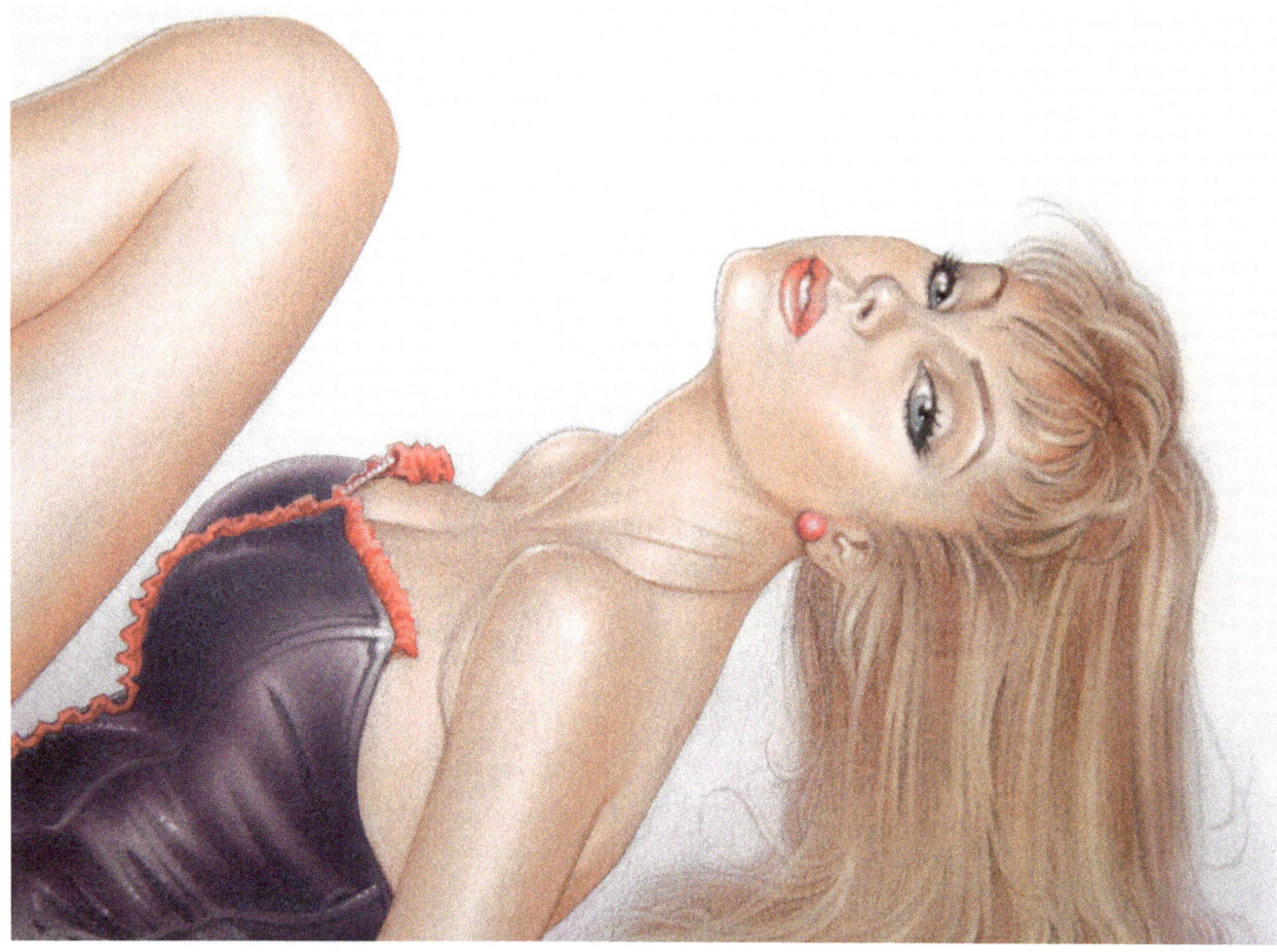

To create a sexy pin-up image you need photos of a great pin-up model - Jacki Morrison in this case.

drawn pin-ups before he starts in with the airbrush. And, instead of completely covering the pencil work, the use of transparent paint means some of the drawing can be seen under the paint even after the image is totally finished.

Like a lot of artists, Tom spends long days in his small studio. The release in this case is the gym in the garage. "I was a regular at the local gym," explains Tom. "When they announced they were going out of business I asked if I could buy some of the equipment." For Tom, body building is not only a healthy alternative to long hours at the drawing board, it also gives him a very good understanding of what muscles really look like. "Being a body builder helps me to understand body structure and muscles, and how they change as the body moves. The understanding helps with both my cartoon and my pin-up work."

Despite Tom's success with pin-ups, painting the winners of various beauty pageants in both Minnesota and Wisconsin, in addition to images like that seen here, cartoon work still forms the foundation of his work. Currently, the pin-up work is only twenty percent of Tom's work.

If body building helps Tom draw and paint the perfect pin-up body, it's three summers spent doing caricatures at the local amusement park that serve as the foundation for his ability to capture the magic in a model's face. "Working summers at the park was really good training," explains Tom. "When it comes to the faces, I don't have to be a slave to that projected image, I'm able to simply draw the image, and I can embellish it slightly if I want to."

Working with Tom for four days as he developed this image turned out to be a pretty easy assignment. With the TV in the corner providing a quiet soundtrack, Tom works with a certain ease. Though multiple deadlines loom on any given day, there's a nice vibe in the studio, a sense that this is what Tom is good at, what he is supposed to be doing – drawing cartoons and pin-ups, one panel at a time.

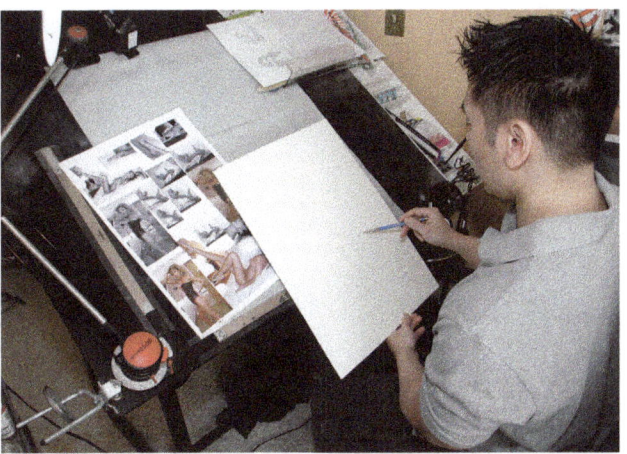

I begin by printing out the reference material on one sheet. Then I begin roughing in the figure on the cold-press illustration board, picking out the best elements from each photo. Drawing lead is normal HB.

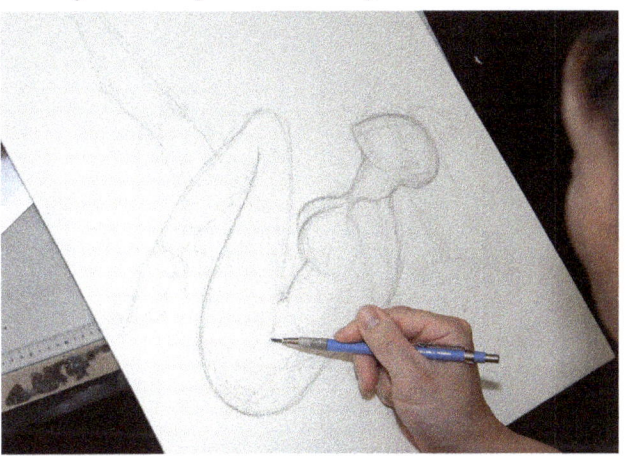

Here I focus on proper construction of the figure and curves. It's important to capture the overall essence as opposed to worrying about little details here. At this stage I can exaggerate certain aspects.

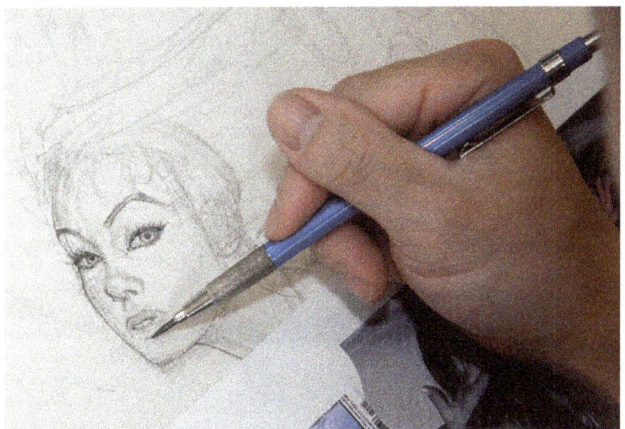

The most important things to me are the face and hands. If I don't get these right, the drawing is as good as dead. Here I'm refining Jacki's face to get a good likeness and proper proportion.

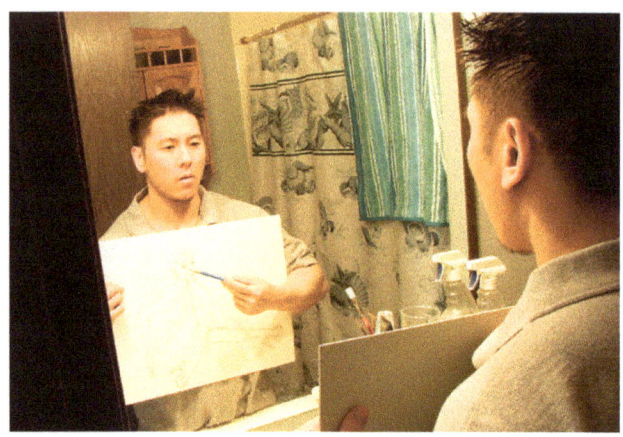

I'm using the good old trick of looking at my drawing in the mirror to help me spot glaring errors in my drawing. Reversing your art will give you a different perspective that your eyes aren't used to.

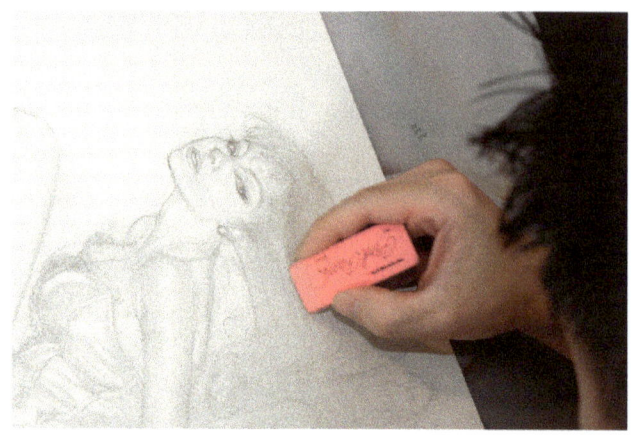

For the hair I'm using the edge of a Pink Pearl eraser which is a good compromise between the abrasive hard electric eraser and the gentler kneaded eraser.

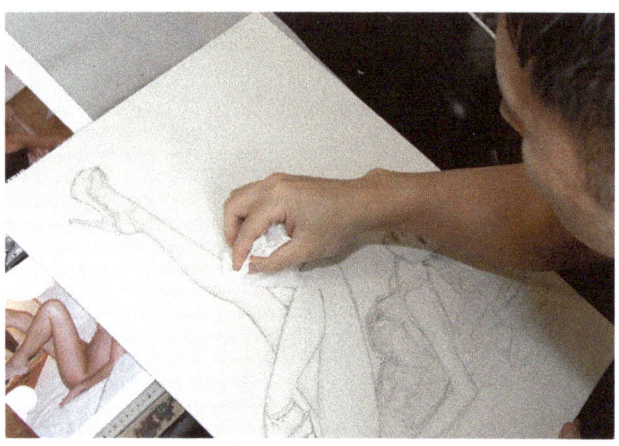

Using a lump of toilet paper (toilet paper!), I gently wipe it all over the drawing in order to purposely smear the graphite around. Although this knocks down the contrast, it also creates a soft gray "wash."

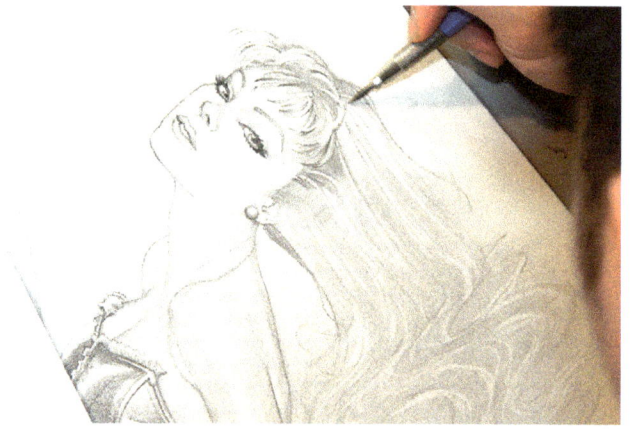

Here I'm going back in with pencil to redefine sharp, dark details that I lost during the smudging stage. At this stage you can really begin to see the pencil art "pop" as the contrast is enhanced.

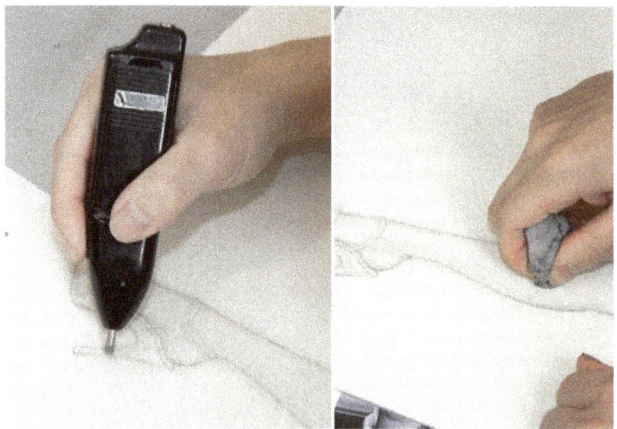

Because of the previous step, I can now use various erasers to create light/highlighted areas on the figure. The electric eraser is good for small details; the kneaded eraser is better for broader, softer highlights.

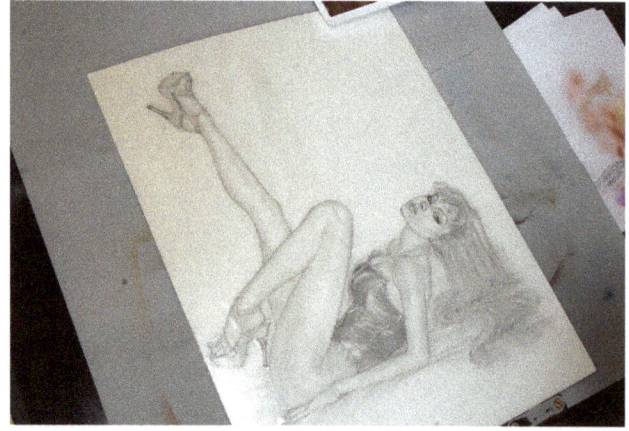

My least favorite stage: applying the matte, low-tack sheet of frisket film and cutting out all the pieces necessary to create masking. Masks are cut for each leg/shoe, the corset, and the entire upper body above the corset - the hair and arm are not separated.

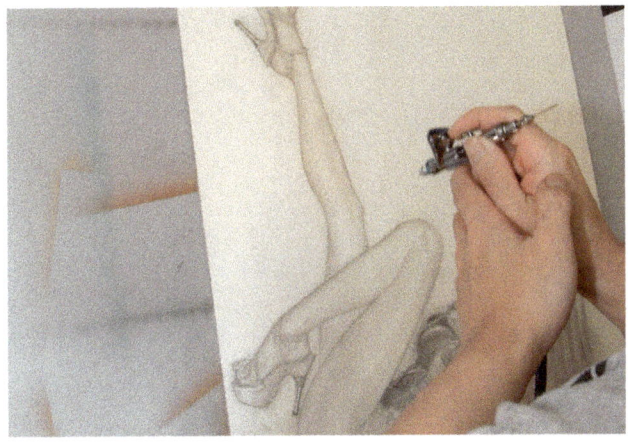

Revealing the back leg first, I spray a very light coat of my pre-mixed flesh tone color. It's important not to get too involved and heavy-handed now - I'm just trying to get some semblance of color on the work.

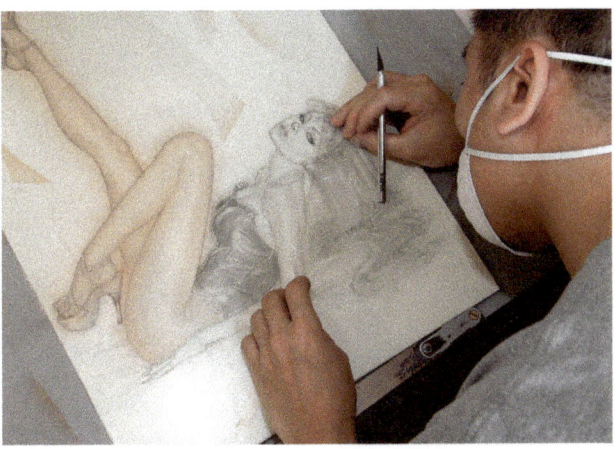

After I remask the front leg, I move on to the upper body and uncover the entire upper body skin areas. You can see that I'm wearing a dust mask so as not to inhale the paint spray.

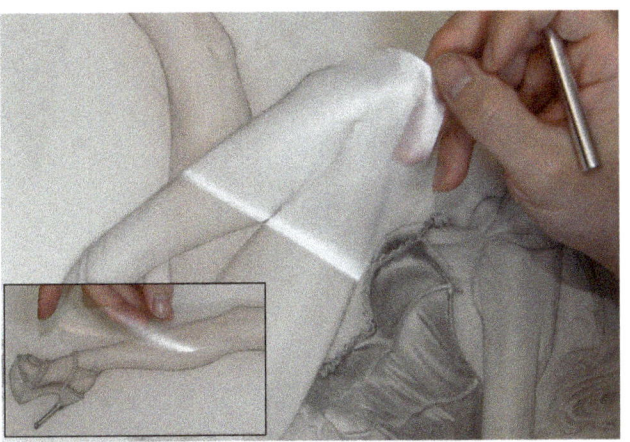

I remask the back leg (to prevent overspray from painting other areas), and reveal the front leg...

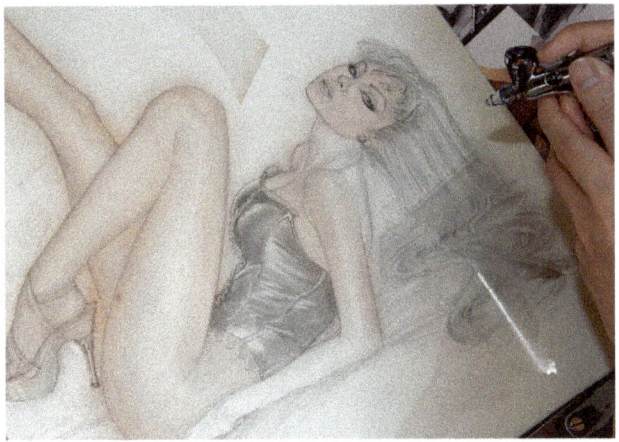

Again, I'm doing a light general spray over the face and shoulders. Remember that I didn't cut a separate mask for the hair to separate it from the skin. This way I don't get a hard transition at the hairline.

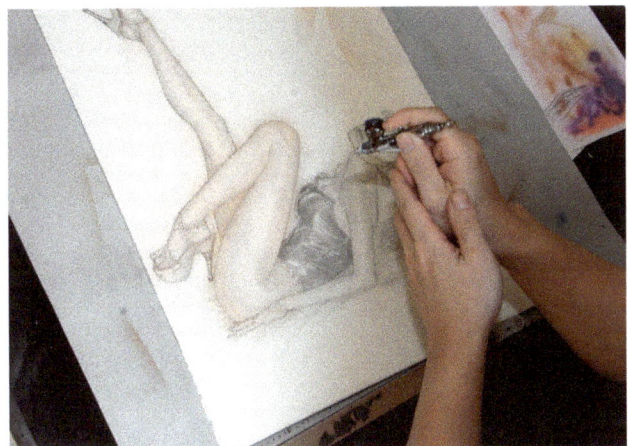

...I now spray the front leg in the same manner as the first leg - with a very light general misting.

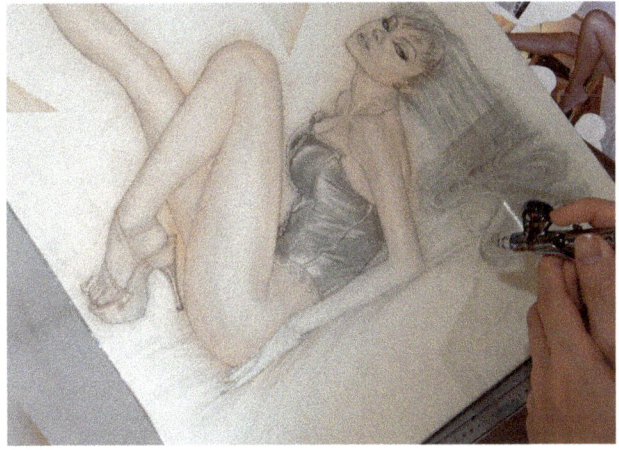

Still working on the upper body, I proceed down to her supporting arm to add a light coat of color.

61

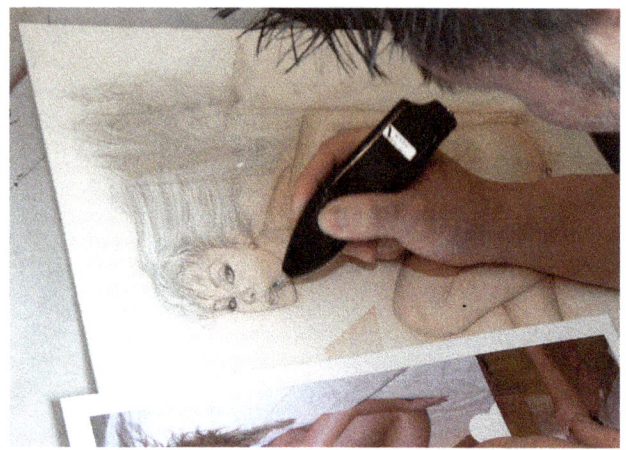

After the first layer of flesh color is applied to the entire piece, I begin erasing highlights. This is like erasing highlights after smudging the graphite.

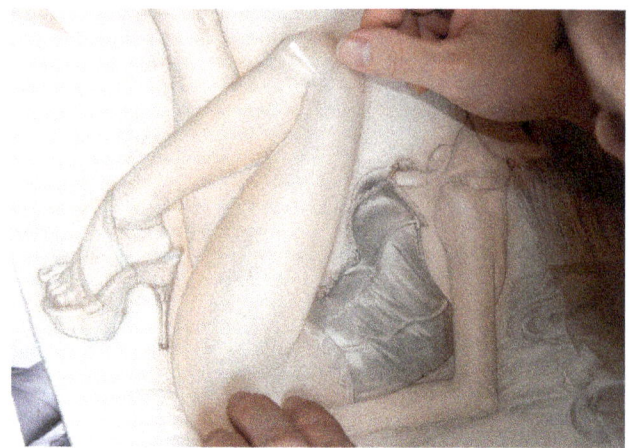

Moving on to peeling the frisket off the front leg again to repeat the erasing.

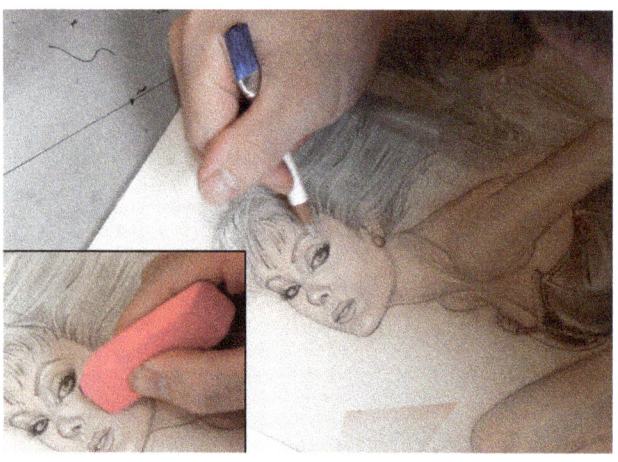

In the main photo I'm using a typewriting eraser called an Eraserstik. It's very abrasive and takes small areas of paint off well, especially in faces.

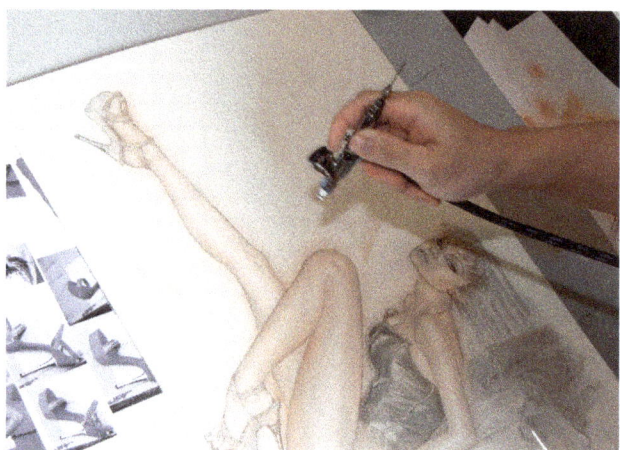

I've remasked the painting except for the back leg. Using my flesh color again, I begin spraying my second round of paint. This time I'm a little closer and more particular with where I'm spraying.

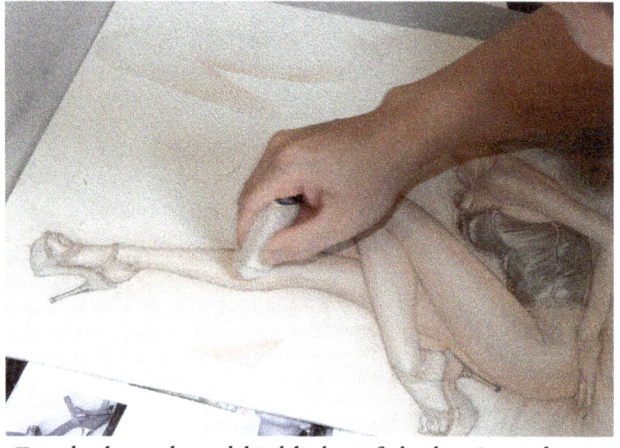

For the long, broad highlights of the leg, I employ yet another type of eraser, a white drafting eraser. This is the least abrasive one in my arsenal, and takes paint off very slowly - perfect for soft highlighting.

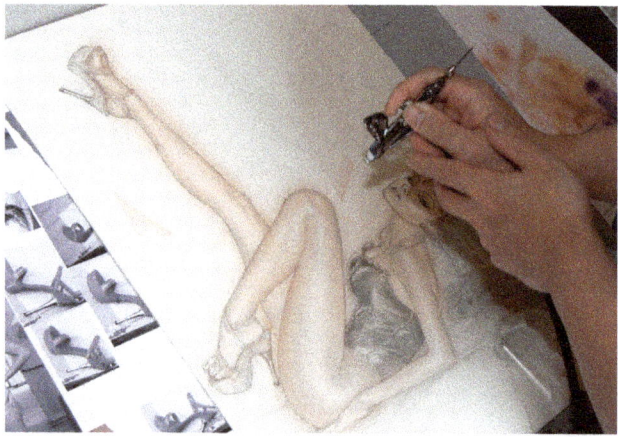

I'm still on the back leg, but working down to the butt.

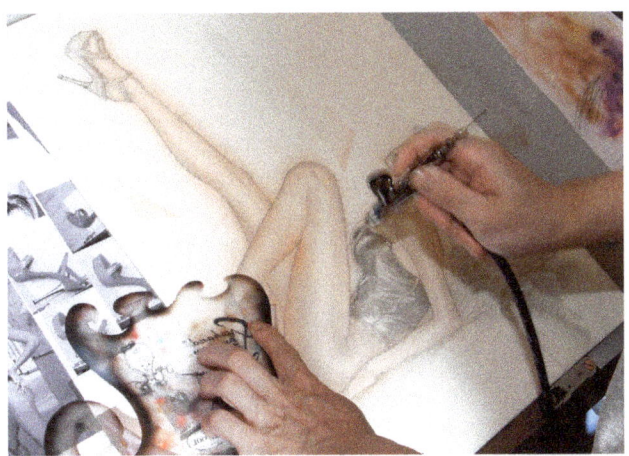

Here I'm just adding a little color to the front leg.

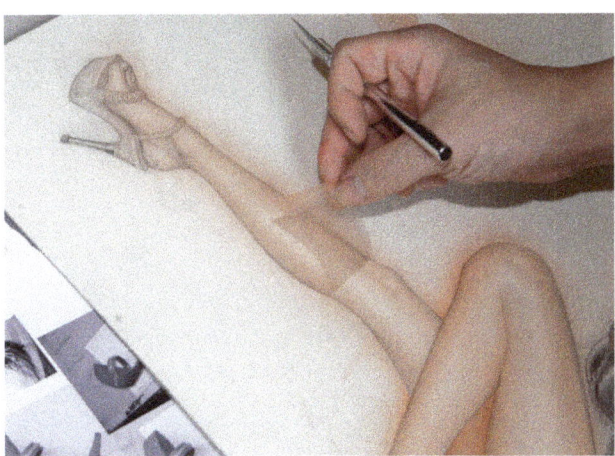

I peel back just a little of the masked, previously-painted back leg in order to check the color contrast between the two legs. Gotta keep things consistent!

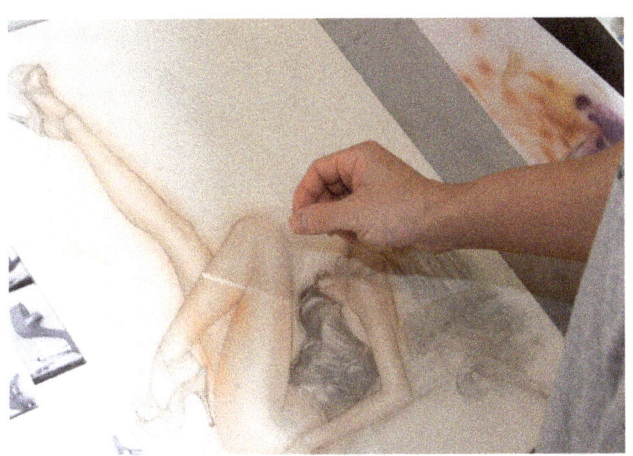

I'm peeling the mask for the front leg as I'm about to attack it next.

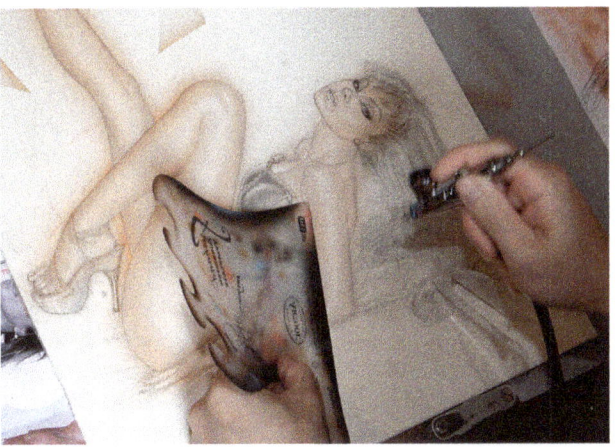

Both legs are completely masked, I move to the skin parts of the upper body again. I'm using a free hand shield to block the area by Jacki's armpit that's right next the area of her arm that I'm working on.

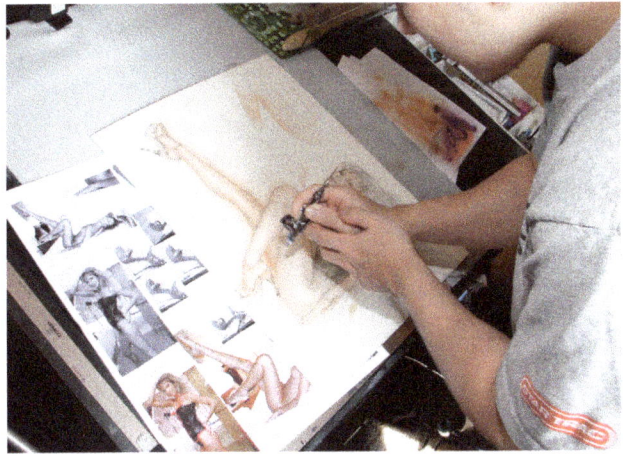

I look at the reference material every few seconds in order to maintain accuracy. I'm working on the near foot.

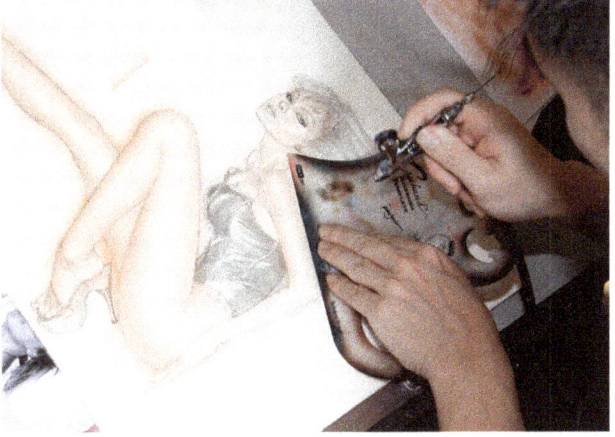

The opposite side of her arm is sprayed in the same manner, as I shield the shoulder blade area. This creates a clearer separation of the arm from the rest of her body since we're dealing with the same color.

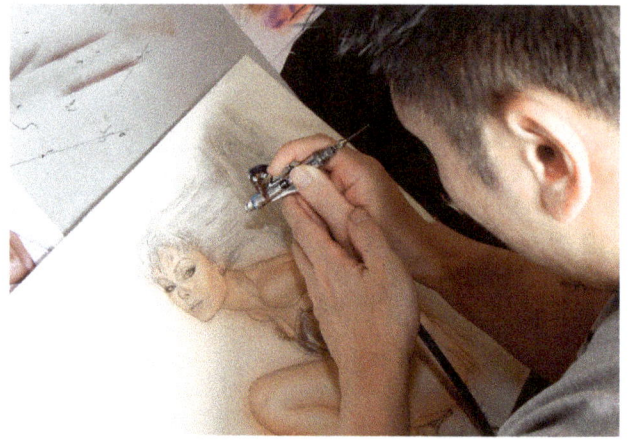

I'm working on the face, adding more color and depth. The hair is unmasked, so I'm more careful getting near it with free hand airbrushing. A little overspray is inevitable, and gives a nice soft transition.

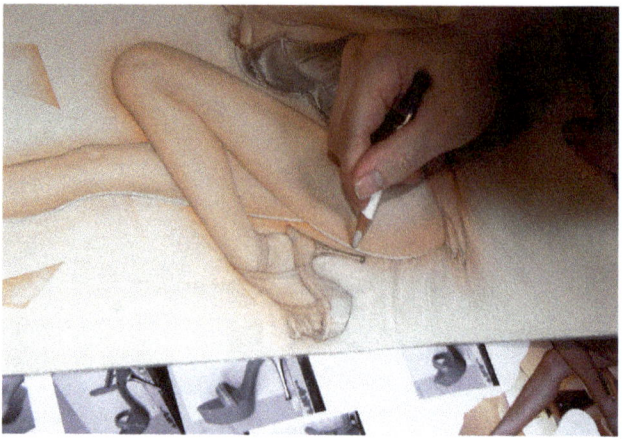

The Eraserstik is perfect for creating thin bounce lighting on the back of the leg. The bounce light is my artistic license; it helps make the figure in the painting more dynamic.

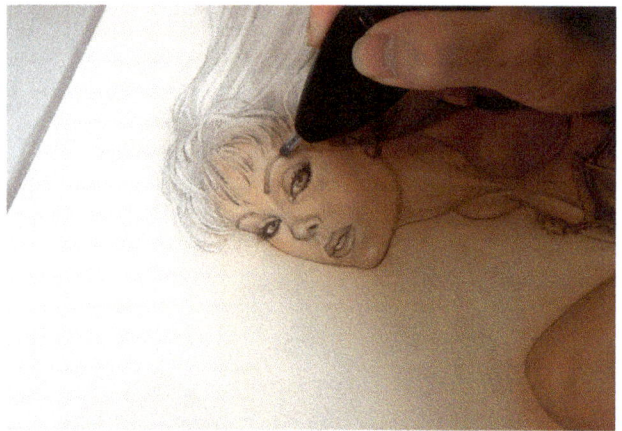

Going back in with the erasers now. This erasing is also a little more fine-tuned and particular, we're gradually getting smaller with the highlight sculpting. Working in layers the way I do helps add depth.

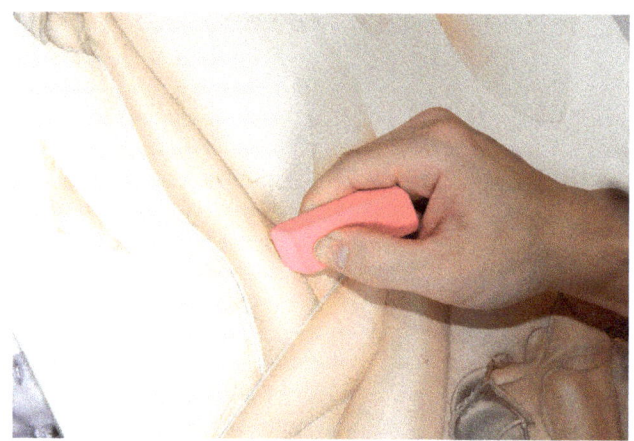

Using the corner of the Pink Pearl eraser, I do some more sculpting on the knee area of the back leg.

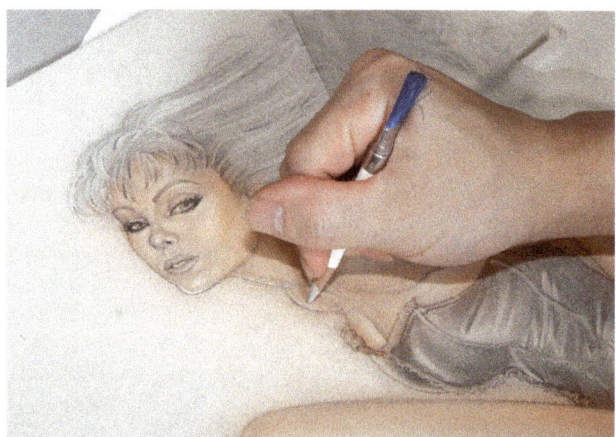

I'm using the Eraserstik again, this time for the smaller highlights on the rear shoulder. The electric eraser would be too small, and the pink-white kneaded erasers would be too big.

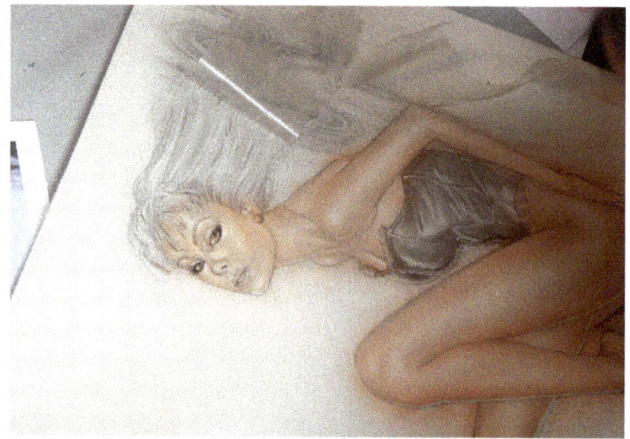

An overview look of the upper body skin area to see that it looks alright, especially compared to the legs.

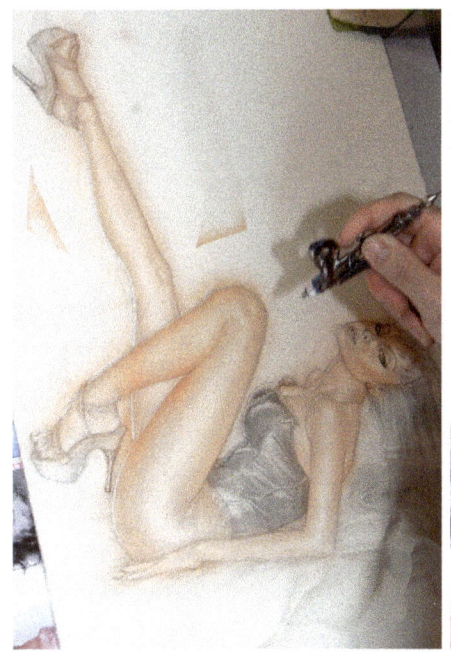 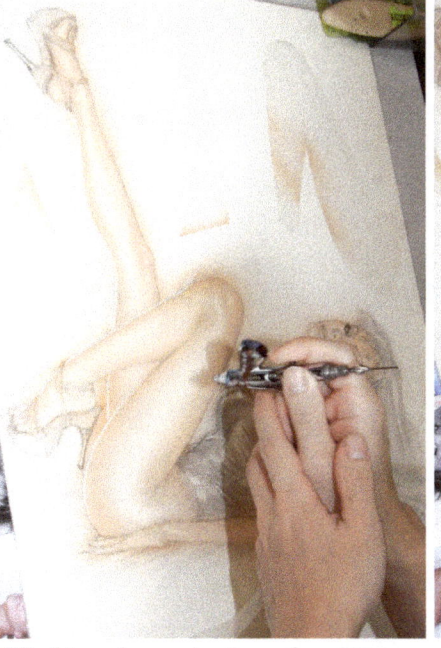 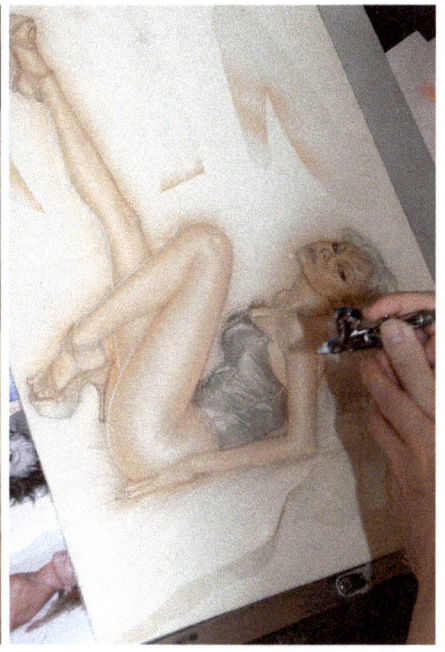

This is my final round of attacking the skin, and this time it's with a darker and dulled down version of my flesh tone. Shadows are the last step to make the skin really "pop." Here I am starting again at the legs.

Working down the front leg, I try to beef up the darkness near the edge. The area between the edge's bounce light and the main highlight is always darkest, and helps bring out dimension.

Still working on the front leg, I'm gradually moving towards the upper body.

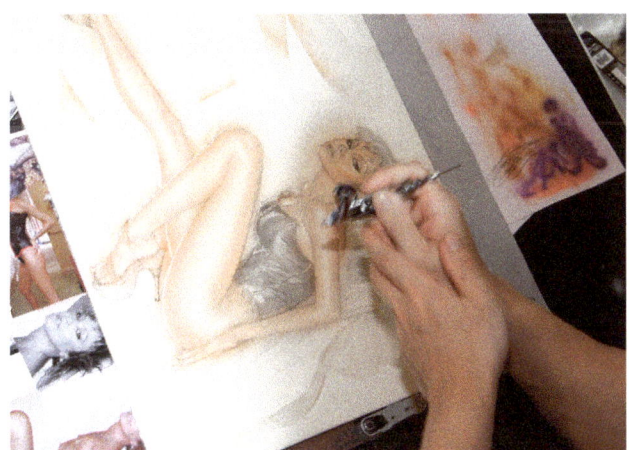 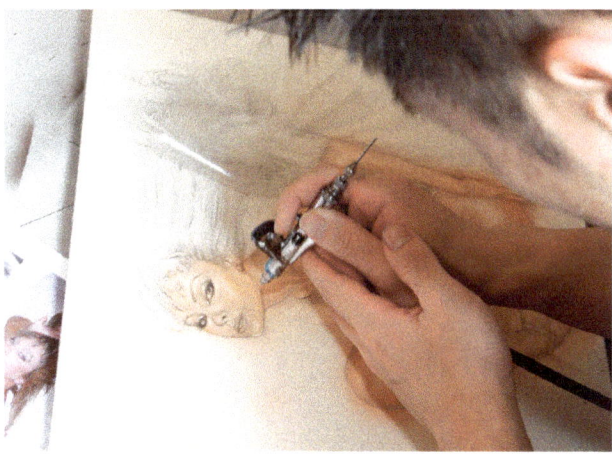

Sculpting shadows around the breast area, being careful not to overspray into her arm and shoulder.

Moving on to the face, I deepen the shadow under her cheek bone.

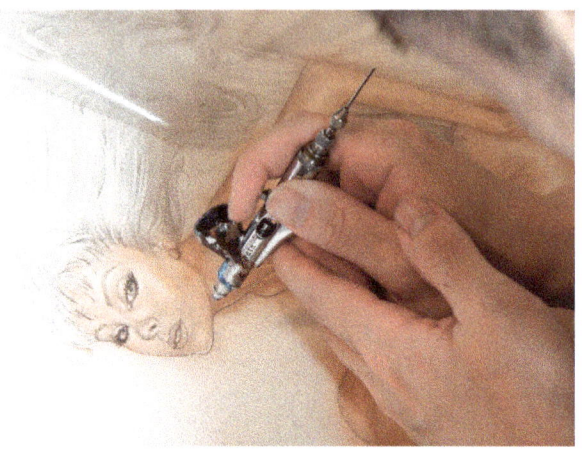

I have to be very delicate here as I'm working the shadows of her chin. My Custom Micron airbrush, along with low air pressure and thin transparent paints, helps me achieve fine, controllable sprays.

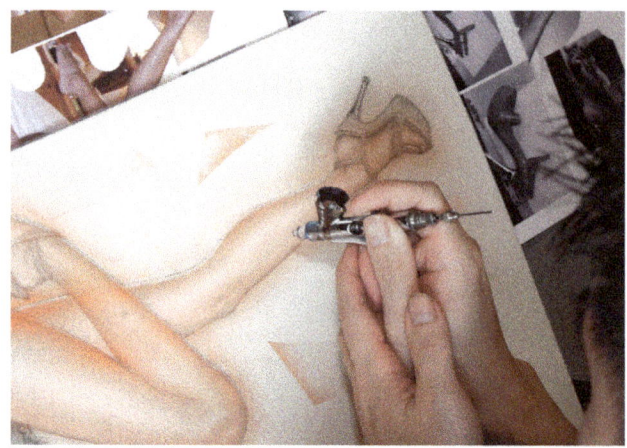

I am fixated on her calf at this point.

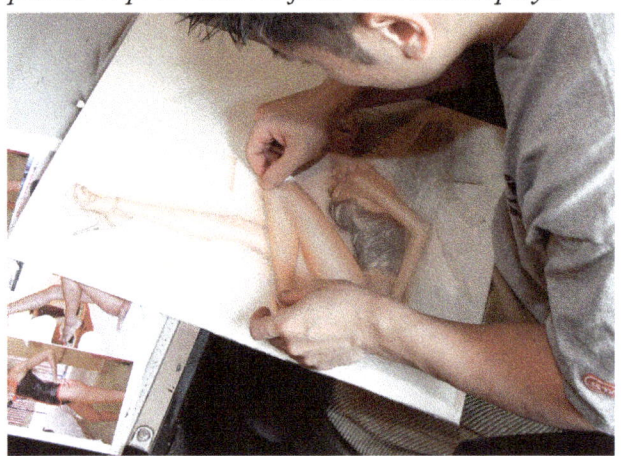

I should go darker on the skin. So I remask the front leg before spraying the back leg. When working with a light background, your eyes tend to get fooled into thinking that tones are darker than they really are.

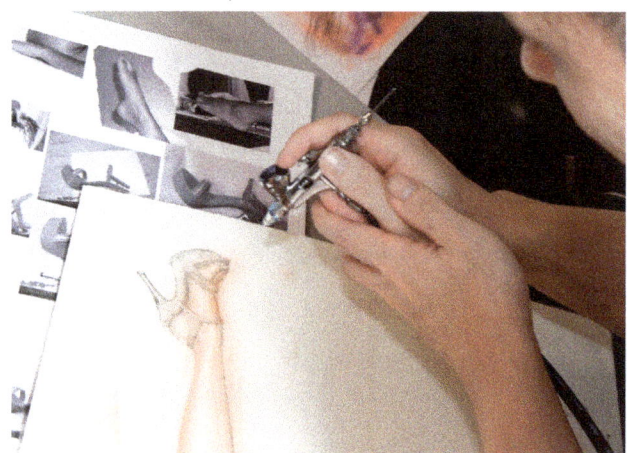

Now I'm working her foot. Close attention is paid to delicate areas such as the feet, hands, and face. As mentioned before, if I mess up on any of these parts, then the painting is ruined.

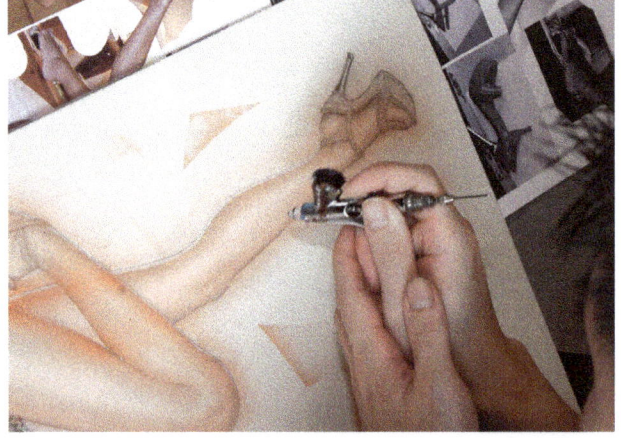

Now I spray the back leg again, attempting to beef up its tone. At this point I'm just concerned with the receding edges of the form and avoiding the highlight. This will enhance the dimensional effect.

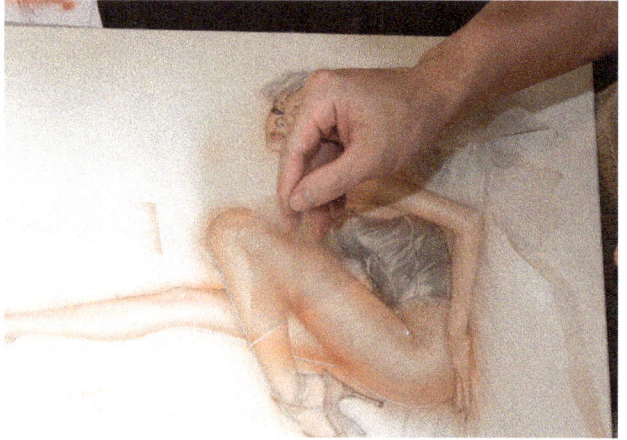

Once again I pull the mask on Jacki's front leg as I get ready to paint it...

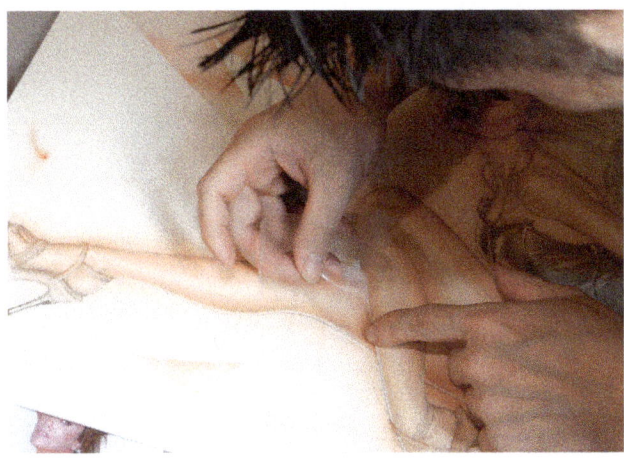

...but not before carefully remasking the back leg that I just finished painting!

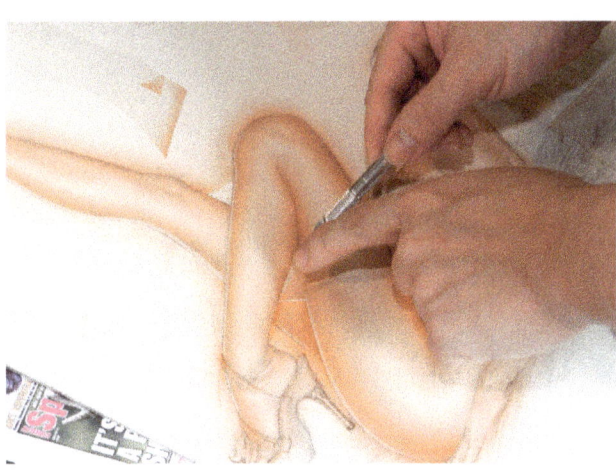

I'm just peeling a corner of the frisket to reveal the back leg in order to make sure the skin contrast is consistent in both legs.

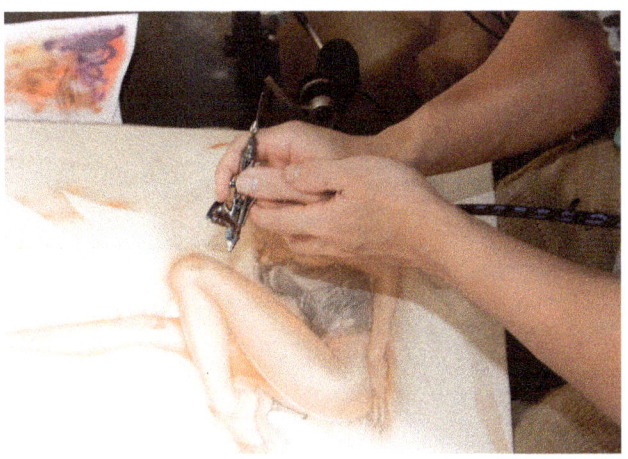

And now the final sculpting begins on the near leg.

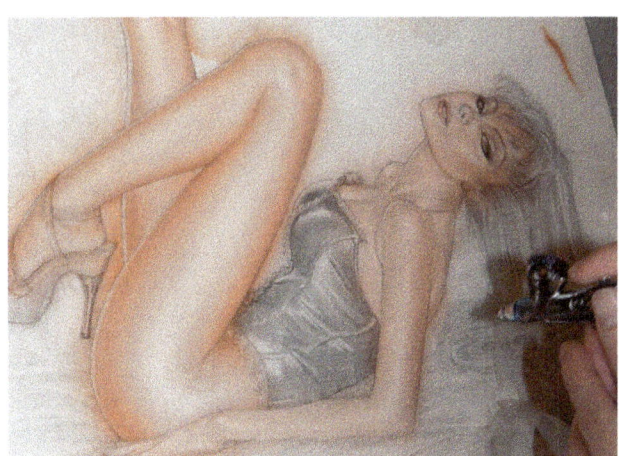

Here I'm working on the upper body, specifically adding more shade and depth to Jacki's arm.

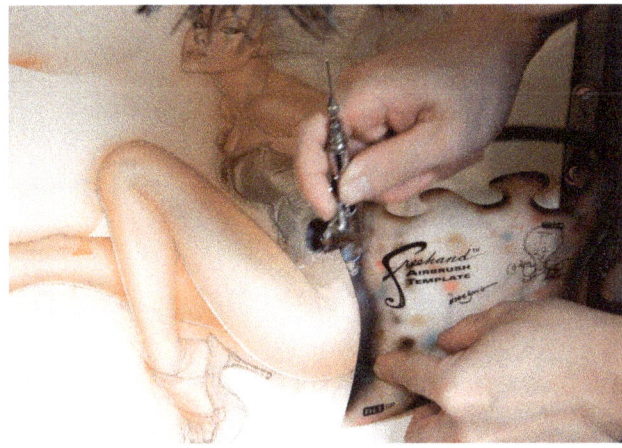

With the aid of the freehand shield, I block the hand as my shadow spraying rounds downward toward Jacki's butt.

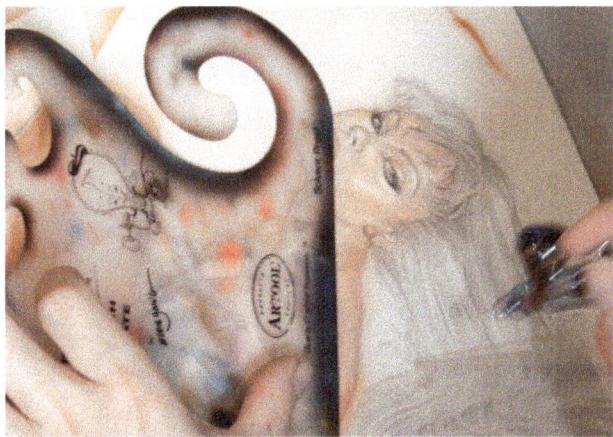

Finished with the arm, I use the freehand shield once again as I work on the rear shoulder area. I pay careful attention not to spray too high or heavily as it would create a line running up her neck.

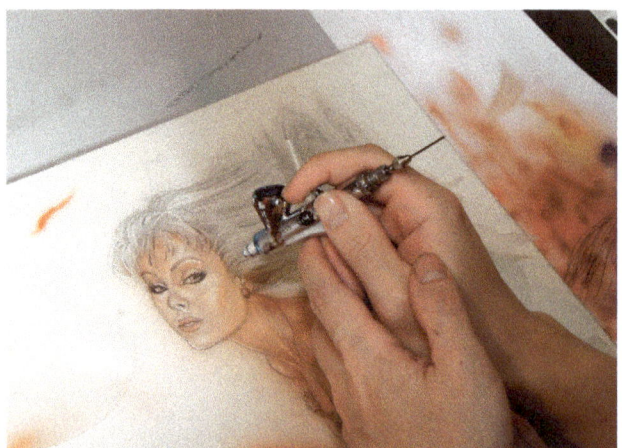

Final shadows are added to the face, particularly around the eyelids and under her bangs. And the area under her cheekbones is darkened slightly.

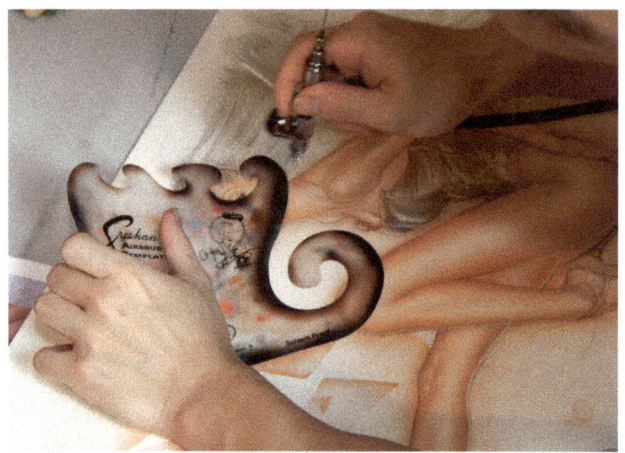

Jacki's face is shielded as I enhance the shadows on her neck.

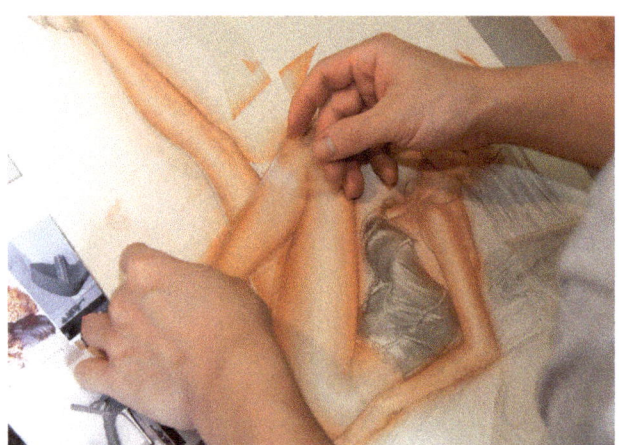

I peel the frisket off of the previously masked legs in order to do my final round of erasing on the brightest highlights.

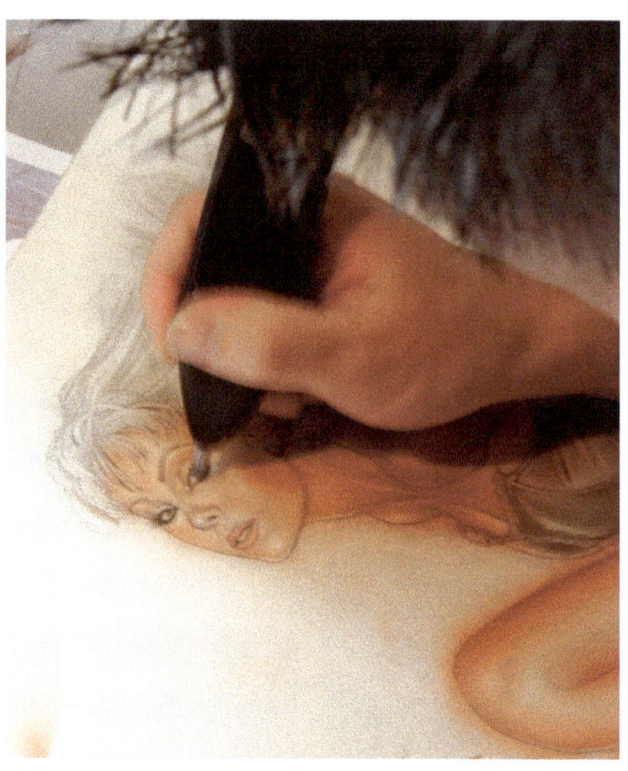

I now add the smallest, brightest highlights in the face (called specular highlights), particularly in the whites of the eyes (shown here), right underneath the eyebrow, the tip of the nose, and on the chin.

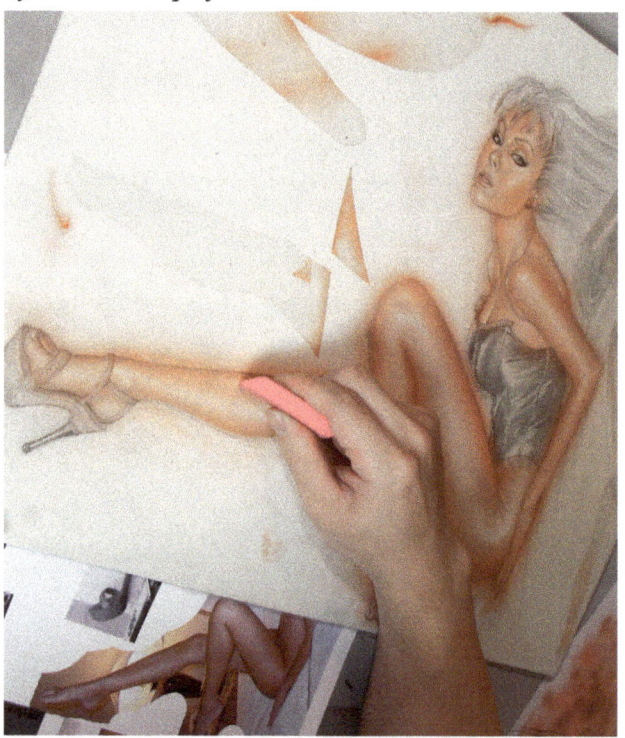

I do the same thing with the rest of her body. Here I am using the pink eraser to work the final middle gleam of highlight on the leg. It's important to note this highlight isn't as strong as a specular highlight.

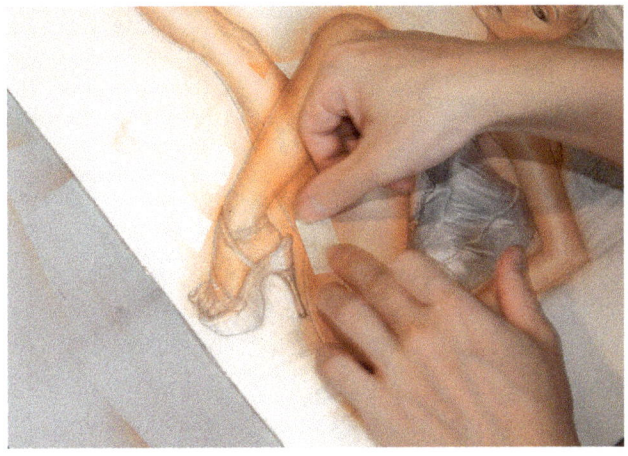

I'm done with the airbrushing portion of the skin. So I recover them and begin sealing the edges with masking tape.

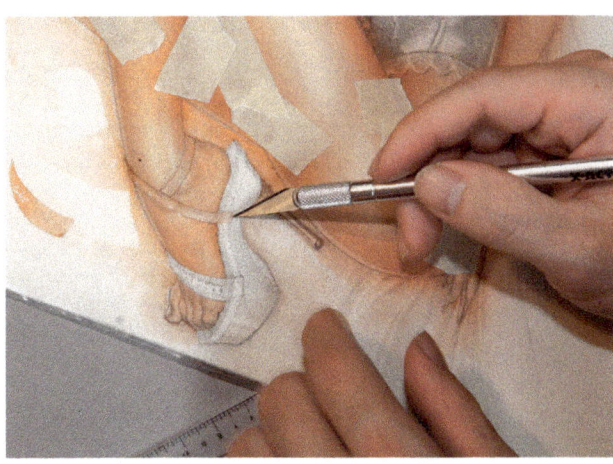

An Xacto blade (the same one used to cut the frisket) is used to more easily lift off the tiny pieces.

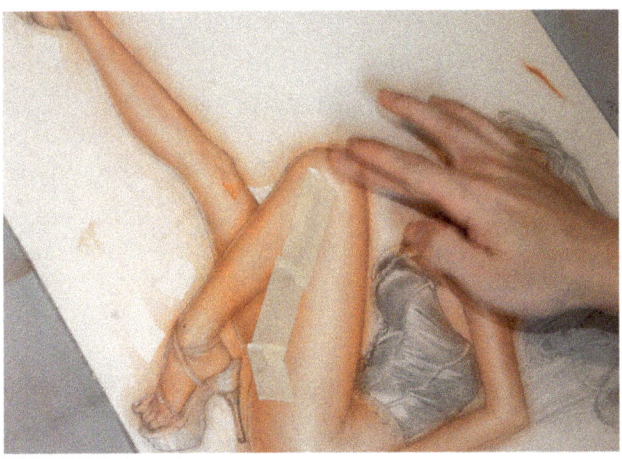

By sealing the edges of the frisket, I'm assured that any upcoming paint won't leak into the hard work already done.

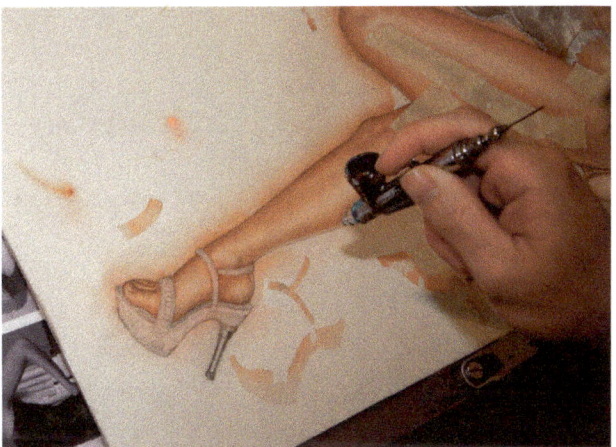

I begin spraying a light tone of red on the shoe. Spraying too heavily right off the bat will prevent effective erasing.

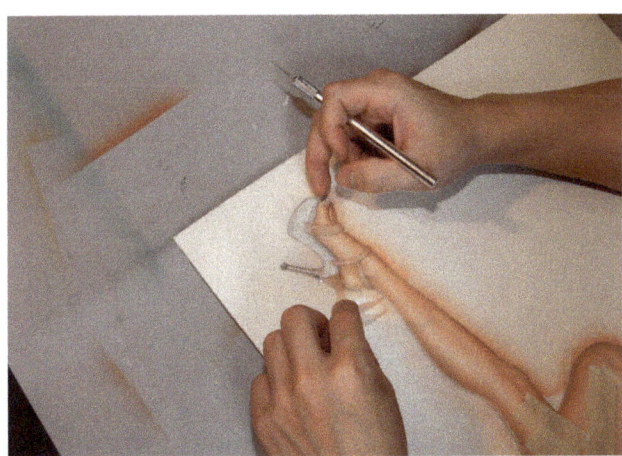

I begin peeling the frisket off of the heels prior to painting.

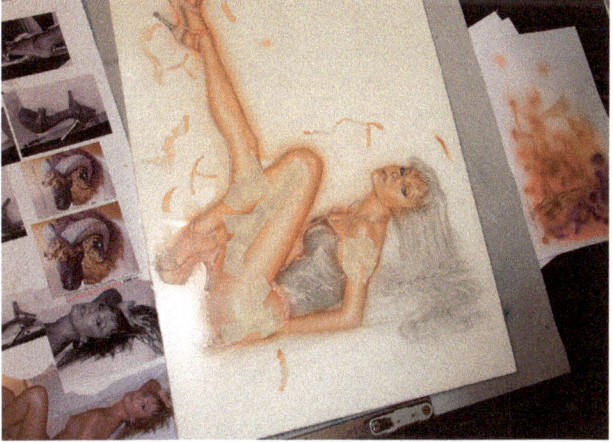

A broad overview of the heels after the initial spray. Again, reference material is always right next to the piece as I'm constantly looking back and forth.

Tom Nguyen Q&A

Give us a little background on you, how did you get started in art, and are pin-ups the main focus of the work you do?

I am self-taught, no art classes other than what was required in school. I followed artists and I always liked comic book art. In my early teens I did portraits and caricatures. Eventually I developed the ability to capture a likeness, it forces you to study the features of the face. It's a nice skill to have and means I don't have to rely on a projector to get a good likeness. I didn't pick up an airbrush until I was 15. About a year later I applied at Valley Fair, the local amusement park, to do caricatures. They started me out doing face painting, then I did caricatures. I worked every day in the summer for three years, and it really pumped up my skills. In 2003 Steve Driscoll and I went to Glamourcon just as spectators, even though I was doing some pin-ups before that. After Glamourcon I decided to use my skills as a comic book artist to develop my own pin-up style.

Who inspires you, who do you look up to?

Sorayama, he is my favorite, Olivia, is the best female illustrator. I owe a good chunk of my knowledge to Steve Driscoll, he and I met at Valley Fair. I took his advice and put my own twist to it. Steve is the man as far as I'm concerned. My paintings are heavily drawing based, his are heavily paint based. He has unbelievable control with the airbrush.

What do you use for an airbrush?

I use an Iwata, Custom Micron B. It can create fine lines, the trigger is super smooth, and it feels good in my hand, very solid, never had a problem. Handles all the paints, the line quality is impeccable.

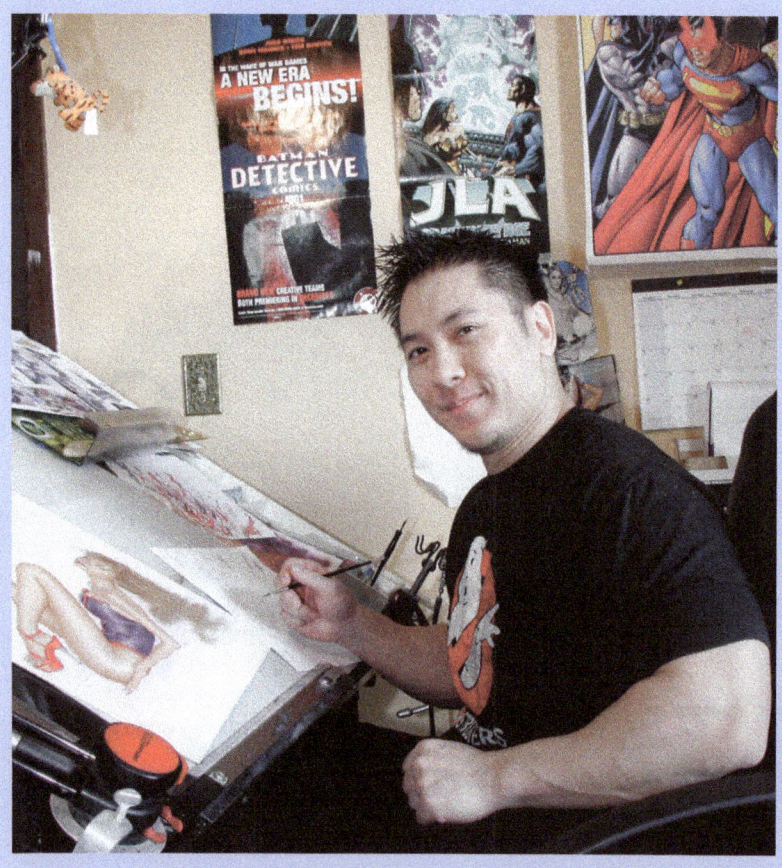

Tom at work in his small studio, surrounded by some of his comic-book posters.

And what do you use for paint?

Com.art usually, mostly transparent, some opaque. Transparent because it's less likely to clog up the airbrush, also because my illustrations are so based on the drawing, I want the pencil work to show through. You do have to be careful with transparent paint, it's hard to cover up a mistake.

Do you always mix your own colors?

Yes, I studied color theory when I was young. It takes practice and you really have to know and understand the color wheel.

Can you talk a little about your method of creation: the fact that you sketch the image out first, and then come back in with the airbrush?

I think I was always good at drawing. I feel it is one of my strengths. Even before pin-ups I wanted to add color to my drawings, I liked the effect of blending the two methods. This is a good method for me because it utilizes both of my skills. This method allows me to add

Q&A continued

a lot of detail because of the drawing underneath. It's mixed media.

How do you create believable skin tones?

For basic generic skin colors I start with a yellowish or ochre color, and slowly build it up. Adding a little magenta or sienna brown is a good way to darken it. If it's too saturated then I try dulling it down with some green or blue. A drop of purple is a good way to create a darker, shadow version, of the skin tone. You can modify the skin tone with a little of something from across the color wheel. So if it's on the orangy side, add a cool color for the shadow. Then mix the color to taste. You also have to consider the color of the light source and the surrounding colors of the environment. Realistic skin tones will pick up color from its environment.

How do you find models, and do you do your own photo shoots?

My first model was a friend of my sister. At Glamourcon 2005, I found Jacki Morrison (the model seen here). Every time I go to Glamourcon I meet more models who are anxious to work with me. And I've worked with a number of top pageant winners and competitors. For example, I'm a prize sponsor for the Mrs. Minnesota, Mrs. Wisconsin, and Mrs. Iowa pageants. I paint the winner each year, and that networking provides more models from the pageant area.

Any tricks of the trade, something you've learned over the years?

A little change in posture can help a lot. I use an old drawing technique, the S curve, it makes for a much more interesting image that way. For example, avoid using straight, stiff posing in the figures. With women, you want to utilize a lot of slants and angles - something that is already naturally appealing in their figures as opposed to the male physique. Because of this, I use a lot of "S" curves when constructing the figure, and even use it to exaggerate the female form.

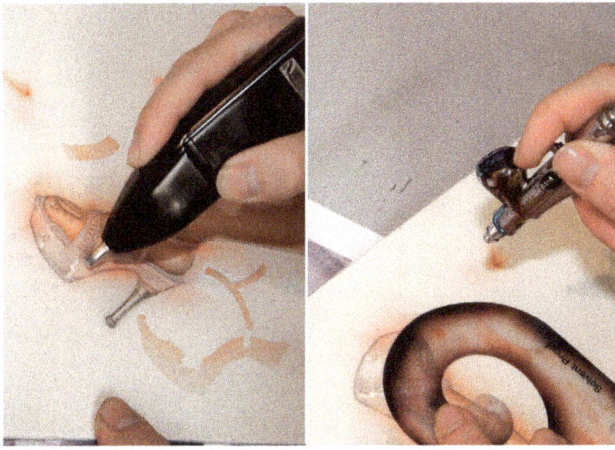

The highlights are smaller and harsher on the shoes, so I whip out the electric eraser to do the job. Right: The freehand shield allows me to cover the lip at the top of the shoe while I add more tone around it.

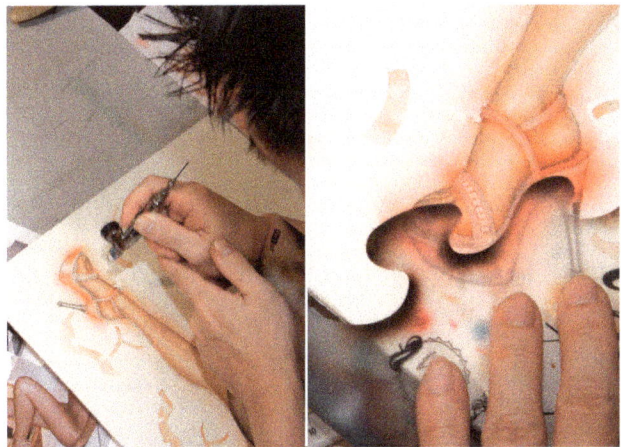

I took several reference pictures of the high heels so that I can pick the best elements from each. Right: Some parts of the freehand shield match up with the curves of the shoe to make my job a little easier.

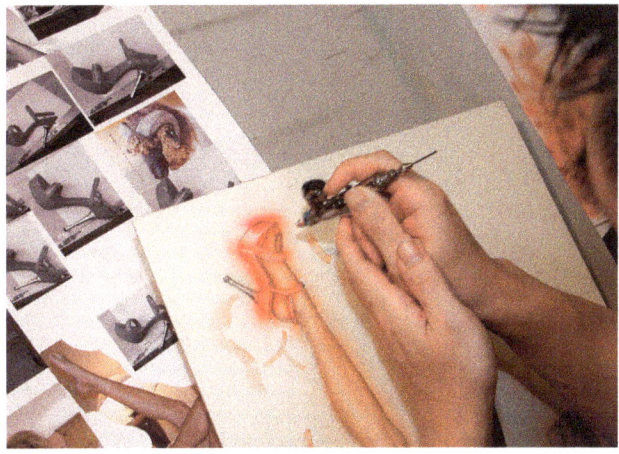

Going deeper with the red so that it's not so light and pink. Again, building up the red with erasing in between makes for good depth.

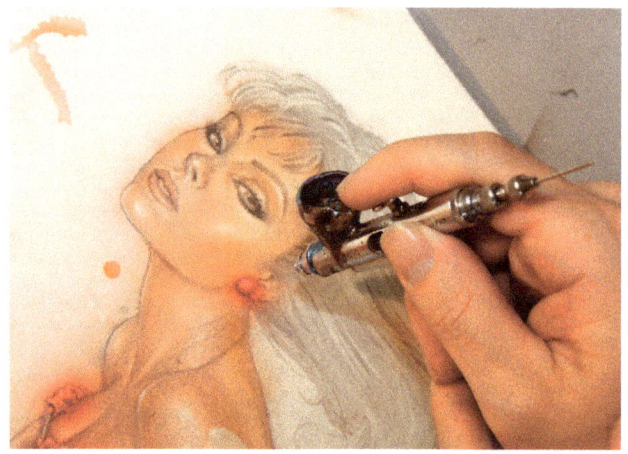

Using the same red, I remove the previously cut masks from the earring and red lace and begin laying down color.

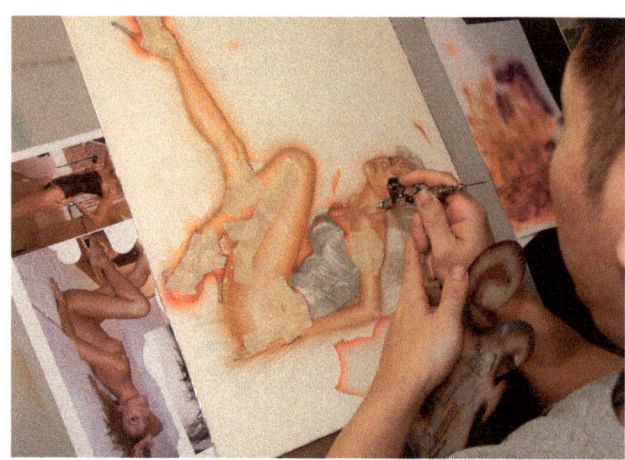

After sealing the edges of the heels with masking tape, I peel the mask off her corset and begin to lay down its color.

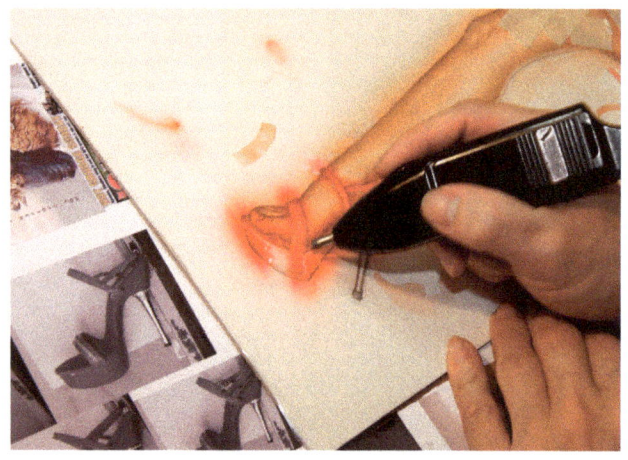

I'm now doing the final specular highlighting on the shoes before I cover them up for the last time.

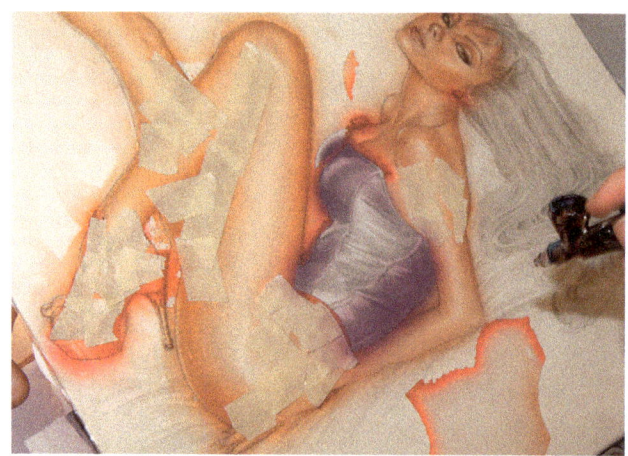

The first light layer of my pre-mixed dark purple tone is sprayed gently. It's not a flat wash to start, there is a soft highlight that I left.

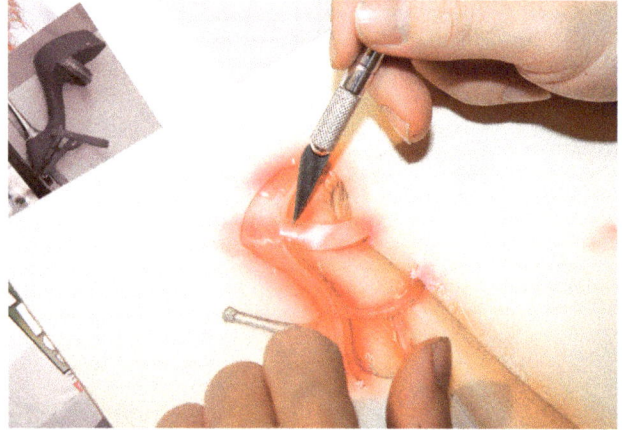

I carefully remask the high heels now that I'm finished with the airbrushing part. The razor blade helps me align the masking a little better than I can with fingers alone.

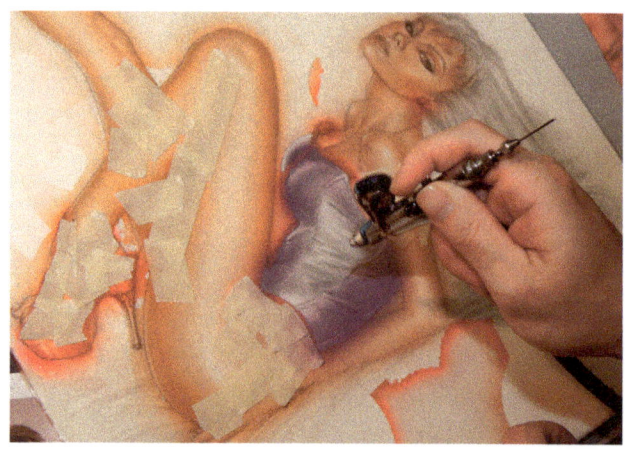

I move in just a bit closer to loosely sculpt some of the wrinkling, but I'm still not going too dark.

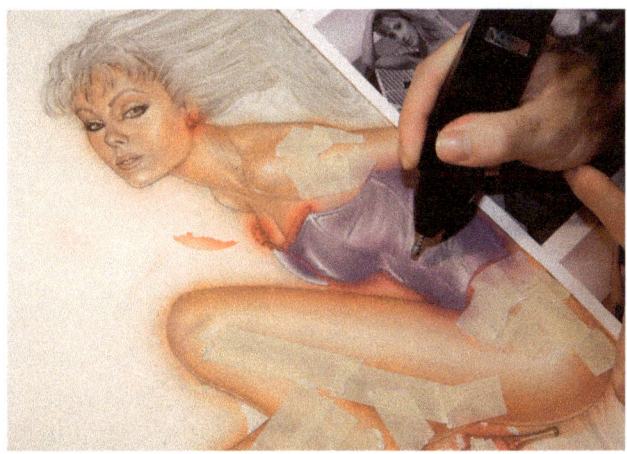

The highlights on this texture are small and particular, so I use my electric eraser to do the job.

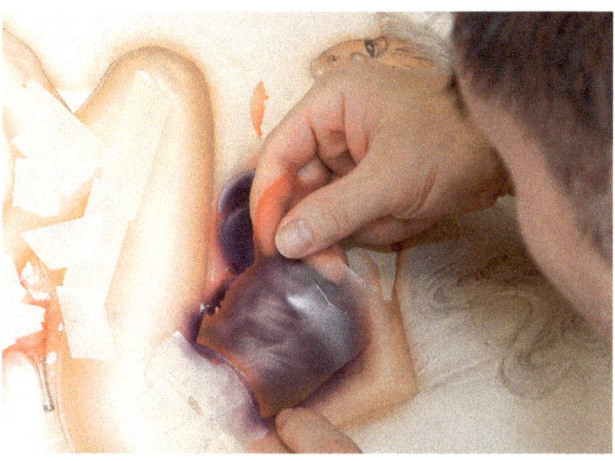

Done with the corset, I remask it and will eventually seal its edges with masking tape again.

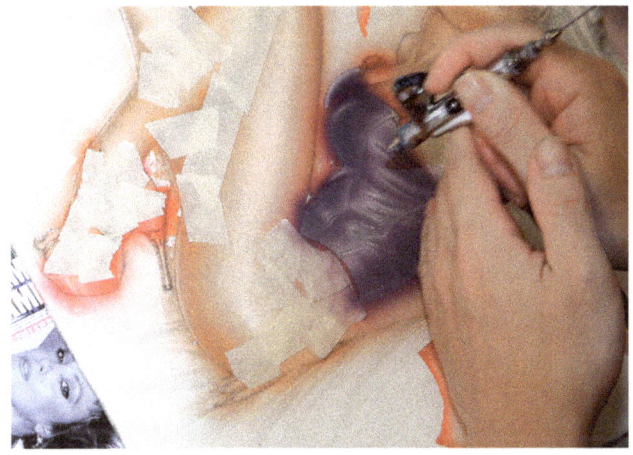

I go in with a another blast of dark purple to deepen the corset.

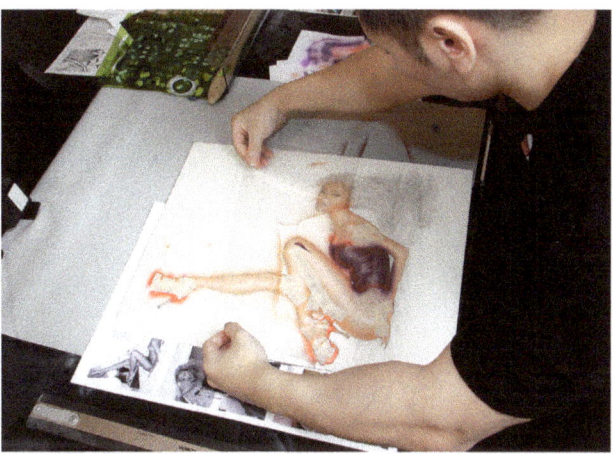

Remember how the mask for the hair was all one piece with the upper body? Well, it's actually connected to the whole background, too. Here, I remove it.

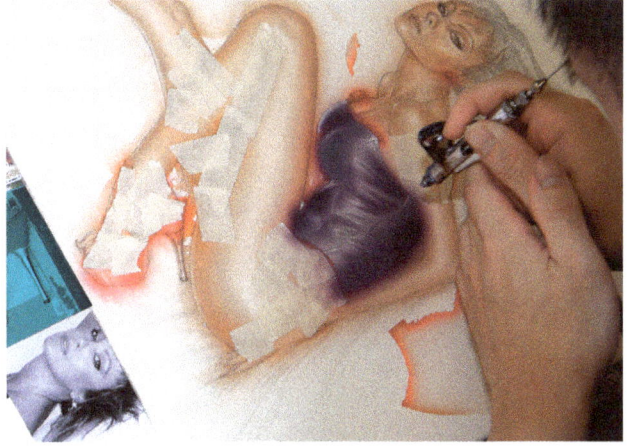

Focus is placed on the darkest of darks as I now avoid the highlight areas.

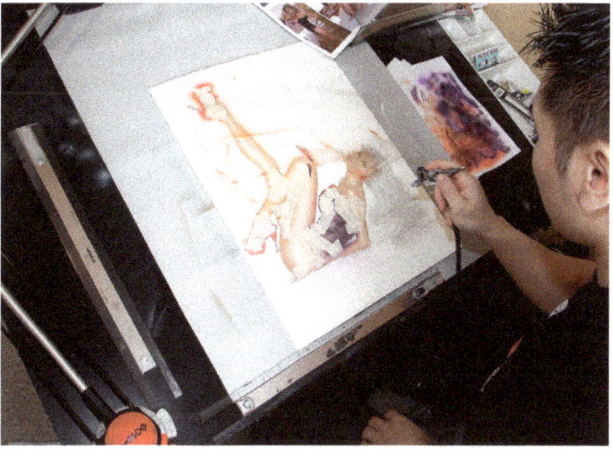

A broad, light-purplish wash is applied to the sheets that Jacki is lying on.

73

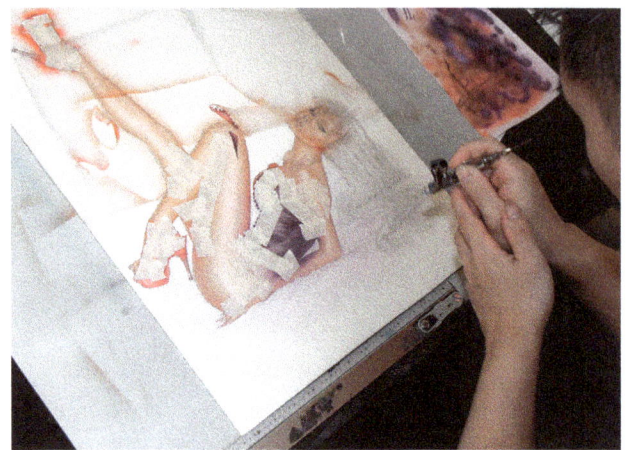

I'm still working underneath her arm and building up the color.

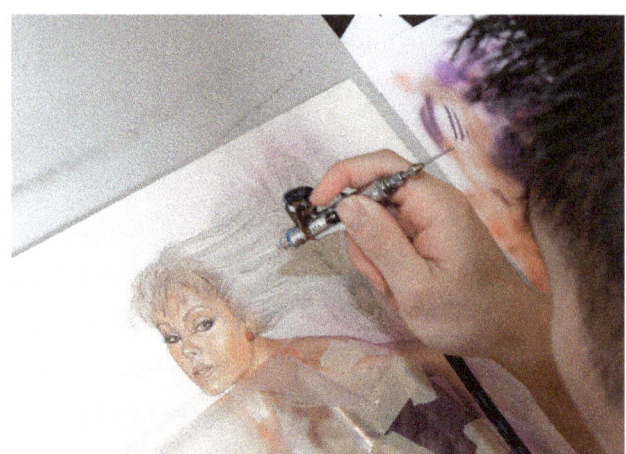

Finished with airbrushing the sheets (it was light and easy), I move on to the hair. The sheets are still unmasked.

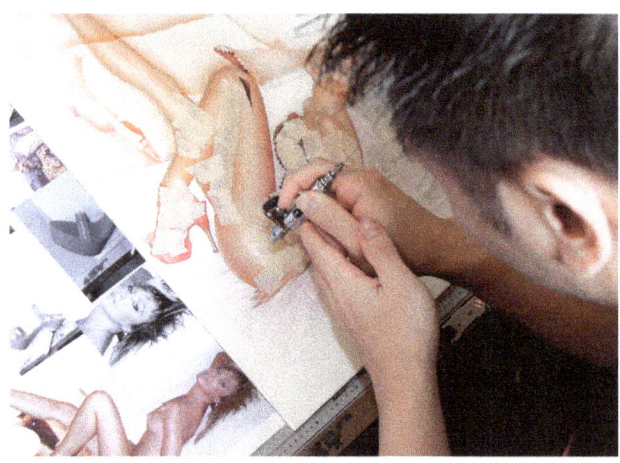

I'm working on the other side by her butt now. I pay careful attention to fade the purple off behind her.

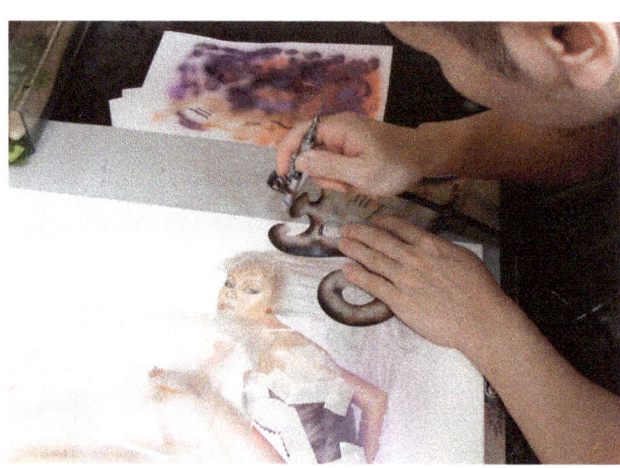

I'm careful with the area of her bangs as it's right next to Jacki's uncovered face. I do want the soft transition, but not too much overspray.

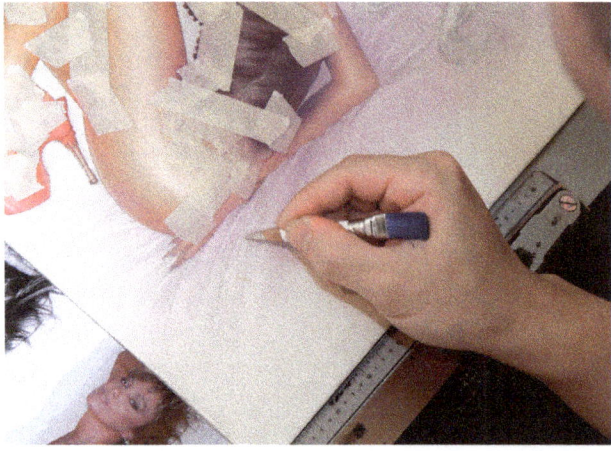

The first layer of purple is done. Here I'm using the Eraserstik to scratch out highlights and begin bringing out the wrinkles.

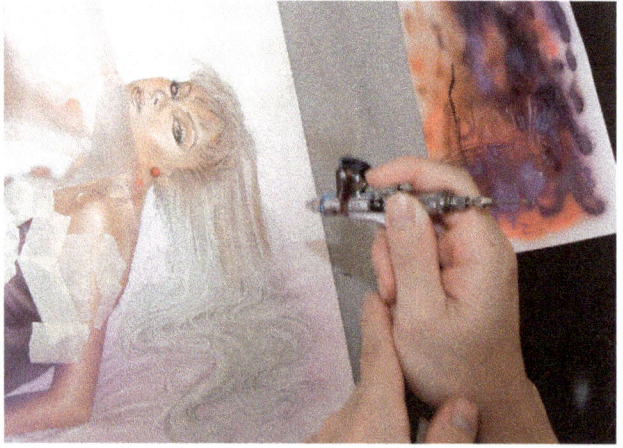

I move down the length of her hair with vertical strokes. Again, I do want to control the overspray that spills onto the sheets.

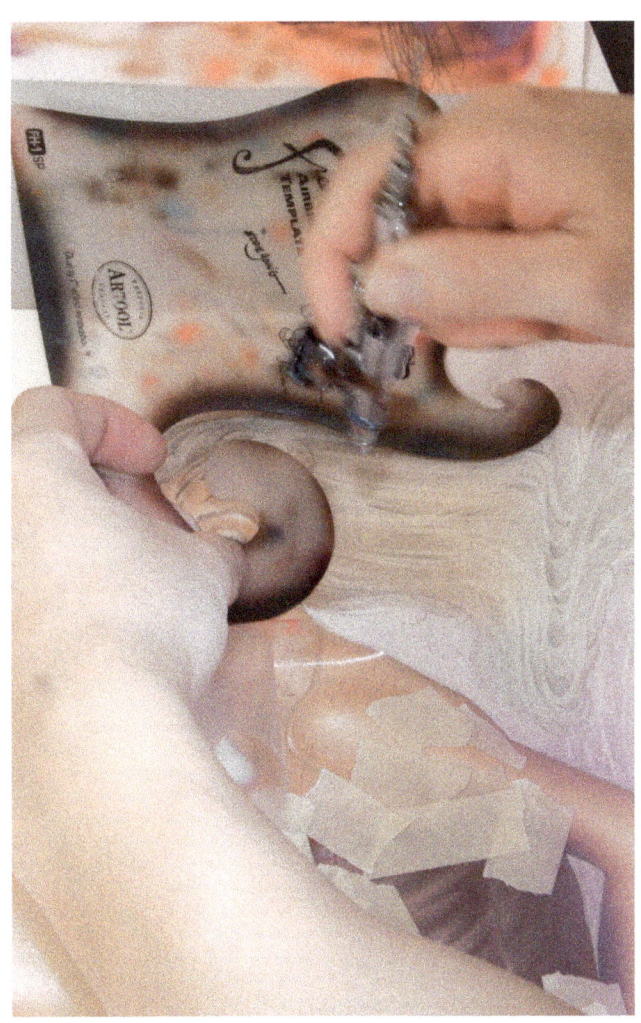

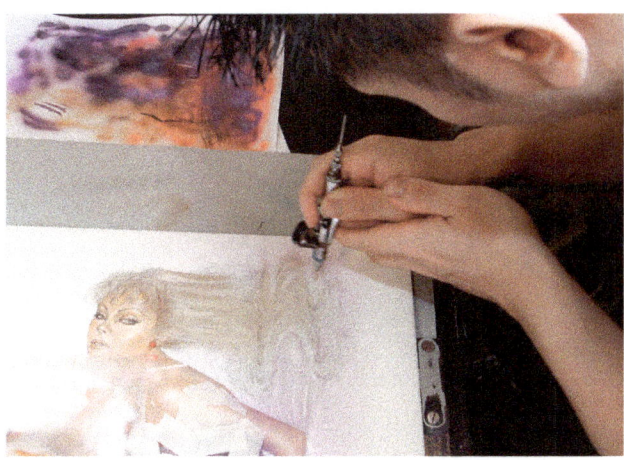

The swirly bottom part of the hair flowing on the sheet is carefully sprayed. These strokes are finer and more deliberate.

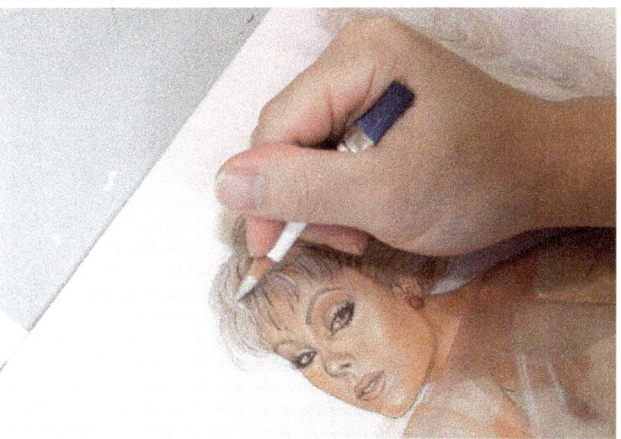

Done with the first round of hair spraying, I now go in with the EraserStik to bring out highlights in the bangs.

The bottom of the ear is shielded while I focus on the darker part of the hair that flows out underneath.

Continuing down the hair, I keep picking out my highlight areas, while trying to be careful so I don't overdo them.

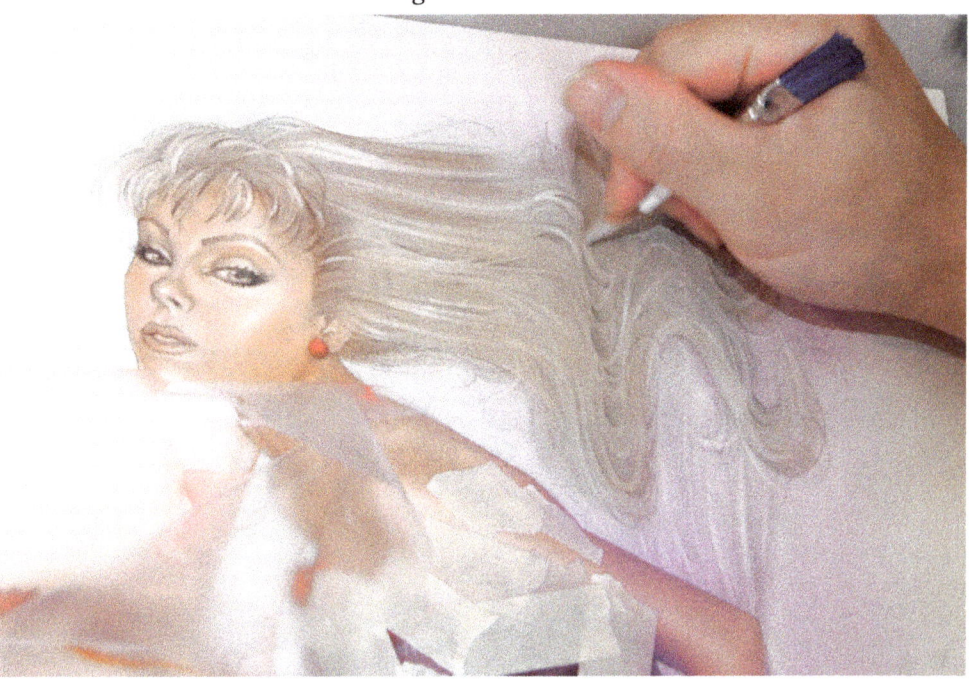

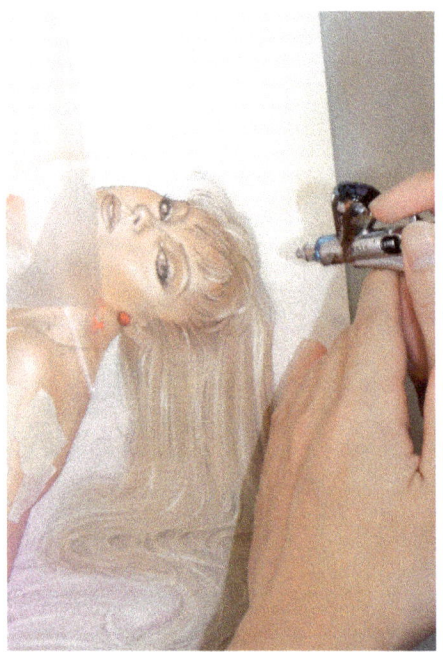

Going in with another round of light brown, I deepen the tone of the hair to help give it depth.

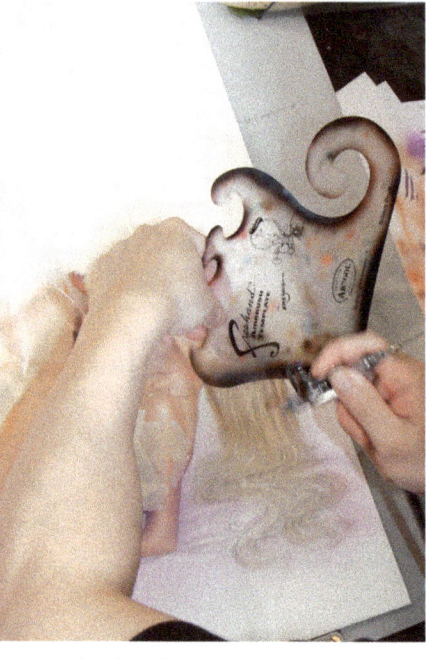

I use the free-hand shield again to protect the ear from the heavier spraying.

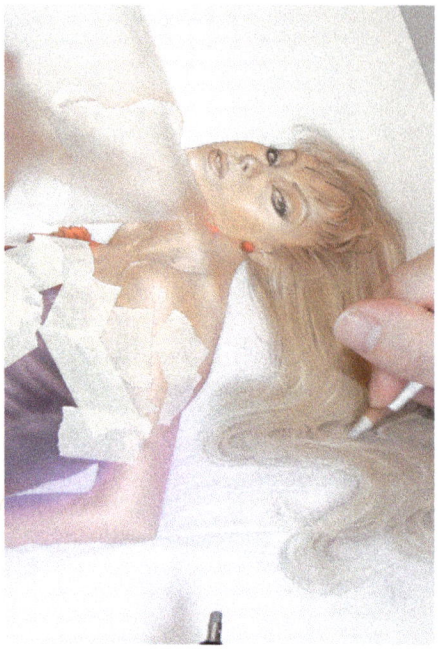

Redefining the highlights again with the EraserStik. Later I'll actually use a sable brush with white for the specular highlights.

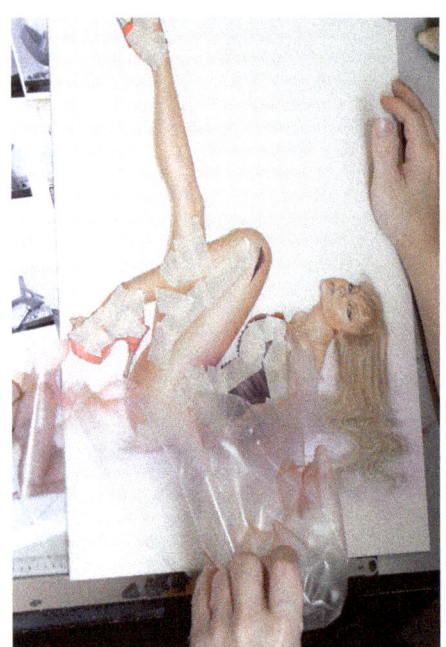

Feeling fairly done with all of the actual airbrushing, I start to peel off all of the frisket (my favorite part!).

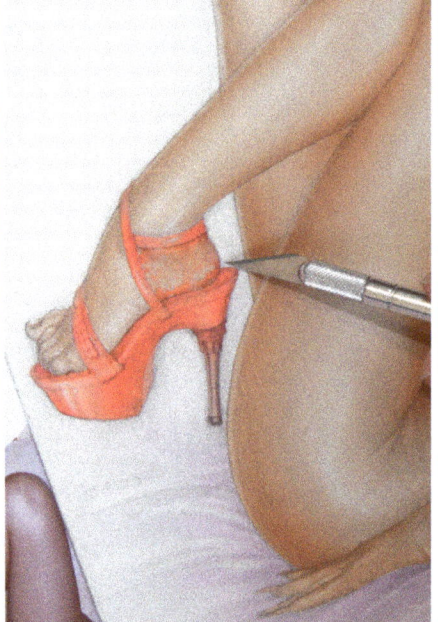

Again, the Xacto knife if used for removal of the smaller pieces.

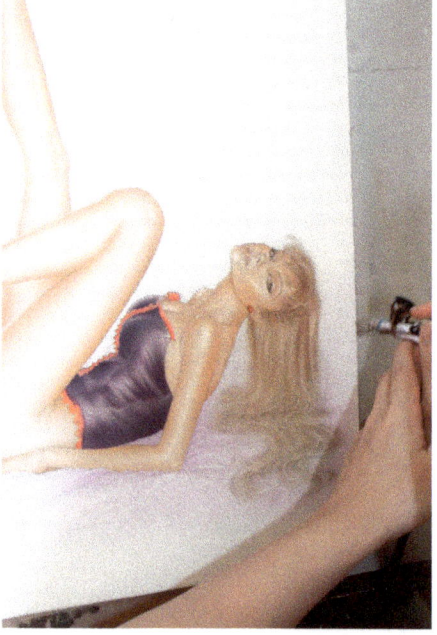

I decided that the hair could be even darker, after looking at the whole piece. So, in I go again with the airbrush.

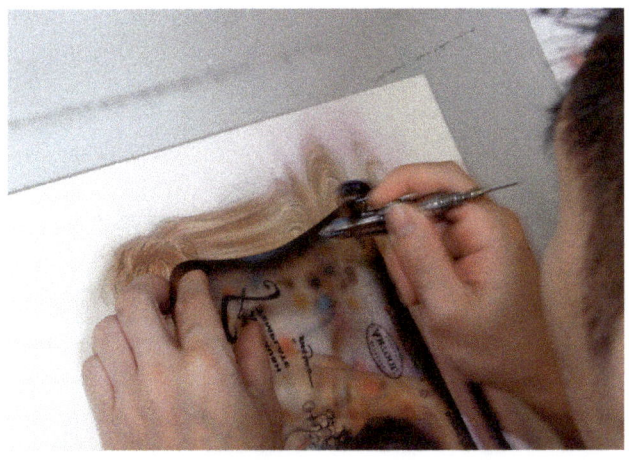

The free-hand shield helps me make random defined lines...

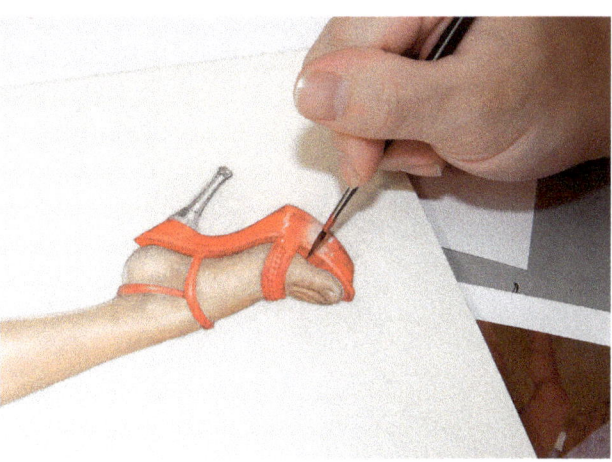

The final step in the painting is the brushwork to bring out the final details and finishing "pop."

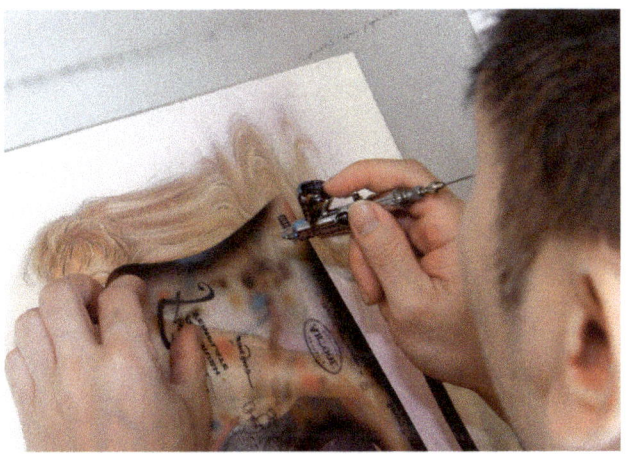

...within the hair to break up the softness.

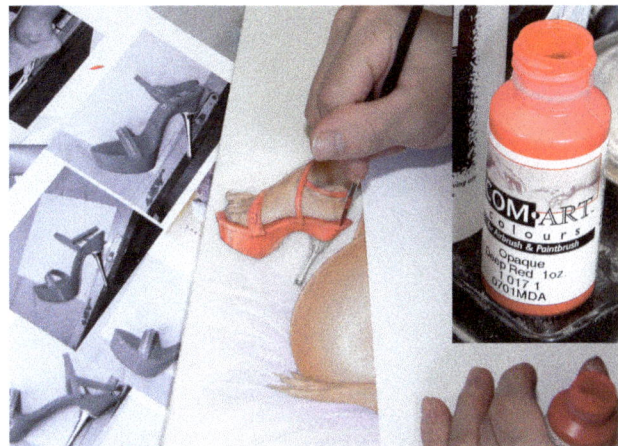

Here I'm using the red straight out of the bottle to bring out the deepest parts of the highheel. But, I'm watering it down just a bit.

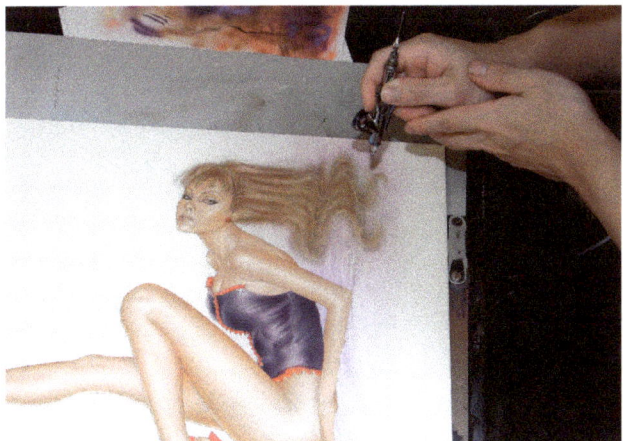

Of course I have to move right down the hair to keep the overall tone even with what I just sprayed in the previous step.

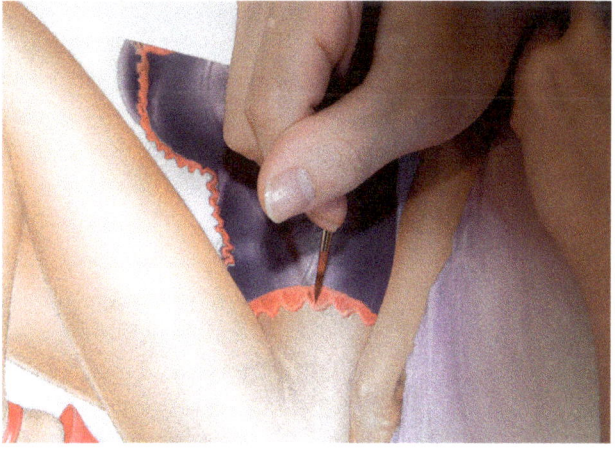

To keep things consistent again, I'm using the same red to detail the lace. At this point I'm making up the detail as the photo was too small.

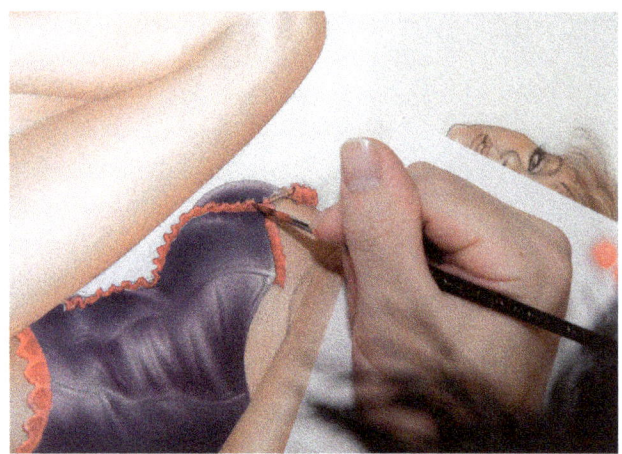

I concentrate on keeping the textures consistent throughout the lace pattern of the entire corset.

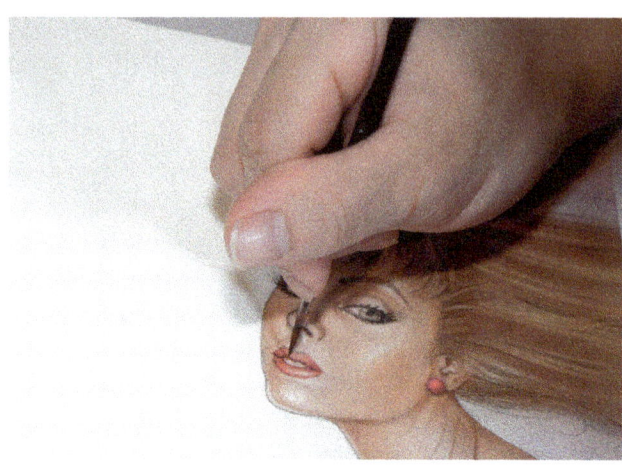

I return to the lips to do more refining, particularly around the gums/teeth. I must have missed it before.

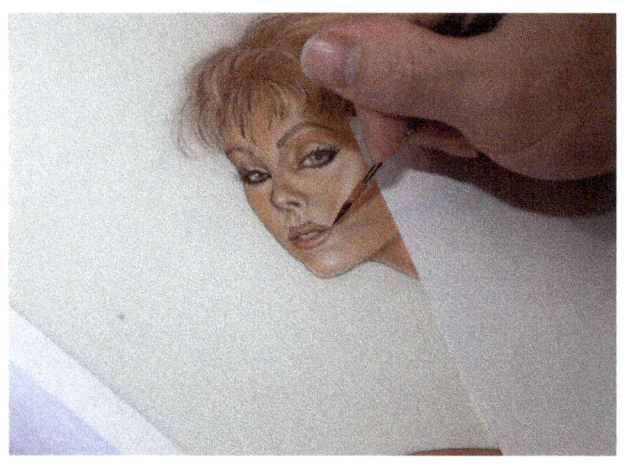

I water the red down in various shades to hand paint the lips.

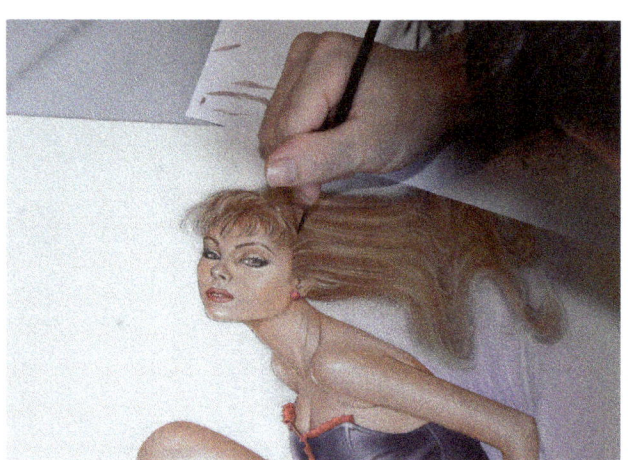

Now to bring out the hair. I'm using a dark mixture of my hair tone to hand brush in individual strands.

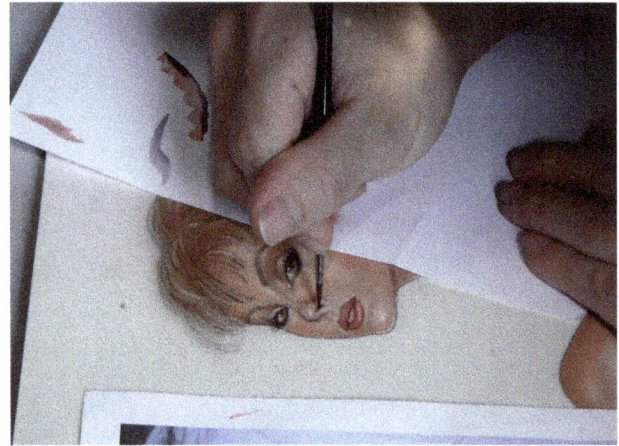

Using the previously mixed shadow flesh tone, I water it down a bit and carefully begin sculpting the nose.

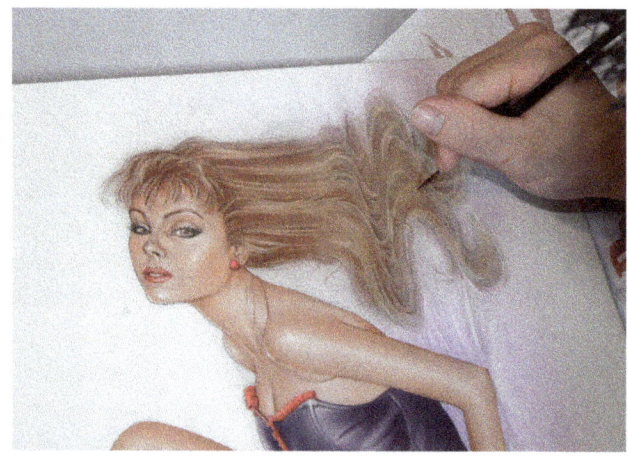

Working down the hair and into the swirlies. Free hand airbrushing can't get lines these sharp; I have to keep the pattern random.

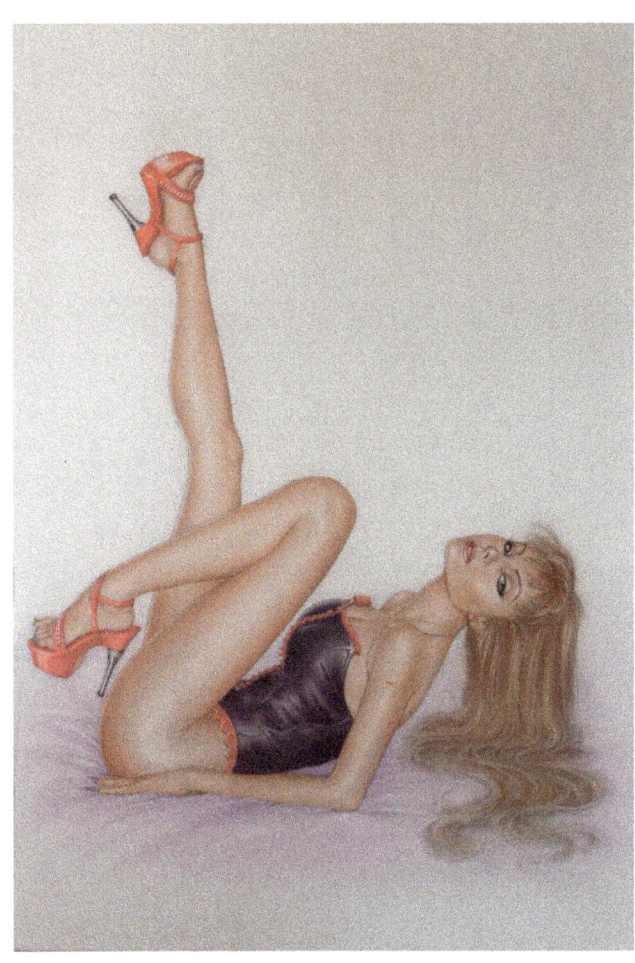

For final specular highlighting I use my sable brush with opaque white on the lips and earring. I think it's time to call it good with this painting. Thanks to the beautiful Jacki Morrison for posing for me!

Still on the eyes, I use Smoke (it's not as strong as straight opaque black) to define the eyelashes. Don't overdo and outline every single little hair!

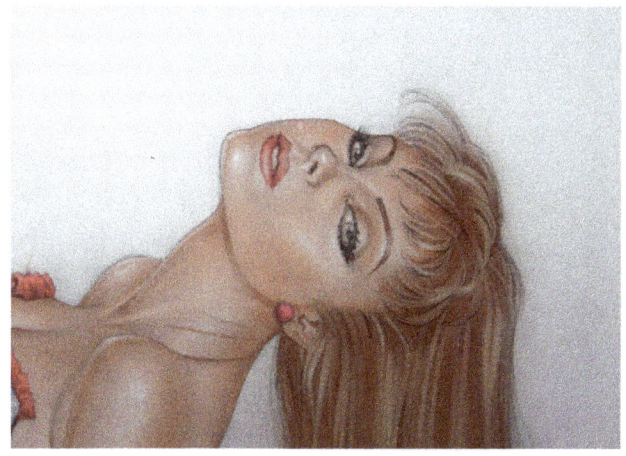

An overview of the face area to see where I'm at, and whether I need to put more work into it.

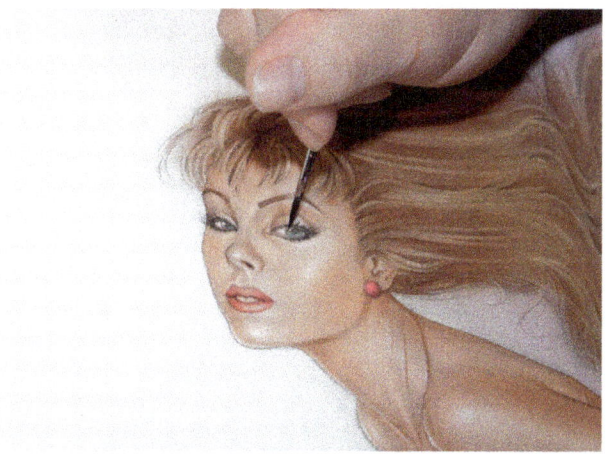

The eyes are very important since they draw the viewer in. Here I'm applying a bright royal blue to Jacki's eyes.

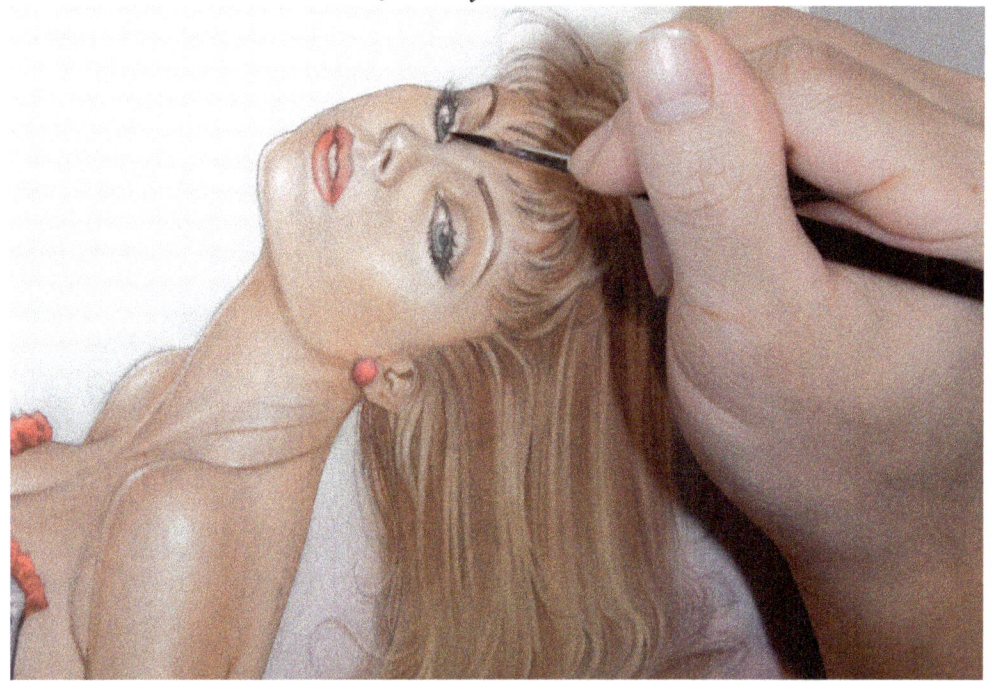

Chapter Five
Steve Leahy
Working on a Small Scale

Part teacher and all artist, Steve Leahy is as gracious as he is talented. Able to paint children's faces at a local Bike Night on Thursday, create a pin-up image on Friday, and teach airbrushing classes all weekend, one of Steve's special talents is his ability to airbrush on a scale so small you need a magnifying glass to appreciate each tiny creation. When Steve "doodles," he does things like render an image of an airplane on a razor blade, or paint more skulls than you can count on a popsicle stick that just happens to be sitting nearby. Though his art degree is in

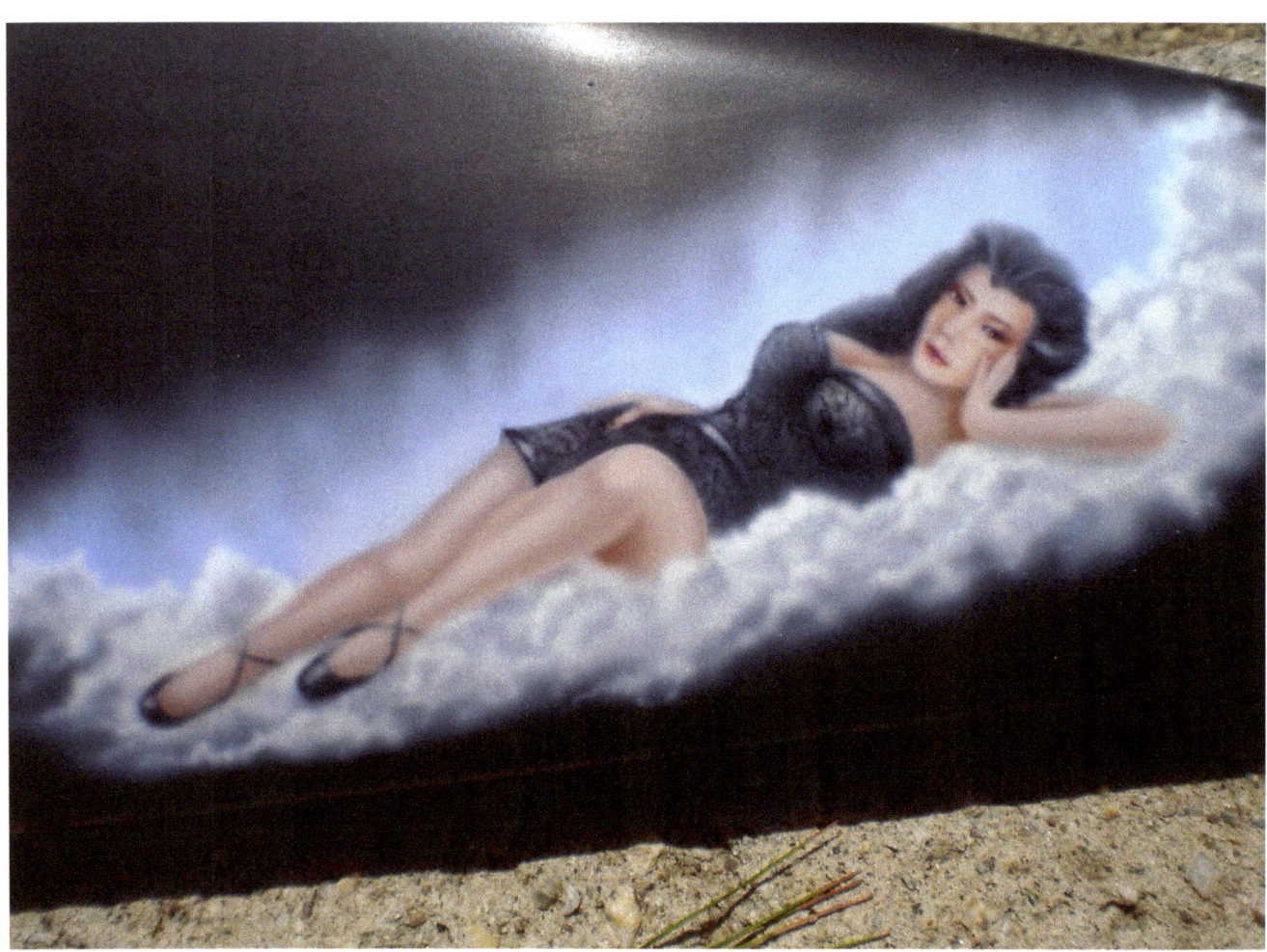

The ability to paint on a small scale opens many new opportunities. By altering a few common airbrushing techniques, painting on this scale becomes much easier.

Illustration, there doesn't seem to be much that Steve Leahy can't do.

This is not Steve's first collaboration with Wolfgang Publications. Steve not only contributed a complete step-by-step still life chapter to another ArtKulture book (Airbrushing 101), he wrote an entire book of his own: How Airbrushes Work, published in 2009. This is an artist with a thorough understanding not only of the art and the color, but of the tools of the trade as well.

Steve's skill at working on a small scale makes him the perfect person to put a pin-up on a gunstock. The project illustrates the challenges of working in a small scale, on a surface that's anything but flat.

Steve starts with an initial drawing and then makes a series of photo copies. As shown in the sequences that follow, the copies are useful in making all of the masks and cut-outs that Steve uses throughout the project. Masks that Steve uses the same way that some artists use frisket film.

The paints used here are automotive grade materials. Steve is partial to PPG's new waterborne line of basecoats and candies.

As you might expect, Steve does very little detailing with a hand brush. Preferring the seamless look of an image that is uniform in texture and appearance, Steve does nearly all his work, including small details, with his trusty airbrush. Besides, when you're talking about an artist with the ability to work on the very tiny scale Steve sometimes does, who needs a small hand brush?

Because of scheduling issues, the final steps in the creation of this image occurred after the photographer was gone, so there's a gap in the photo-record. For an explanation of how he finished the image, be sure to read Steve's explanation at the end of the chapter.

Otherwise, just pretend you're at one of Steve's seminars, a seminar on painting pin-ups. Class is in session so pay attention.

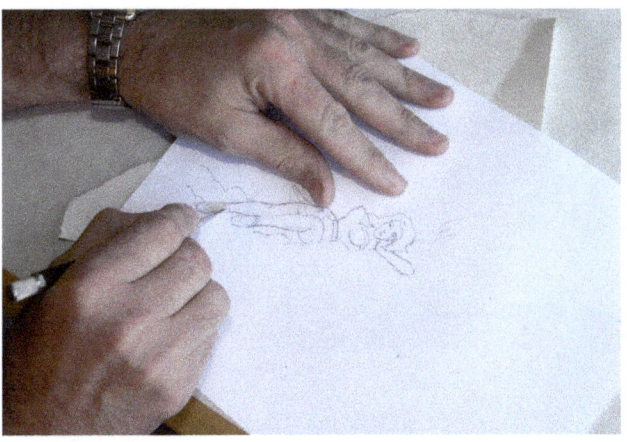

After the initial drawing is completed, several photocopies are made to be used as stencils. The first one to be cut is for the clouds. A standard #11 knife works very well for these tight turns.

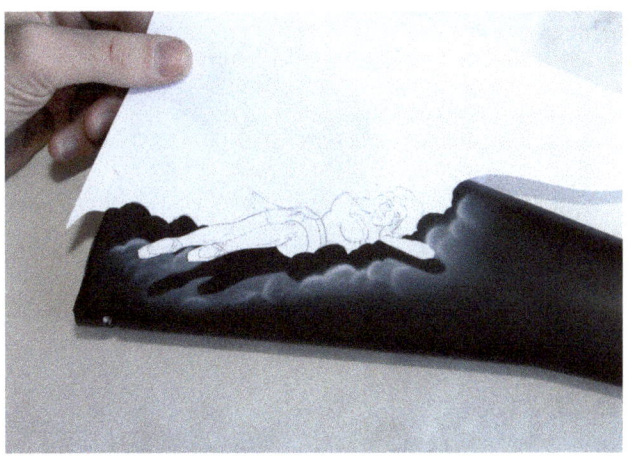

Using PPG global white highly reduced, and the paper stencil, the clouds are roughed in. The paint needs to be applied in light, dry layers to avoid soaking the stencil.

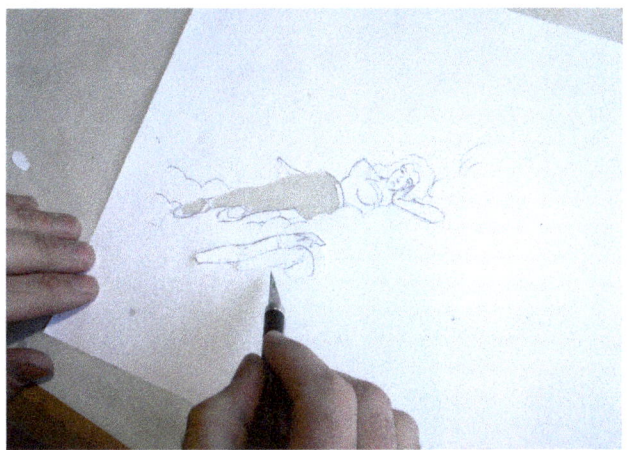

With a new copy, the areas that will be skin tone are cut out. Even though I plan on using the larger sheet as the stencil, I save the smaller cut outs to be used later.

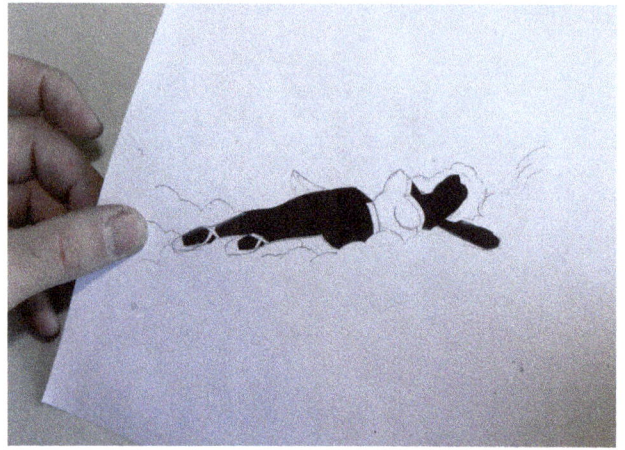

This is the skin tone template completely cut out.

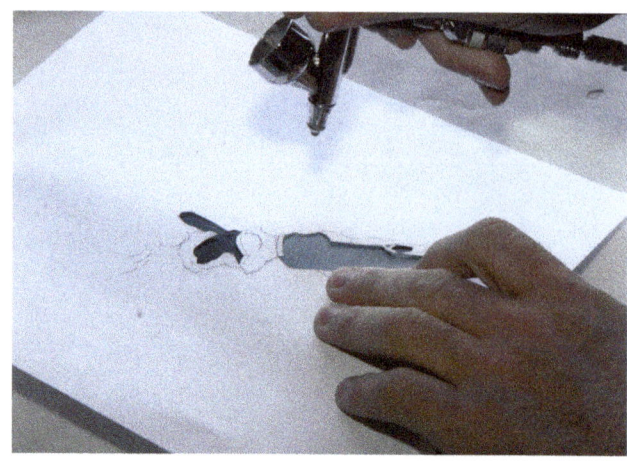

When working with a non-adhesive template, try to spray with the edge of the cut out to hold it down, just using the color to block in the shapes.

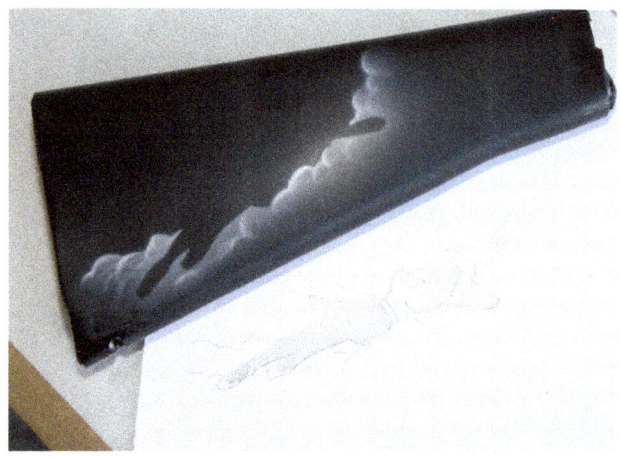

With the clouds roughed in, the placement for the skin tone is easily apparent.

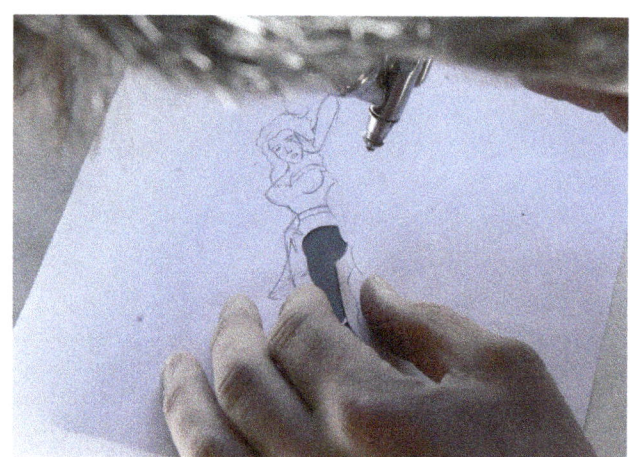

Keeping the airbrush at a distance of about 4 to 5 inches from the surface ensures even, soft coverage.

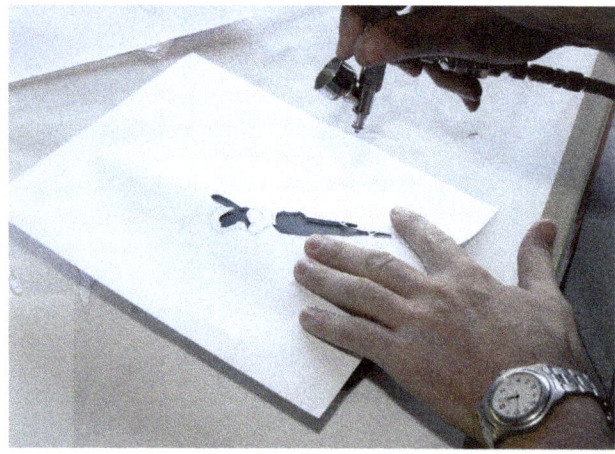

The skin tone that is mixed is very light in color. Mostly white with a touch of brown and red toner. Toners are dye based automotive colors, also known as candies.

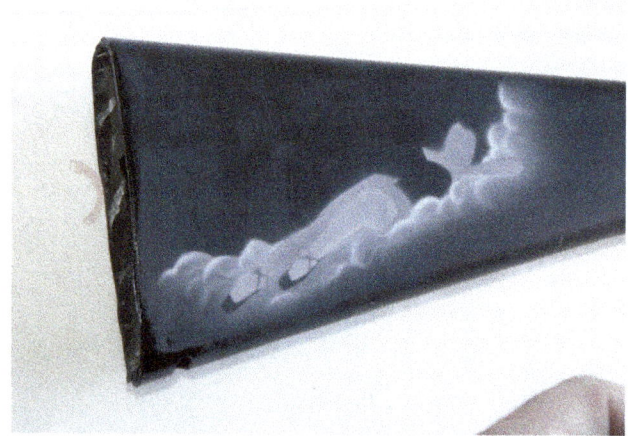

The light skin tone is now blocked in. Any slight misalignment of the image will be easily adjusted as the painting progresses.

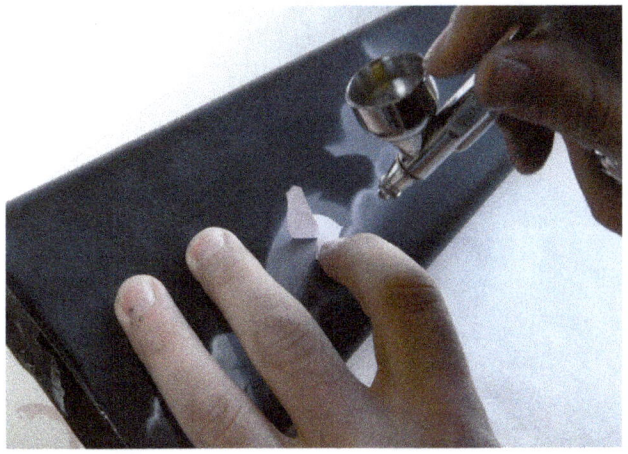

Here is where the positive cut-outs from the template are used. The leg cut-out is used to start defining the upper edge of the leg.

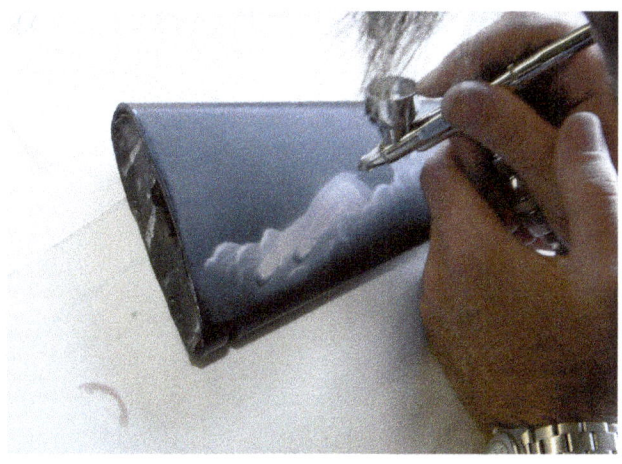

When painting freehand details, I always use two hands. More control is achieved by steadying my airbrush hand.

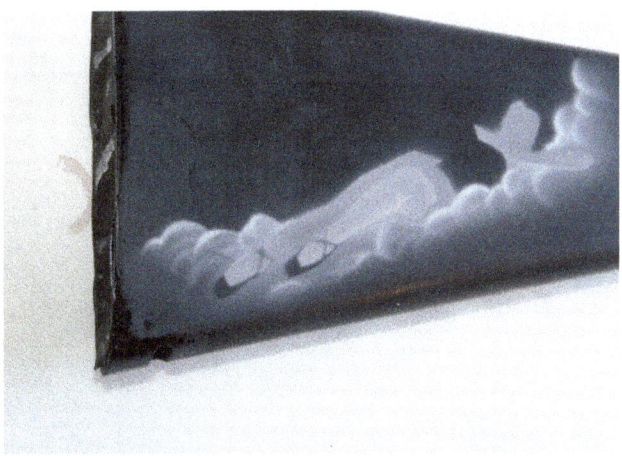

The same light skin tone is used to begin defining the edges within the skin tone areas.

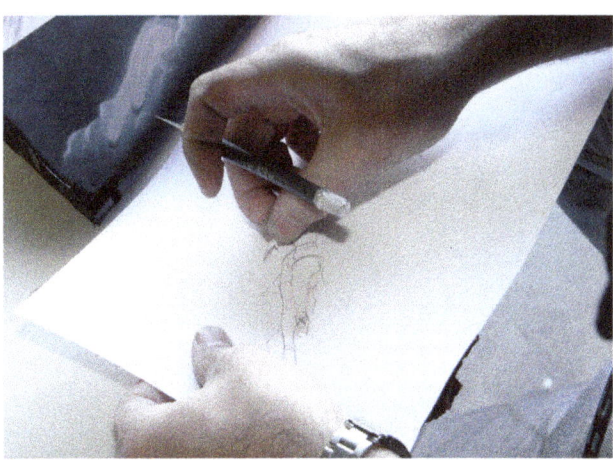

The next area to be cut out is the hand. With areas this small, keep the cut-out simple. Details will be added later.

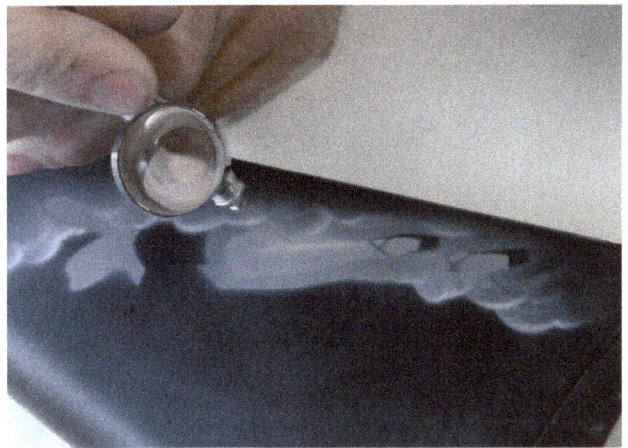

Working without the shields allows me to adjust the edges and soften transition areas.

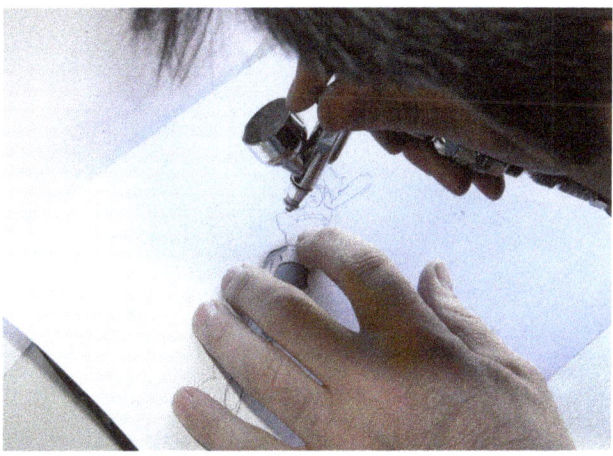

The cut-out for the hand area is smaller than the leg area which allows me to get much closer to the surface without worrying as much about under spray.

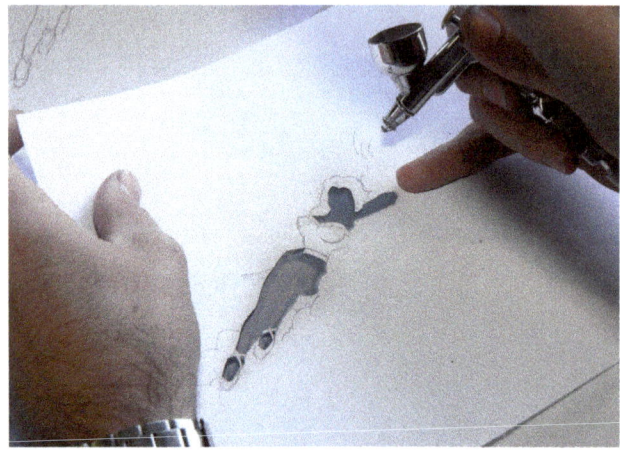

The main skin tone cut-out is now used to begin to define the arm.

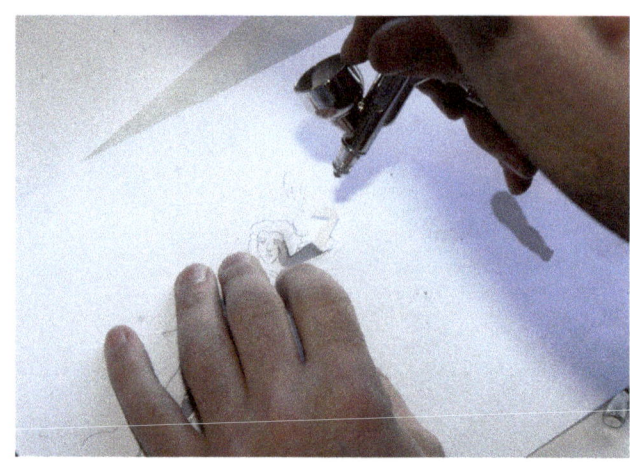

Detail and definition are slowly worked into the hand and forearm. The color being used is still the light flesh tone.

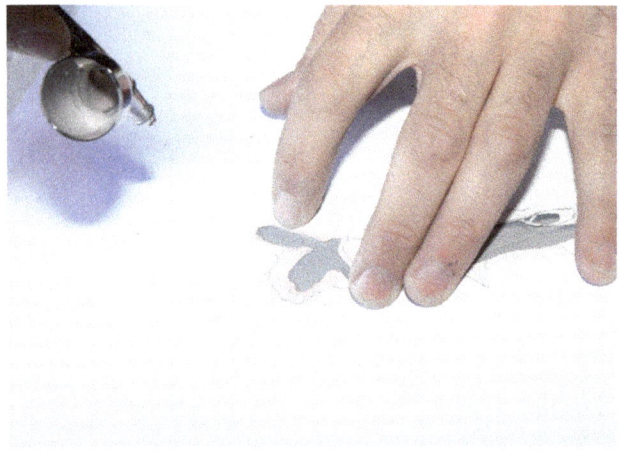

Holding the template down with my fingers allows me to get closer to the surface and develop the details.

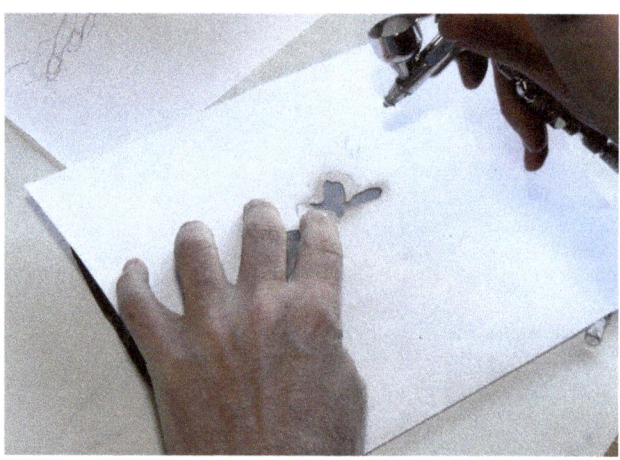

Jumping back and forth between two templates allows all the edges to be defined. Because they are cut from a photocopy, they all align perfectly as well.

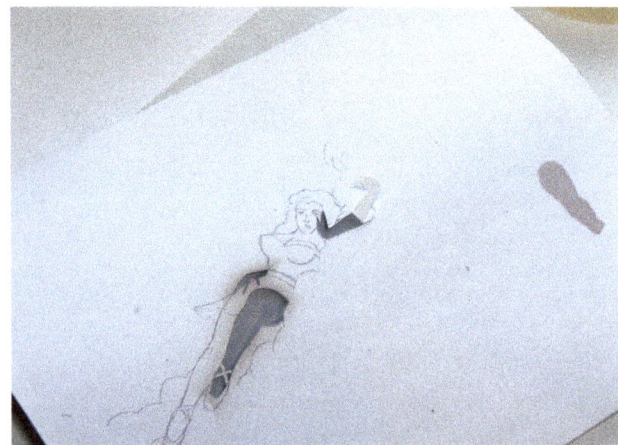

This template shows the cut-out of the forearm and the hand, as well as the left leg. One stencil can often be used for multiple parts as long as they are not too close together.

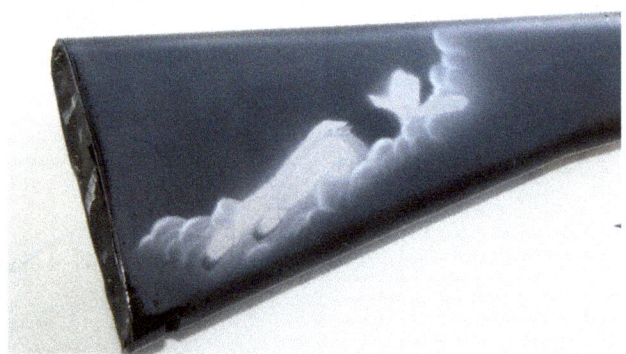

The lightest skin tone is completed and all the edges are defined, making this ready for some shading.

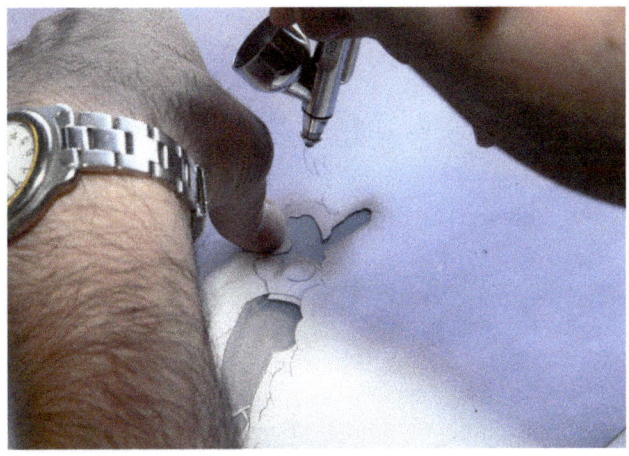

The next skin tone will be made up of the same colors, only increasing the percentage of brown and red. Using the cut-out, a sample is sprayed.

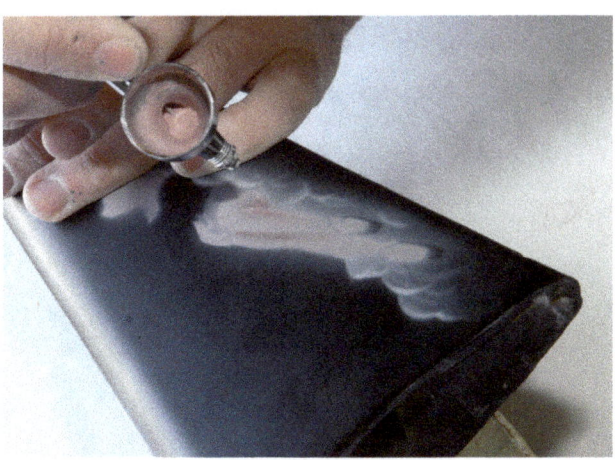

This new color works well when starting to define the shading. It is not so dark as to overpower things, though.

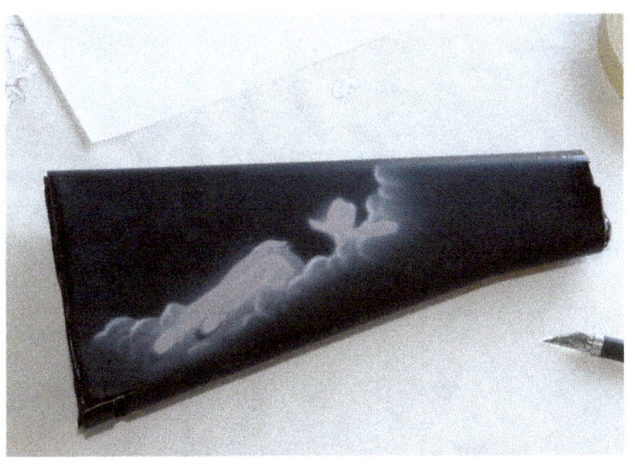

Taking a step back and looking at things helps to give a clear view of things. Looking at the color that was mixed makes it apparent that it can be a bit darker for more contrast.

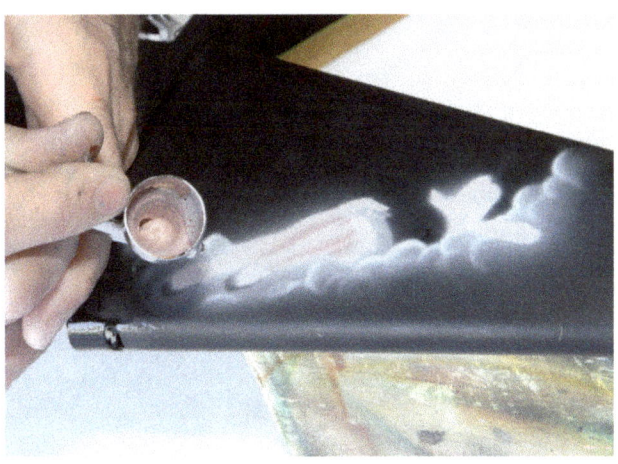

Freehand application of the darker tone is much easier now that all of the shapes have been blocked in with the lighter tone.

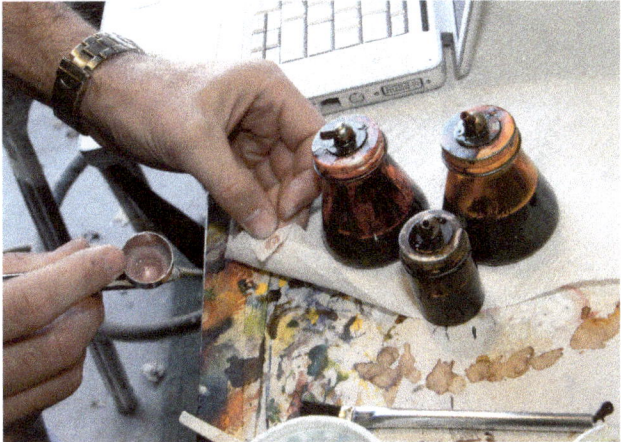

Back at the bench, a slight amount of brown, red and orange toner are added to darken the color.

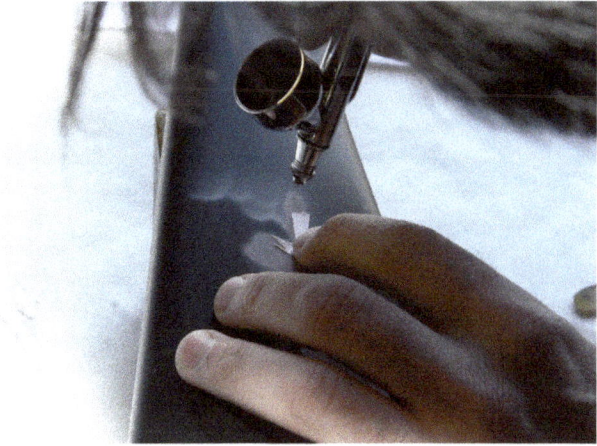

Very defined edges, such as on the hands and fingers, are still easier to grab using the cut-outs from the template.

85

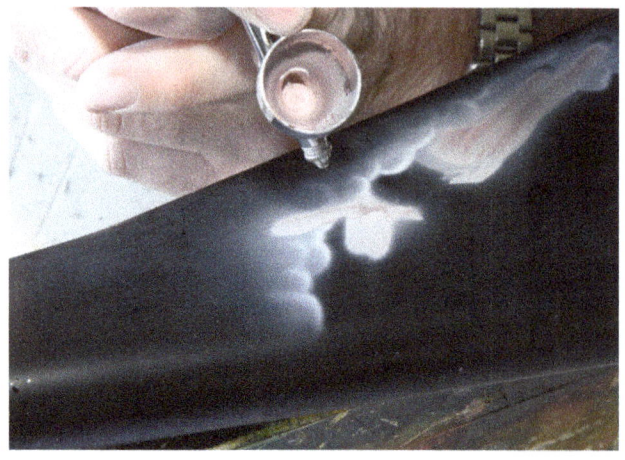

Since this early part of the painting process is generally geared towards blocking in shapes, it's important to constantly look at where edges meet. Adjustments are much easier to make now, than later.

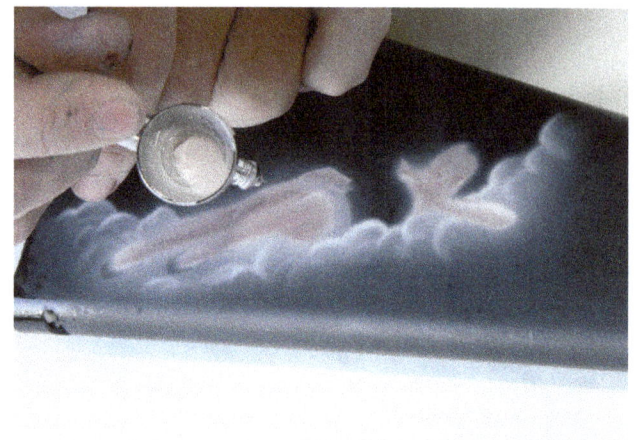

Internal shapes, such as the knees, are pulled out with this color as well.

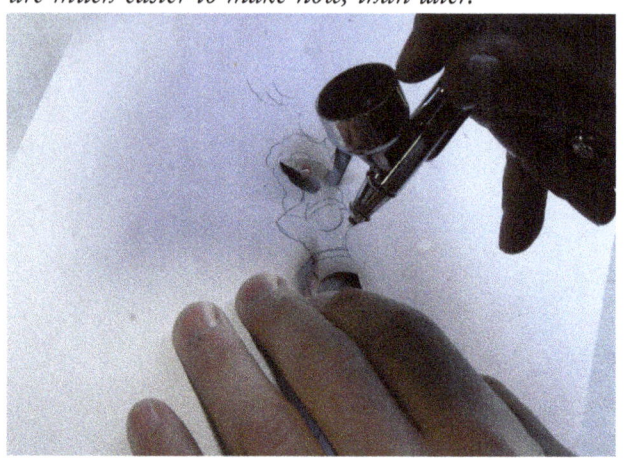

Template cut-outs can also be left connected, creating a "door" that can be folded out of the way, such as in the face cut-out here.

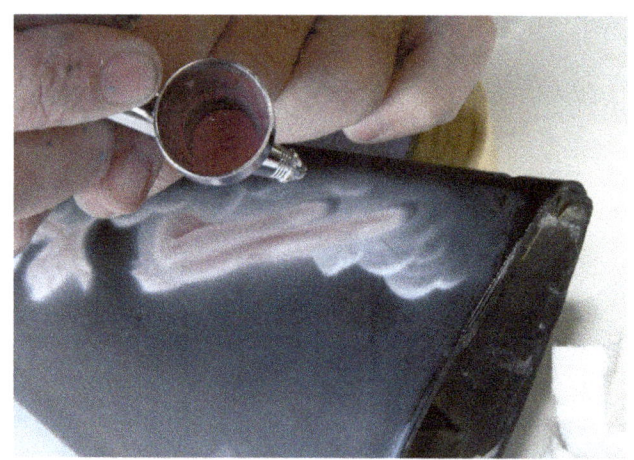

Finally, a dark skin tone is mixed again using the same colors, but with a lower percentage of white. This color is used to define the darkest areas.

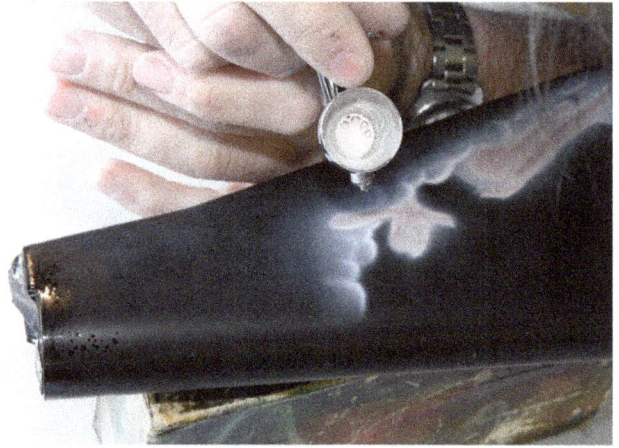

Jumping back to the lightest skin tone color allows the light source to be added to the upper edge of each shape.

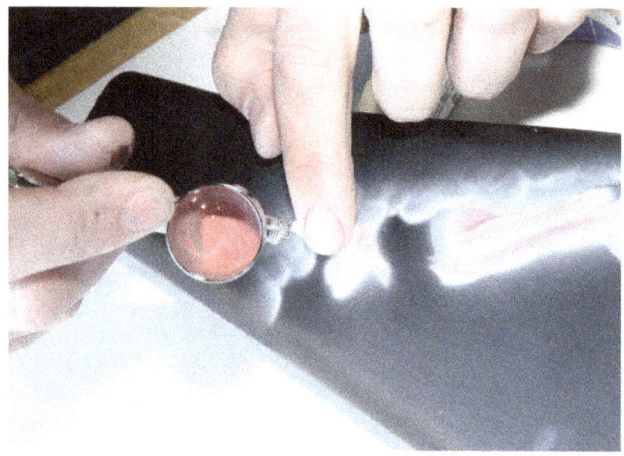

Sharp areas of contrast can be created with this color, so work very slow and be patient here.

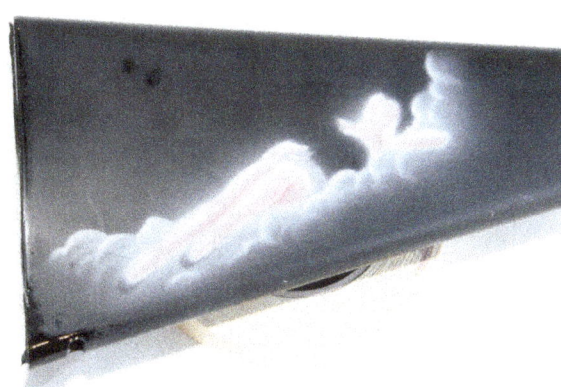

The overall skin tone areas have been defined and are ready for detailing. For now though, it is important to block in the rest of the areas.

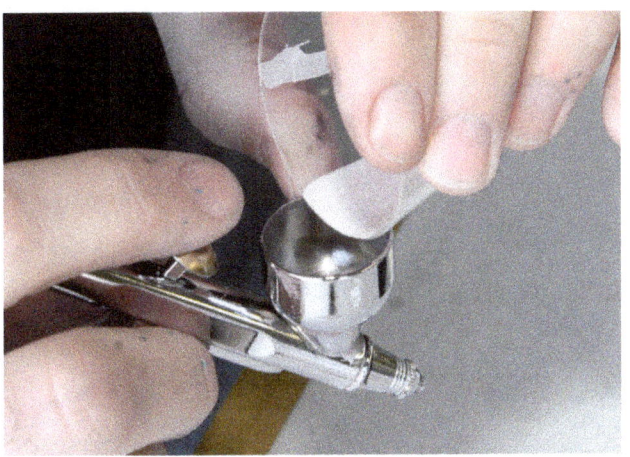

The airbrush is cleared and reduced white is mixed for the next area.

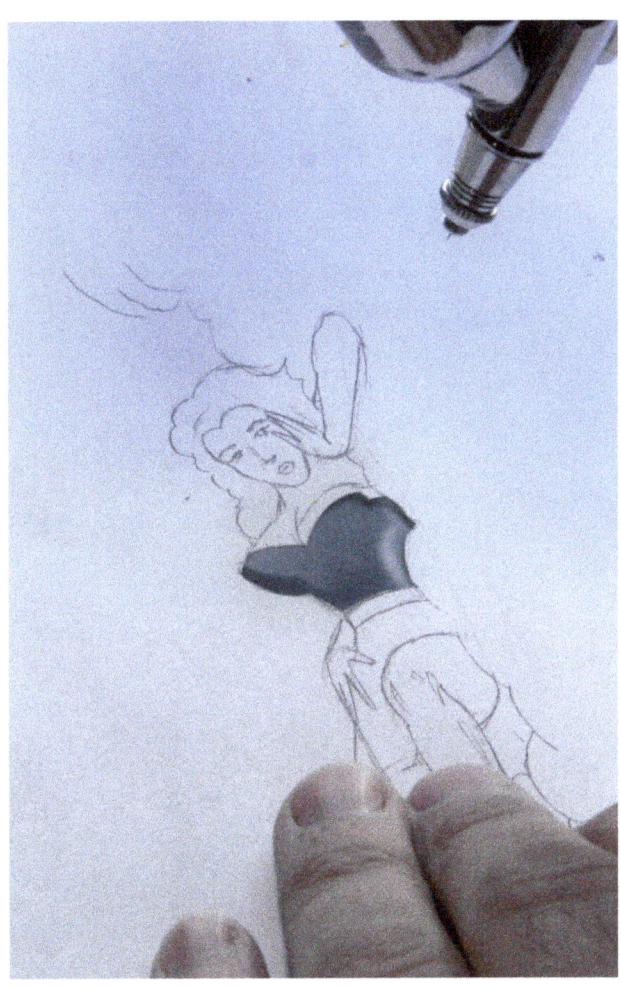

The outfit the pin-up is wearing will ultimately look like lace, so a base of white is painted in. Keeping in mind the light source gives the shape its form.

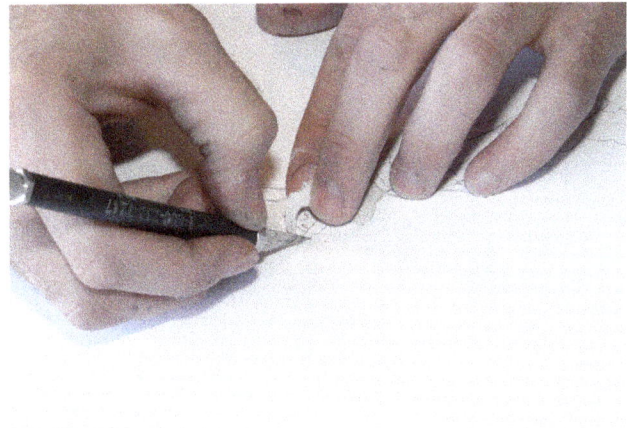

A new photocopy is used to begin painting the new areas.

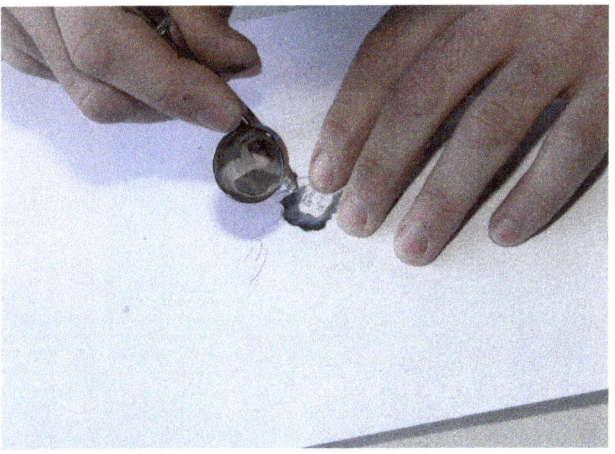

The foundation for the hair is also blocked in. Here the focus is not on the individual hairs, but the larger, general shape.

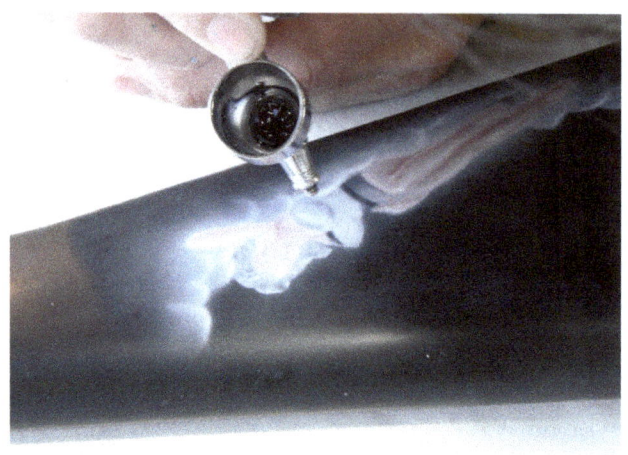

The white is replaced with a reduced black toner and the dark areas of the clothing are defined.

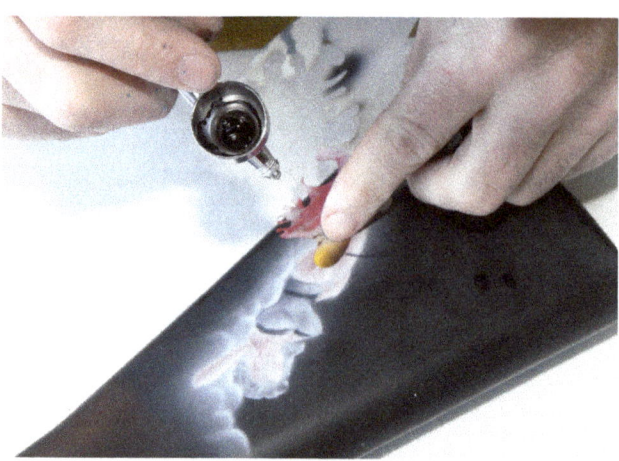

Precut shields can play a huge role as well in defining a specific edge.

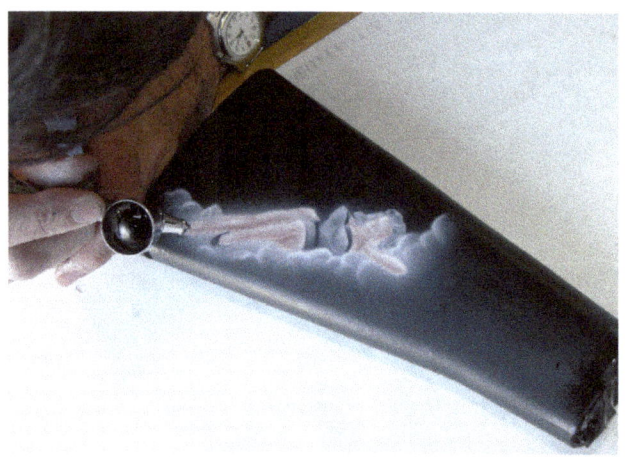

Details like the straps of her shoes are easier to paint in free hand than to try and line up the specific cut out.

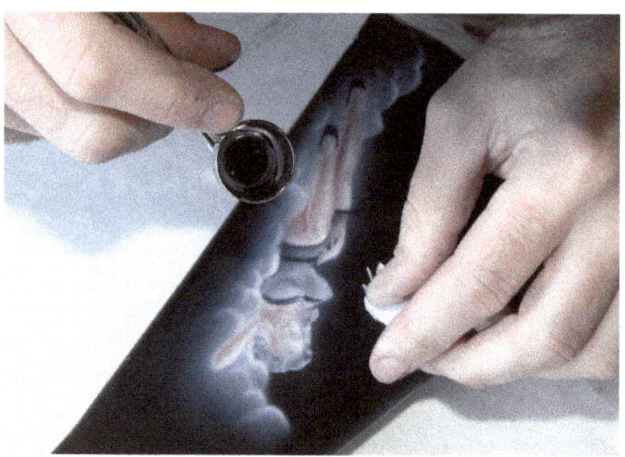

Regardless of the mask that is used, great care must be taken not to get black overspray on the skin. Straight black toner on skin tone turns a sickly gray and would need to be repaired.

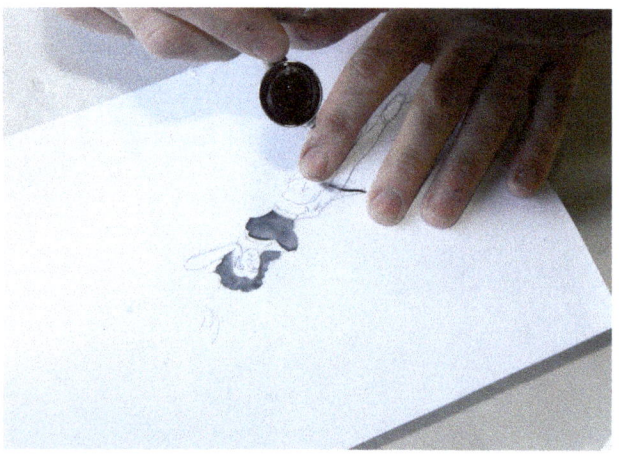

Sometimes there are areas where using the stencil helps to quickly place a detail, such as on the hem of the lace.

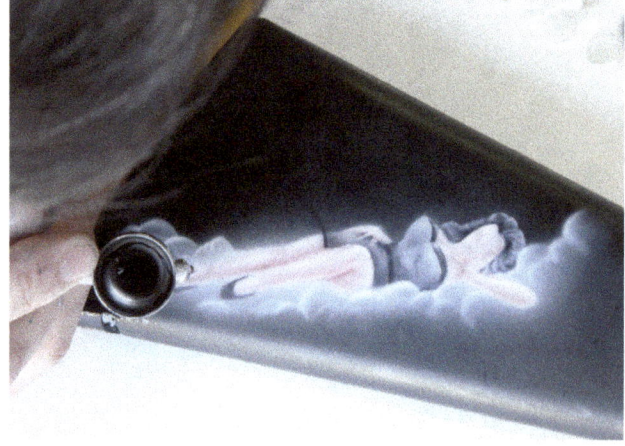

Detail on the shoes is added allowing some areas of the clouds to overlap and come forward.

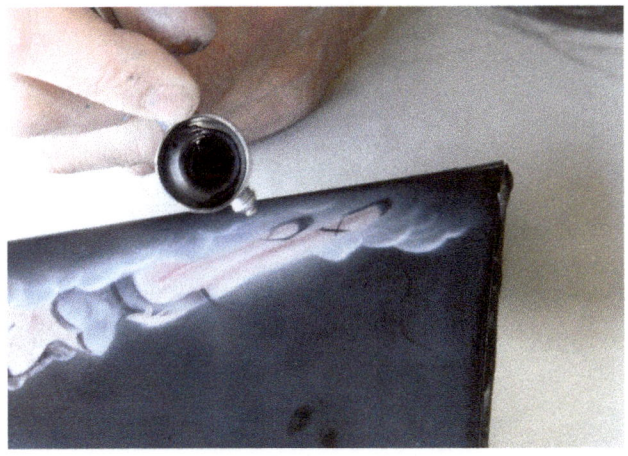

Here working without shields gives me the ability to quickly make decisions concerning the edges. The cloud edges will be redefined in the end as well.

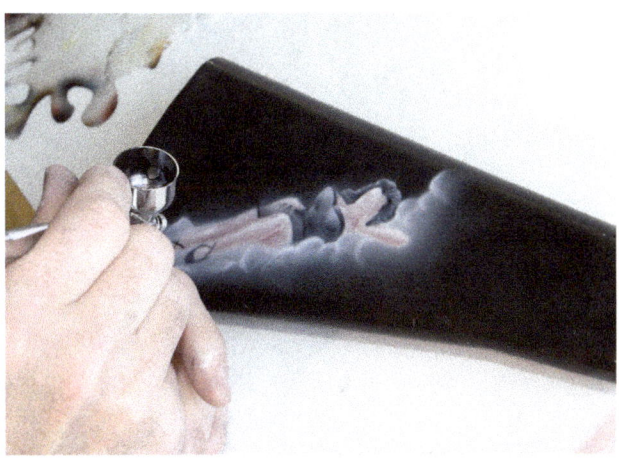

Since the basecoat of the gun stock is black as well, I can use this same black to clean up any stray overspray and marks.

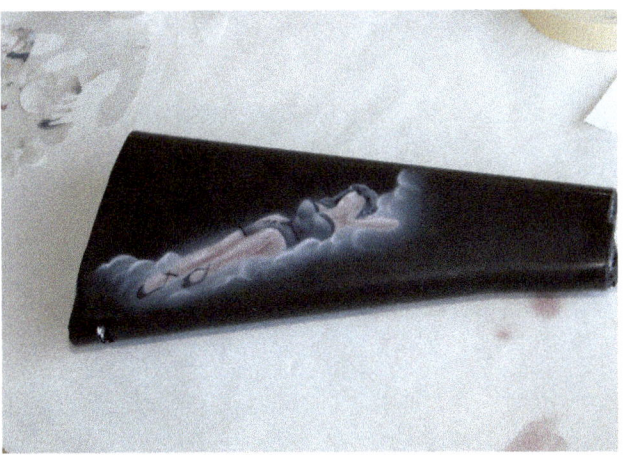

Here the majority of the black shapes and form are locked in.

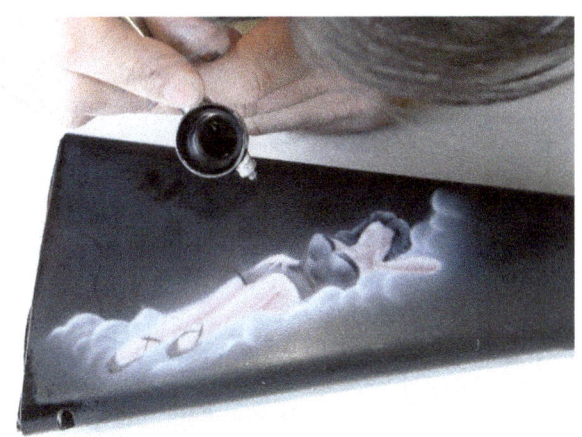

Reduced black toner is used carefully to eliminate overspray around the hand, and also to define the edge.

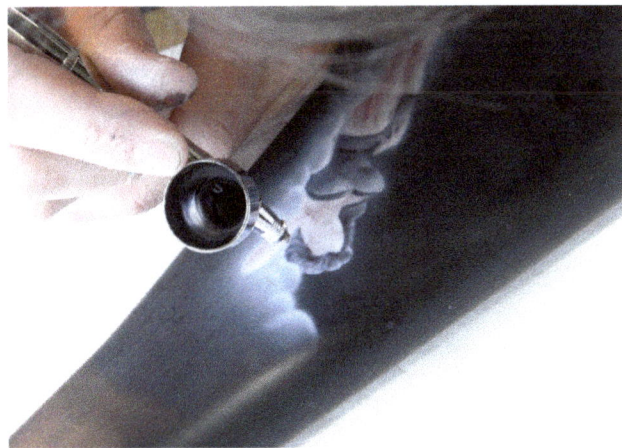

Before moving on, I use the black to start adding form to the hair. Again, at this stage I am dealing with the overall shapes, rather than individual hairs.

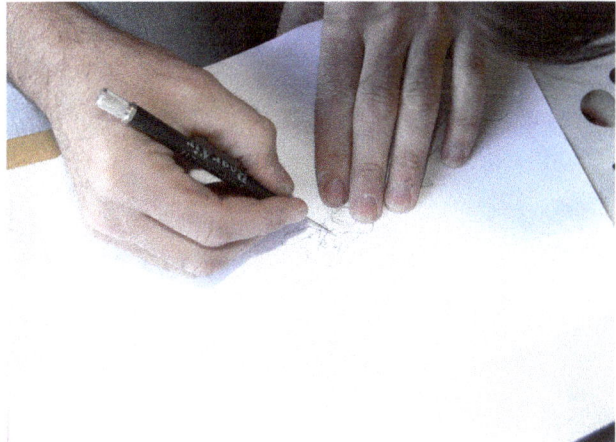

Finally, a stencil is used to cut out the eyes for placement.

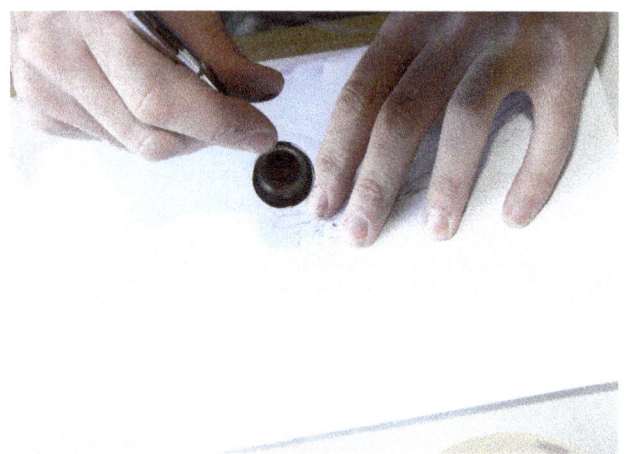

Working extremely lightly, the placement for the eyes is sprayed in. The eyes receive a lot of attention at the end of the painting, so this is only to put them in the right place.

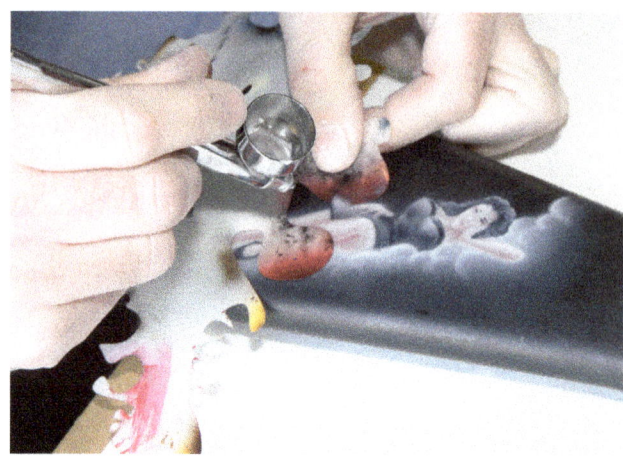

Using a very light skin tone color, highlights are added to the satin on the lace. Using this slightly tinted color helps to visually tie the image together.

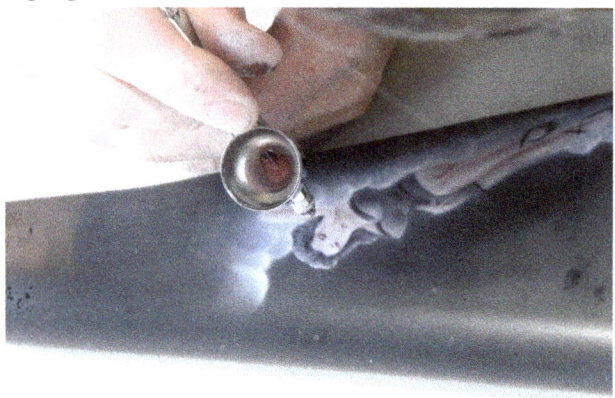

Jumping back to the mid-tone skin color, some of the overall facial forms are put in areas like below the chin and the shaded side of her nose. This color is also used to place the mouth.

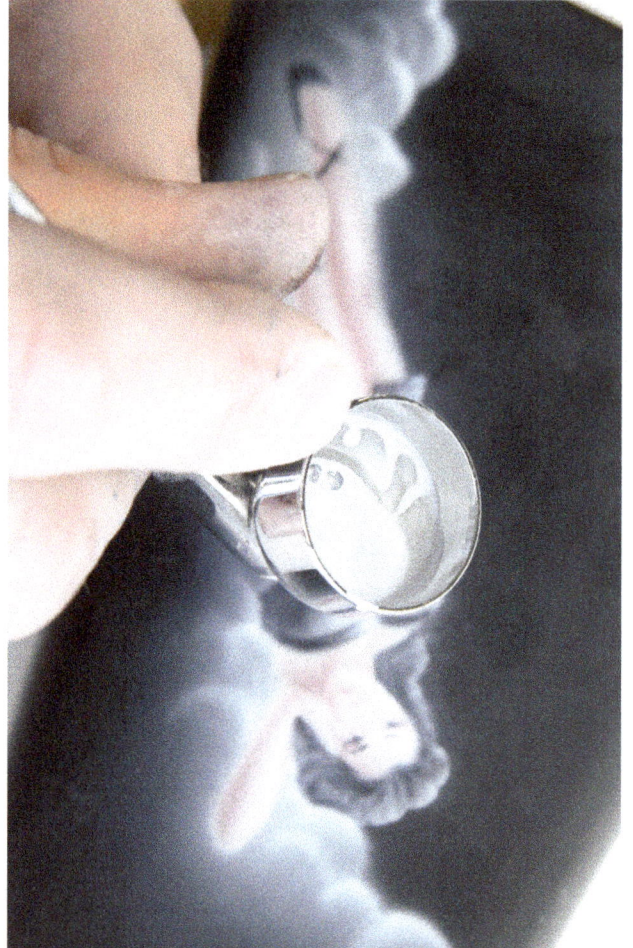

The eye placement can be adjusted as well with this color easily. It will be nearly completely covered later on, so this allows a lot of room for adjusting.

This same color is used to bring out some of the highlights on the skin. Again, work very slowly. These stronger colors have far more impact on the painting and need to be used sparingly.

Note from the Artist

The last 5% of the painting process delivers 90% of the impact. At this point the details are put in. The lace is created with reduced black and a simple fine squiggle line. Because the form is already laid out, all that is needed is the texture to make it work. The eyes get makeup which is a super reduced brown toner and highlights. The lips turned out to be too low on the face. Because the original placement was done with a mid skin tone color, moving them was very easy. The overall change in her expression though is dramatic. Once the lips were properly placed, a slightly darker skin tone was used with a slightly increased amount of red. Simple white highlights make them jump out. Once all the details are set, the image gets a light coat of intercoat clear before heading over for the final clear coat.

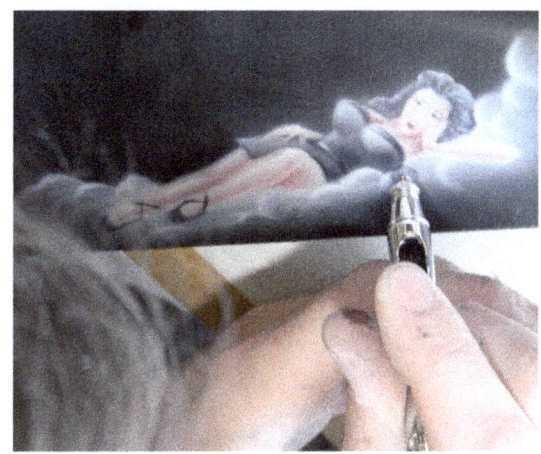

Here a retired Richpen 212A is used to cut in some of the finest details.

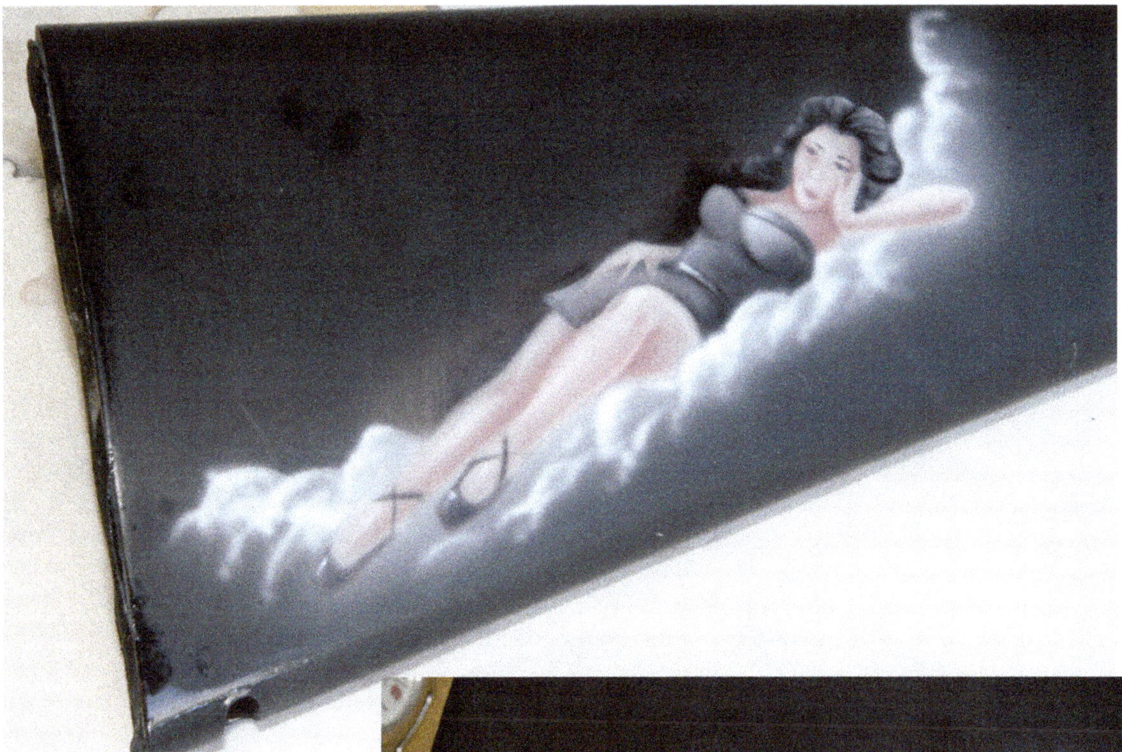

Everything is now in place and ready for the blue background and the detailing.

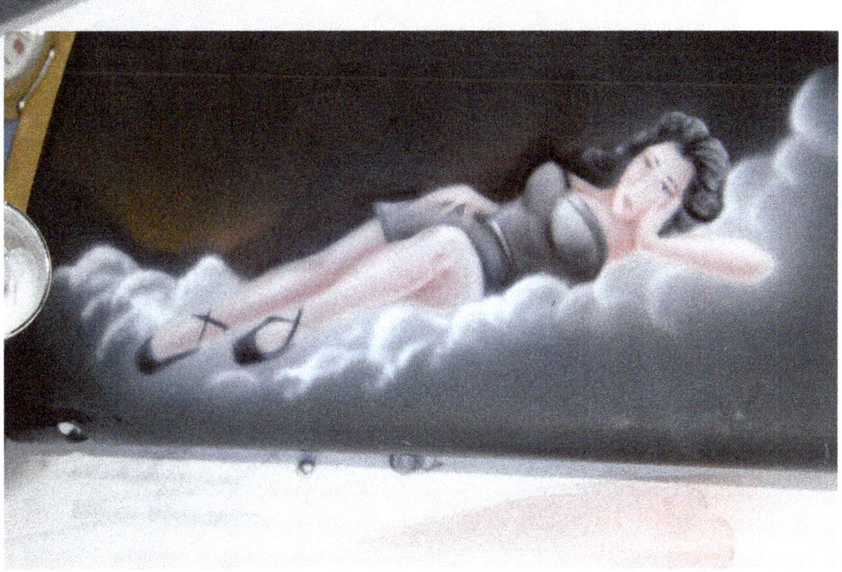

The black is also used to make overall adjustments to the upper edge, before the background is put in.

Steven Leahy Q&A

Give us a little background on you, how did you get started in art, and are pin-ups the main focus of the work you do?

I can't remember a time that I was not into art. I grew up in a very artistic family and everyone always encouraged my art. As far as the focus of my work? Anything is fair game. Taking on different challenges stretches what I am able to do and keeps things interesting for me.

Did you take art classes? How did you learn to sketch and airbrush?

My formal art education was in college. I was an illustration major so we were exposed to many different techniques. It was the airbrush, and what it was able to do, though, that really got me hooked.

Who inspires you, who are some of the artists you look up to?

The list is long but at the top of my list are the photo-realists. Robert Bechtle, Charles Bell and my favorite, Richard Estes. I draw a lot of inspiration from Vermeer as well.

Novice artists sometimes have trouble rendering believable skin tones, how do you achieve life-like skin tones?

The challenge is to paint what you see. Human skin can reflect so many colors. Sometimes the most unlikely of colors is the one that really makes things work. Sometimes we need to turn off our brains and trust our eyes.

I like to start with the lightest skin tone that I can see on the reference picture. This is often a very pale skin tone made up of white, brown and a small touch of red oxide. Each layer then builds on that, getting darker and darker until the final darkest color is applied. The impact that the darker layers have is great, that I find the darker the color I am applying, the less of it I use. Near the end of the painting I am literally dusting the color on. This method allows for the greatest control of the boldest colors.

Another area where people have trouble is with faces, are there tricks or particular methods you use to create a good portrait?

Having multiple abilities allow Steve to paint on almost any surface or scale you can imagine. The gun stock project is just one example of his ability to work on a very small scale.

Steven Leahy Q&A

Proportions play a major roll. Simply getting the features in the right spot on the head can make all the difference. Once again, painting what you see is extremely important. Sometimes an eye or a mouth is not shaped like what out brain is telling us it should be shaped like. Trust what you see.

How about the equipment you use, which airbrush do you typically use and why? And what do you use for a compressor?

Painting on a small scale demands a lot of control. Small needles, and nozzles atomize the paint to an extremely fine mist, and smooth trigger control eliminates surprises. For my detail work I use a Richpen 213 and for extreme detail, I use the smaller Richpen 212B. The compressor that I use is the SilentAire 50-6.

Paint, which brand of paint do you use and why?

It largely depends on the project. For the majority of my work now I have been using the PPG Aquabase Automotive paint. It is waterborne so it thins and cleans up with water, yet performs better than any waterbased paint I have used.

How did you learn to mix paint to create unique colors?

Mostly trial and error at first, yet the color theory classes in college helped tremendously in teaching me what really happens as we mix colors together.

Do you use other media like hand brushes to add detail, or achieve effects that are hard to do with an airbrush?

I find that I have a more continuous look to the piece when I do everything with the airbrush. Occasionally I will use traditional paint brushes and colored pencils, but those are always followed by more airbrush work to blend them in with the rest of the work.

How do you find the models, typically who does the photographs that you use for reference?

It is far easier for me to take my own photographs for reference. Models are often people that I know, they are accustomed to having me rely on them for this kind of thing.

What makes a good pin-up?

Emotionally, the image has to be inviting yet still have some mystery about it. It has to tell a story. The model needs to be physically attractive, and needs to be rendered well. Other than that, the sky is the limit.

If you were going to give ten words of advice to someone just starting out, what would that advice be?

Don't get discouraged. Educate yourself and always push yourself. Paint!

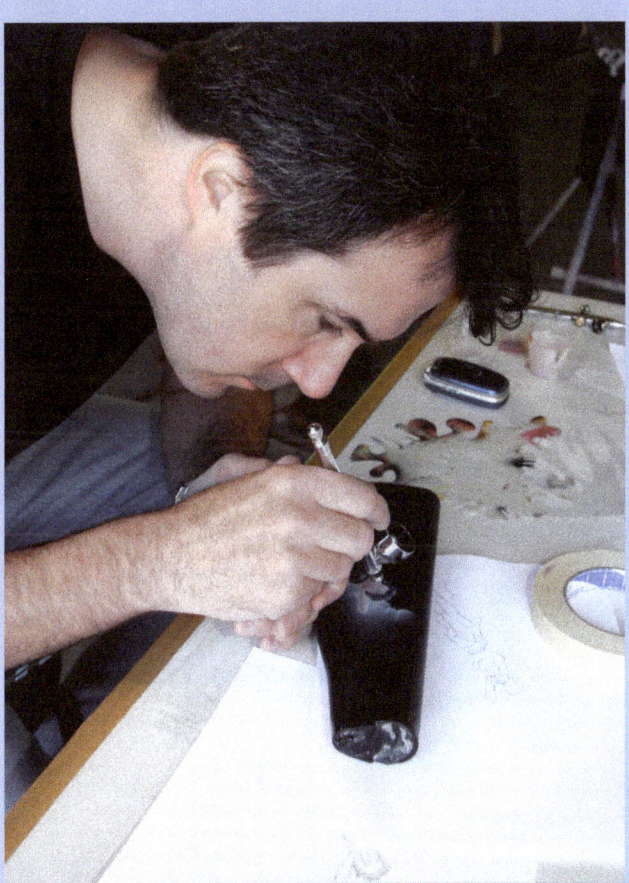

For this project Steve worked without any reference photo, just his initial sketch.

Chapter Six

Susan Heidi

Quality Takes Time

They say engineers think only linear thoughts. That their brains are logical and orderly to the point of boredom. Pretty much the opposite of what you expect from an artist in other words. So it might come as a surprise to learn that Susan Heidi's training, and her first career, was in engineering.

In Susan's case, engineering was the vocation, art the avocation. "I always did portraits as a hobby," recalls Susan. "Eventually I began coloring in the portraits, and then I became intrigued with pin-ups."

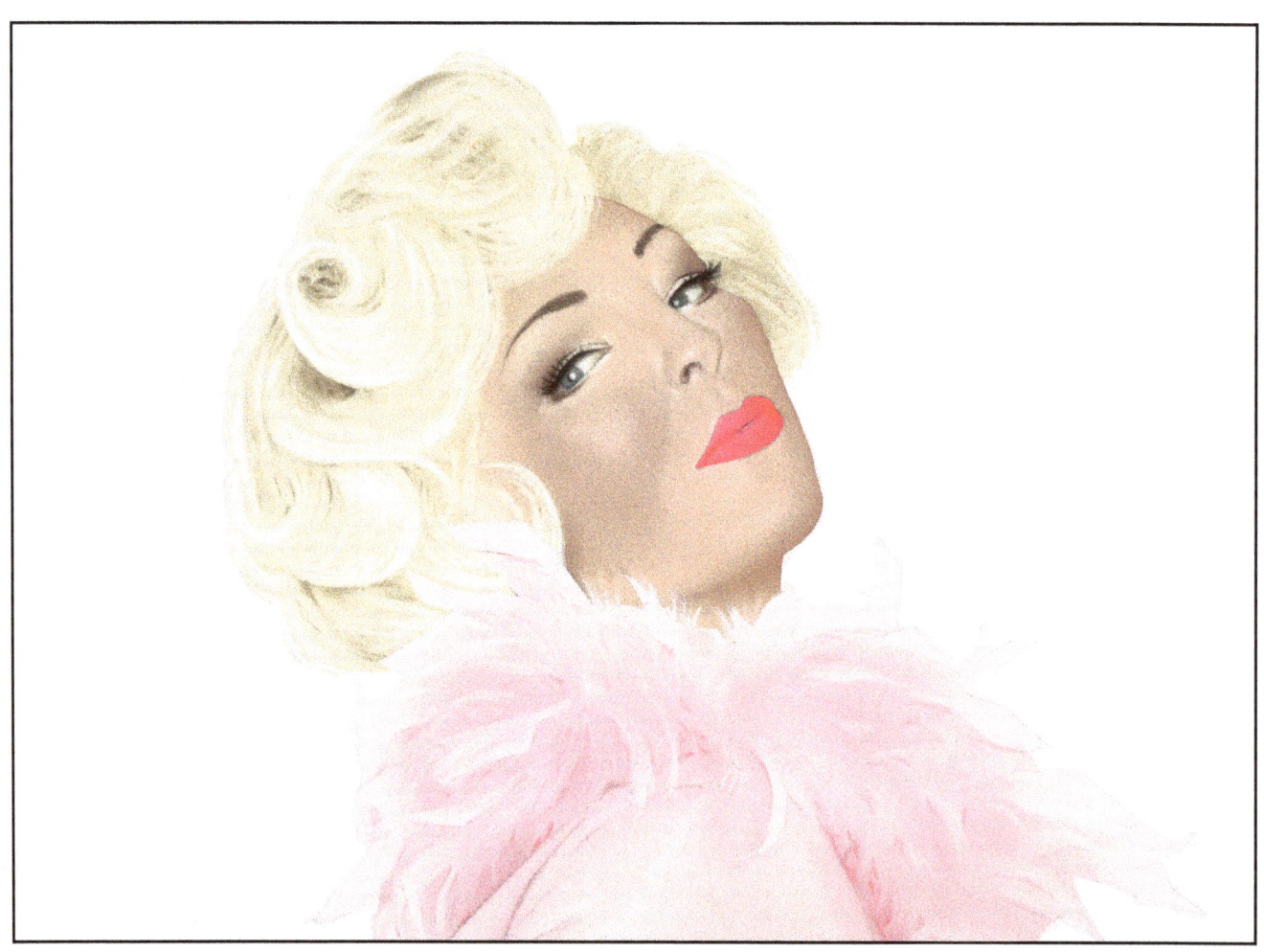

This painting is based on a photo of retro pin-up model Kay O'Hara. Working with retro style pin-ups gives me an opportunity to render lots of fun (and challenging) clothing and accessories. For me, the focus of any pin-up is the expression, which for this painting is an archetypical come-hither look.

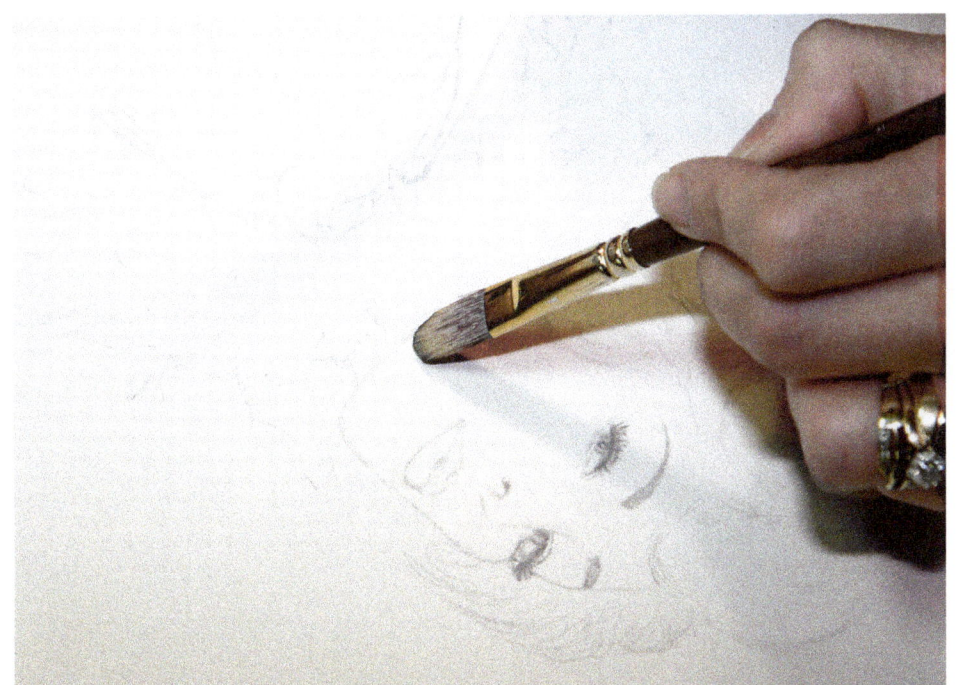

A completely rendered graphite drawing on Strathmore illustration board is sealed with Myston workable fixatif and then dilute gesso. After drying overnight, this under drawing can be painted over with dilute acrylic washes using sable brushes.

If you look at one of Susan's pin-ups, it's not hard to believe that she started out doing portraits. What grabs most viewers are her faces, and in particular, her eyes. Inanimate eyes with the ability to bore right through you, the most beautiful eyes you've ever seen.

Though it took Susan years to make the conversion from engineer to pin-up artist, she's making up for it now. Once she decided to make the move, it took Susan less than five years to go from total unknown with her first pin-up image to a well-respected and well-known pin-up artist. Which makes for interesting speculation as to what the next five years hold for Susan Heidi.

Patience might be the one word that can be used to describe Susan at work. No detail is too small to warrant intense concentration as Susan works slowly to get each one just right. In Susan's art-world, good work takes as long as it takes – you can't rush the process.

Susan is of the subtractive school, creating her images with transparent paint, erasing her way to highlights. Her skin tones glow, the eyes sparkle. Though she doesn't display very often at pin-up conventions, she reports that when she does, print sales are good. In the case of Susan Heidi's art, seeing truly is believing.

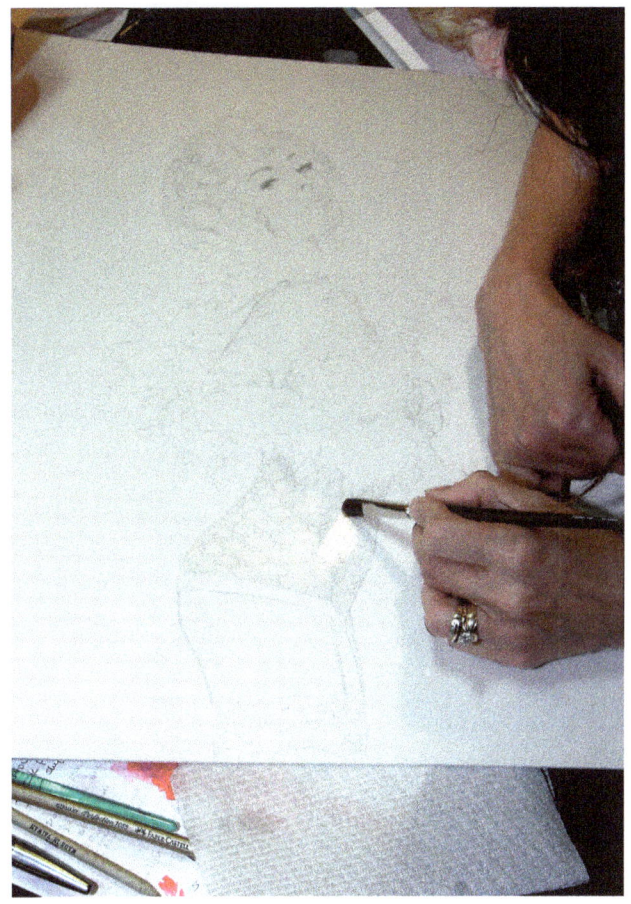

Before laying down the washes, the board is wet thoroughly using a sable brush that will be used for water only. All areas of the painting are painted lightly with pre-mixed color washes that will be used throughout the painting process.

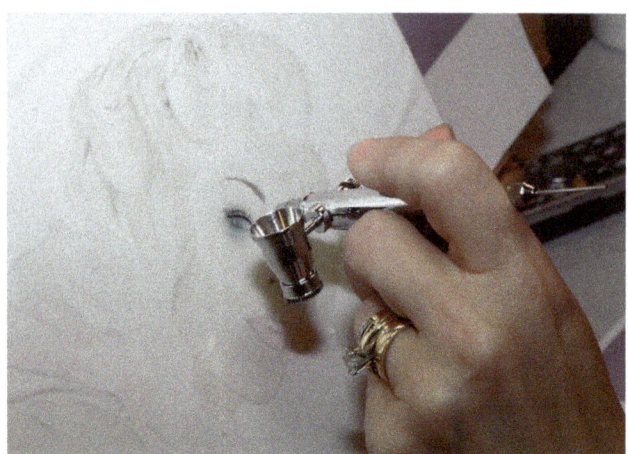

The darkest areas of the painting - in this case the eyes and lips - are painted first to set a value comparison.

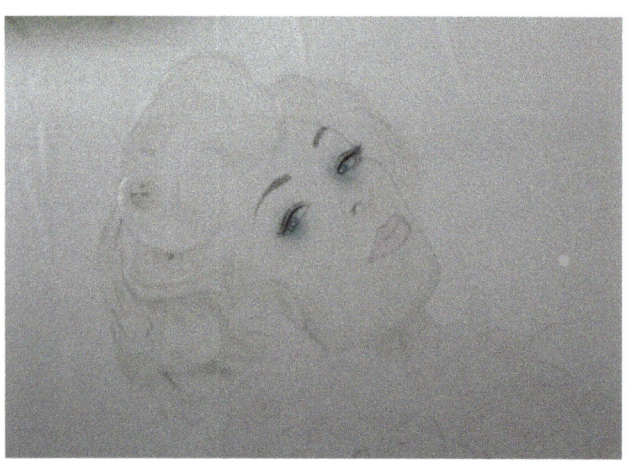

This painting is all about the model's expression, so a great deal of time is spent building up the tiny details of the iris.

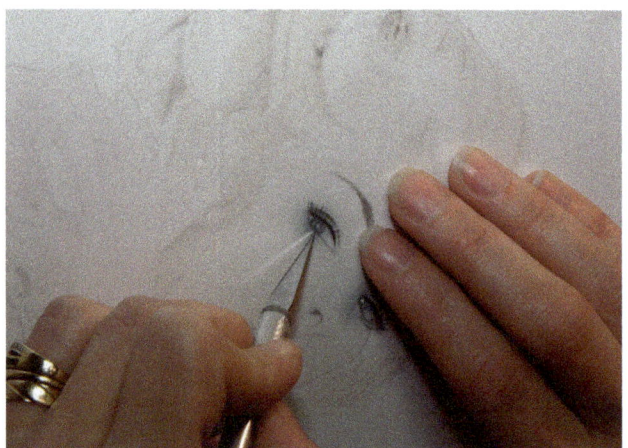

Erasing or scraping the highlights in the iris, layering paint, and repeating the process creates depth and texture.

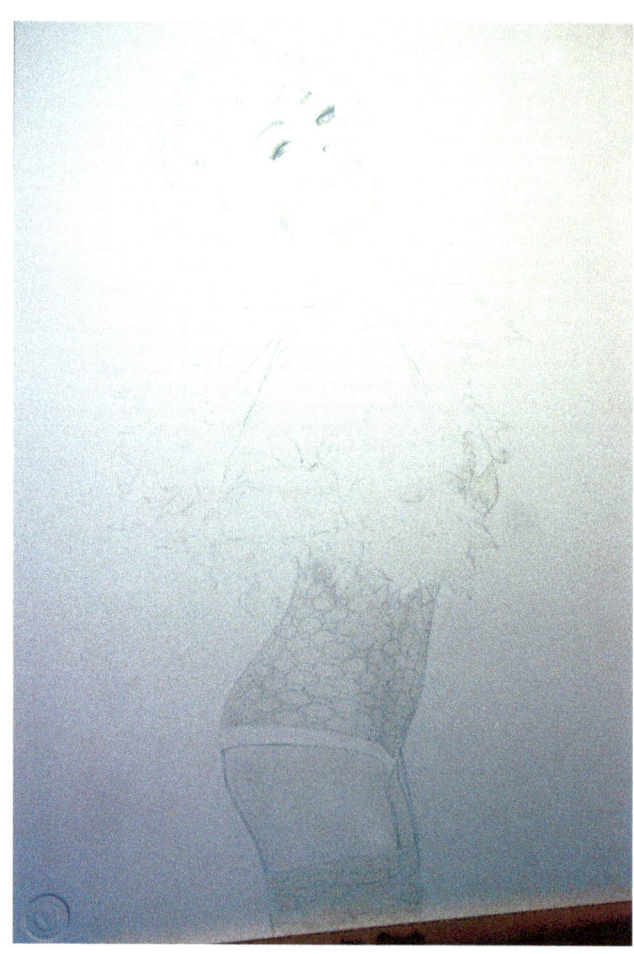

After the under painting dries overnight, the entire piece is covered with frisket. The outer edges of areas that will be painted are cut with a very sharp Xacto blade, changing the blade often. Care is taken to "cut into" the hairline to create a natural transition.

Though most of the details are created with the airbrush, positioned so close it almost touches the board, Susan also uses hand brushes to create details or hard lines difficult to achieve in any other way. Fisket is her friend as well, though she more commonly uses plastic masks and templates to achieve the necessary separation without a hard line.

If you ask Susan what makes a good pin-up, she talks about the sexual ambiguity. Susan is an artist who understands the notion that what you can't see may be more important than what you can.

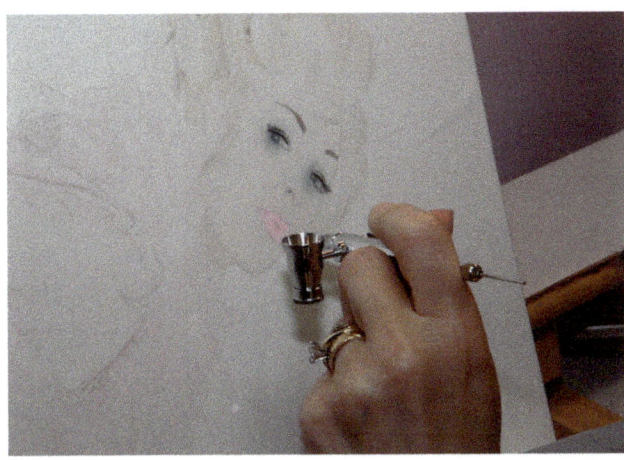

The lips are painted using much the same technique as the iris. A small amount of liquid frisket covers the white area where the lips are parted.

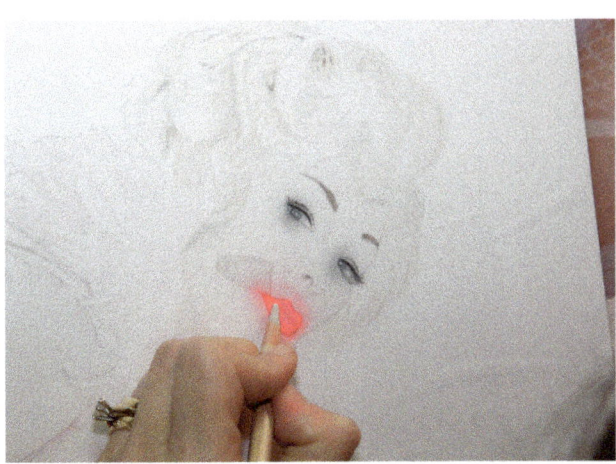

By concentrating the paint in the center and erasing highlights on the outer area, I create the line that separates the two lips.

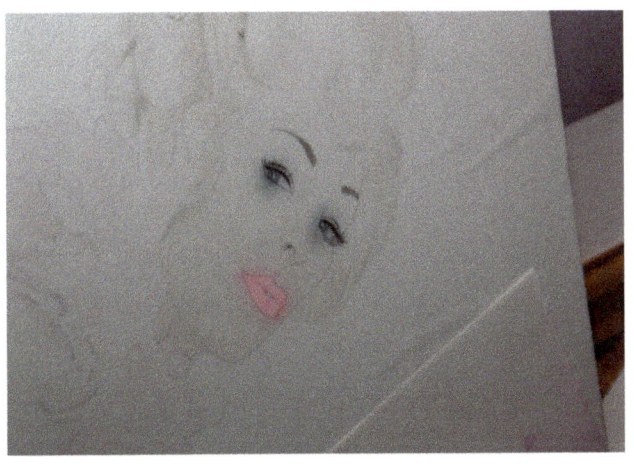

By layering thin layers of paint, erasing highlights, then adding more paint, I get a more realistic, subtle look.

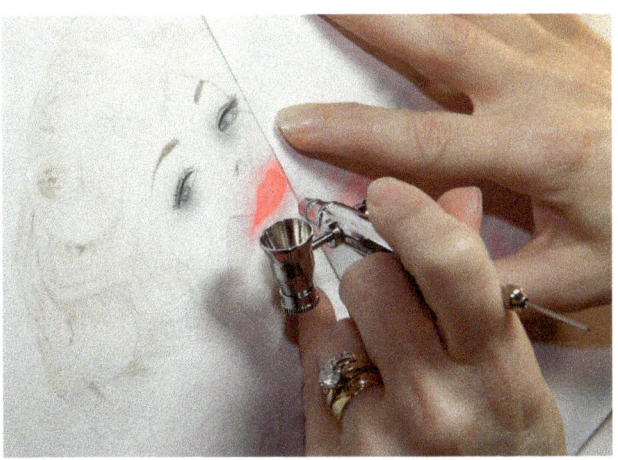

At this point you can start to see the fullness of the lips, like she's pursing her lips.

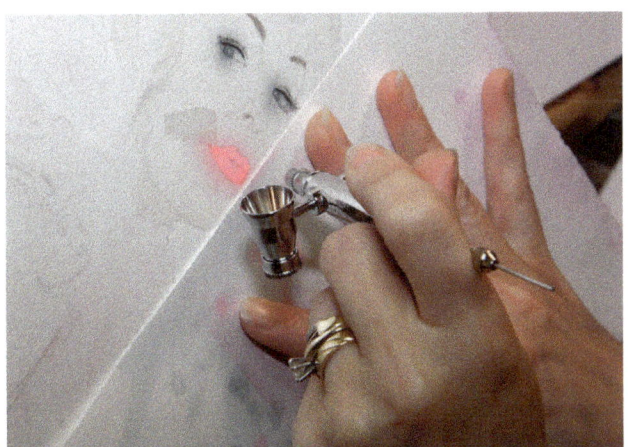

I'm careful to not create too harsh a line where the lips meet the face, softening that edge with an eraser while painting the lips.

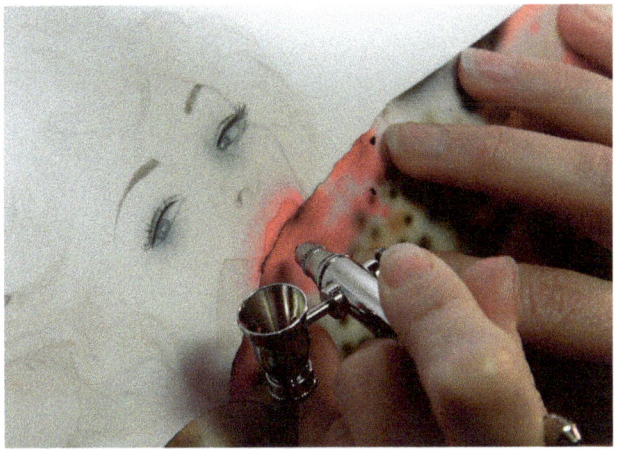

Using a handheld mask, I darken the line between the lips and sharpen that edge.

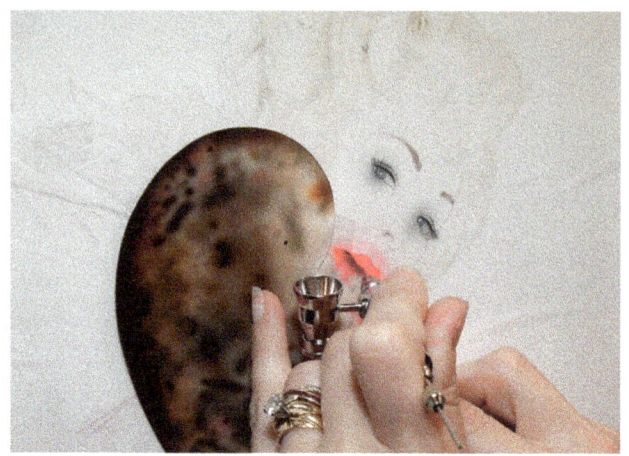

I'm working very close to the board when creating these details.

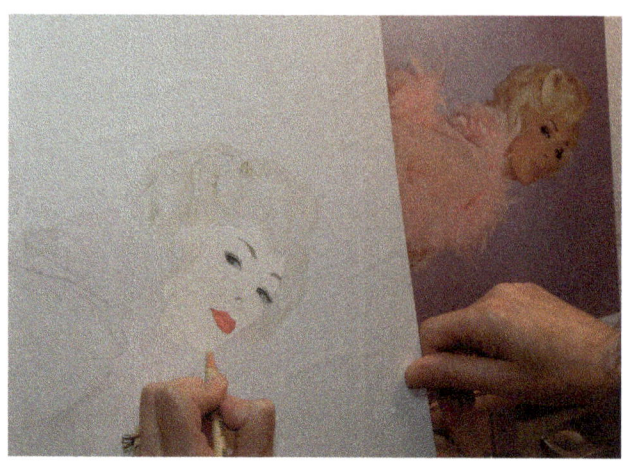

To begin rendering bone structure, lighter areas are broadly erased.

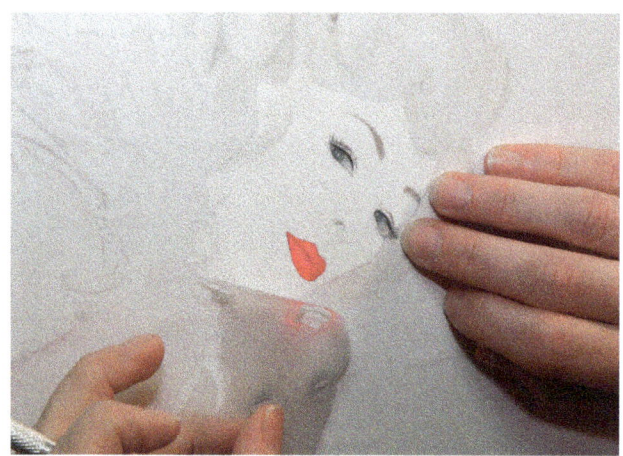

The frisket is removed from all the flesh areas. For this painting they will all be painted at once, but that's not always the case.

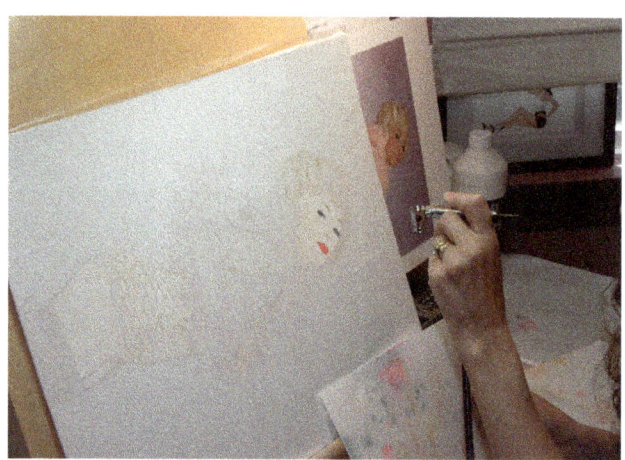

Another layer of light skin tone is added.

A premixed light flesh tone is used first, dusting it over the flesh area.

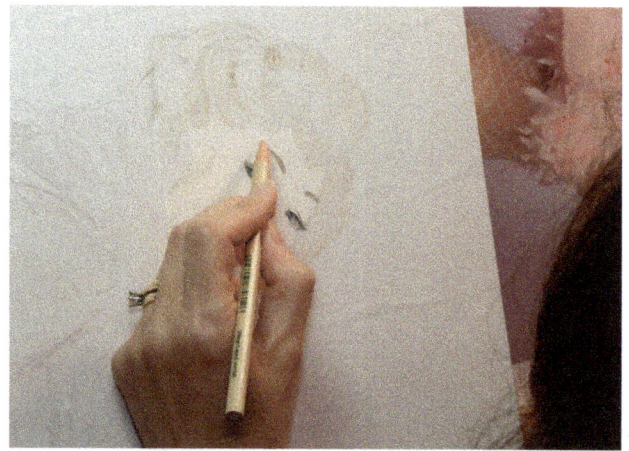

Erasing over the light areas early on creates a more subtle effect than if I went back at the end to remove the highlights.

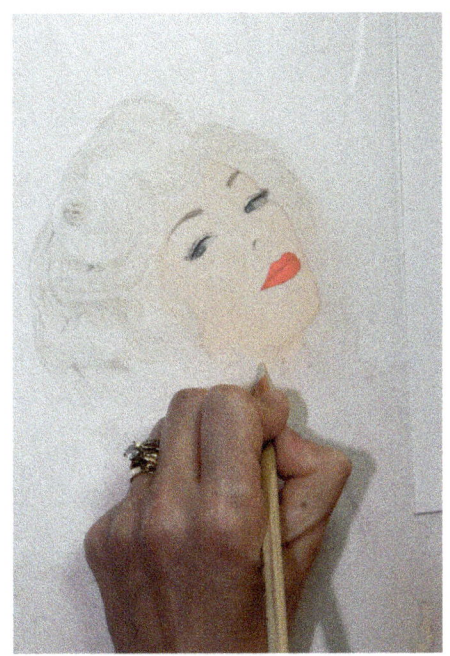#
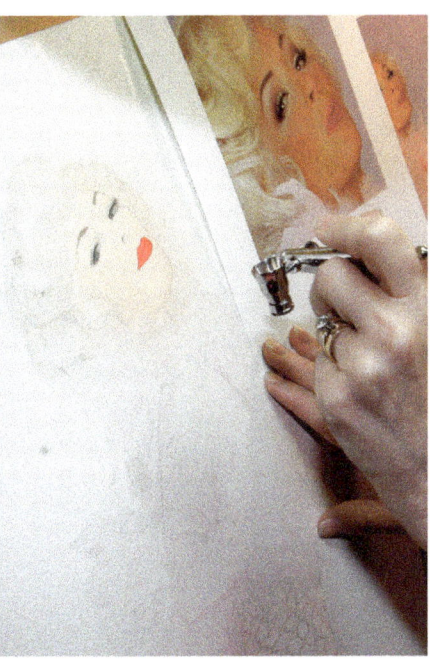
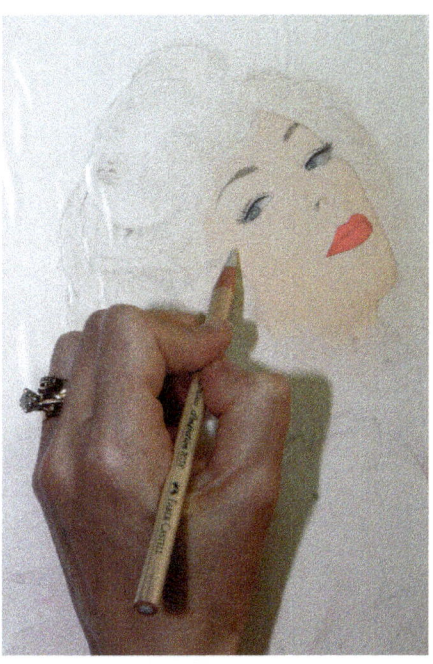

Time is spent using an eraser to soften the line where the hair and feathers meet the skin.

Layers of skin tone can be painted more broadly at this stage, working farther away from the surface of the board.

The process of erasing out the bone structure continues.

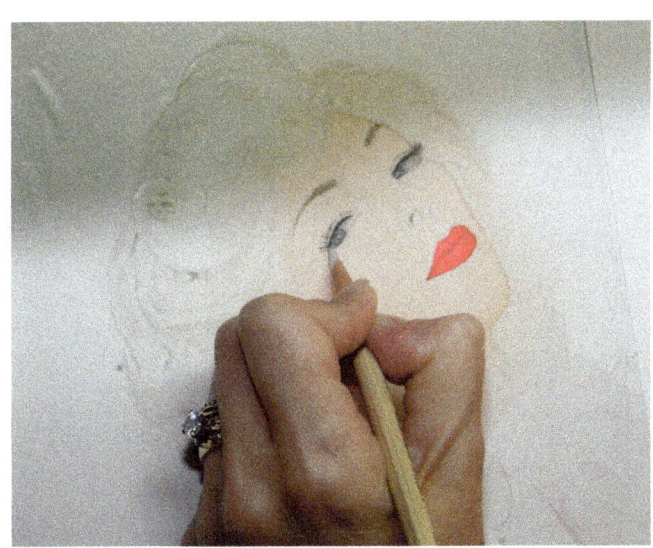
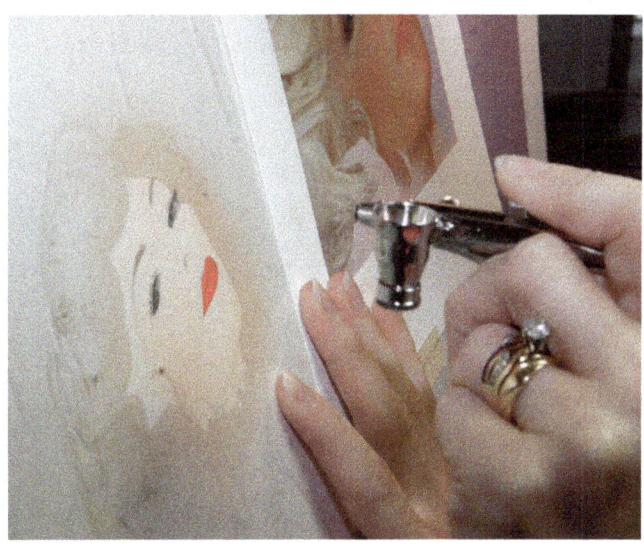

Attention is paid to even the smallest areas, like the lower lids of the eyes.

Additional application of light skin tone.

99

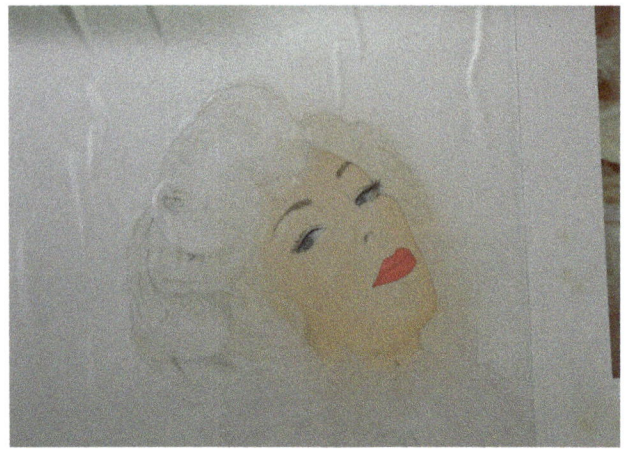

At this point you can see the structure of the face quite clearly. The shadows and highlights are subtle but there.

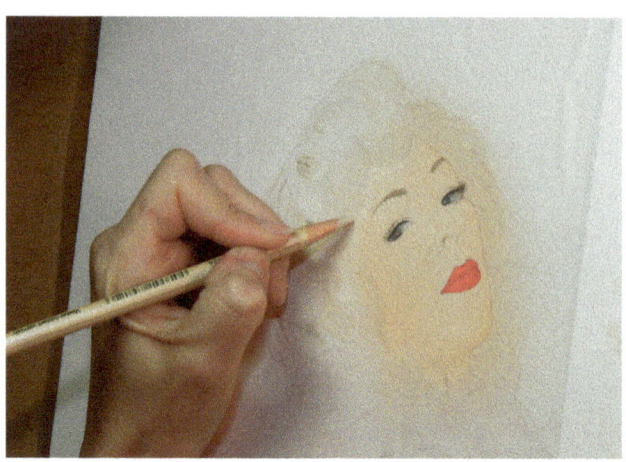

The hairline is kept soft by erasing the edges where the hair meets the face.

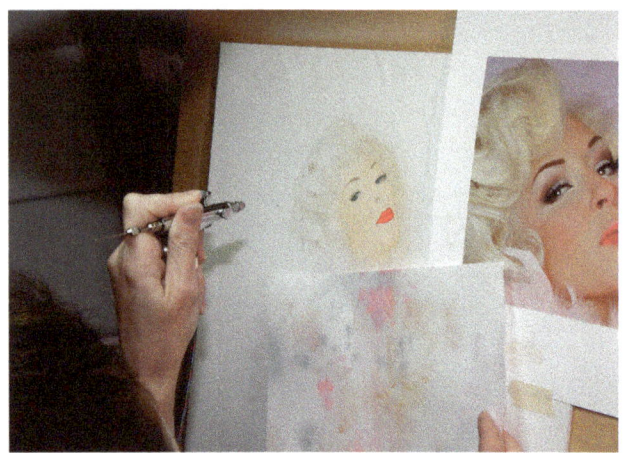

A light dusting of skin tone darkens the face.

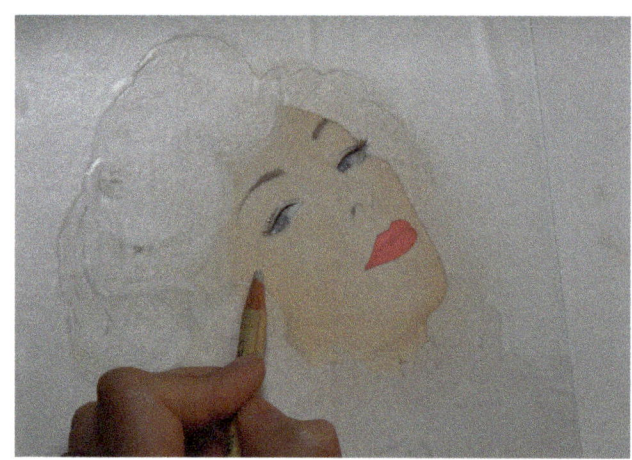

Some small stray hairs can be created by carefully erasing fine lines.

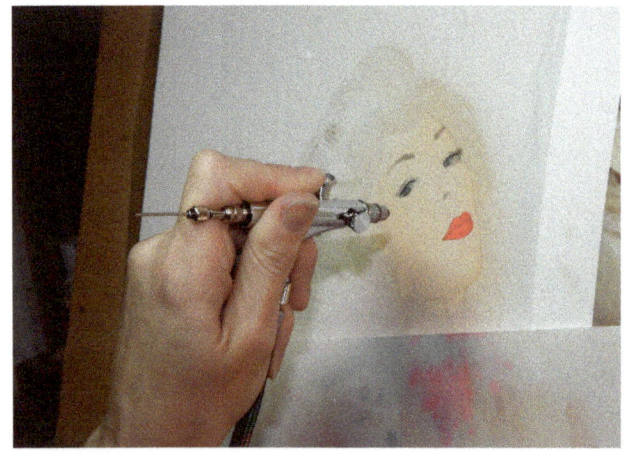

Working closer to the board gives more control. At this stage shadows are being created by controlling the application of the skin tone.

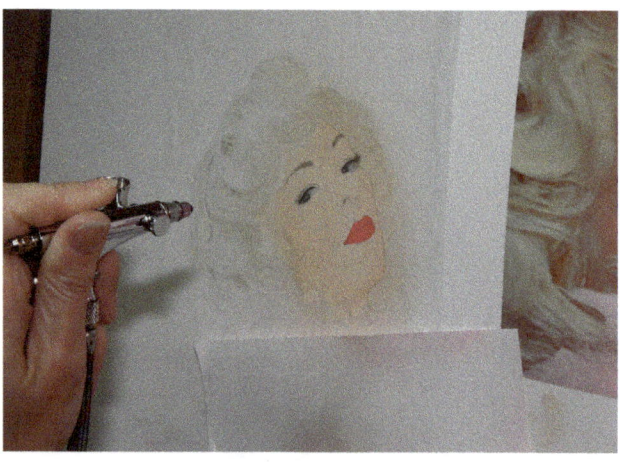

A thin wash of violet is lightly sprayed over the flesh areas to add more depth to the color.

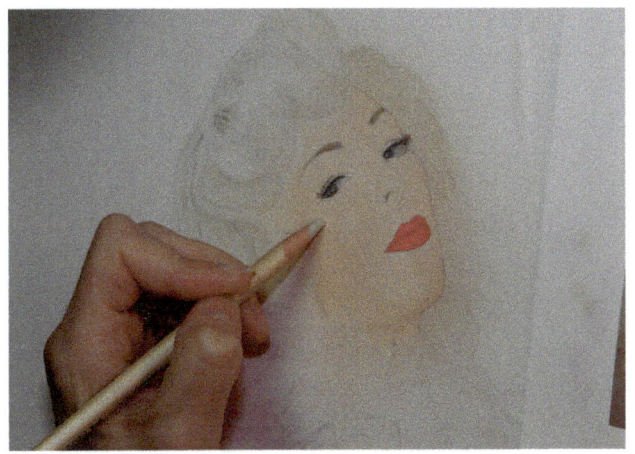

It's important to retain the highlights after every application of color.

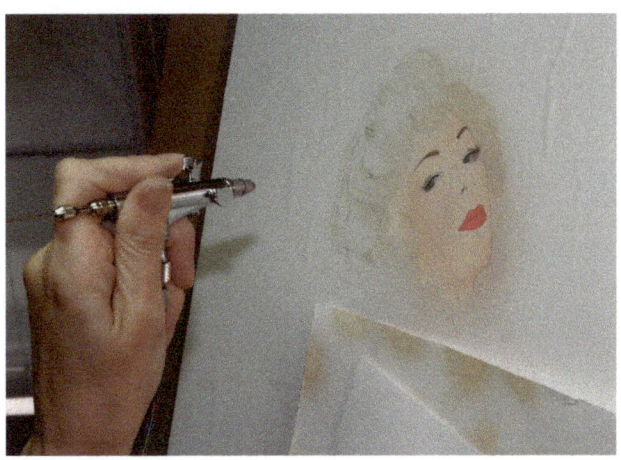

A scrap piece of paper is kept close at hand for testing the paint before adding it to the painting.

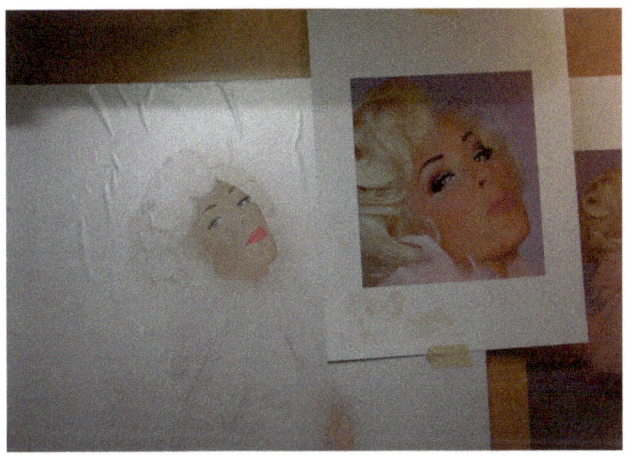

To create a likeness, the reference photo I'm working from is kept close.

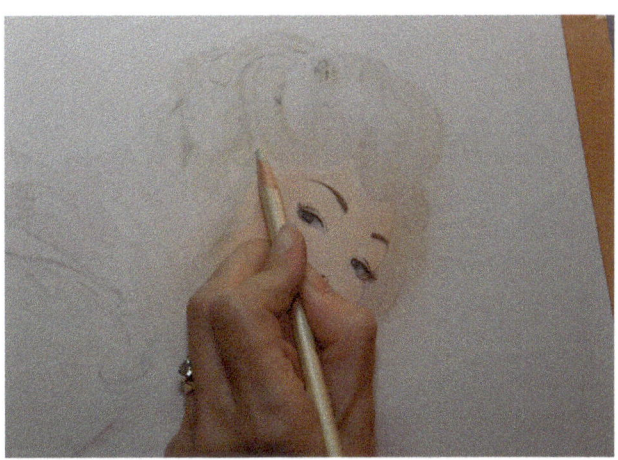

Care has to be taken throughout the painting process to keep edges soft.

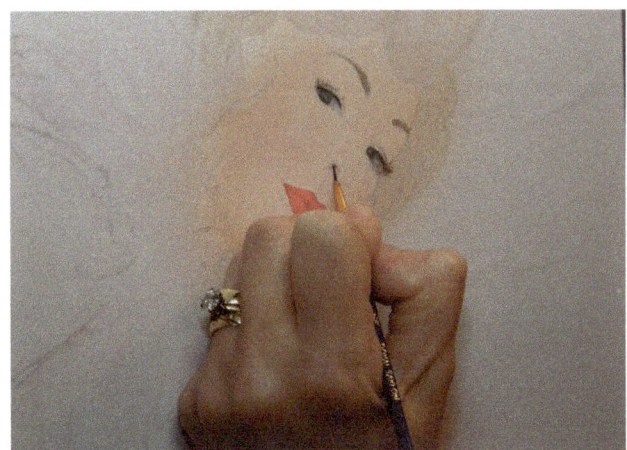

The tiny details of the nostril are done with a fine brush. Here the shadow in the nostril is darkened using diluted sepia.

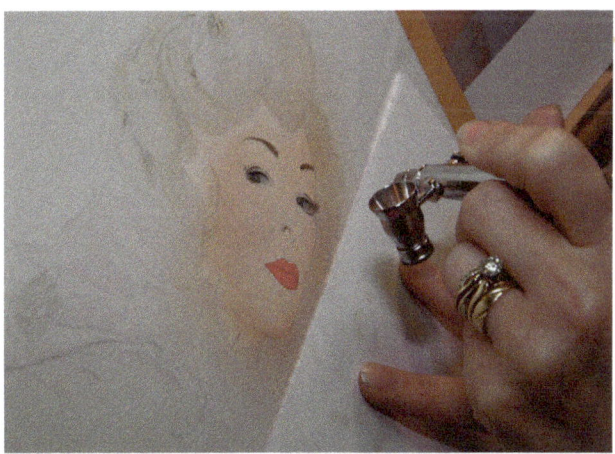

Turning the painting sideways helps me look at it differently, to see a shape as a shape and not a body part.

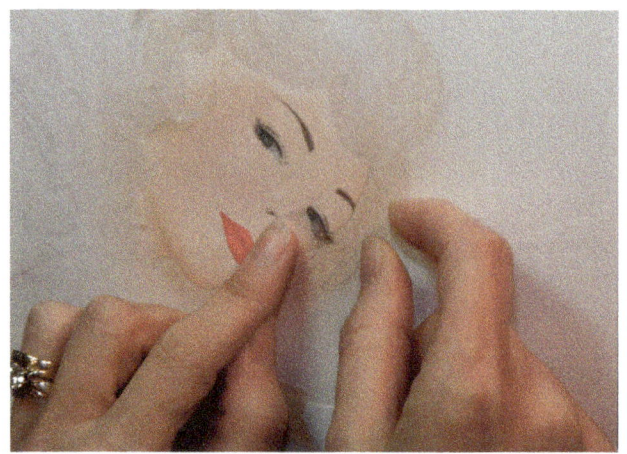

Once the painting has progressed to this point, it's important to keep more control of where the paint is going by working closer to the board.

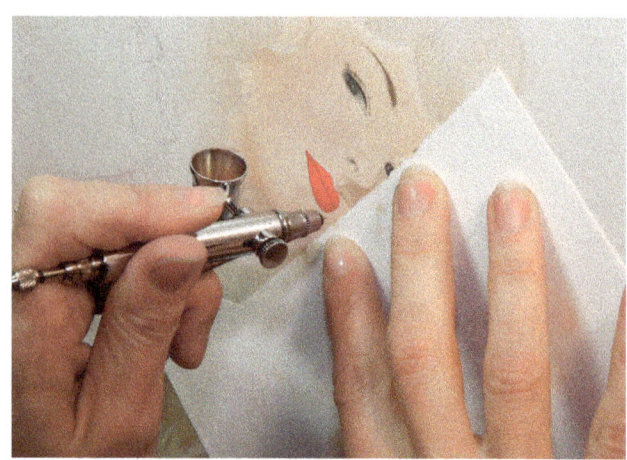

The shadow under the edge of the nose is created in the same way.

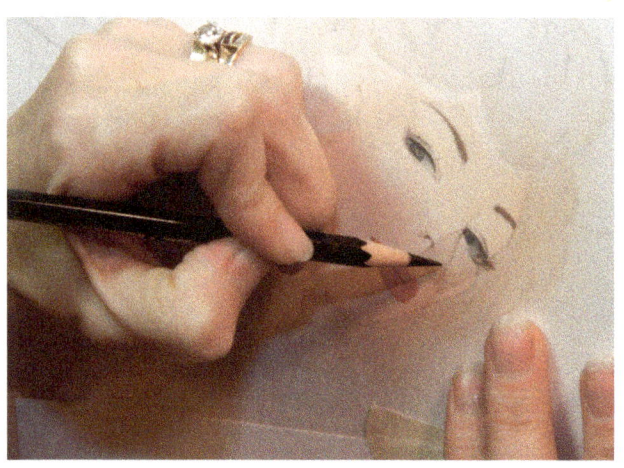

Hard edges like the bridge of the nose can be created by making a mask with frisket. I've switched to using a darker pre-mixed skin tone for these shadows.

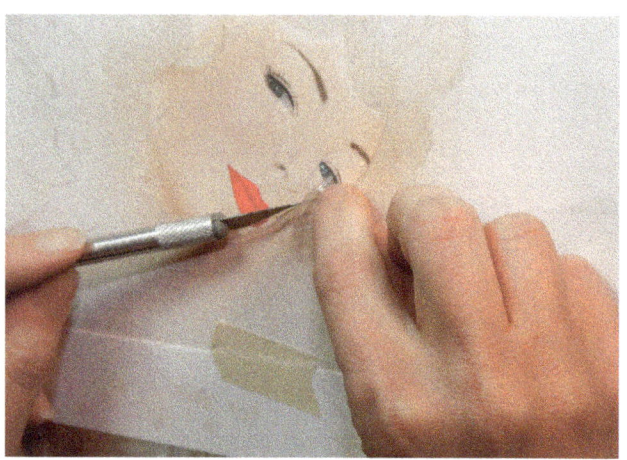

The point of an Xacto can be used with care to help pull the frisket off the painting.

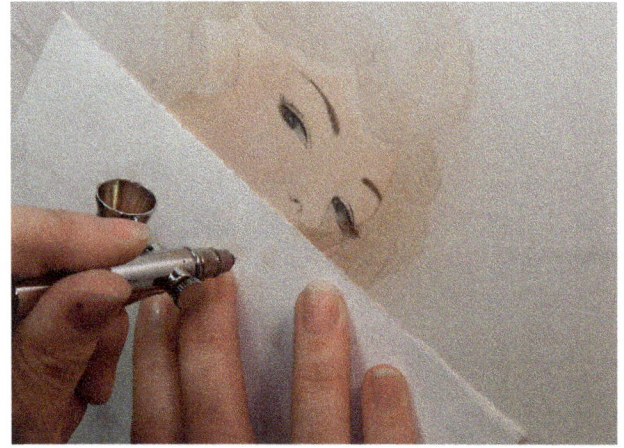

First, a piece of frisket is laid on the area and marked with pencil. The frisket is removed to a worktable and the edge is cut with an Xacto blade.

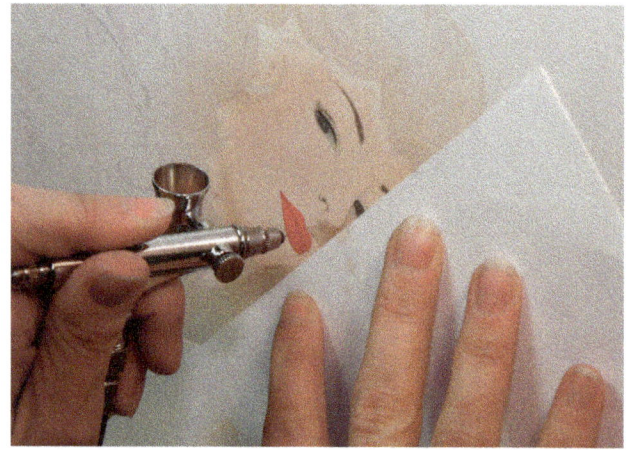

The process can be repeated if the shadow needs to be darkened.

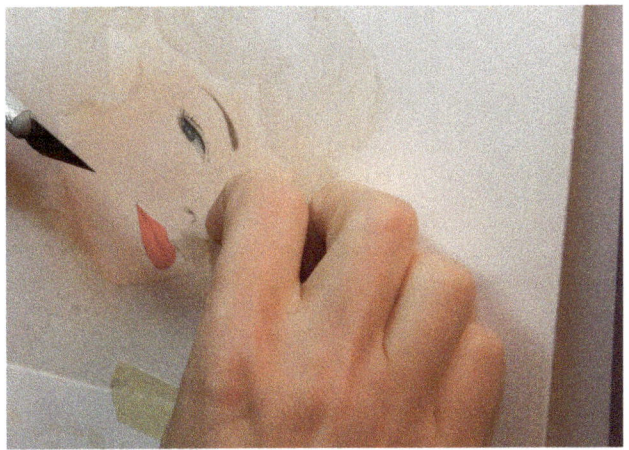

The small frisket mask is removed very carefully from the surface of the board.

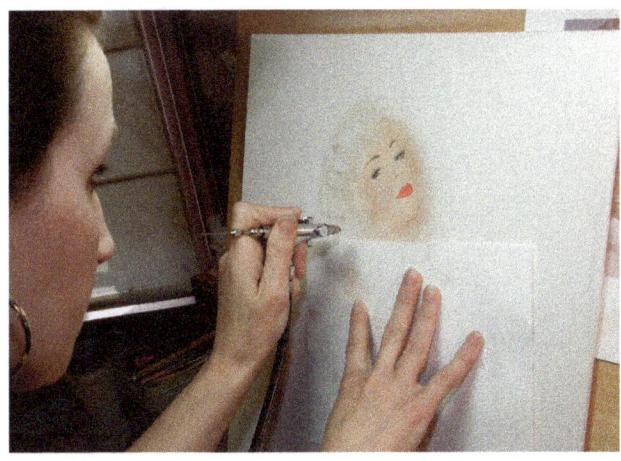

A plain piece of paper can be used to create a straight-lined edge.

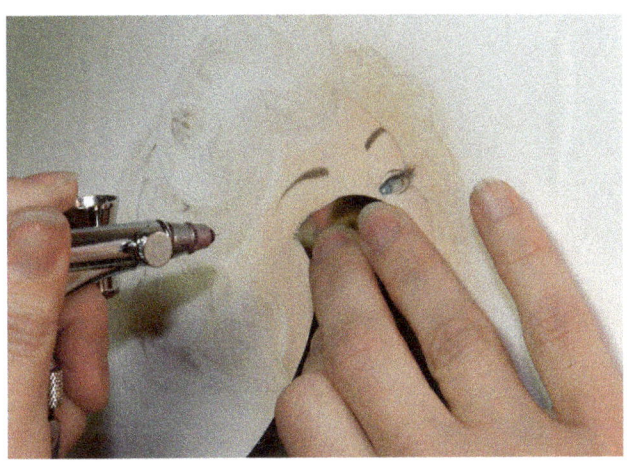

A handheld shield made using heavyweight bristol and a french curve, helps me create hard edges where I need them. Care needs to be taken not to create hard edges where I don't want them.

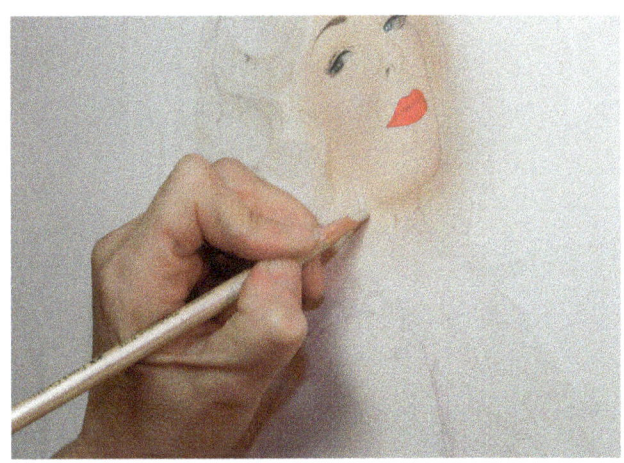

Erasing with a sharpened eraser helps to establish this edge of a feather.

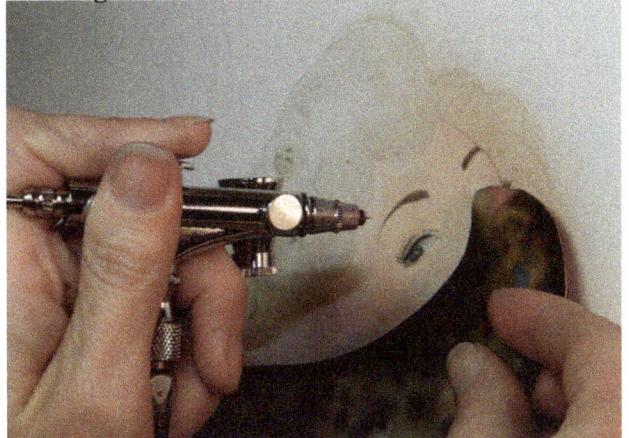

The same shield has mostly all of the angles and curves I need for creating the hard edged shadows around the eyes.

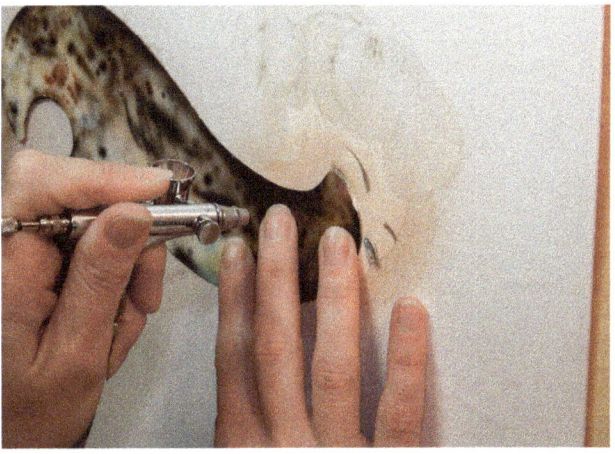

Going back to the eyes, I darken the shadow in the crease of the lid. I like to move around a painting - working on one area and then jumping to another.

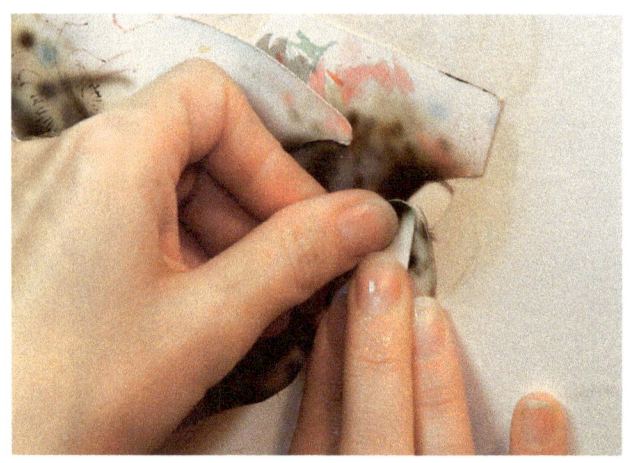

There are times when more than one shield is needed to create just the right shape. That's when dexterity comes into play.

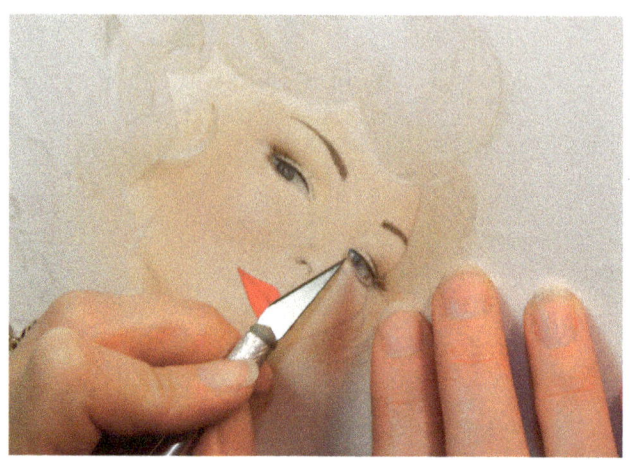

The highlight of the pupil is carefully placed using an Xacto blade. Placement of this highlight is critical to achieving the gaze I want for the model.

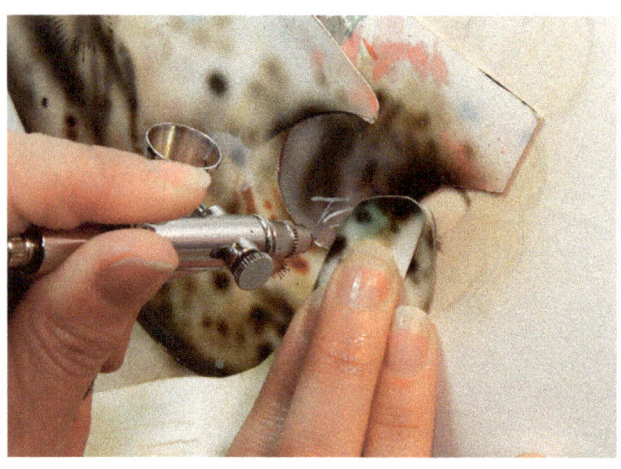

Holding several shields against the board with my right hand, I pick up the airbrush and paint with the left hand.

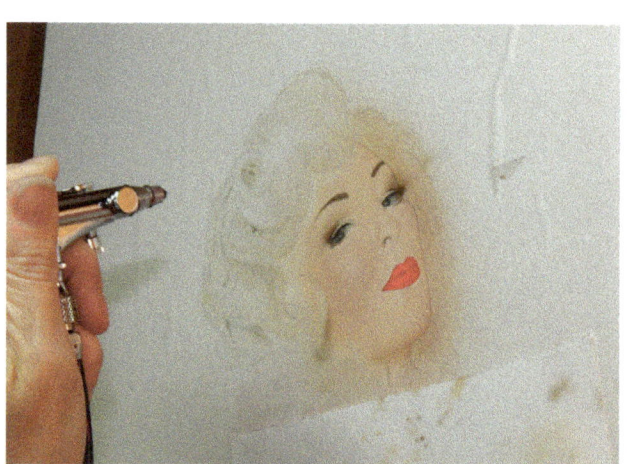

Now that the area around the eyes is darker, it becomes apparent that the skin tone needs to be darkened.

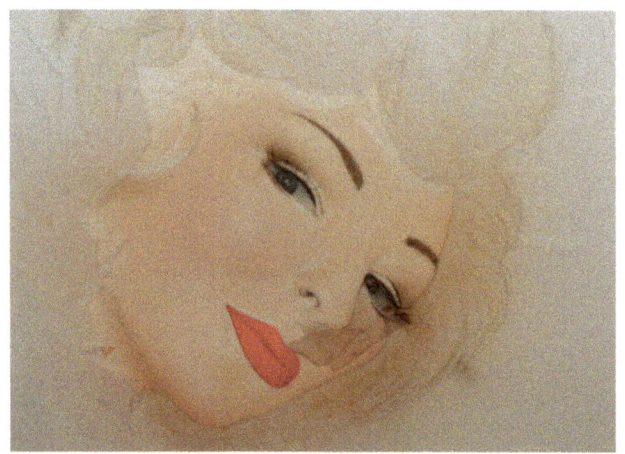

Smoky shadows on the eyelids help create that dreamy effect.

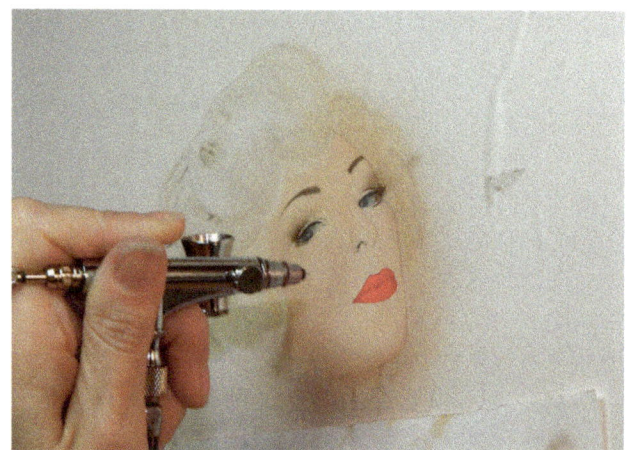

Shadows are added to the face free-hand. At this point, avoid erasing all but the brightest highlights or too much texture will be created.

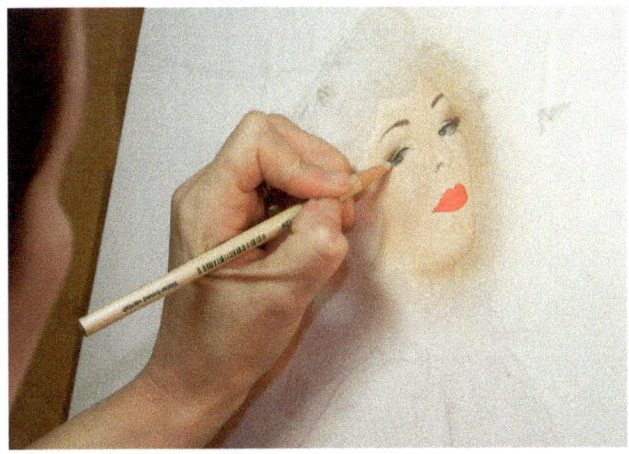

Whenever I see something that needs adjusting, I do it right then to keep the painting unified.

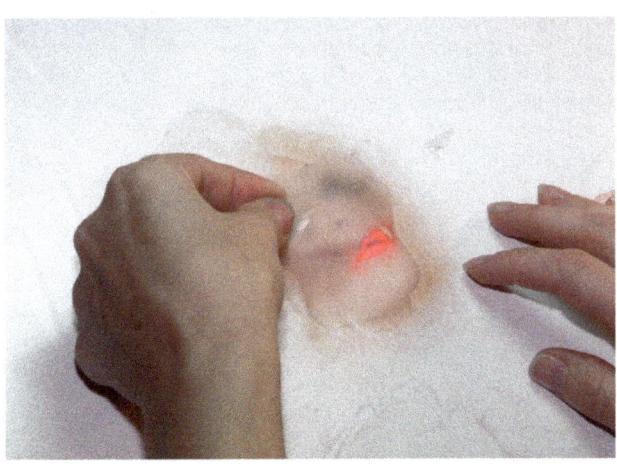

Ready to move on to the feathers, small pieces of frisket that were stored on the original backing paper are placed over the painted face.

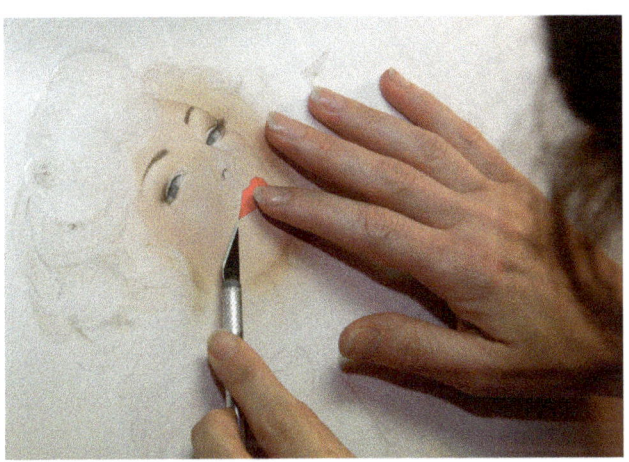

The sharp point of an Xacto blade can be used to help replace small pieces of frisket

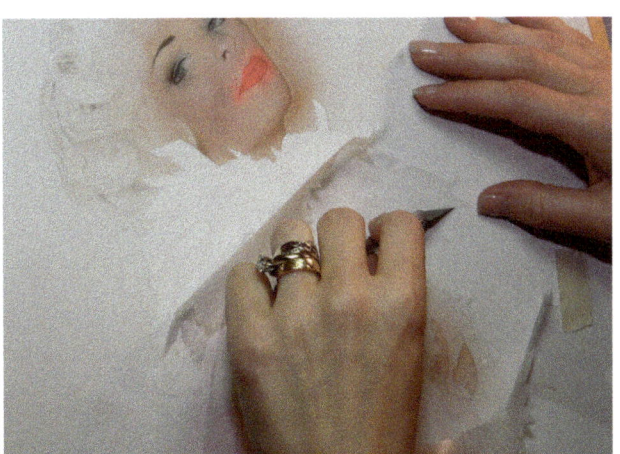

Frisket is carefully removed from over the feather boa wrap, taking care not to tear the surface of the board underneath.

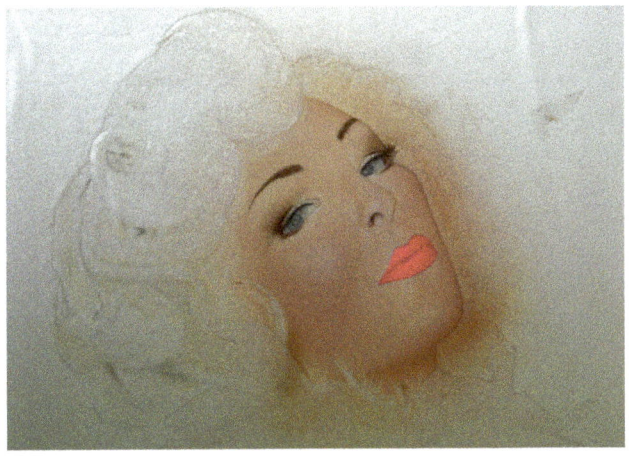

It's a good idea to stop occasionally and assess the progress of the image so far.

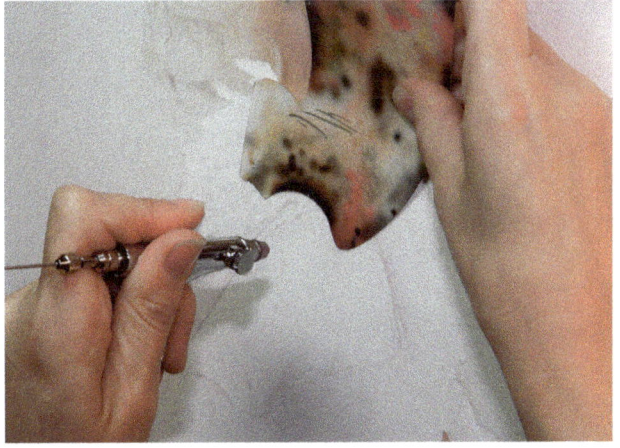

To start painting this area, I first mark in the hard edges using the pre-mixed pink wash and a hand-held shield.

Masking With Liquid Frisket

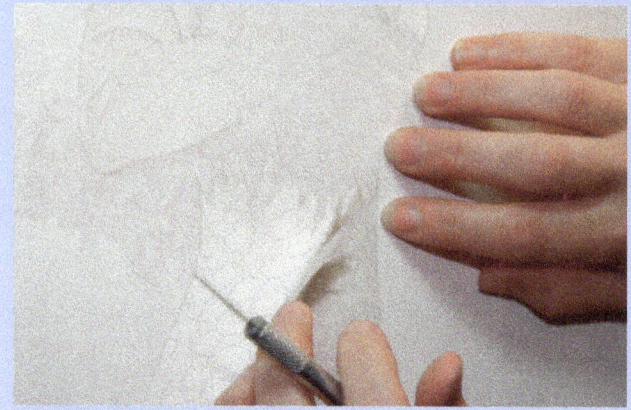

Liquid frisket can be used in situations like this to mask off irregular areas. To start, carefully remove frisket film from the area to be painted.

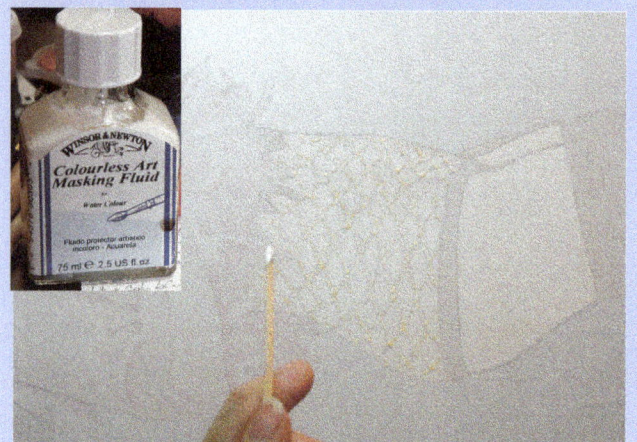

Mix liquid frisket with water, half and half, then "paint" areas that you want to keep unpainted. Use an old brush that you don't care about ruining for this technique.

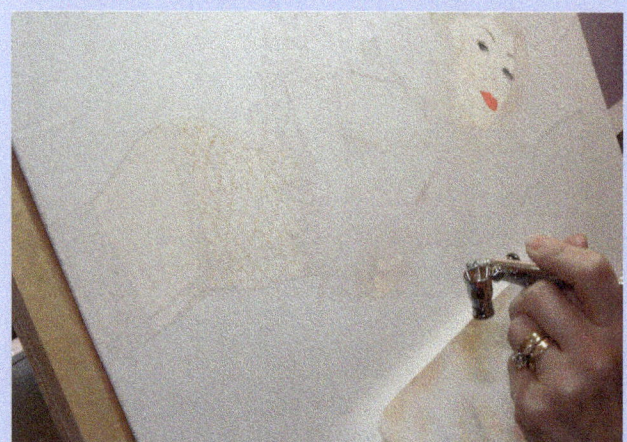

Dust light skin tone over the entire area.

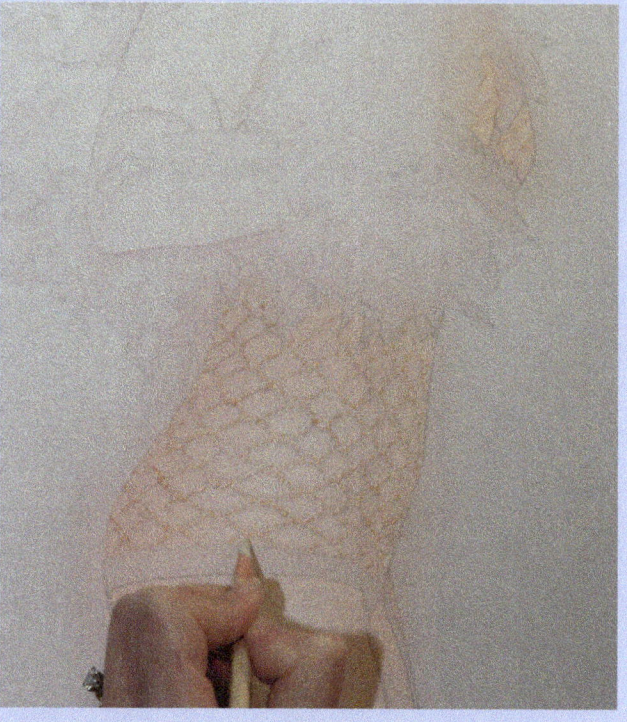

As with the face, start erasing lighter areas early on in the process to keep the highlights subtle.

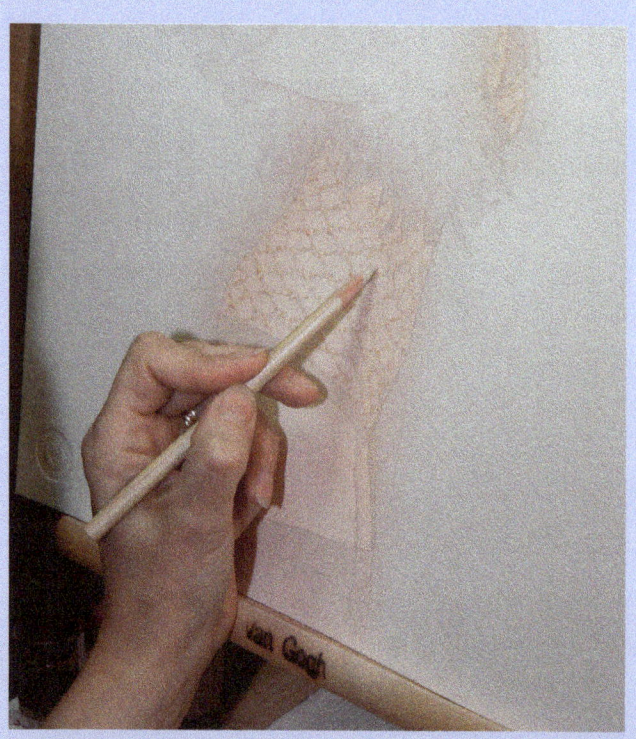

Continue to dust, erase, dust until the bone structure starts to appear.

Masking With Liquid Frisket

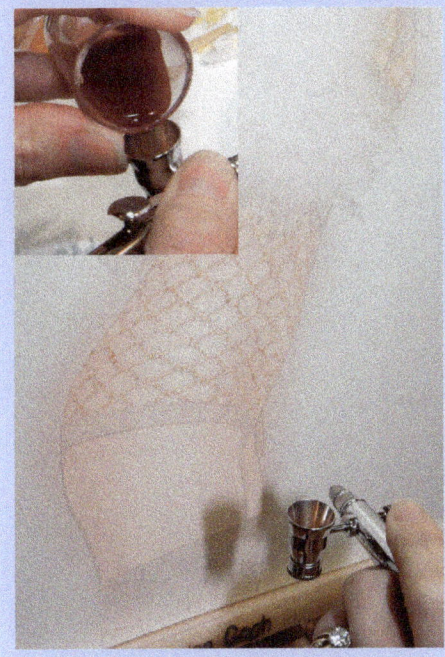

I notice that the color of skin on the body is redder than the face, so violet is added to the light skin color for this area.

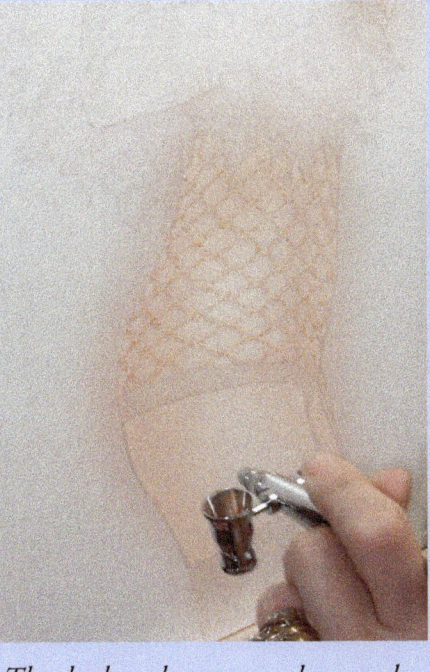

The shadow that creates the roundness of the form is reinforced using the darker skin tone.

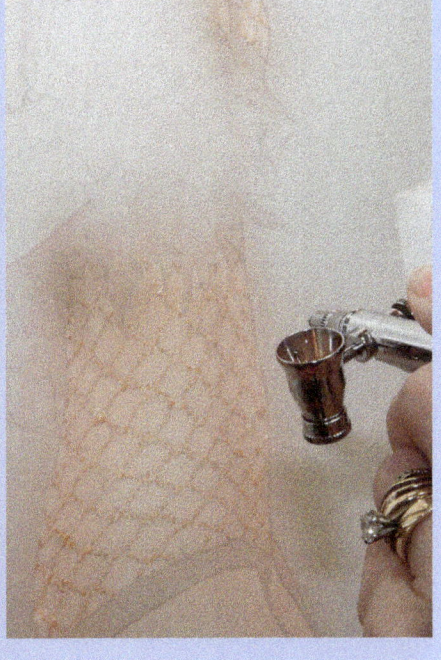

The dark shadows under the feathers are created first using dark skin tone.

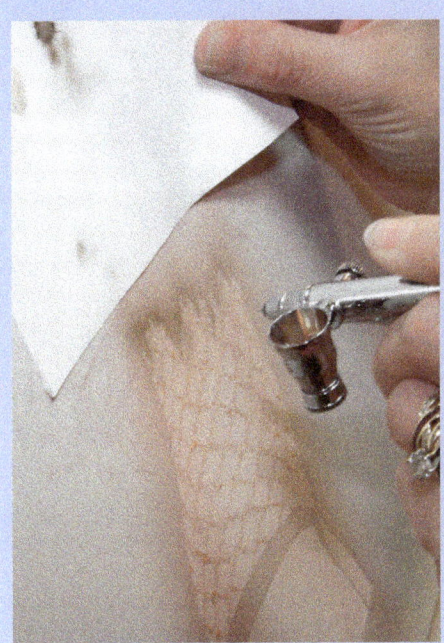

A harder edge and darker core of the shadow are created using diluted sepia.

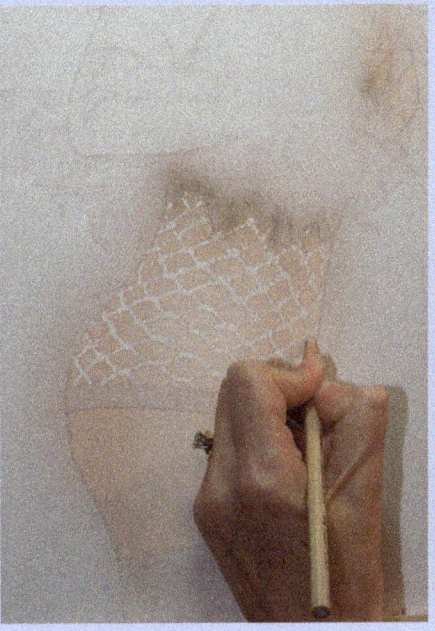

Once the skin areas are done, "erase" off the liquid frisket. The contrast was more than I wanted, so the strands of fishnet...

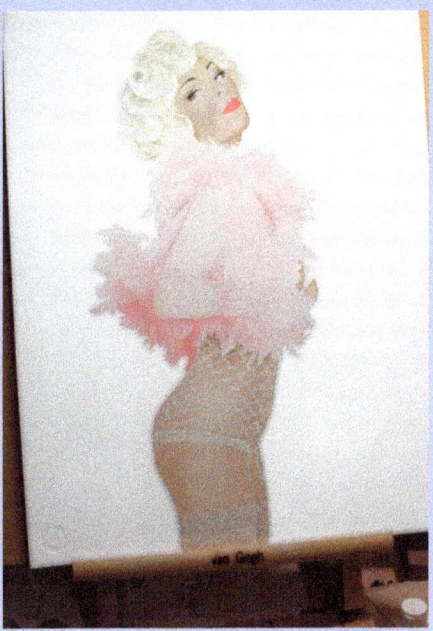

...had to be painted over by hand using dilute sepia and a fine detail brush, leaving the painting with the effect seen here.

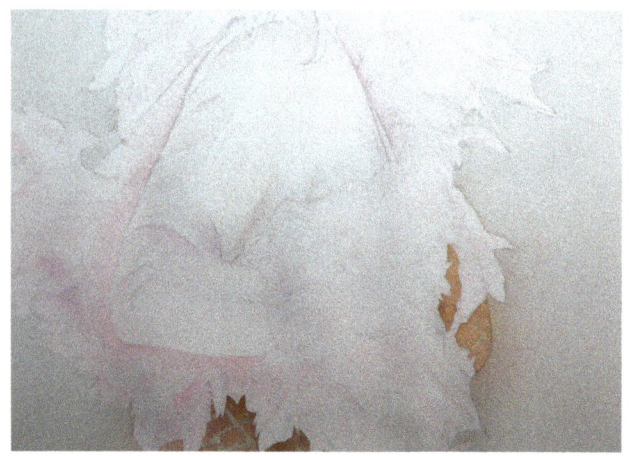

It's easy to see how light this area appears compared to the already painted skin tones.

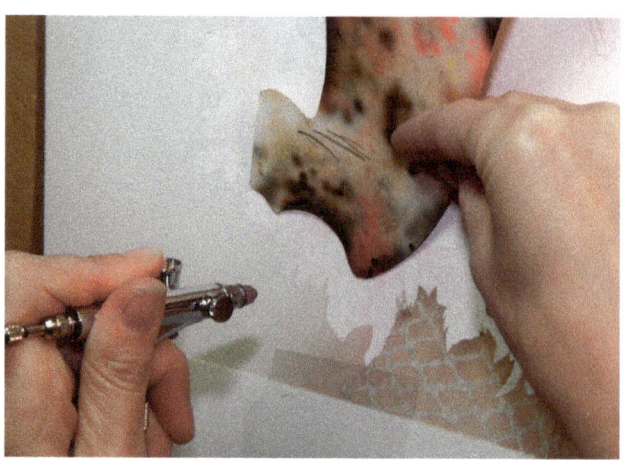

Mark more crisp shadow edges using the handheld shield.

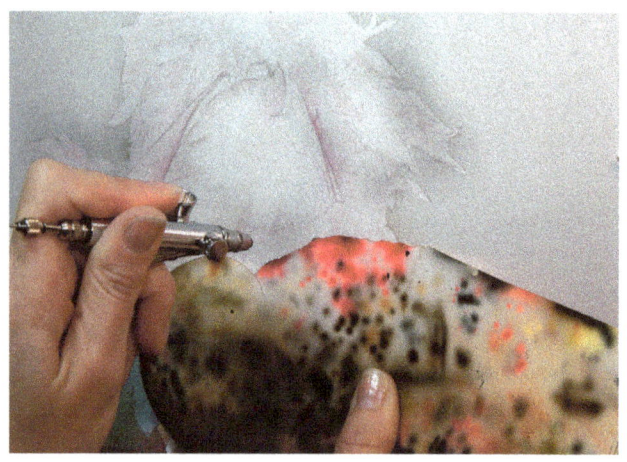

A torn area of the shield can be used to create ragged edges.

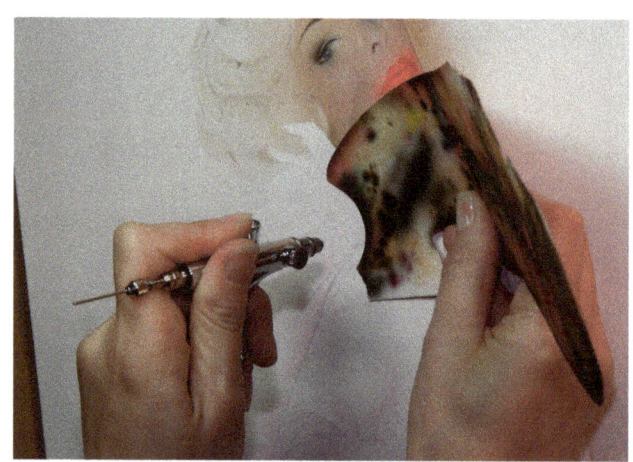

The shadows have to be placed just right so they make sense visually and contrast with the highlights.

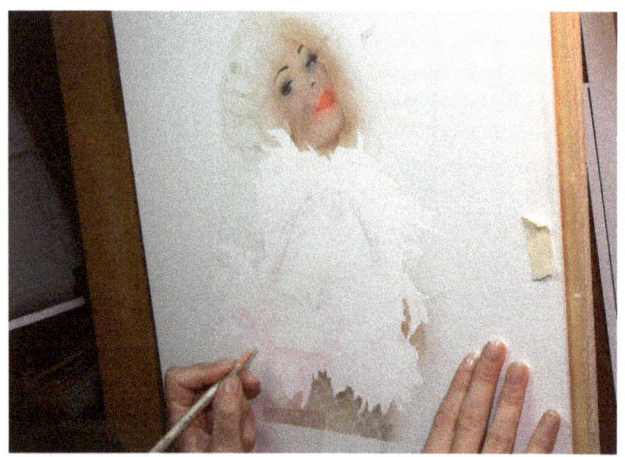

After dusting the entire area with color, highlights can be erased. This area has much more texture than the model's smooth skin.

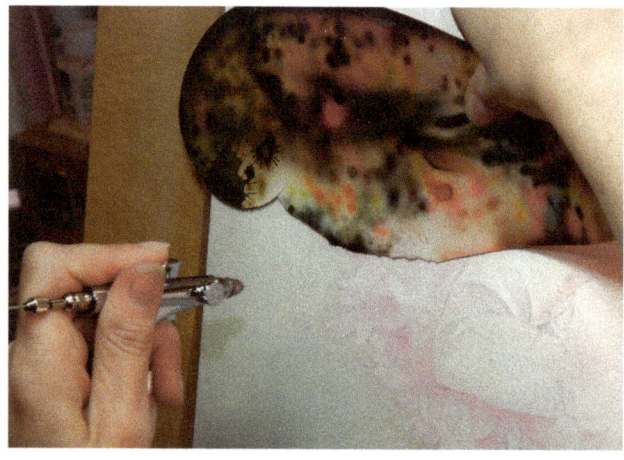

Continuing this way, the "feathers" start to appear to float away from the boa.

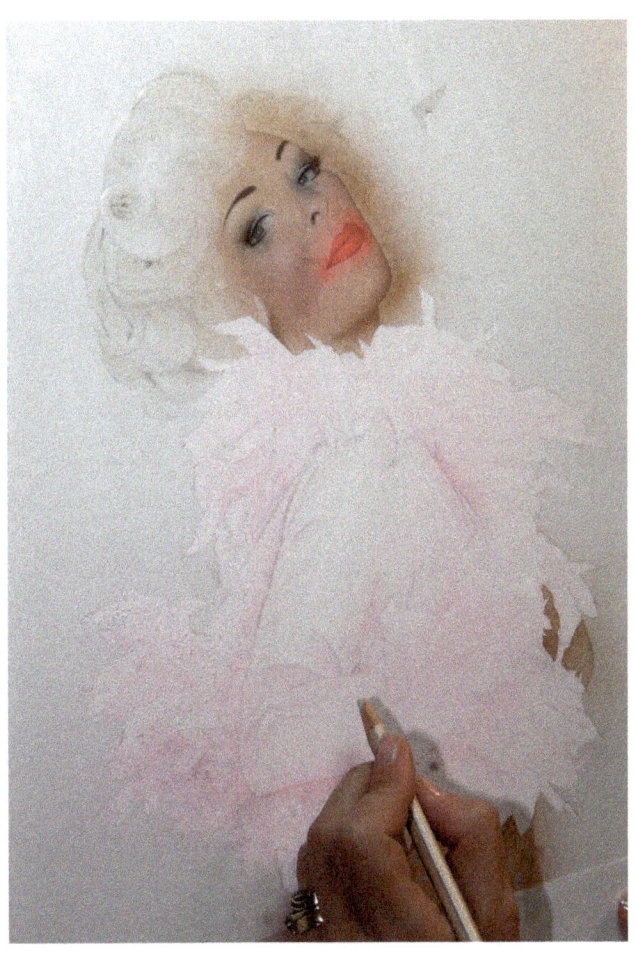

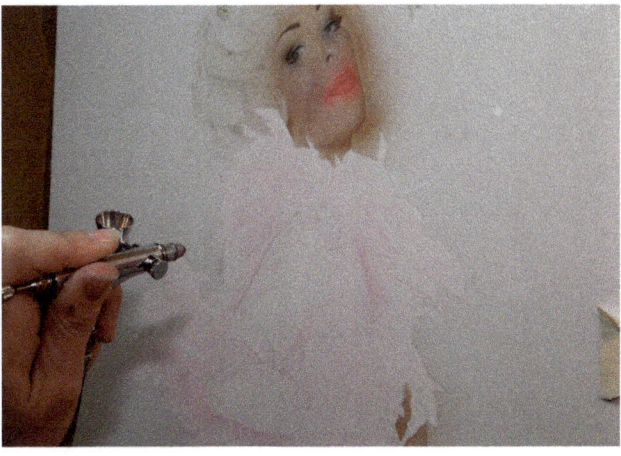

Some shadow areas are "fluffier" than others and don't require the hard edges that the handheld shield will create.

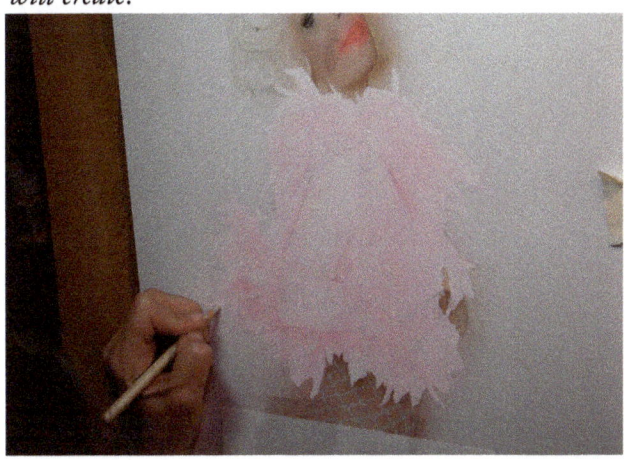

Even these areas have some of the soft downy feathers that stand away from the model and need to be highlighted.

Rendering her arm under the chiffon wrap requires attention to detail. The seam of the garment and soft highlights make the arm look solid under the fabric.

Despite a lot of overspray on the frisket around the figure, it's apparent that the feather boa wrap is beginning to take shape.

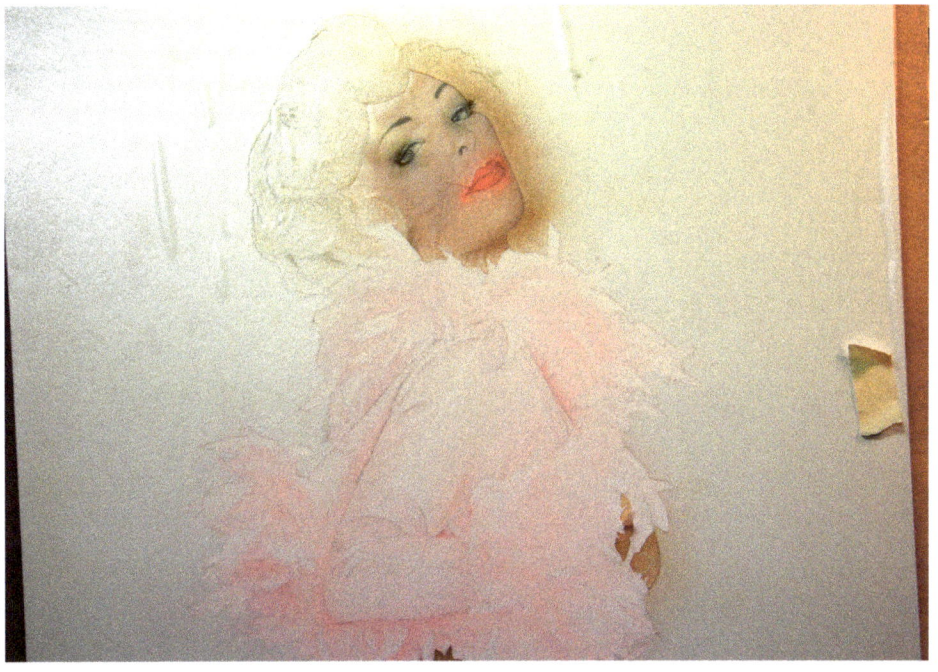

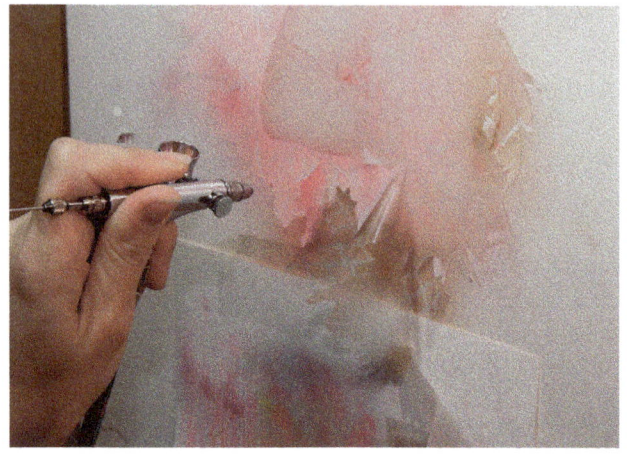

Some areas stand out as being much darker than others, but to get depth in these areas it's important to build the color slowly with layers of diluted paint.

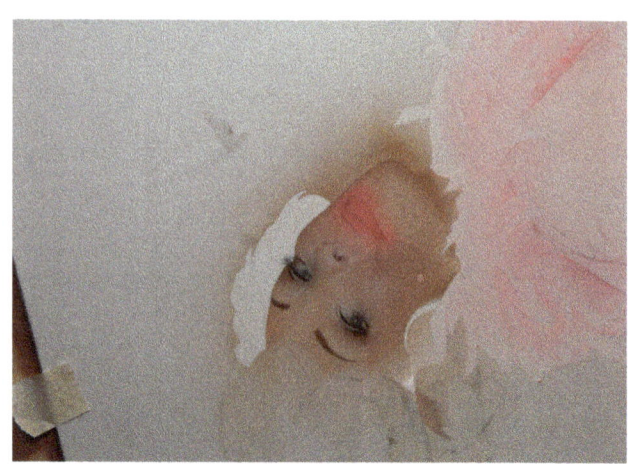

It's obvious how much painting has gone on next to this area once the frisket is removed.

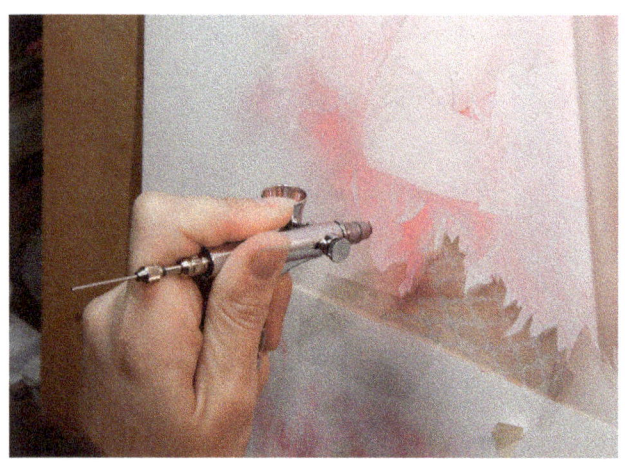

The shadow edge under the arm takes on more form by keeping the edge soft with a freehand application of paint.

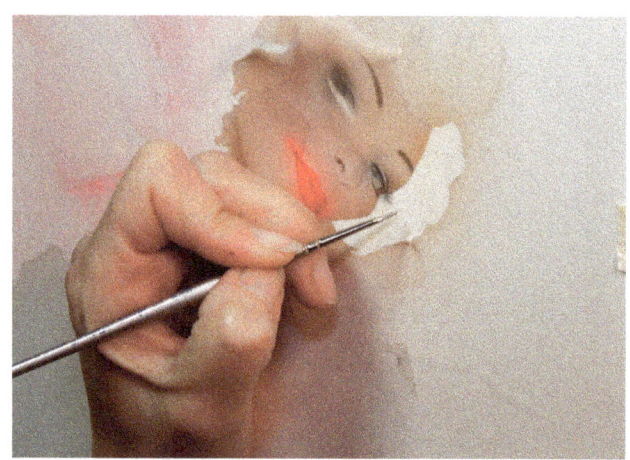

Painting the hair begins by applying diluted liquid frisket with an old brush on the lightest strands.

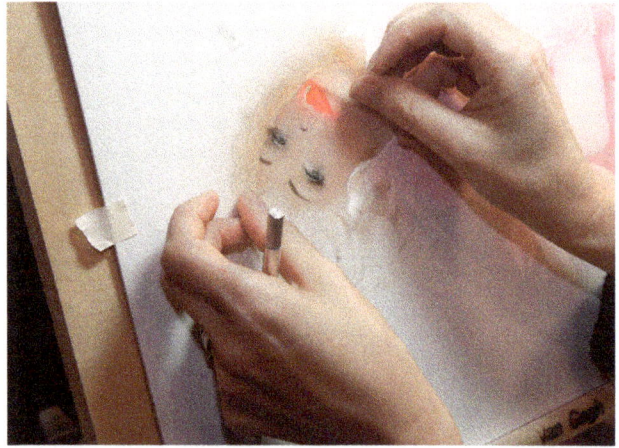

The hair is the last to be painted. Frisket is removed from the hair on the right side of the painting first, because it is darkened by the cast shadow of the face.

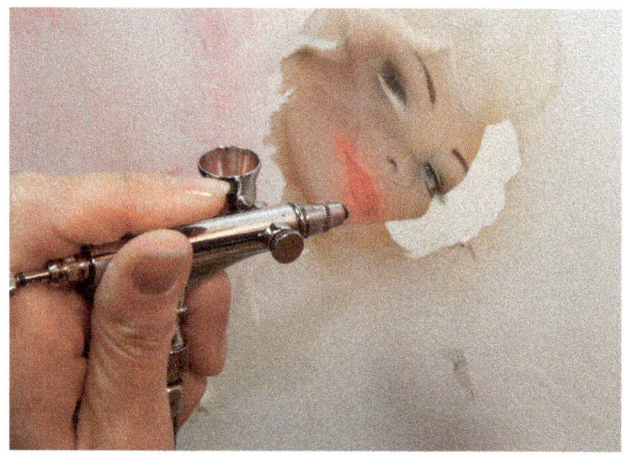

The pre-mixed hair color is dusted over the entire area.

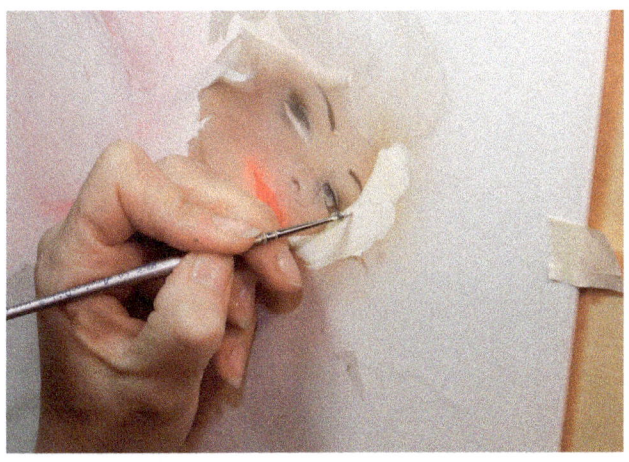

Repeat the process of applying liquid frisket, overlapping some highlighted areas and keeping other areas covered with liquid frisket and dust with paint.

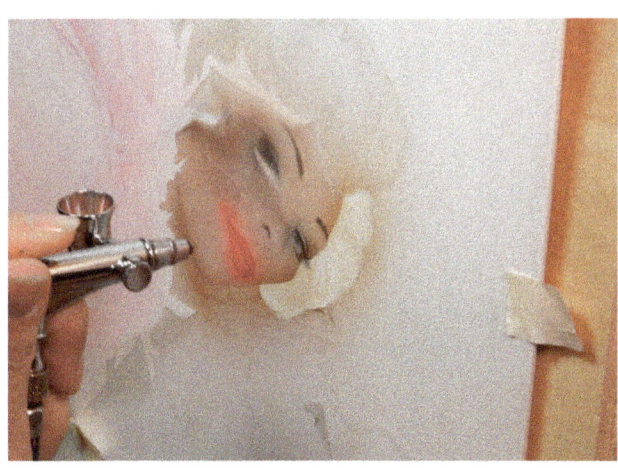

Continue to build the hair color slowly.

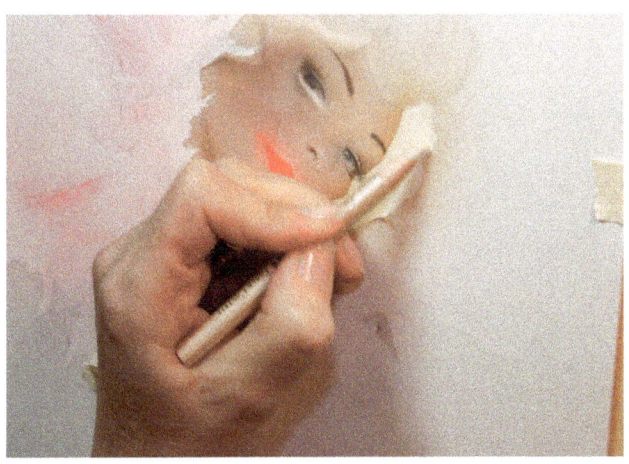

After repeating a few times, "erase" off the liquid frisket to see how it is going.

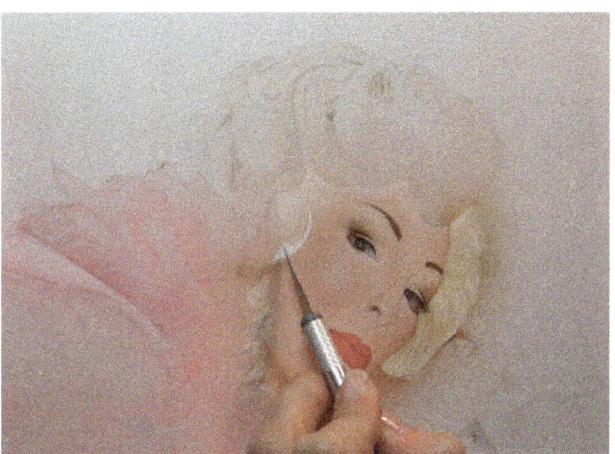

The hair on the left side of the painting overlaps the face, so the frisket is removed from the face to render this area. An Xacto is used to sharpen the contrast of an overlapping curl of hair.

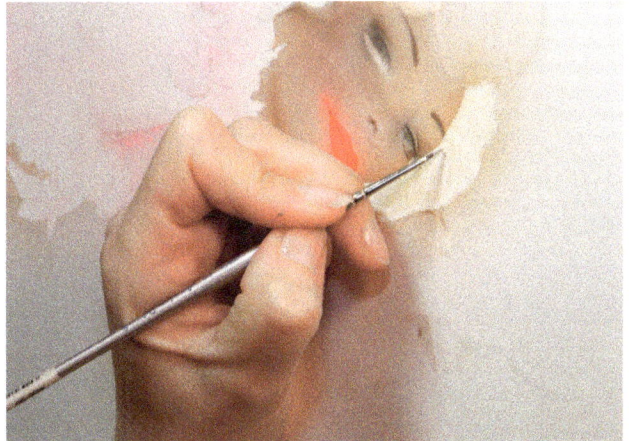

Paint the liquid frisket on again to increase the light-dark contrast. Be precise with some highlights and random with others. Don't have all the strands lined up in a row.

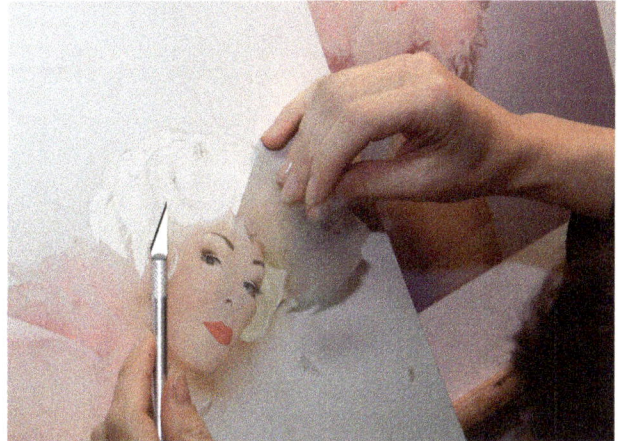

Removing the frisket from the hair on this side makes it apparent why these edges were kept soft to blend the hairline into the face.

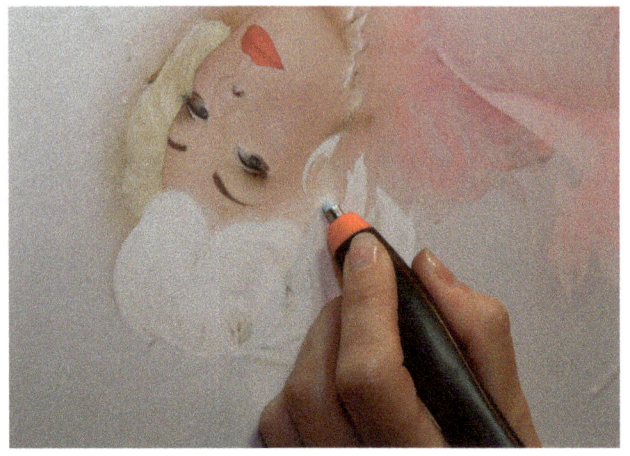

An electric eraser is used to create larger, softer areas of highlights.

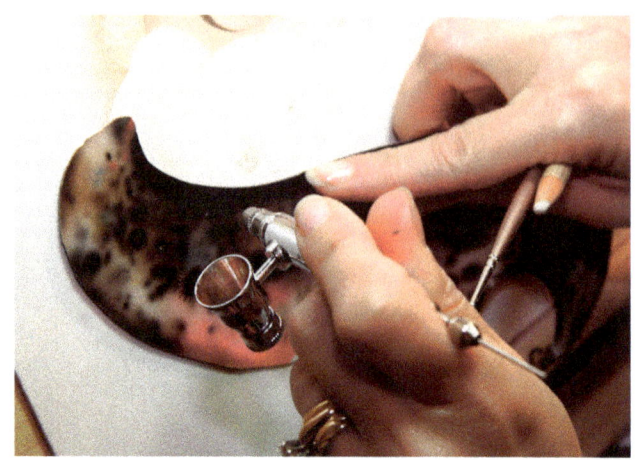

The handheld shield is used to mark out darker shadows with sharp edges.

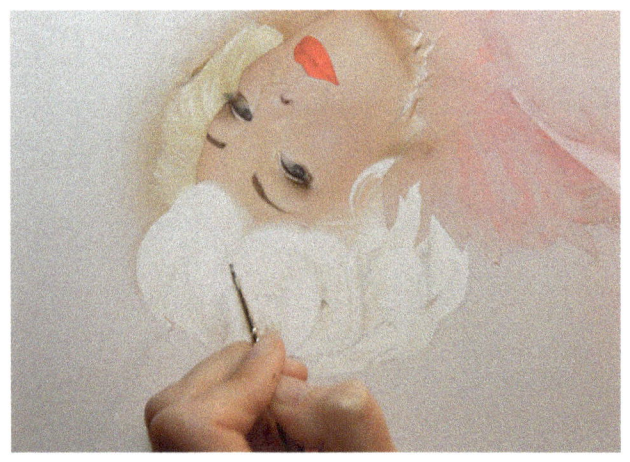

Once again, liquid frisket is "painted" on to retain lighter strands of hair.

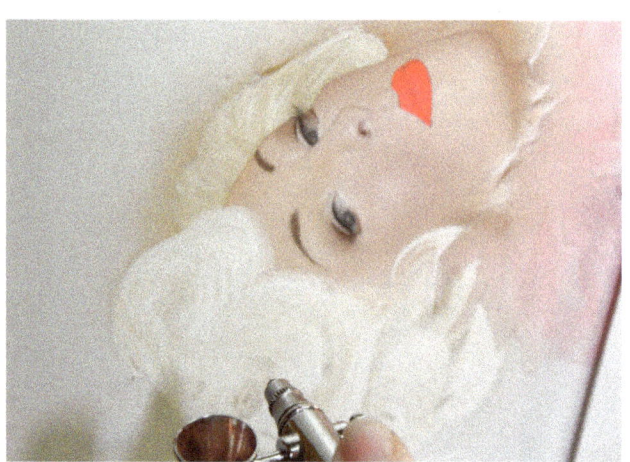

More hair color is applied over the entire area.

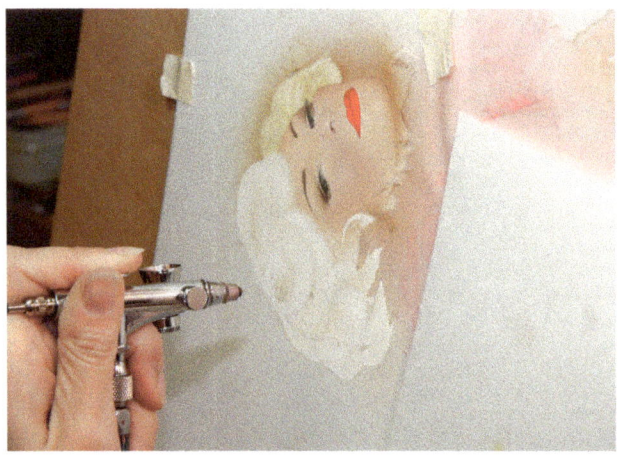

Hair color is sprayed broadly over the area.

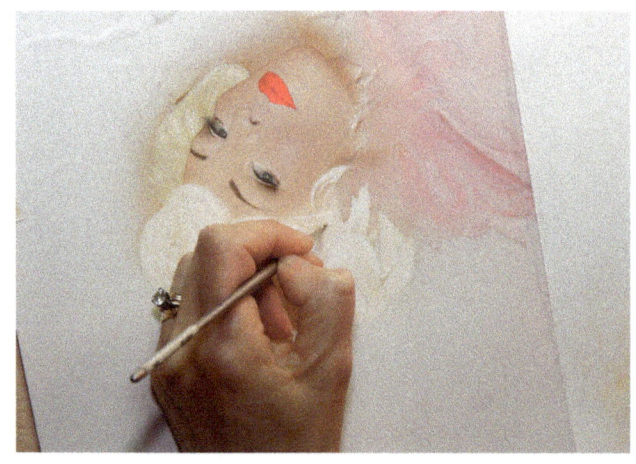

Areas are erased to sharpen the highlights.

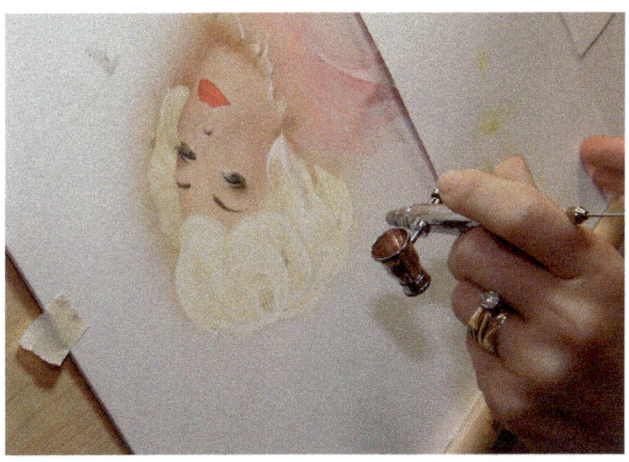

The hair color is built up some more with heavier applications of paint on the darker areas.

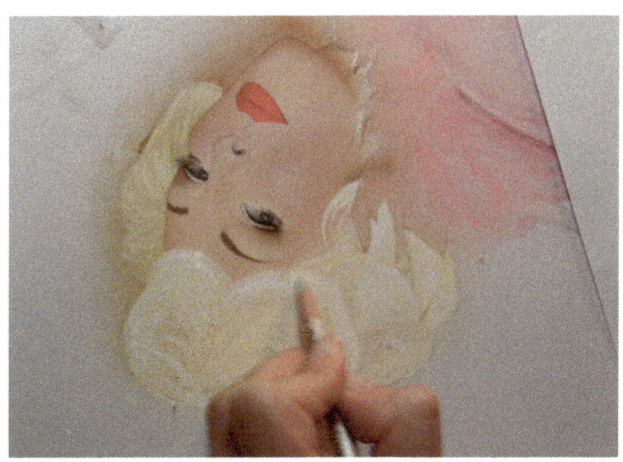

Highlights are reinforced with an eraser.

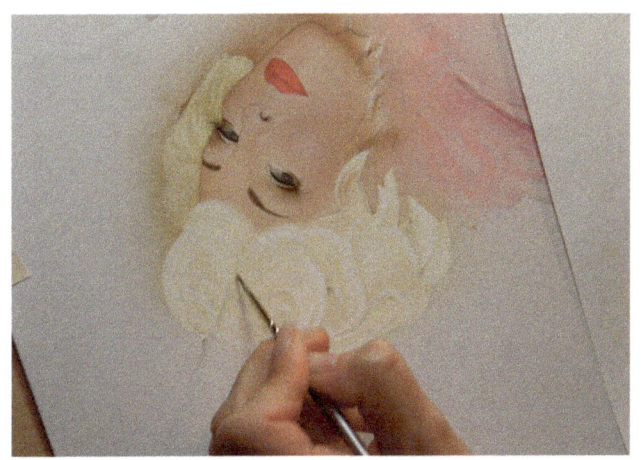

More liquid frisket is "painted" directly over the previous layers of frisket and paint, to build depth.

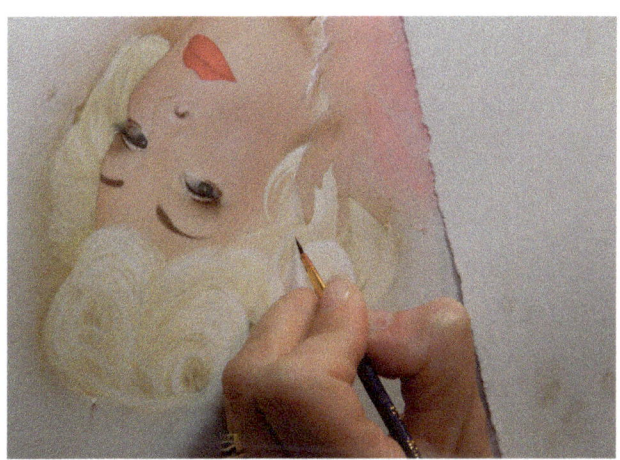

Some of the hardest edged areas of shadow in the hair are created by hand using a fine detail brush and diluted sepia.

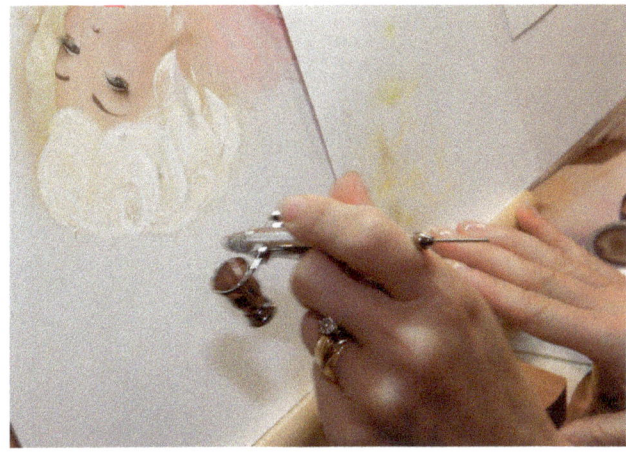

The hair color is sprayed again.

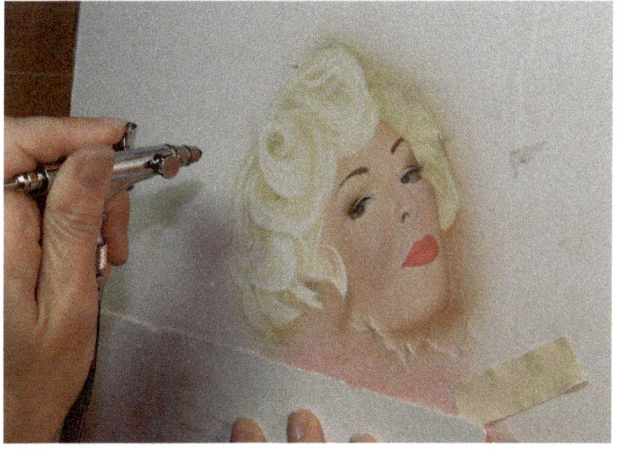

The same dilute sepia is sprayed to create the darker areas at the center of a curl.

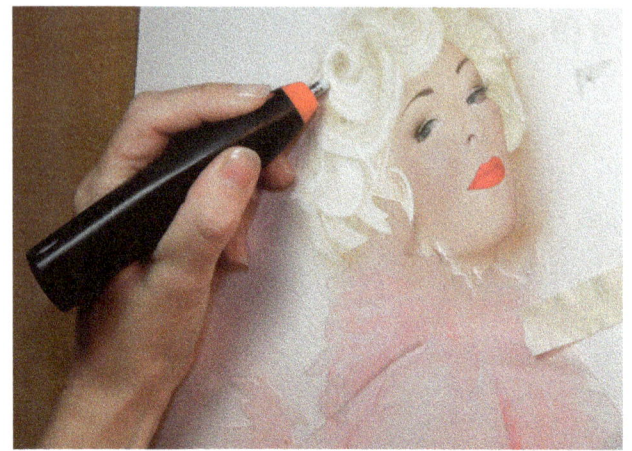

The shape of the curl can now be emphasized by erasing highlights on the outer most strands of hair.

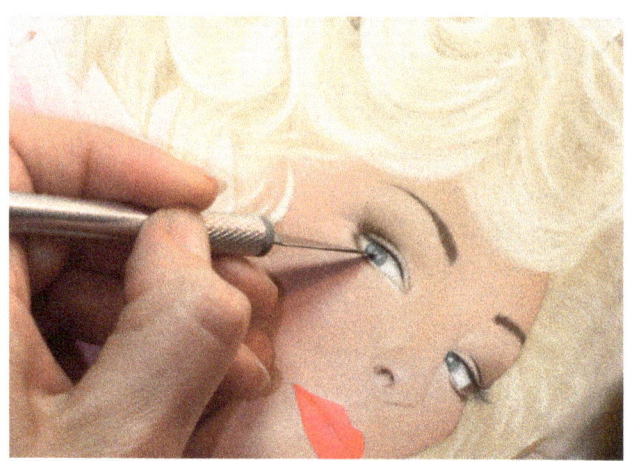

Using an Xacto to define the catch lights of the eyes.

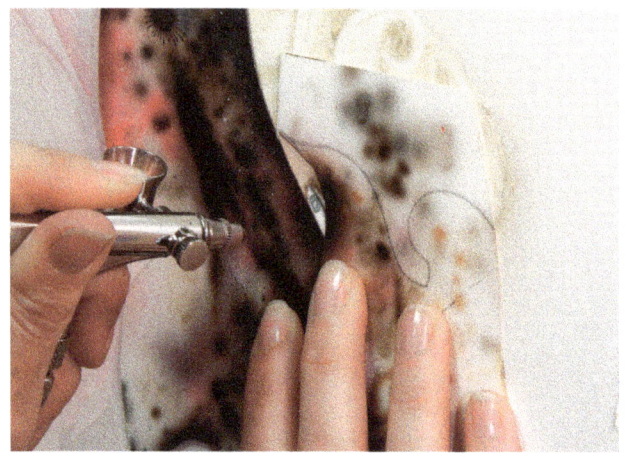

Once the hair is done, I want to go back over some details of the eyes. Two handheld shields are used so the inside corner of the eye can be darkened.

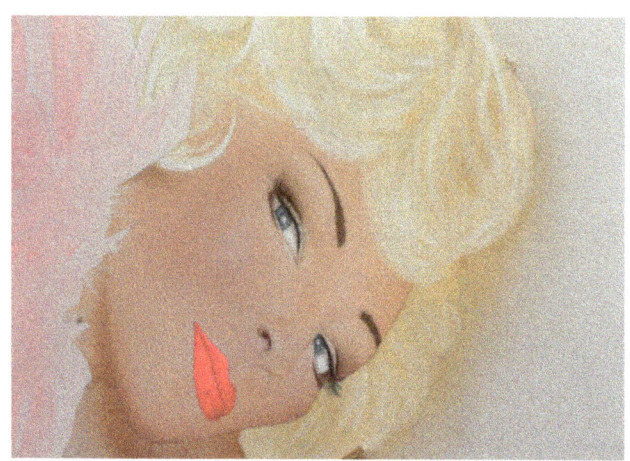

Placing the pupil and highlights just right creates a smoldering eye focused on the viewer.

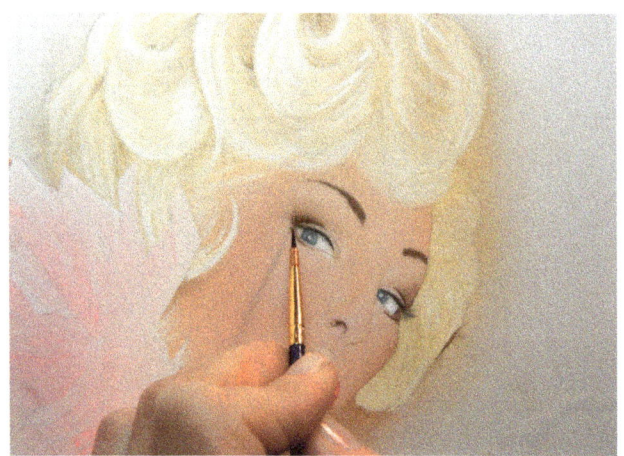

A small detail brush is used to darken the dramatic black eyelashes.

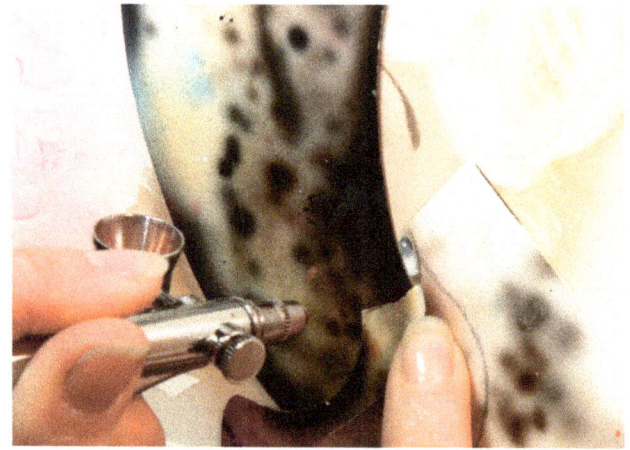

Two shields are used so that the outer corner of the model's left eye can be darkened.

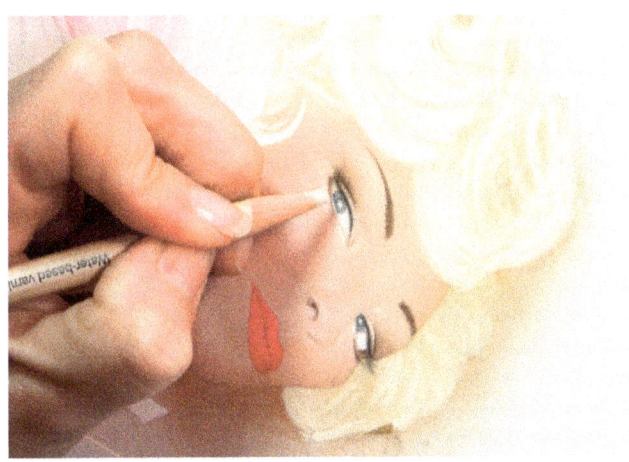

More erasing is needed to emphasize the catch light in the iris. Making this highlight stand out creates the illusion of sparkling moist eyes.

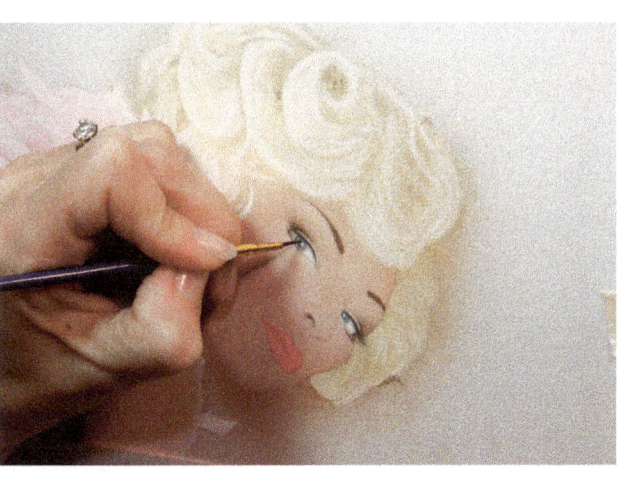

The pupil is painted by hand. Placement is critical to getting her sideways gaze just right.

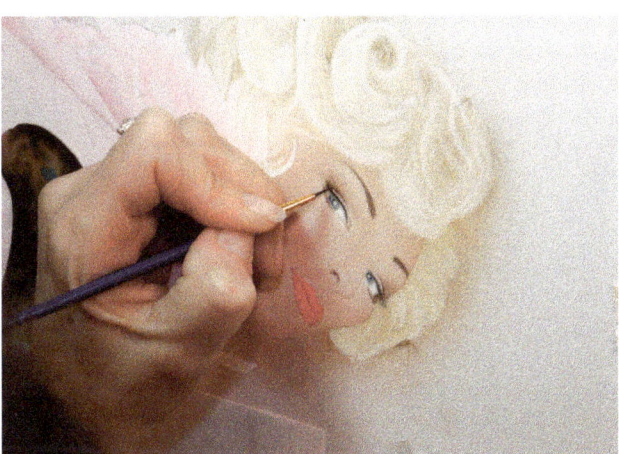

Using a small brush to hand paint the eyelashes, be mindful that some areas appear to clump together as they would naturally. Don't paint them all lined up like the teeth on a comb.

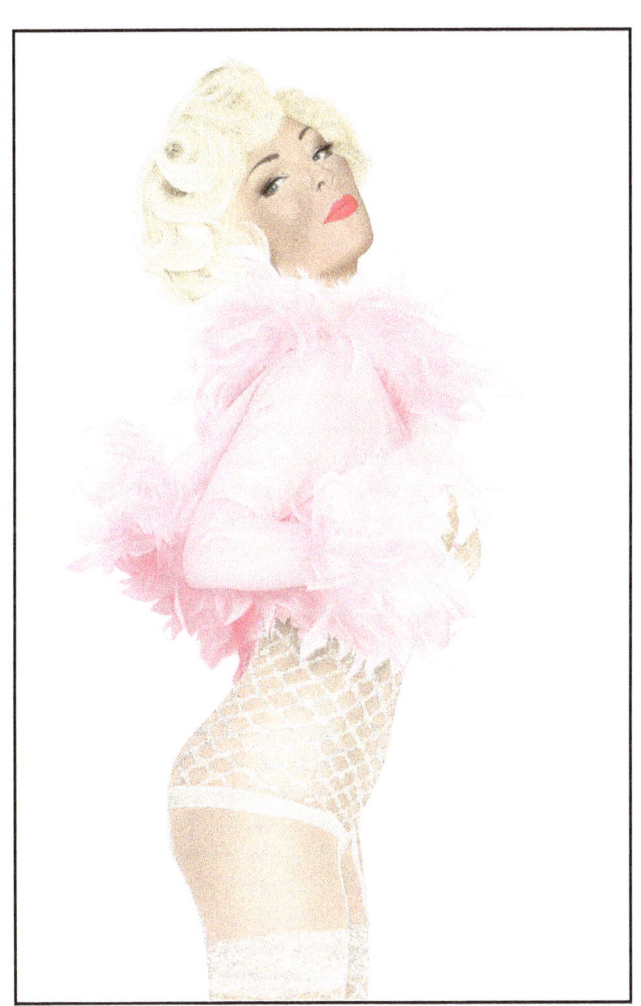

Once the frisket is removed from around the figure, the outer edges need to be "feathered" into the background. Some edges are kept hard while others are lost into the background.

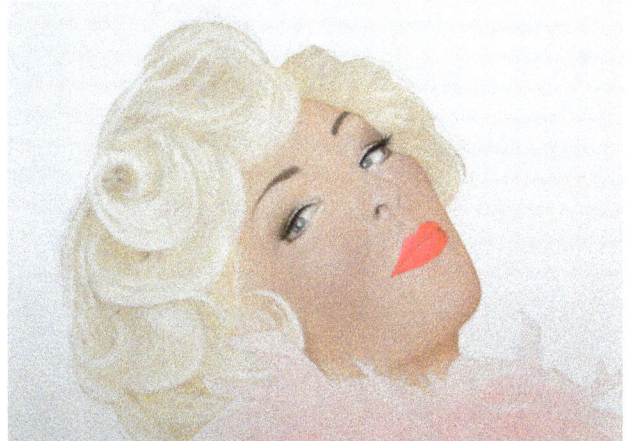

The last few minor adjustments make a huge difference in the final piece. At this point I like to let the painting sit for a few days to see if any other adjustments are needed.

115

Susan Heidi Q&A

Give us a little background on you, how did you get started in art, and are pin-ups the main focus of the work you do?

I've been doing pin-ups for three years. In 2006 I did my first full pin-up. I have always liked portraiture. Before doing my first pin-up, I did black and white portraits with charcoal or pencil as a hobby. Then I started coloring in those sketches with watercolors. I've always been fond of the glamour era of the 1940's and 1950's…. so pretty soon I wanted to do full-figure paintings like the artists did back then. I took Dru Blair's portrait class to learn how to use the airbrush and create photorealistic images. I highly recommend his classes.

Currently I sell prints through my website (www.susanheidi.com) and at trade shows and galleries. I usually keep the original paintings, but original studies and sketches are sold at the shows. I do commissions working from photographs. Sometimes a client wants an image of his wife or girlfriend, or a company wants a pin-up for their logo.

My work also lends itself really well to the hot rod, pin-up, and kustom kulture shows.

Who inspires you, who are some of the artists you look up to?

When I started to study pin-ups, the work of Alberto Vargas stood out to me. His style is different from Elvgren's - there's a sensitivity in his use of watercolors that I relate to. I started studying his work and found a book that had a how-to section written by Vargas. I like the way he used washes of color and built up layers of paint. He typically used an airbrush to finish off paintings, but when he went to Esquire he used the airbrush more, to speed up production.

How do you find the models, typically who does the photographs that you use for reference?

I work with professional pin-up models as reference for my paintings. They are all very much into the retro lifestyle and have studied the hair, makeup, clothing, and poses that make a classic pin-up. Either I take the photos or I have their photographer take the pictures, usually to my specifications.

Novice artists sometimes have trouble rendering believable skin tones, how do you achieve life-like skin tones?

Well first, I pre-mix my paints and dilute them with water to create washes. I don't use anything directly out of the bottle. I mix light and dark skin colors first. The light is burnt sienna, with a little alizarin for the red, a little red violet, and cobalt blue, (blue is opposite of orange so it knocks down the saturation and makes it more natural).

Then I'll take some of the light skin tone and grey it down with cobalt blue and a little violet, and use that for shadow areas. I'll usually mix the light and dark skin colors right on the board by over-spraying them for mid-tones.

These are retro pin-ups. They have a rosy soft skin tone that goes with the feel of the era, so I work toward that color to get the vintage look.

Paint, which type of paint do you use and why?

The paints for this demonstration are all transparent acrylics by Winsor & Newton, Liquitex, or Aeroflash. Sometimes I'll use watercolors or oil paints to achieve a different look. I

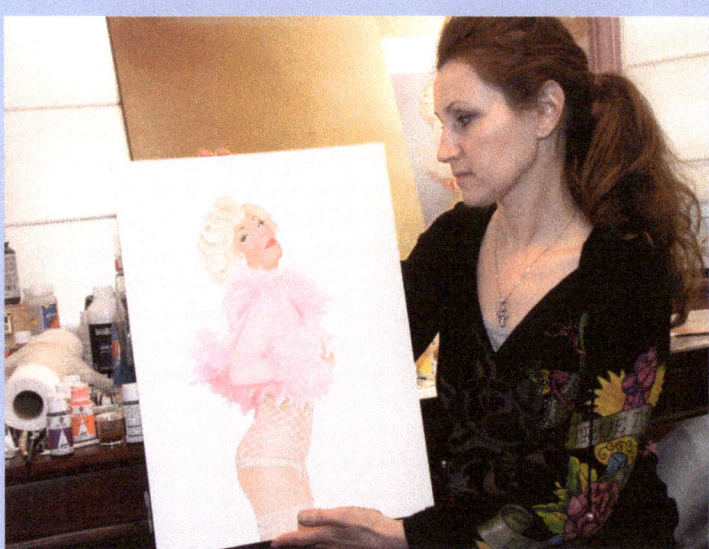

Testimony to the idea that you can make a major career change as an adult, Susan Heidi now makes her living as a full time artist.

Susan Heidi Q&A

like the feel of transparent paints, but they are very unforgiving.

How did you learn to mix your own colors?

It's intuitive for me, but I suppose I understand the color wheel from science class, knowing what you get when you mix colors. I used watercolors first, and mixed those to see what I could get. More formally, I took Dru's class which includes a very thorough treatment of color theory. Chris Saper is a portrait artist whose book on painting portraits was very helpful. It goes into great detail about color theory.

Faces, how do you create such beautiful faces?

I focus on the expression; the eyes, the mouth, and how the model holds her head, all work to bring the image to life. I pay a lot of attention to each of the slightest little curves and angles to get it just right.

Are there some rules or guidelines you follow in terms of your compositions?

I try to pull the viewer through the image. In classic art everything is based on the triangle. I try to keep that in mind when laying out the composition for a painting. I'm also concerned with where the viewer's eye enters the painting.

Why did you pick this image to paint, you talked about the texture of the body stocking, the tension in the pose, the ambiguity?

I usually paint the full figure head to toe for a pin-up because that was traditional for 1940's and 50's pin-ups. The time constraints for this demonstration limited me to painting only part of the figure. I felt that with all the texture going on in this piece it would demonstrate all the techniques that would be used to create a full figure pin-up.

I also like the come hither expression on her face and the tension in her arms as they hold the feather boa. The composition flows because your eye has different things to look at. Her face draws you in first, then the feathers draw your eye down through the rest of the painting.

What equipment do you use?

My airbrush is an Iwata hp sb with a side feed cup that I can switch around because I'm left handed. The The paints I use are acrylic Windsor and Newton, Liquitex, or Aeroflash. I like acrylics because I can use them like watercolors, but they make it a little easier to build up to brighter colors.

Do you use other media like hand brushes to add detail or achieve effects that are hard to do with an airbrush?

An airbrush can be used to achieve just about any effect when used freehand or with frisket and shields, but I'm not a purist when it comes to using the airbrush. I enjoy doing the under painting by hand and some little details are quicker to do with a small paint brush. As long as the edges are controlled properly (soft, hard, or lost), it doesn't really matter which technique is used to achieve the effect.

What makes a good pin-up painting?

For my focus, which is the retro pin-up, it's important to have the right expression and pose. You need that soft vintage look, and that is what I try to achieve

Ten words of advice for someone starting out?

With aspiring artists in any area, the big thing is to slow down and take your time during each phase of painting. You'll end up moving quicker with your skill level. Essentially. you can speed up by slowing down and get things just the way you want them. Think before you put anything on the paper.

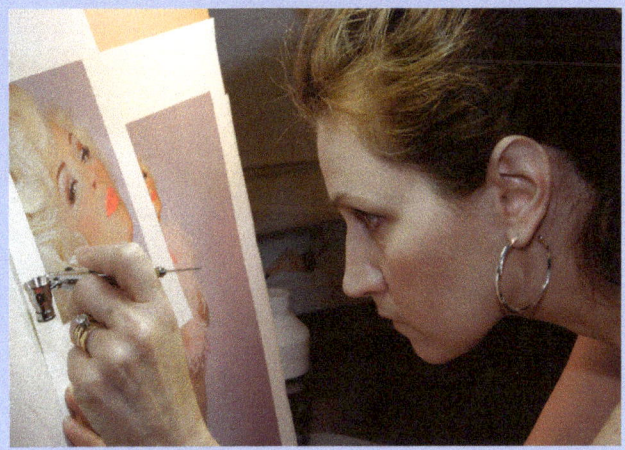

The word intense does not begin to describe Susan at work.

Chapter Seven

Liz Austin

Beautiful Eyes and Great Color

As comfortable with a tattoo gun as she is with an airbrush, Liz Austin is an intuitive artist who just seems to know how much yellow it takes to make a good skin tone. Without any formal art training, Liz simply "gets it." What starts as an outline quickly turns into an airbrush painting that is more alive than many real women sitting nearby.

Like some other artists in this book, Liz starts with a pencil outline, then erases part of that before the actual painting begins. After watching Liz work on a painting over a period

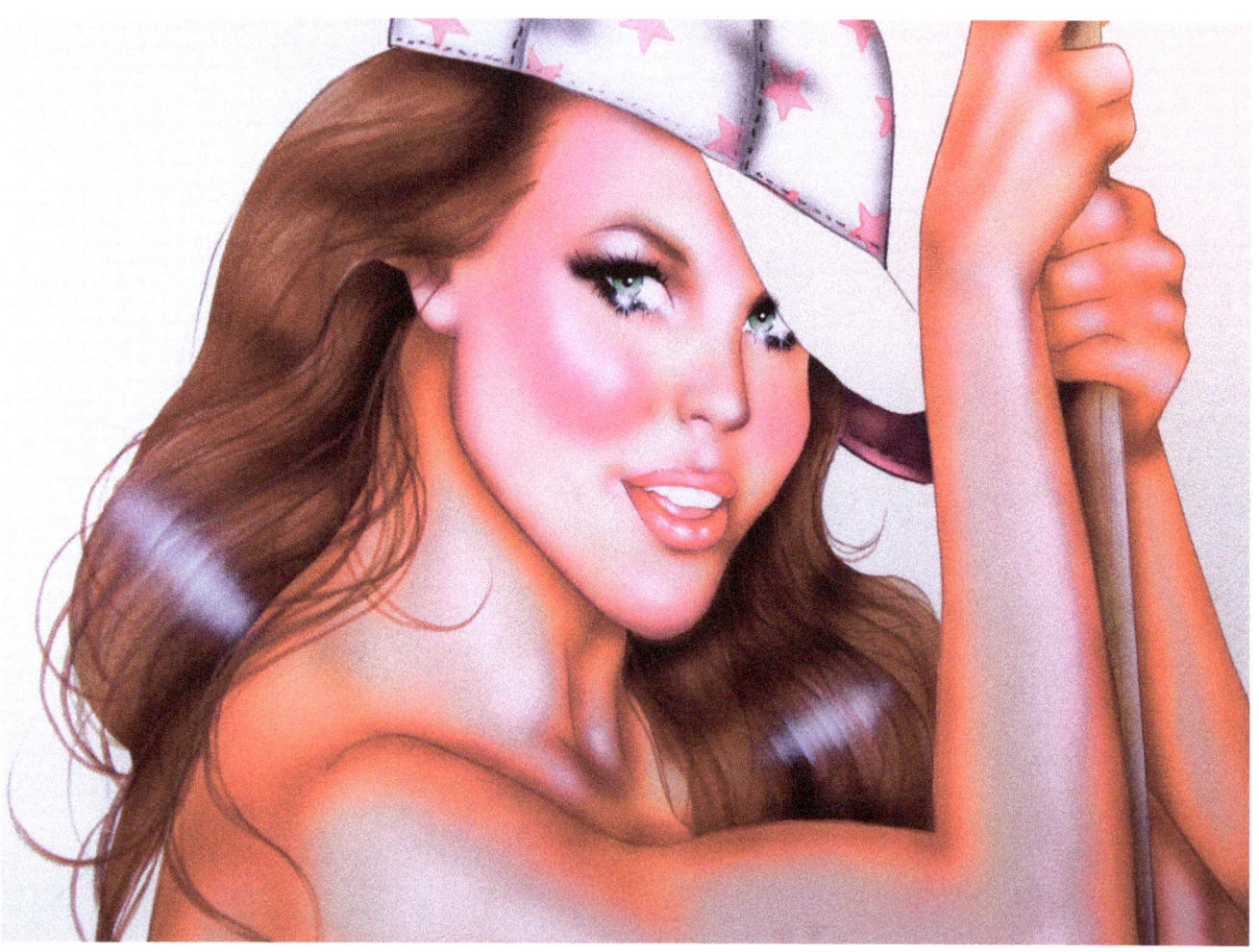

Looking at the finished image, it's not hard to believe that Liz has, "always been focused on the face, it comes naturally to me."

of days, you realize that while pin-ups may be all about sex and a shapely body, it's the face that truly makes or breaks the image. And if Liz has one outstanding ability, it's her skill at rendering some of the loveliest eyes ever seen on canvas. To use her own phrase, "they do follow you around the room."

Working with acrylic paint, Liz switches back and forth from the airbrush to a hand brush with ease. Along the way mixing colors by feel, much the way a good chef knows exactly how much salt to add to the stew without ever referring to a recipe or reaching for a measuring cup.

Because she often uses frisket and masking materials to work on just one section at a time, there are periods, as the pin-up develops, when you wonder how she's ever going to pull it all together into one coherent image. Liz does of course. Near the end the masking comes off and presto, a lovely young woman suddenly appears where only white press board existed just a few days earlier.

The paint that Liz uses is opaque rather than transparent, and she uses it with skill to outline an area before coming back to fill in and add color to the face or the thigh. Highlights are created in white paint, or supplied by the color of the board in areas that she chooses not to paint. Details like eyelashes and hair come near the end of the project. Again, these final components, and the necessary details, are formed with the help of hand brushes. Some of the brushes are larger than you would expect, used in an almost random fashion to build a believable hairdo with all the necessary shading and highlights.

For now, Liz has given up doing tattoos, choosing instead to use her understanding of color and form to create pin-ups that are just as colorful as they are beautiful.

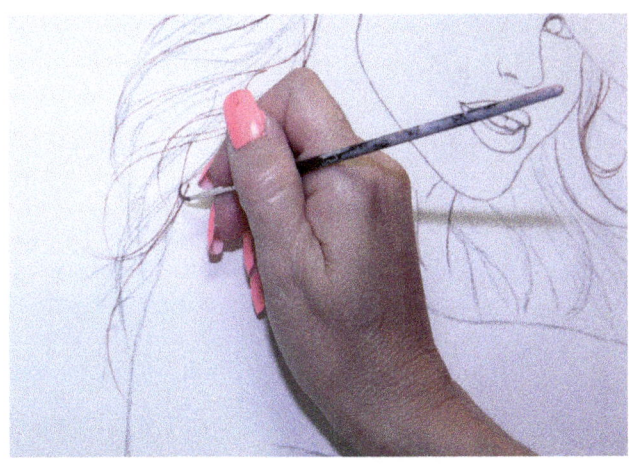

Once I complete the sketch, I outline in paint using a soft brown or beige.

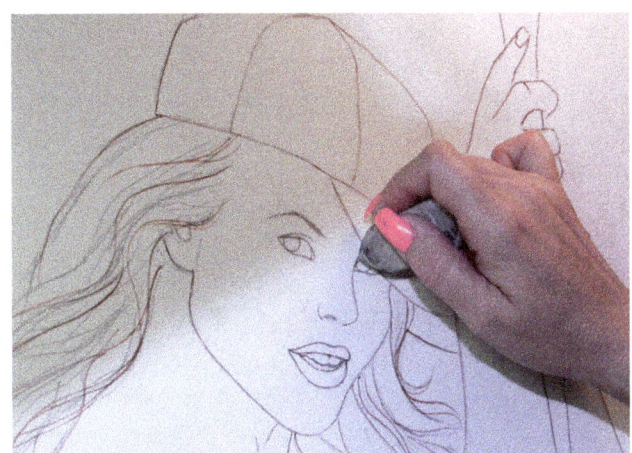

After the paint outline is complete, I erase the pencil lines to eliminate lead smears.

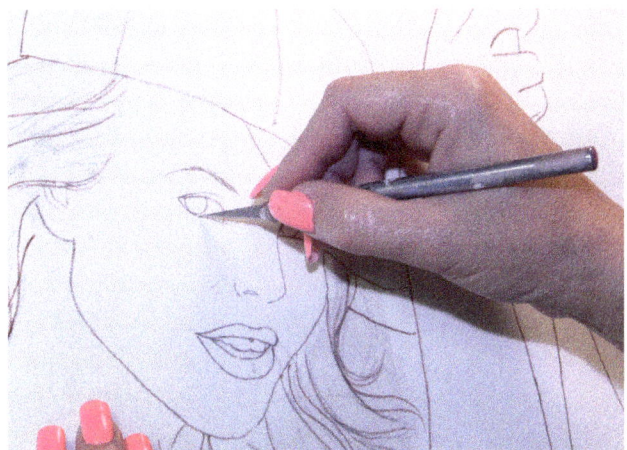

I now lay frisket over the face, and cut around the eyes and mouth.

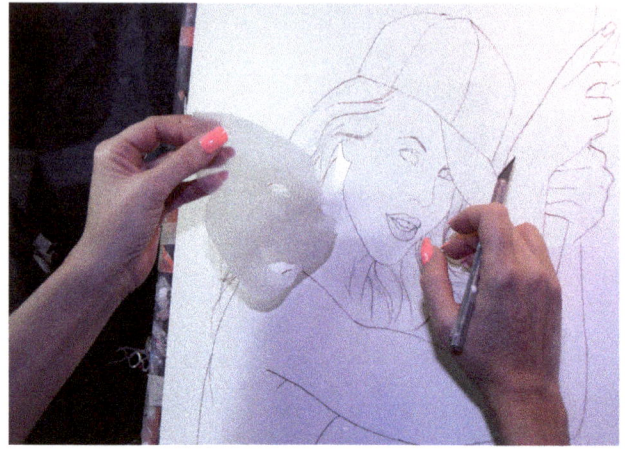

Next, I pull off the main piece of frisket.

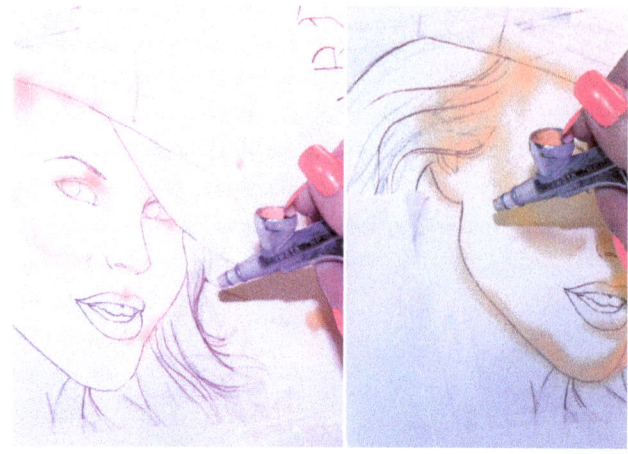

Here I'm defining cheekbones and facial features.

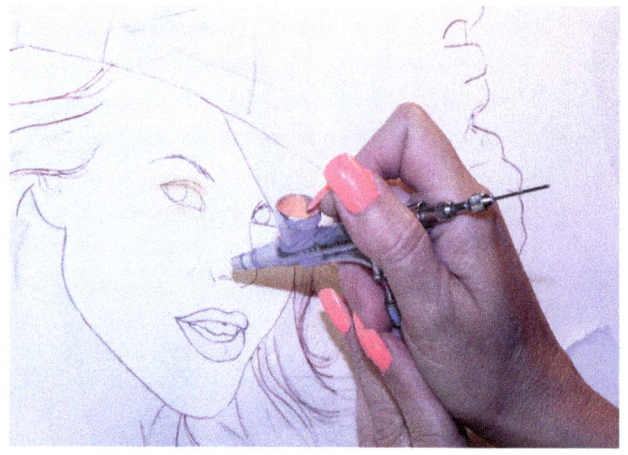

I start with the darkest area and begin to define the nose, eyes, and other features.

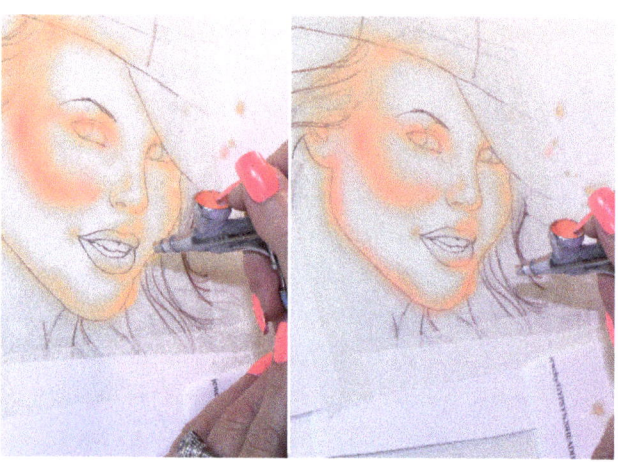

I keep working on the face, after adding a drop or two of pink and flesh to my mix.

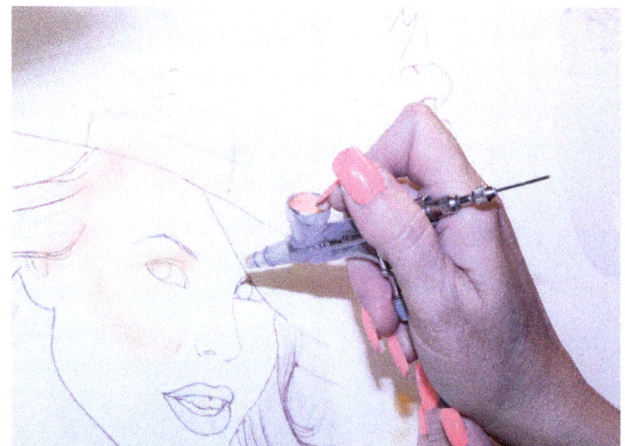

I begin to render the face in a mixture of yellow pink, flesh and white.

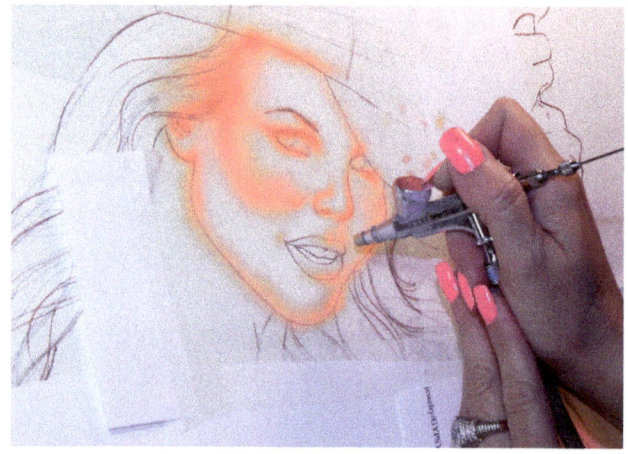

I add pink to the mixture and paint in more definition.

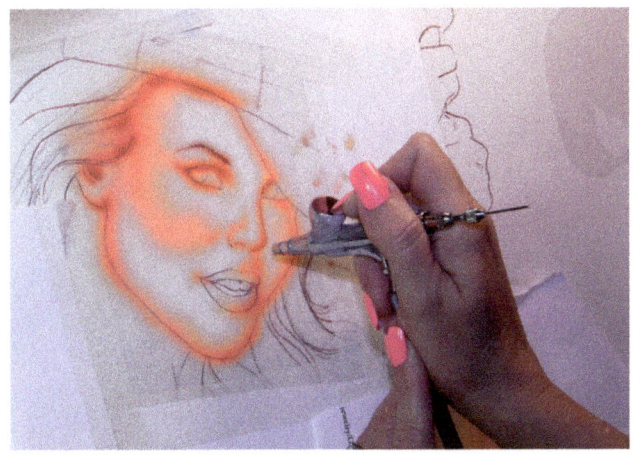

I'm still working on definition, with pink and soft brown added to the cup.

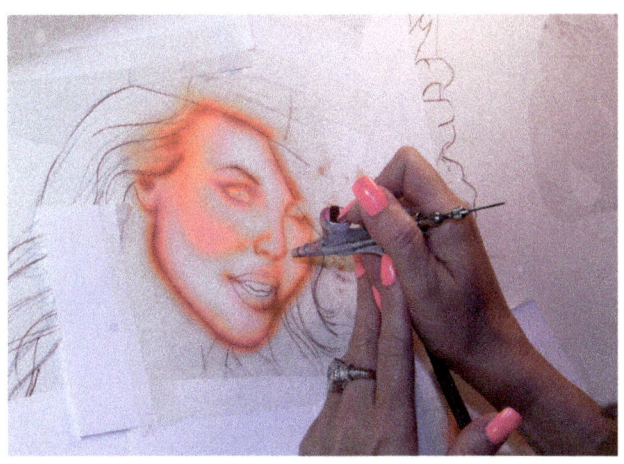

The eyes and mouth are masked off...

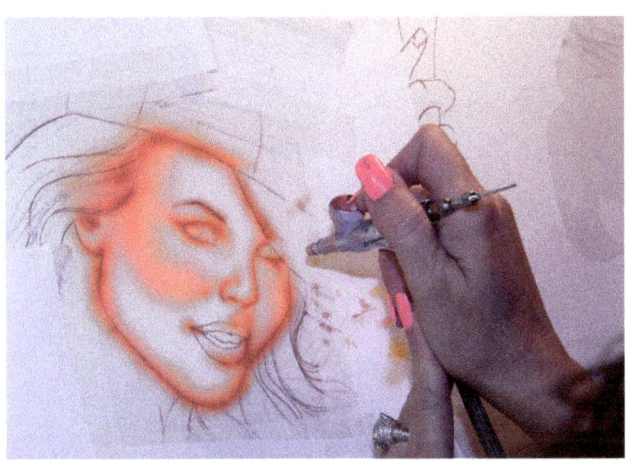

Now I'm adding shadows using brown.

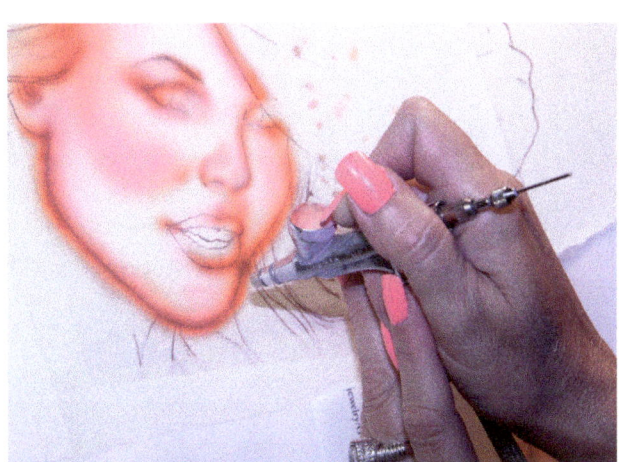

...and I continue working on the outline of her face.

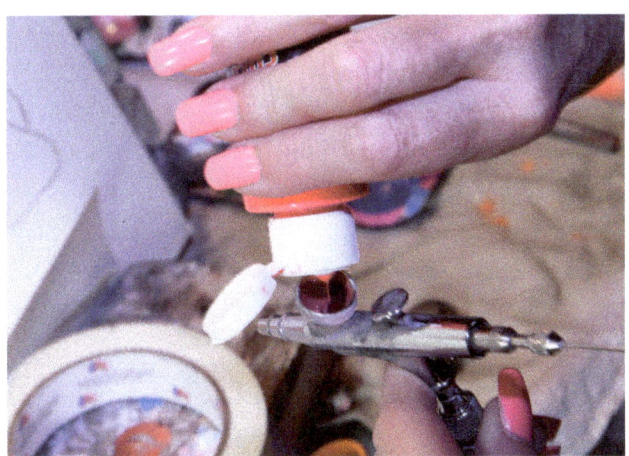

Adding hot pink to the brown mix.

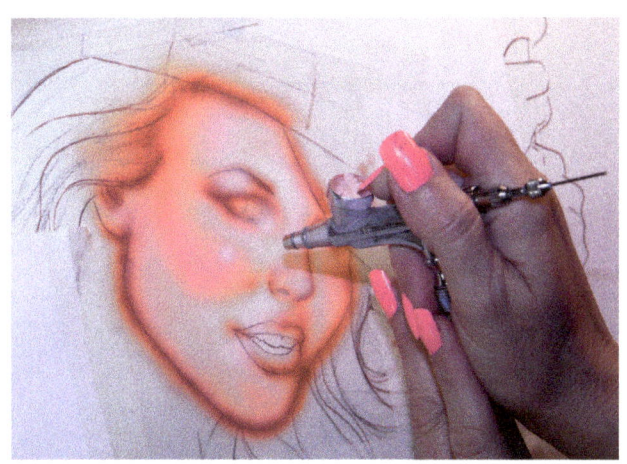

I now add in my flesh tone, and white.

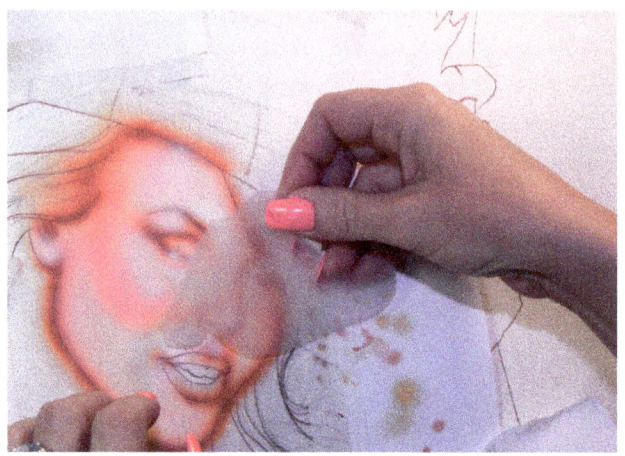

At this point I peel away the frisket.

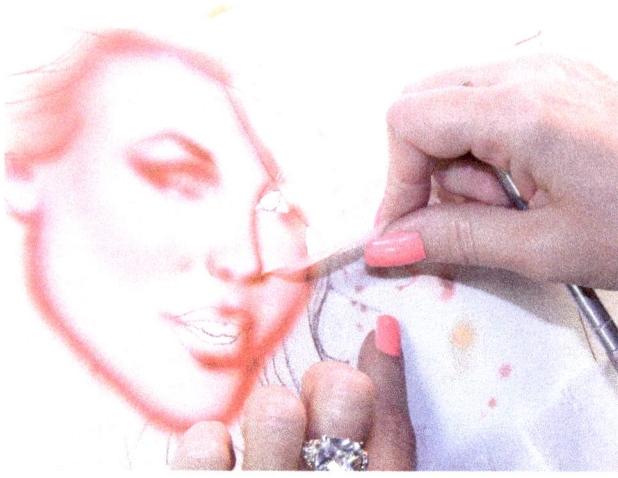

I can now pull the frisket.

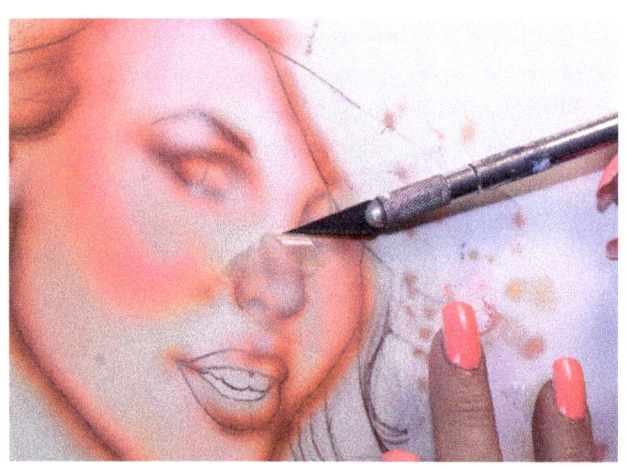

I lay a small piece of frisket over the nose and cut away to create a shadow by the nose.

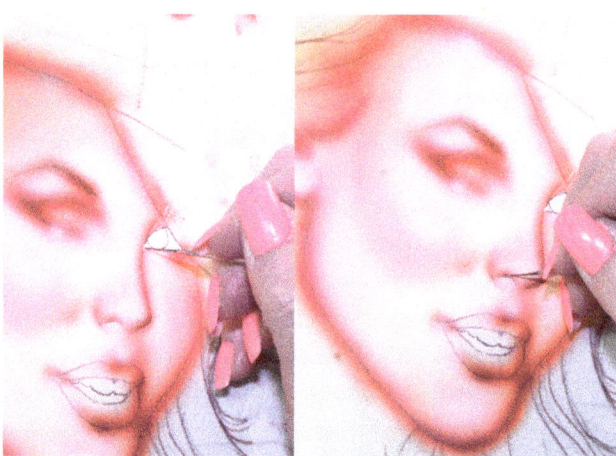

Here I use a very fine brush to outline and define the eyes and nose.

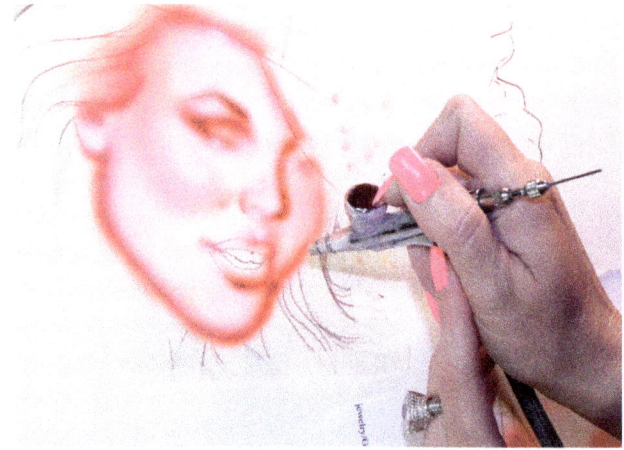

Next I'm filling out shading on the face with a little dark brown.

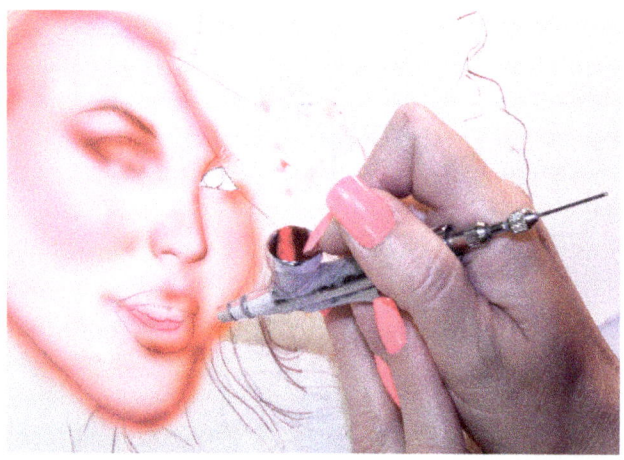

Defining shadows again using brown.

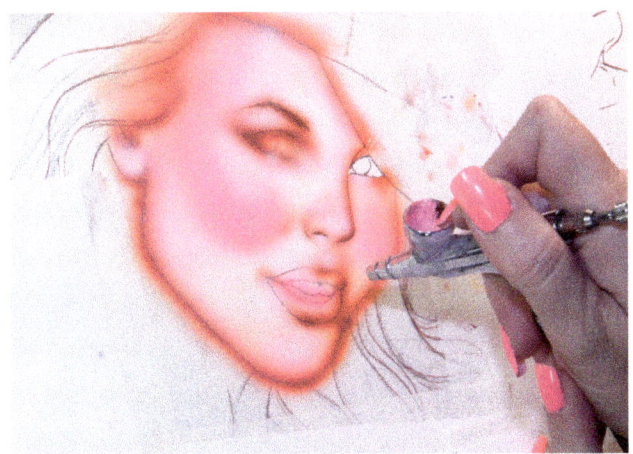

I add pink to give the face warmth.

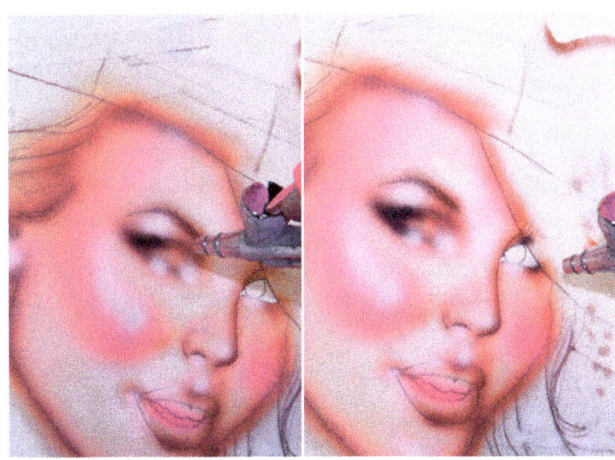

Here I add black around the eyes.

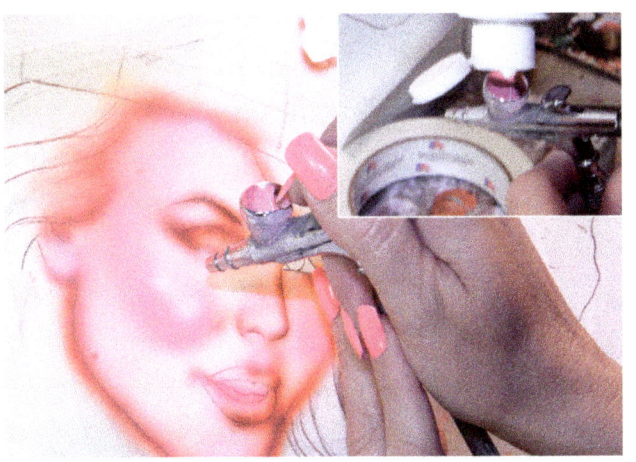

Here I add white for highlights, and to add depth.

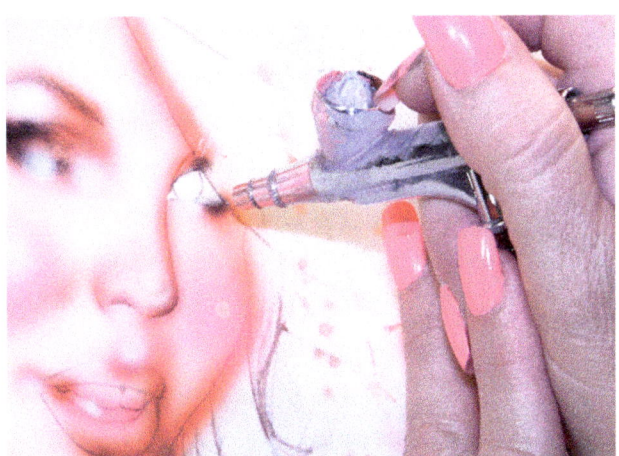

I add tiny white highlights to her eyes.

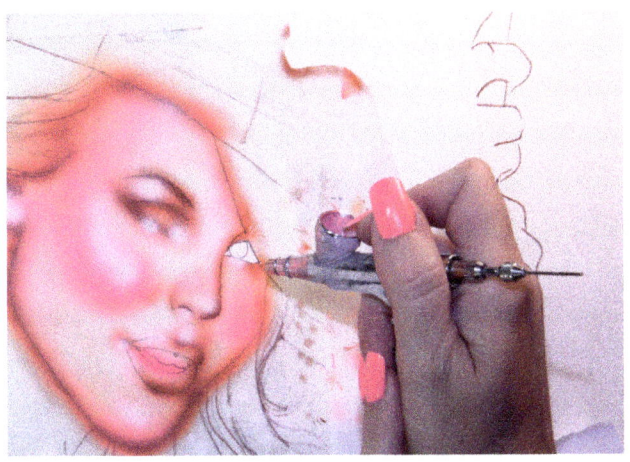

I begin to darken the area around the eyes with brown.

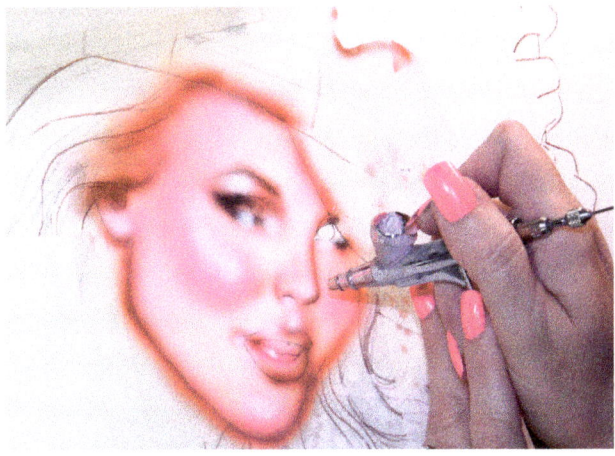

I'm softening, and also defining, the nose with dark brown.

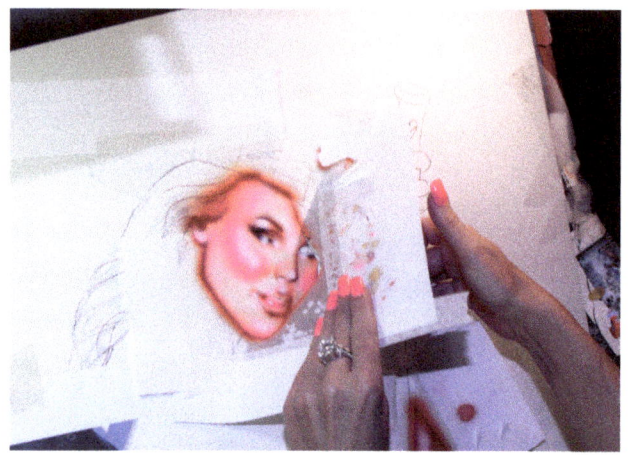

I peel the frisket away.

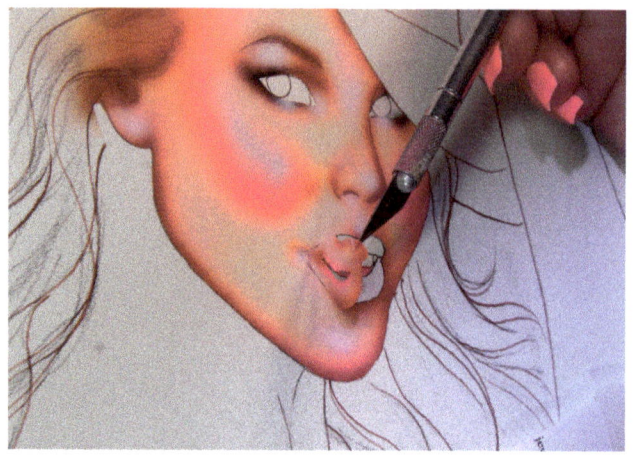

Peeling away frisket from her mouth.

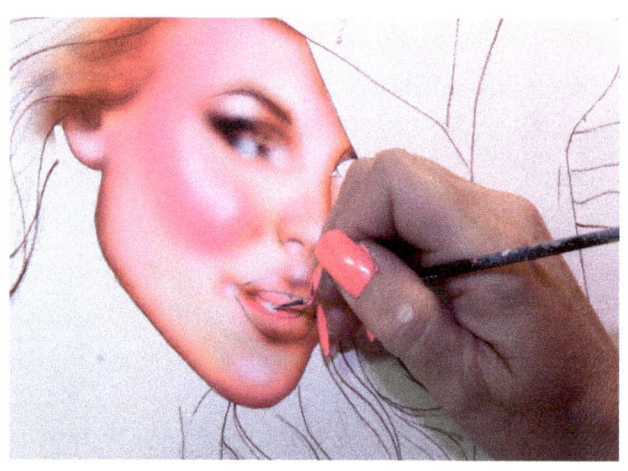

I use a very fine brush to add highlights to the tongue for a "wet" look.

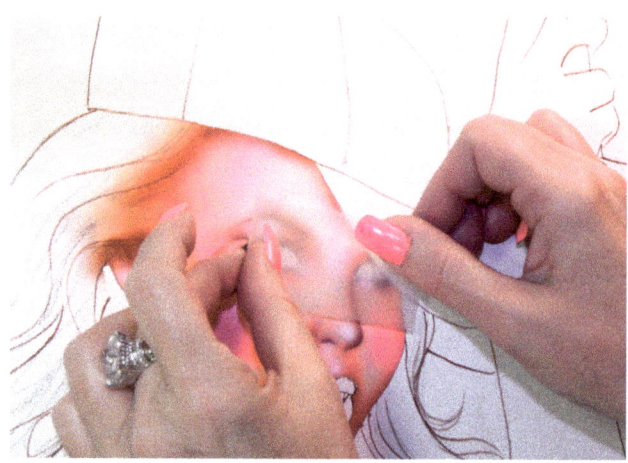

I lay frisket over the eyes...

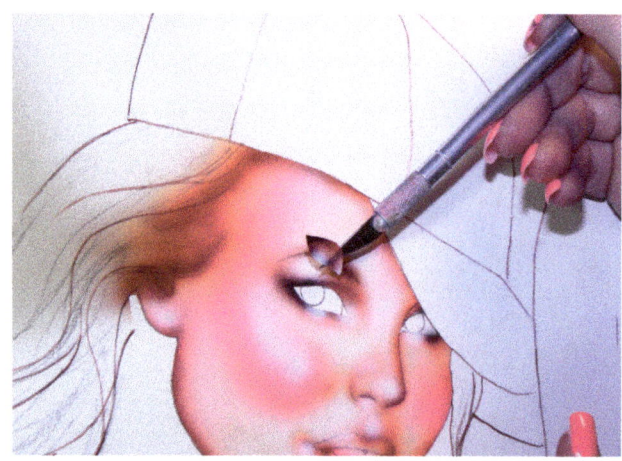

Removing frisket that was covering the eye during the rendering of her face.

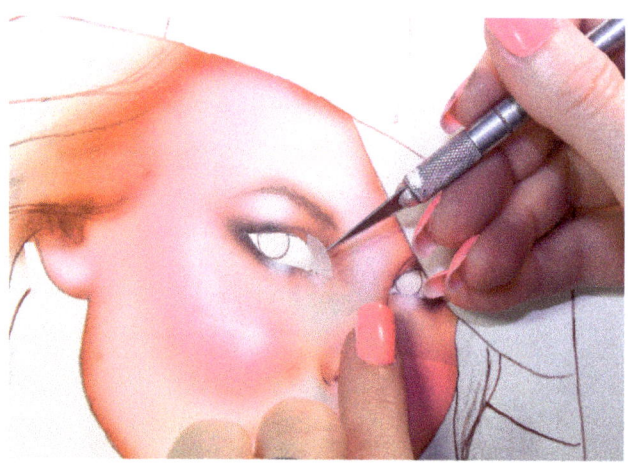

...then cut away the "white" area.

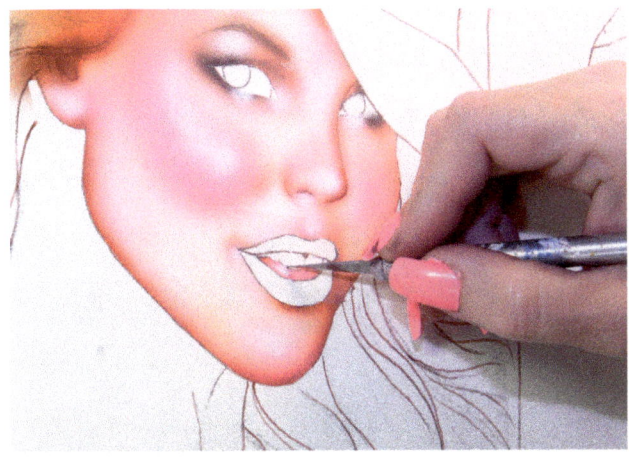

Once I have rendered the tongue, I mask the area off and cut out the teeth.

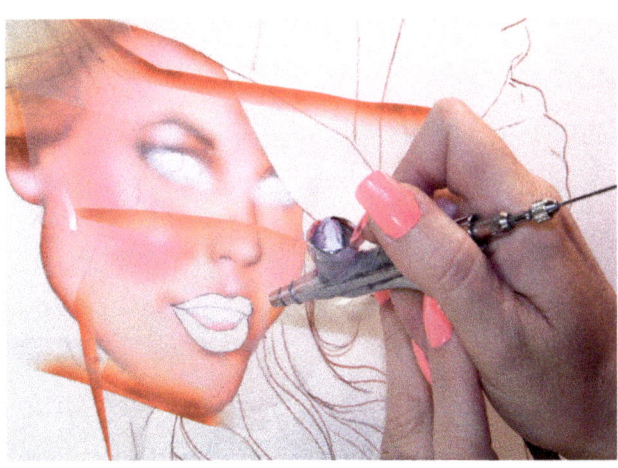

Teeth and eyes are cut away, and I fill in with white.

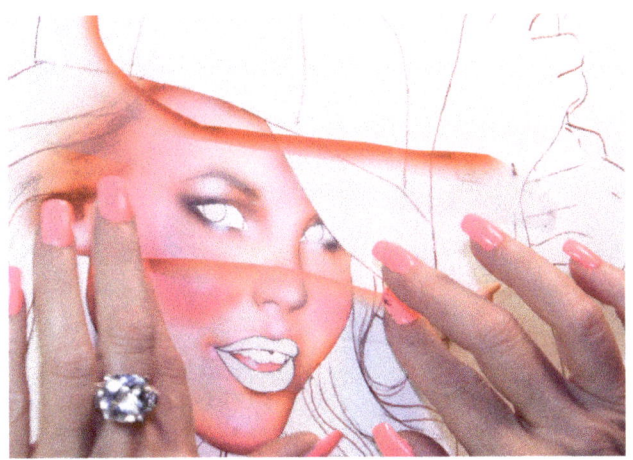

I use large pieces of the frisket saved from the body.

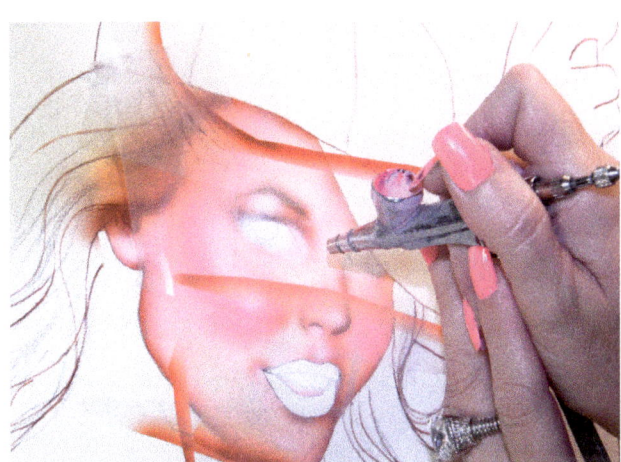

Filling in with more white.

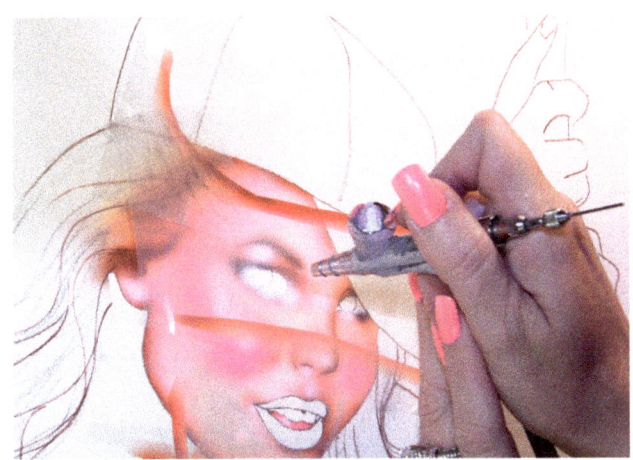

Now I can fill in the eye area.

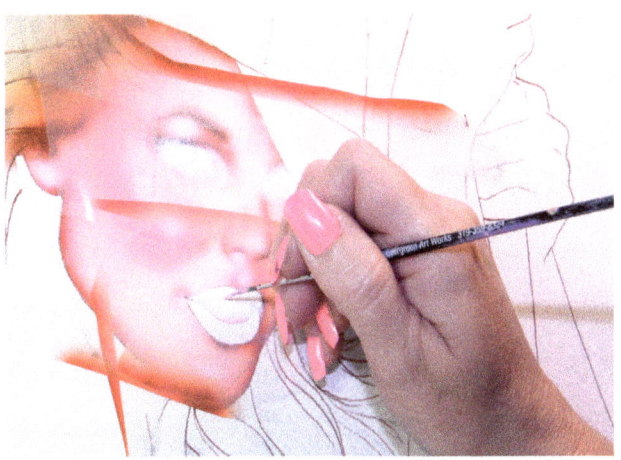

Defining the teeth with white, using a thin sable brush.

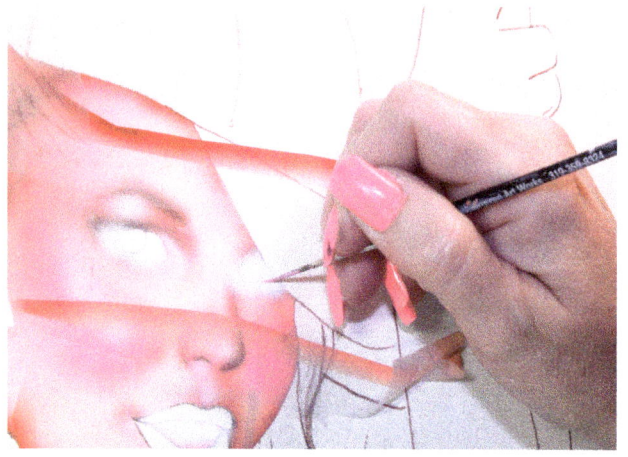

Using a very thin sable brush I add the pink eye membrane.

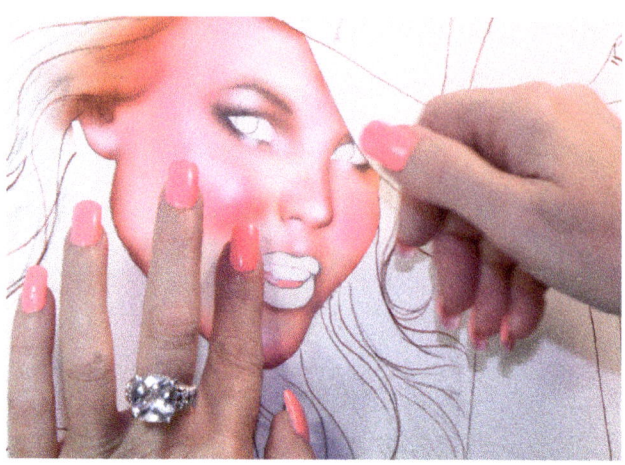

Before going further I make sure the frisket has adhered to the board.

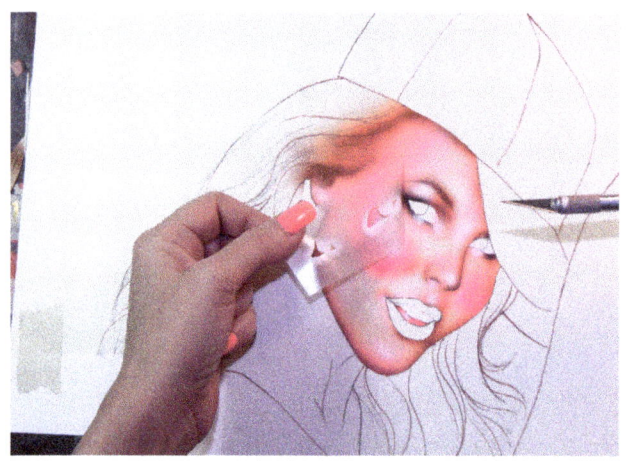

Peeling the mask away from her eye.

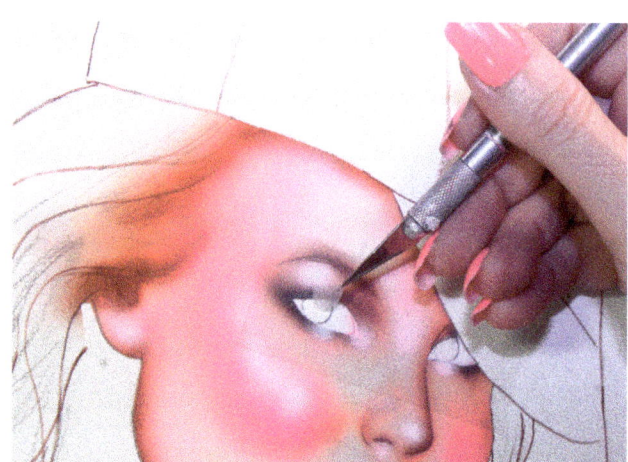

Now I can cut out the iris.

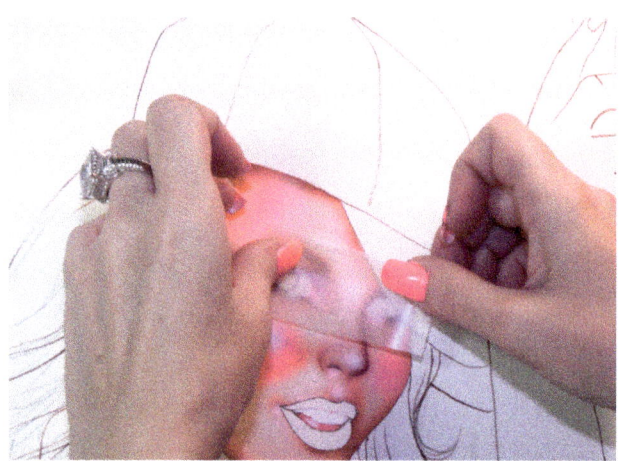

Laying more frisket over eyes to prepare for color.

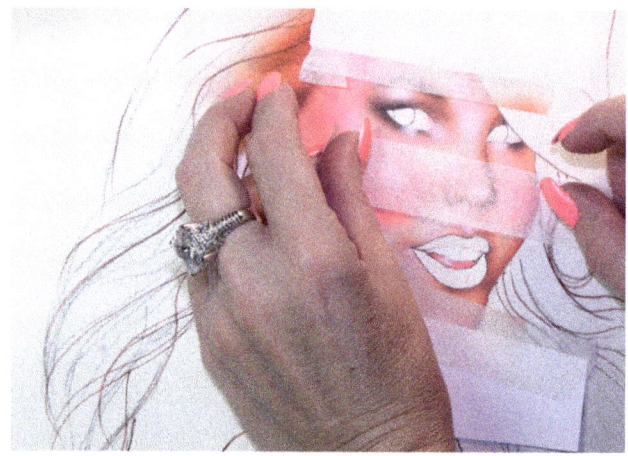

I'm careful to tape off the open areas to protect them from overspray.

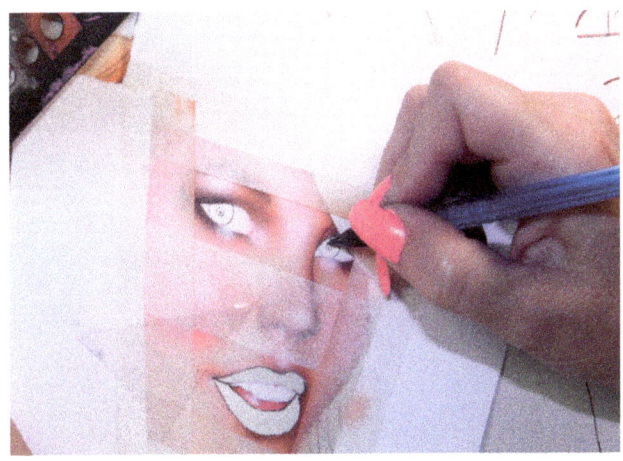

I start the iris color using a blue pencil for highlights.

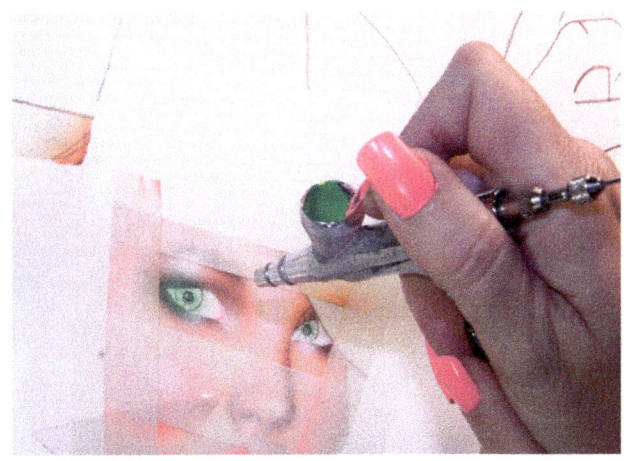

I use a green mixture and spray the eye color in.

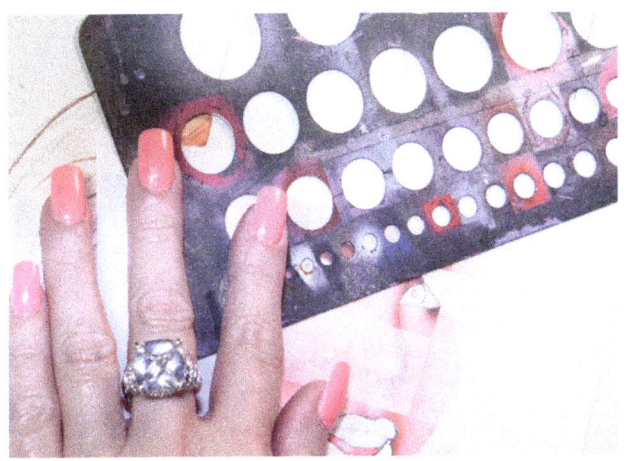

Using a template, I draw in the pupil.

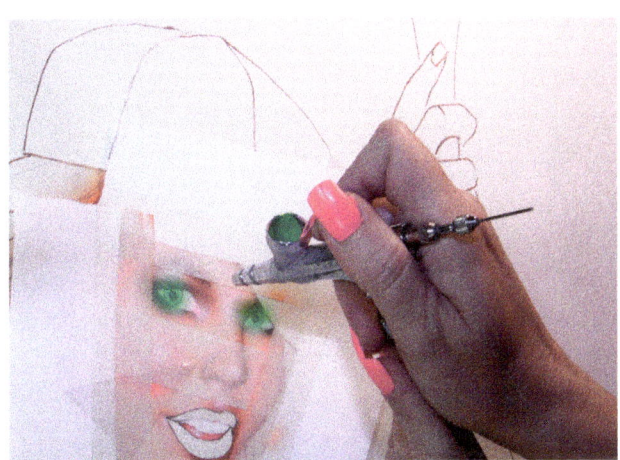

Darkening my green with more eye color.

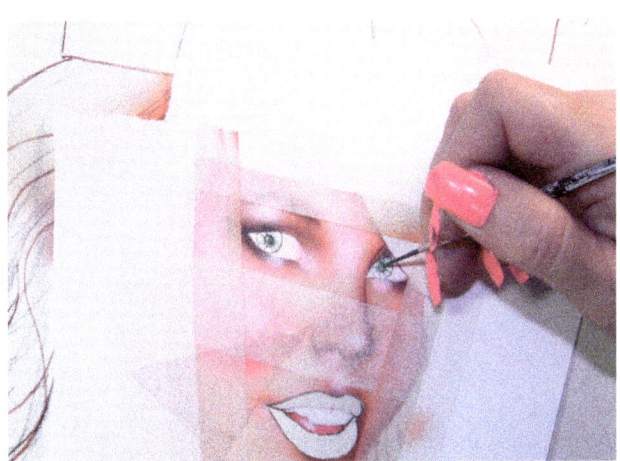

Now, using a fine brush, I add more lines to the iris in a dark green.

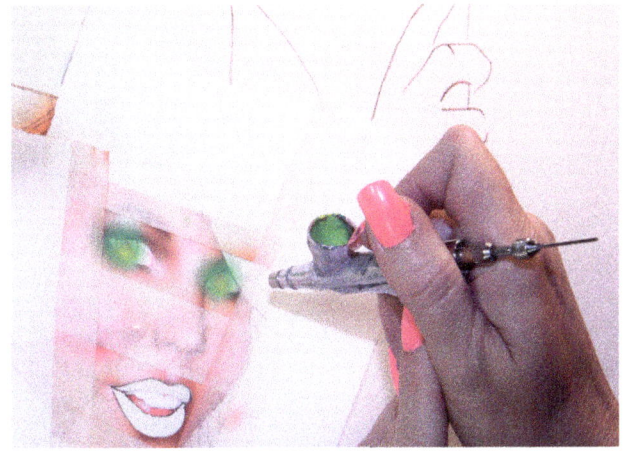

I now add yellow, which creates a lime color and adds depth.

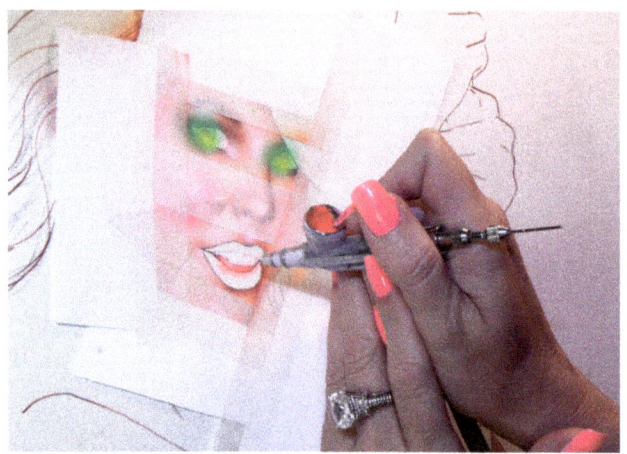

With eyes and mouth cut out of the frisket I begin to apply the lip color.

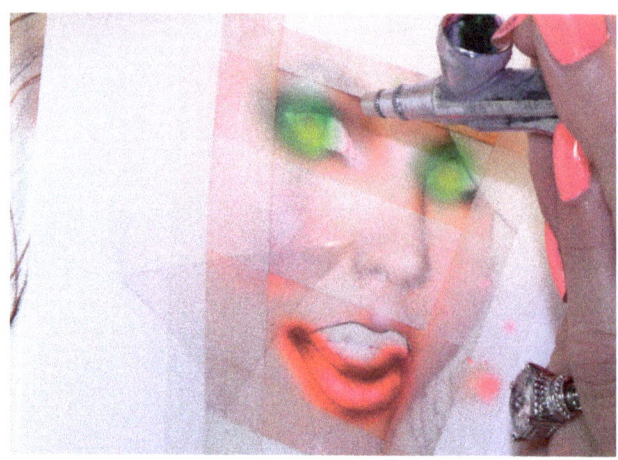

I darken the upper part of the iris with a dark forrest green.

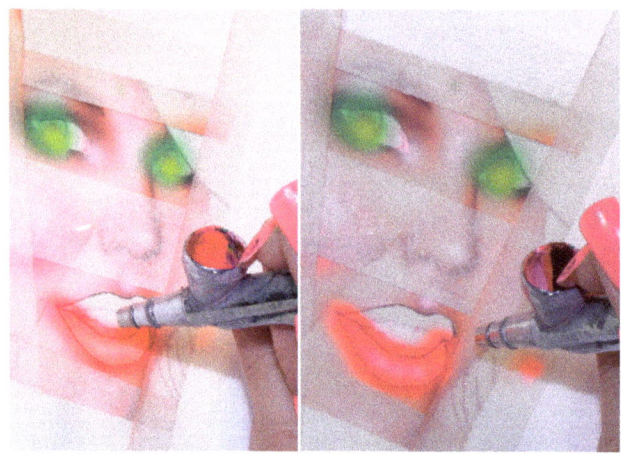

You can see I'm adding more lip color and highlights.

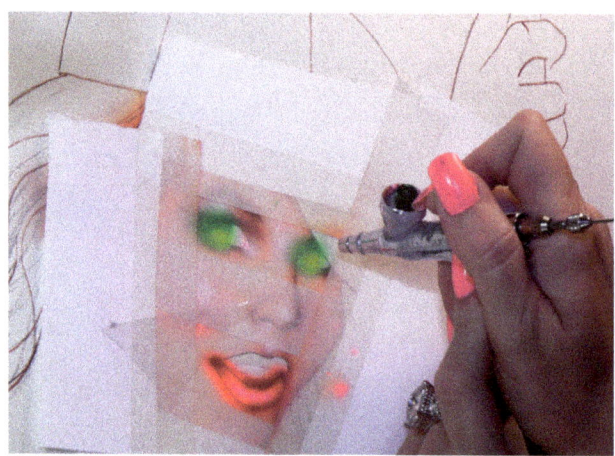

At this point you can see the effect of the dark green.

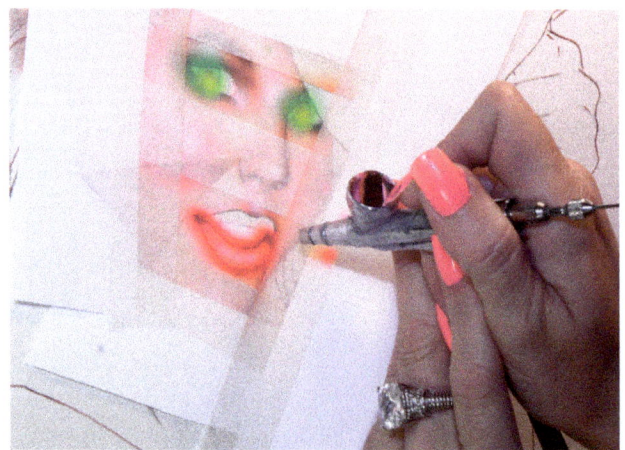

Here I'm using a pink and brown mixture to darken the corners of her mouth.

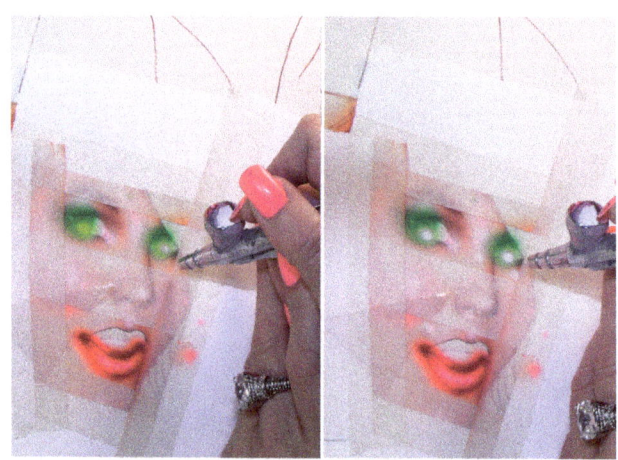

Next, I add white highlights to the lower iris.

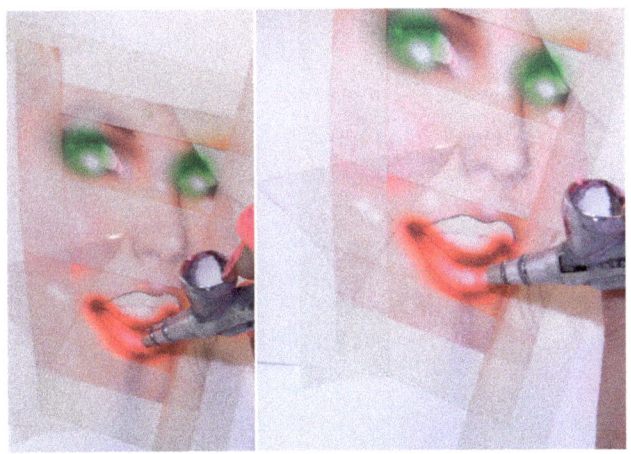

More highlights, added to the lips this time.

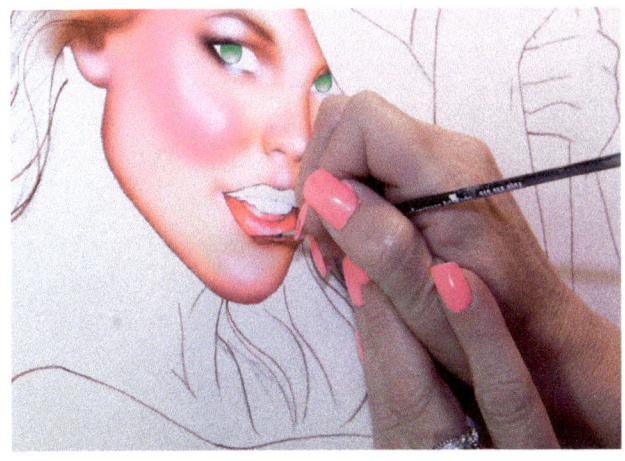

I outline the bottom lip with a pink and brown mix.

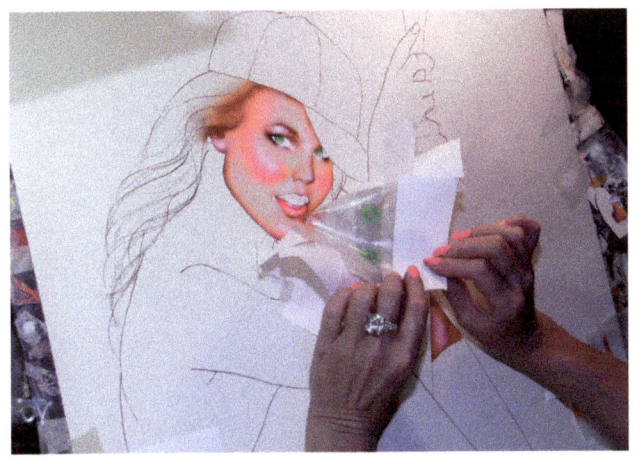

Satisfied with the lower lip and iris, I peel the film away.

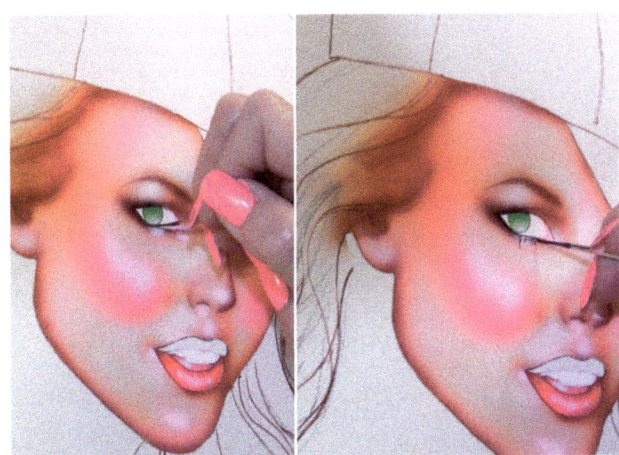

Using a fine brush again I start the eyelashes.

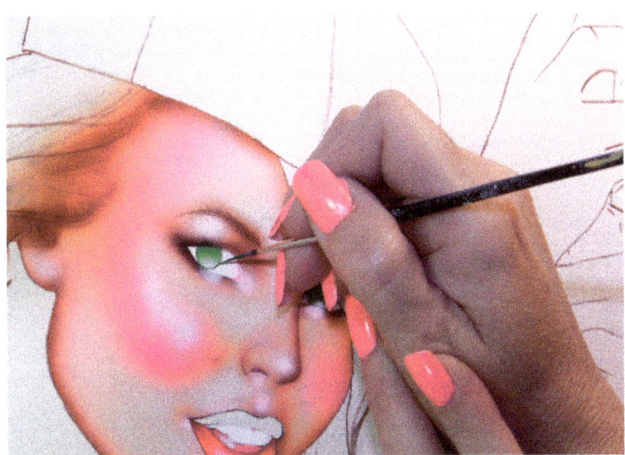

Here I outline the iris starting with a dark green, then black.

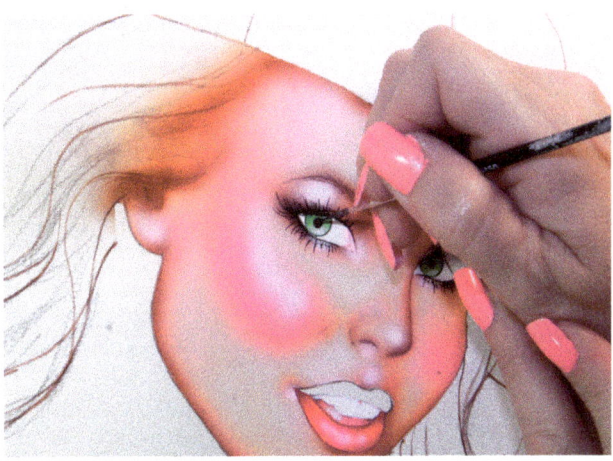

Bottom lashes first, and then I move to the upper lid.

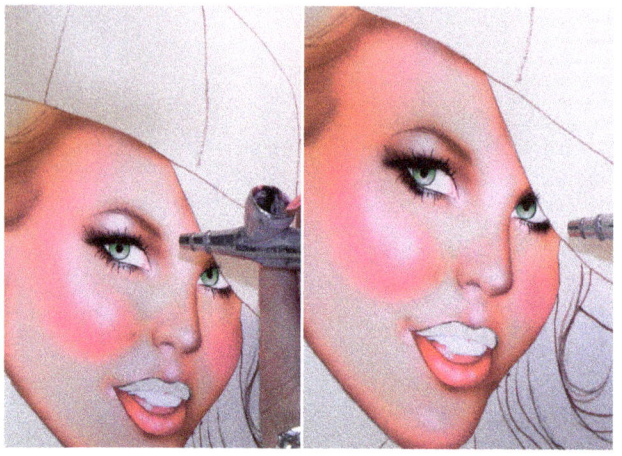

Using black I lightly spray over the lashes to soften them.

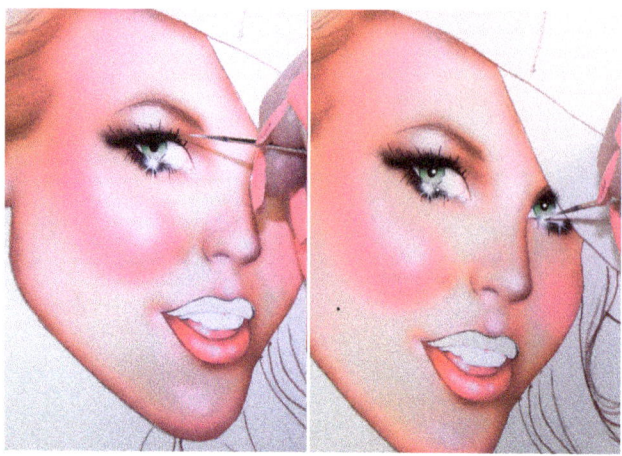

Using white and a fine brush, I add some sparkle to her eyes.

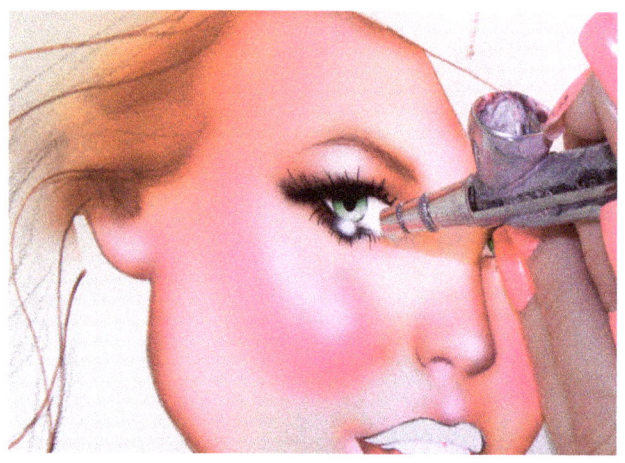

Here I add tiny dots - highlights - with my airbrush, using white paint.

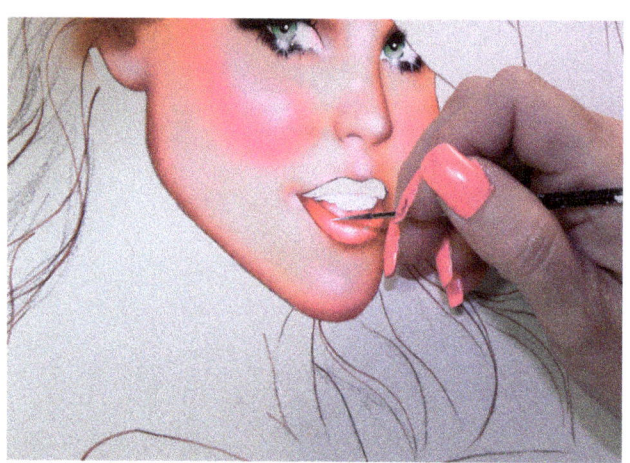

Using a fine brush and white, I add dots to her lip.

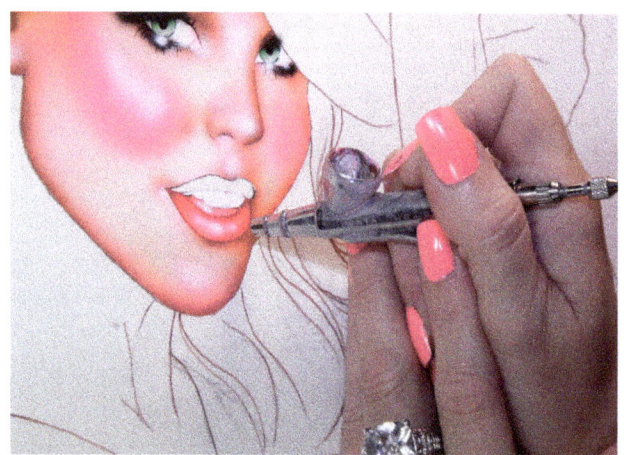

More white highlights on the lower lip.

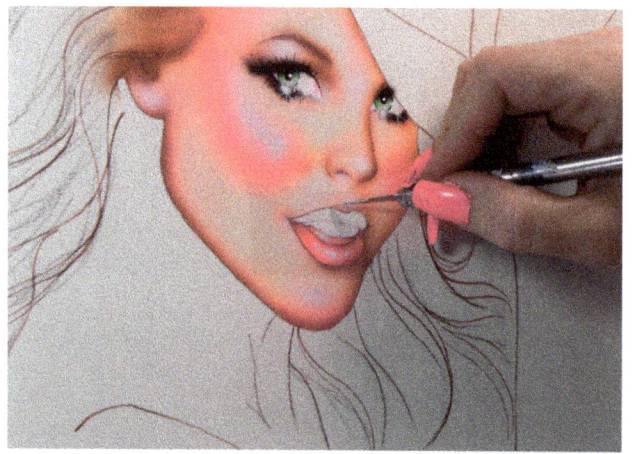

I now move to the upper lip, cutting out the frisket first.

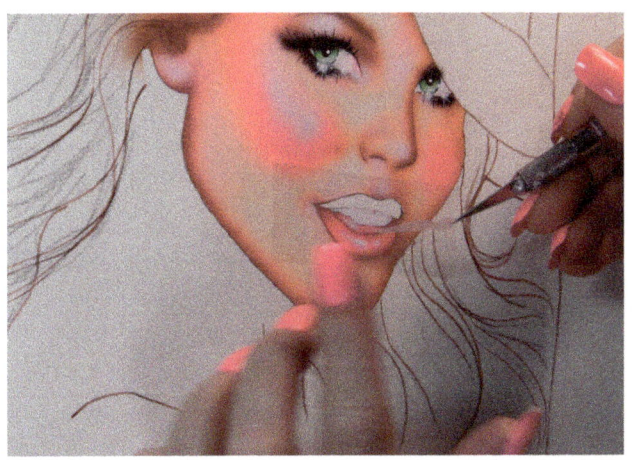
I peel the frisket away from the lip to be painted.

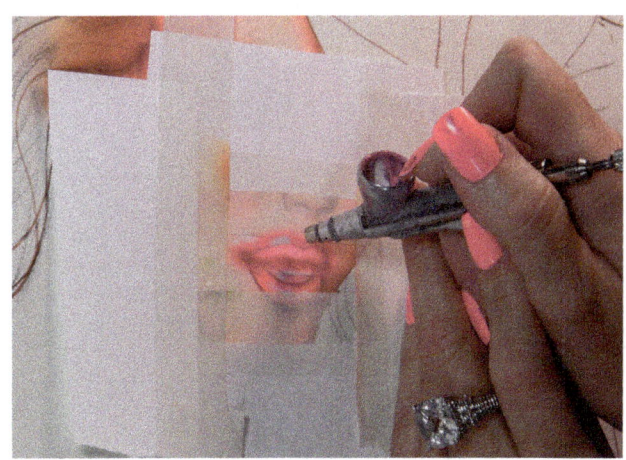
I now put in the white highlights.

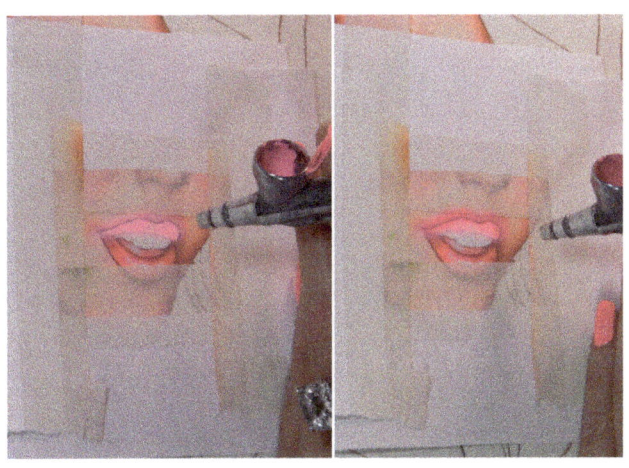
Having masked off the area around the lip, I begin with light pink.

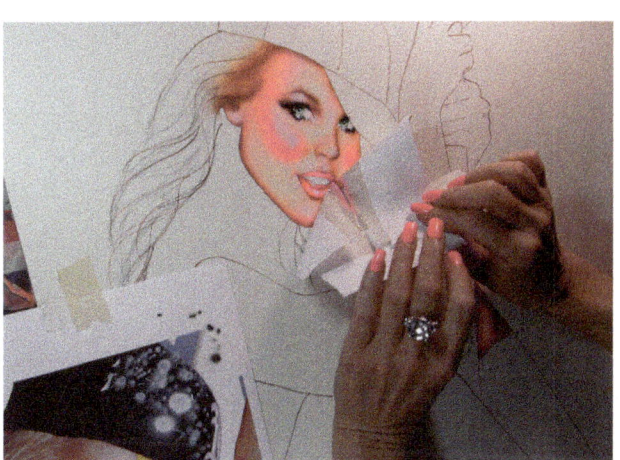
Satisfied - I peel the frisket away.

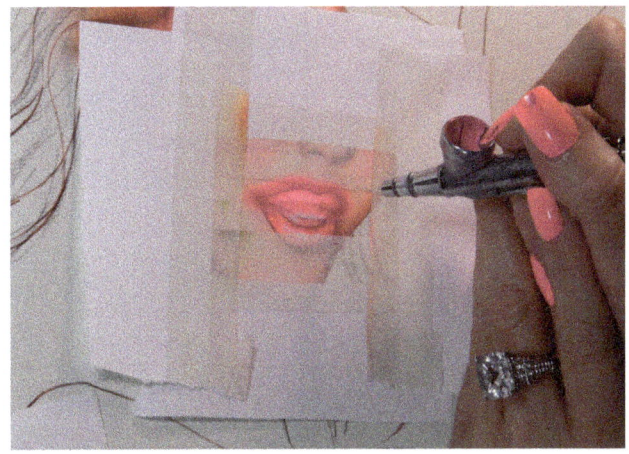
I add more pink with a drop of brown.

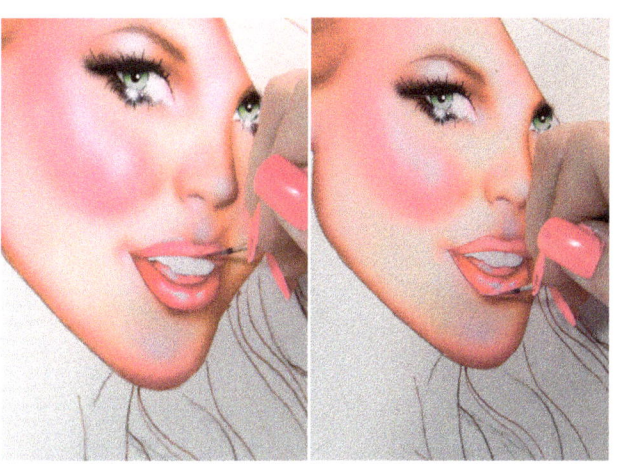
I outline the upper lip in a pink and brown mix.

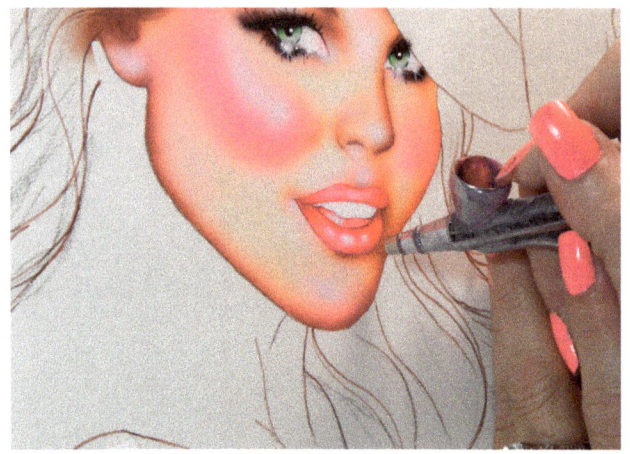

Here I'm adding more white highlights.

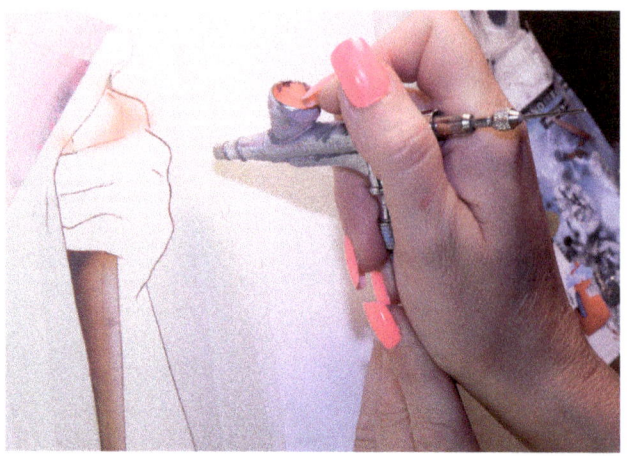

With the surrounding areas masked off, I begin working on the skin tones.

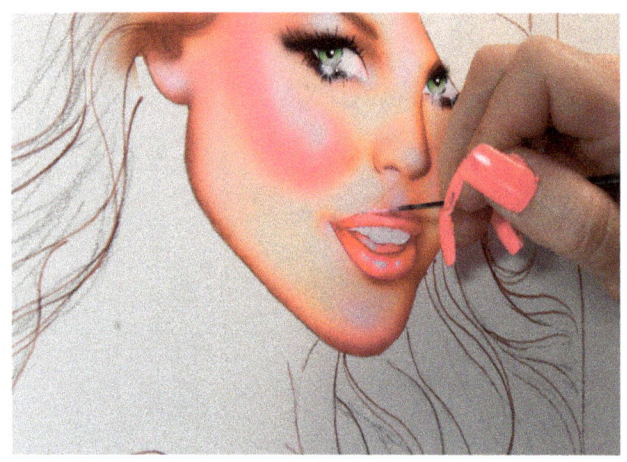

Using a fine brush I add dots in white for that "wet" look.

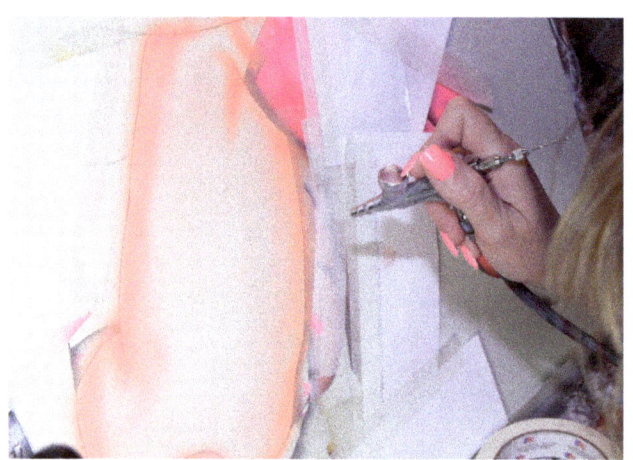

Here, I'm adding in the base tones...

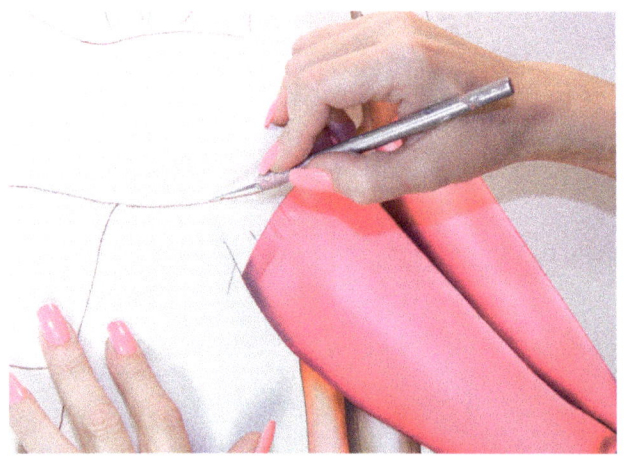

I switch to the body, outlining with a fine brush and light brown paint.

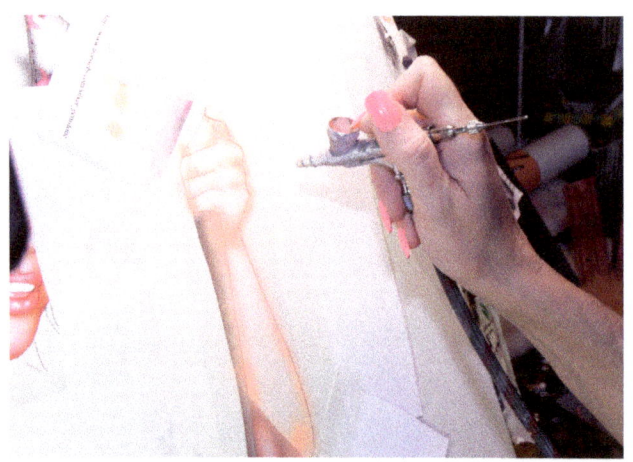

...and defining areas that will be darkened later.

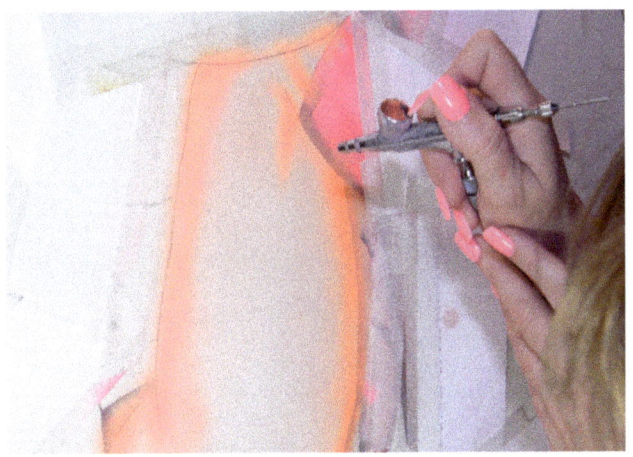

After darkening my mix with pink and brown, I deepen the skin tones...

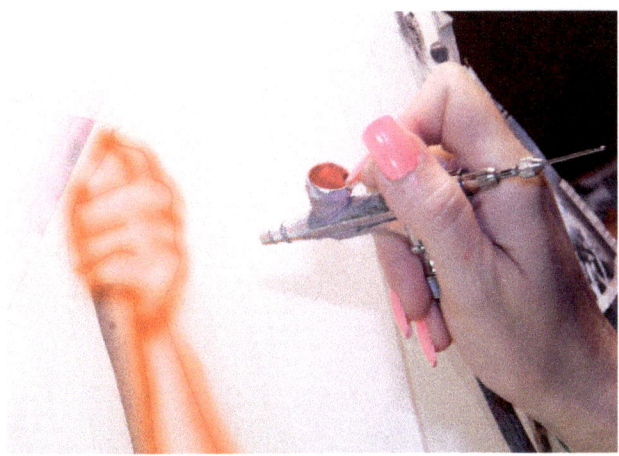

Deepening tones again with the deep pink mix.

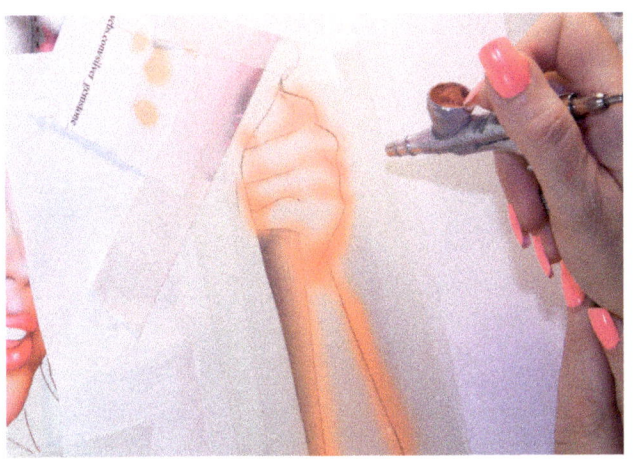

...and better define the knuckles and fingers.

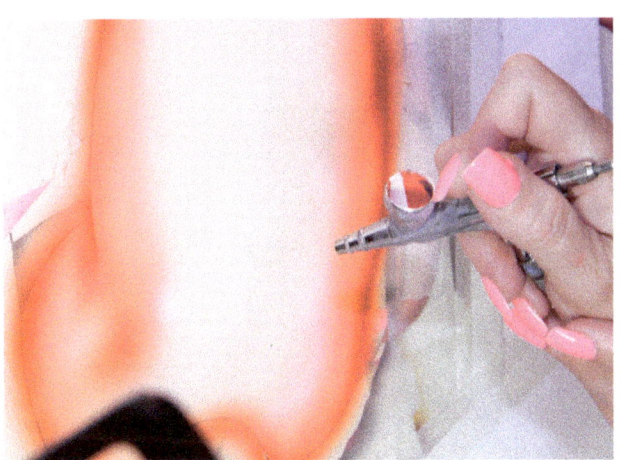

Defining and deepening the muscles and curves.

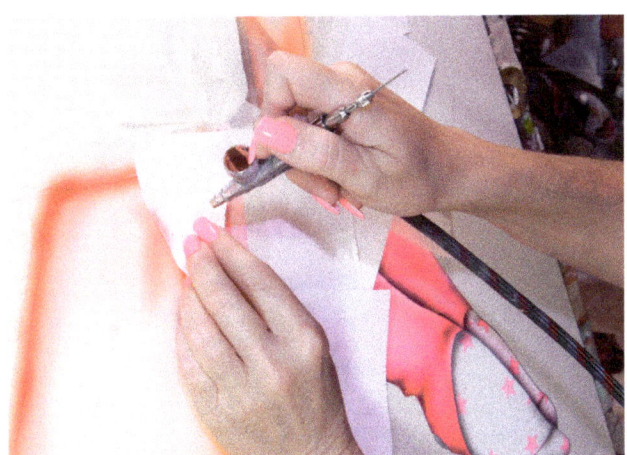

Here I create a simple paper mask for a curve on the leg.

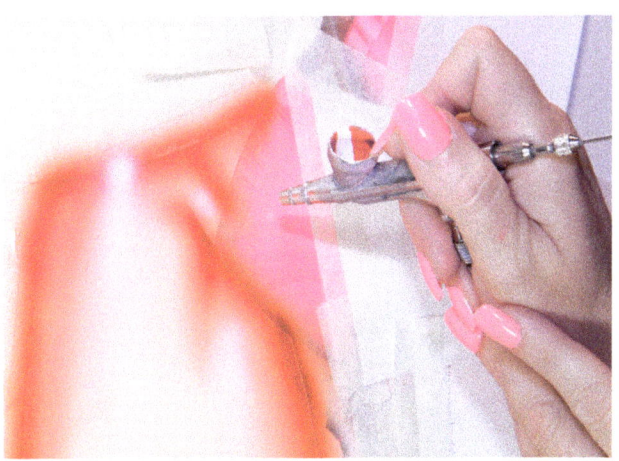

With white, I now add highlights.

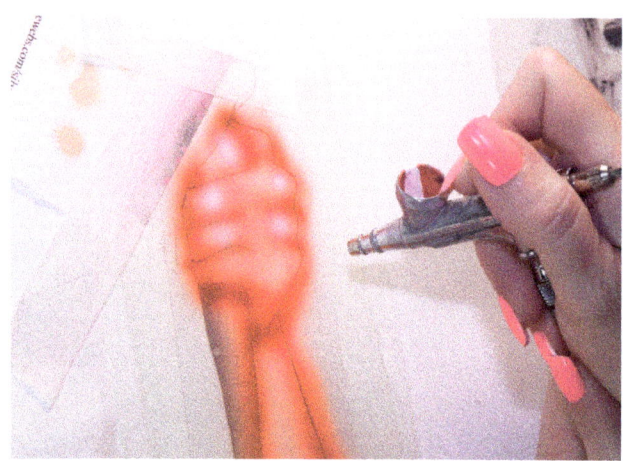

I add white highlights to her knuckles.

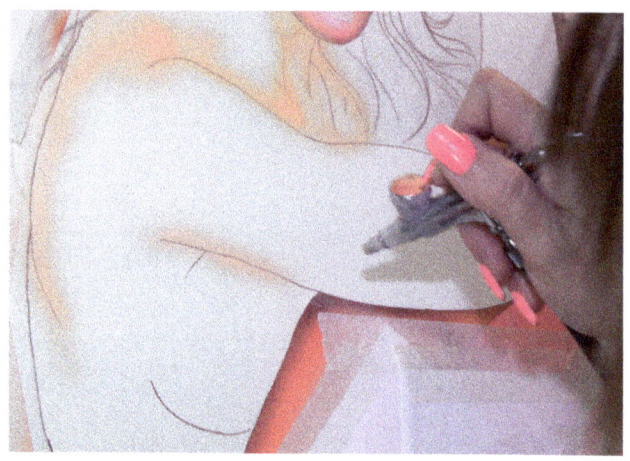

Using a mix of flesh yellow and pink I begin to render the skin.

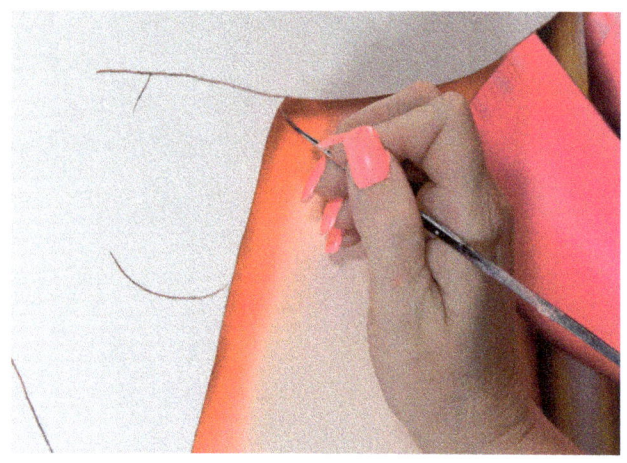

Once the frisket is pulled away I outline her leg with a pink and brown mix.

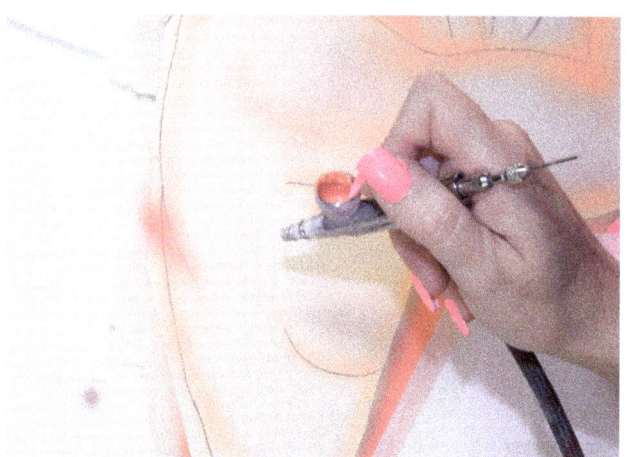

Using a darkening spray mix of pink and brown, I start to work on better definition.

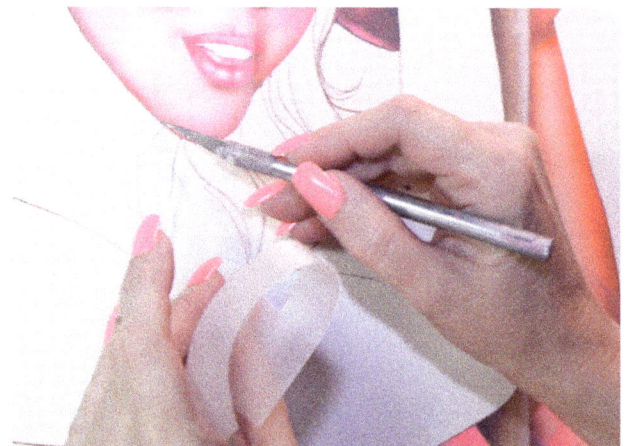

With the face covered and protected by the frisket, I can begin to work on body tones.

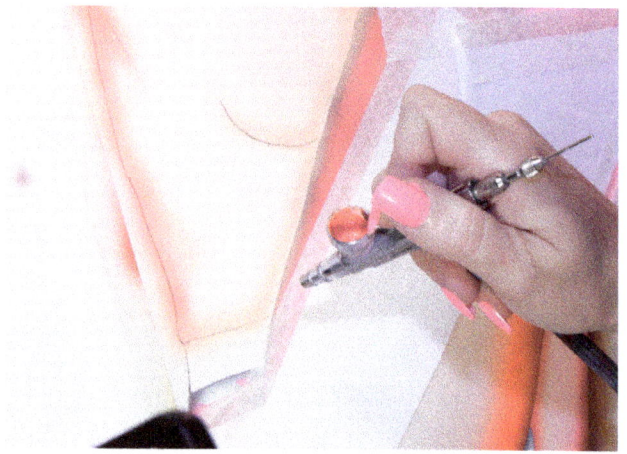

Using brown, I add shading and shadows.

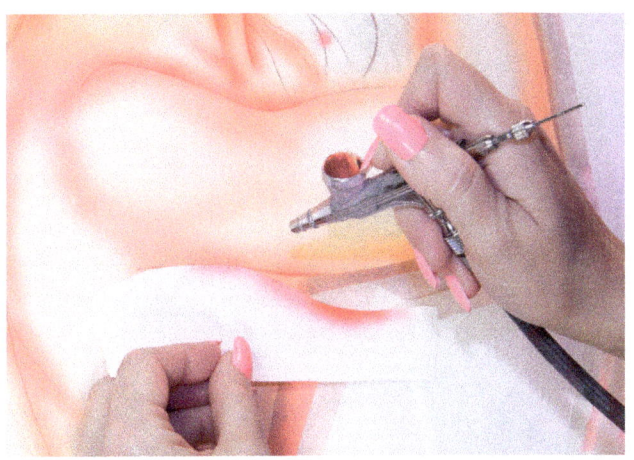

With the help of a loose paper mask I define her arm.

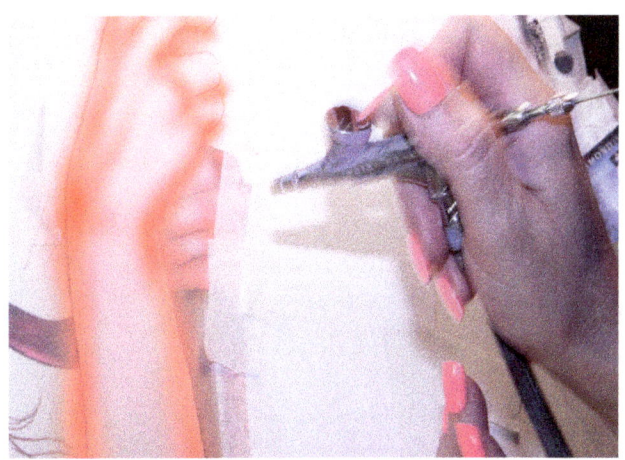

Next, I define her wrist in brown.

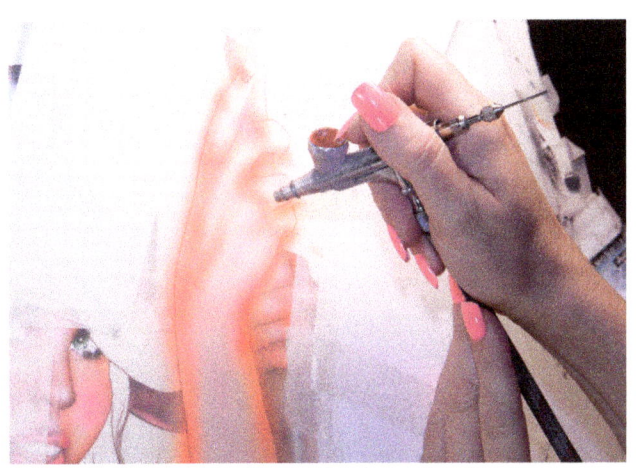

I define the hands with a mix of brown.

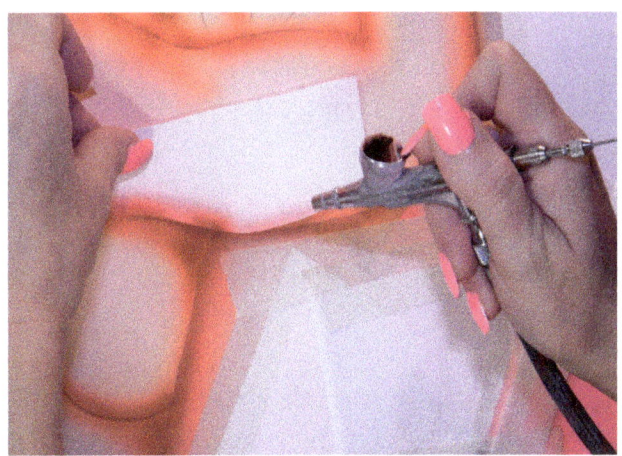

With a loose mask covering the arm, I add shading to the breast.

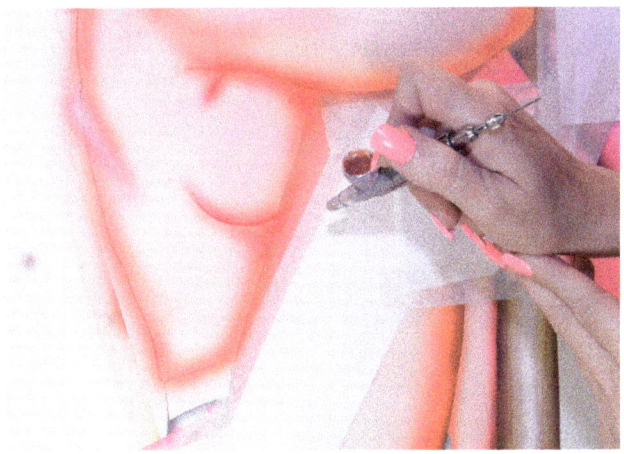

I add more shadows with brown.

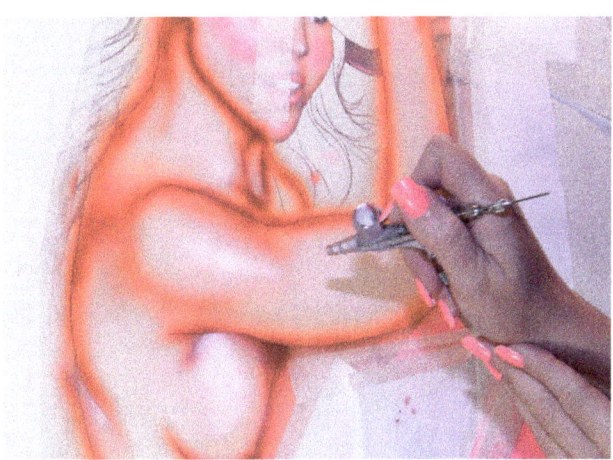

Then I use white to add highlights and define the arm muscle.

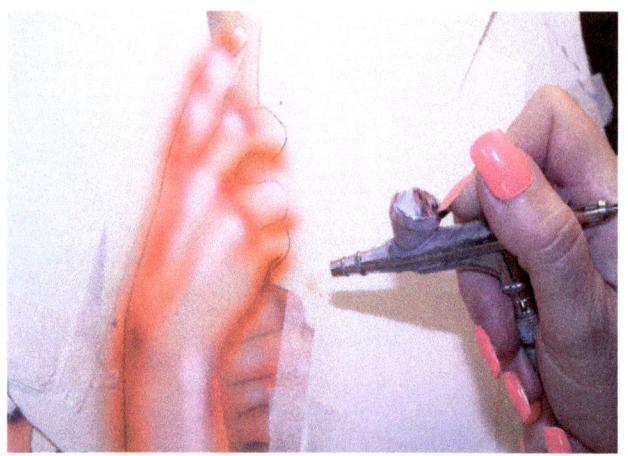

I highlight the knuckles again, and her wrist, in white.

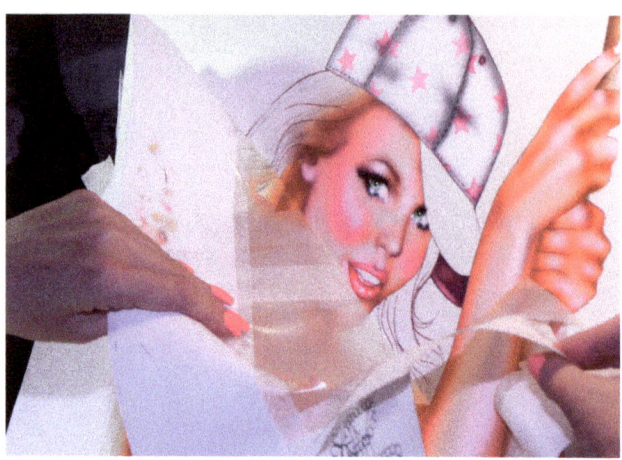

I peel the frisket away now that the body is complete.

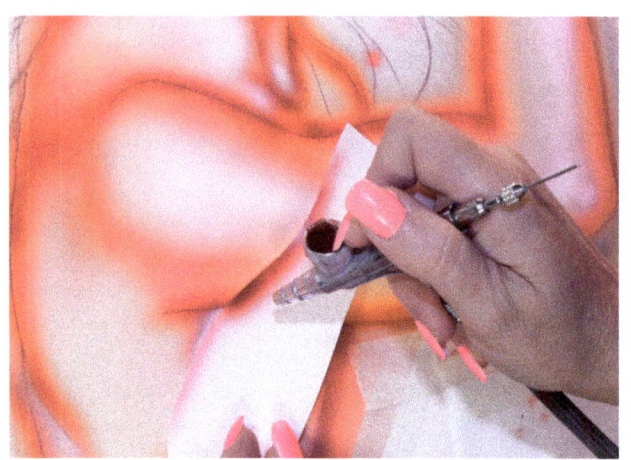

Using a loose mask again to define the area.

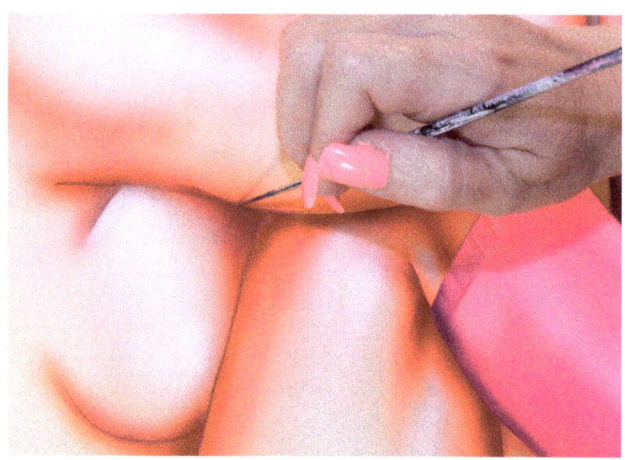

Using a fine brush again, I define the edge with dark brown.

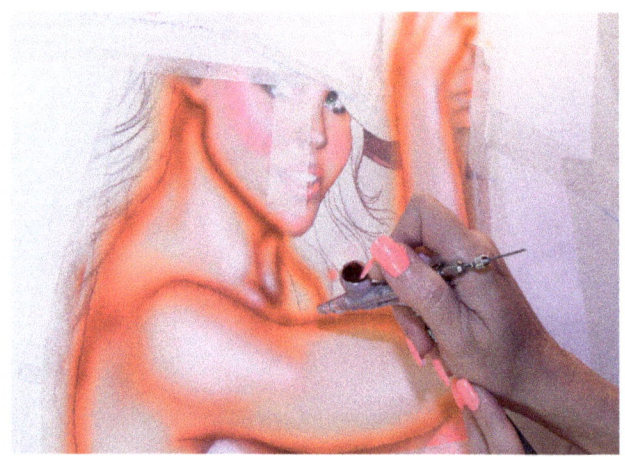

I'm shading here with dark brown.

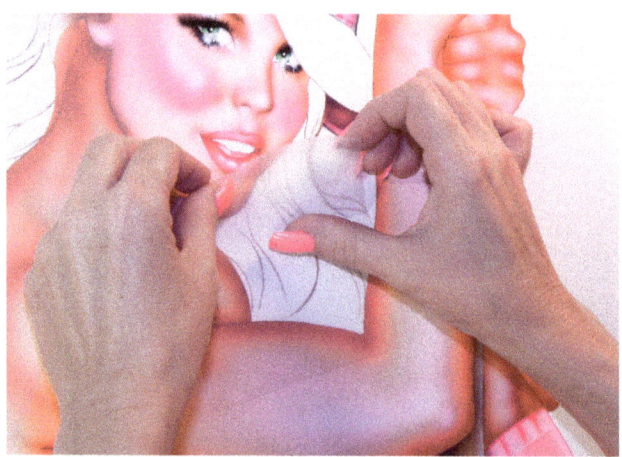

I mask off the face and body to protect them as I render the hair.

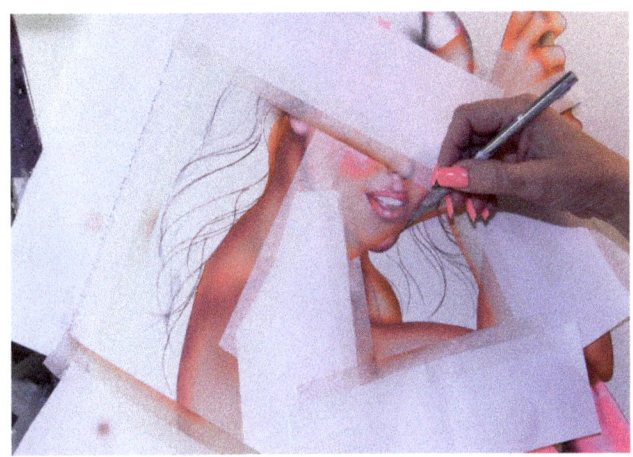

With most of the area masked off, I cut out an area for her hair.

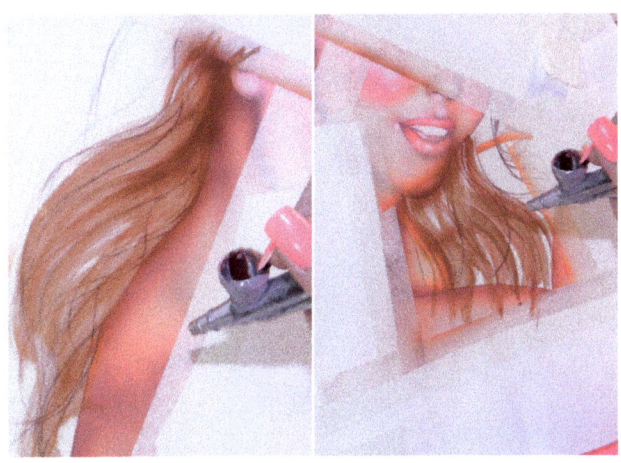

Once the brush strokes are complete, I use brown in my airbrush to soften the hair.

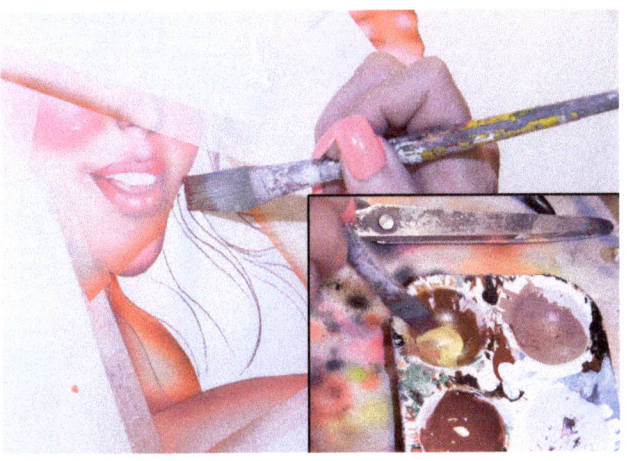

I start with a wide, fairly dry brush, and a mix of brown paint.

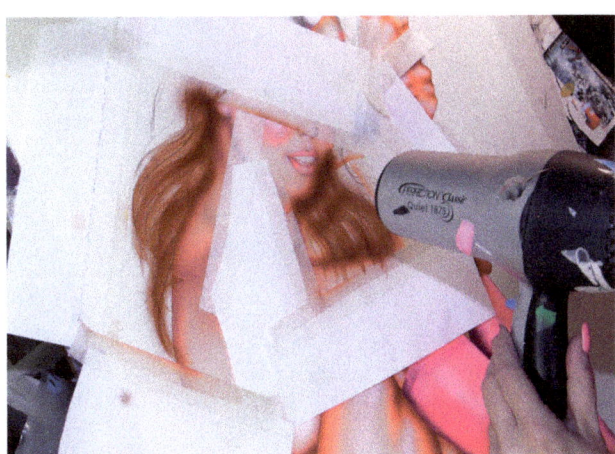

A blow dryer helps to speed the process as rendering hair takes a lot of paint.

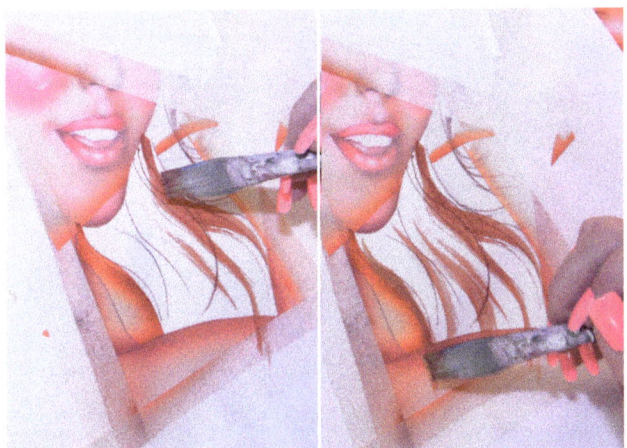

I use the brush in an almost random fashion to create the texture of hair.

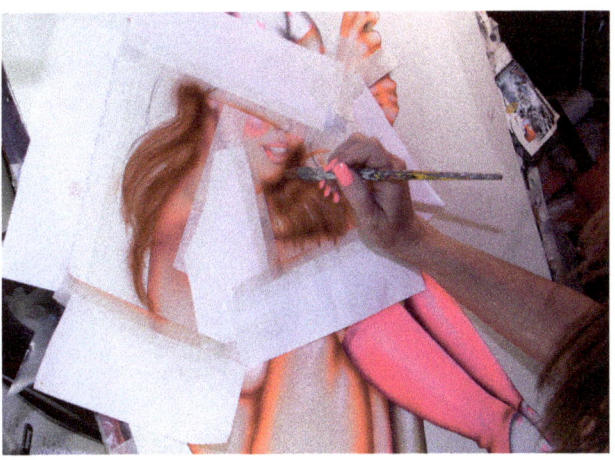

After I've airbrushed to soften, I go in again with the wide brush and add highlights.

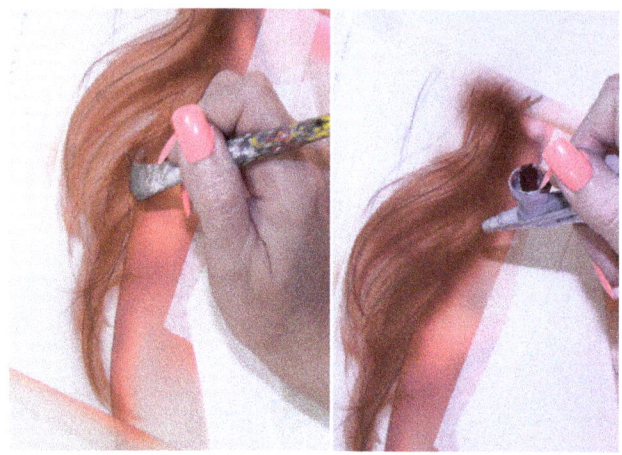

More brush work, followed by more work with the airbrush.

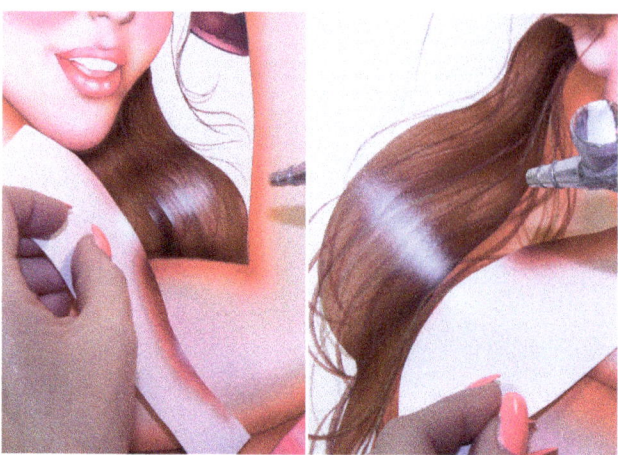

I add highlights to the hair in sections, for a hint of realism.

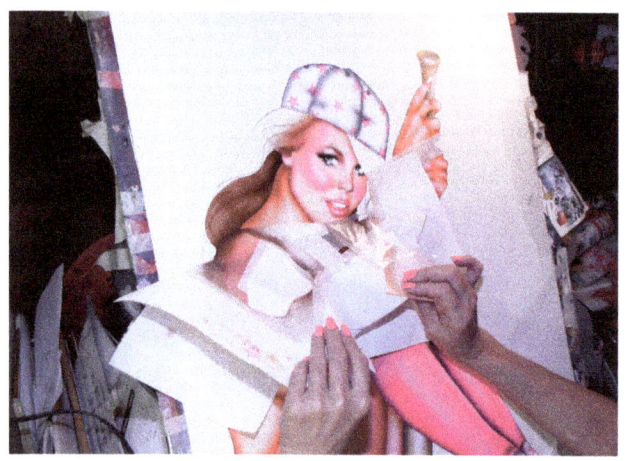

Now I can peel the frisket away from a section of completed hair.

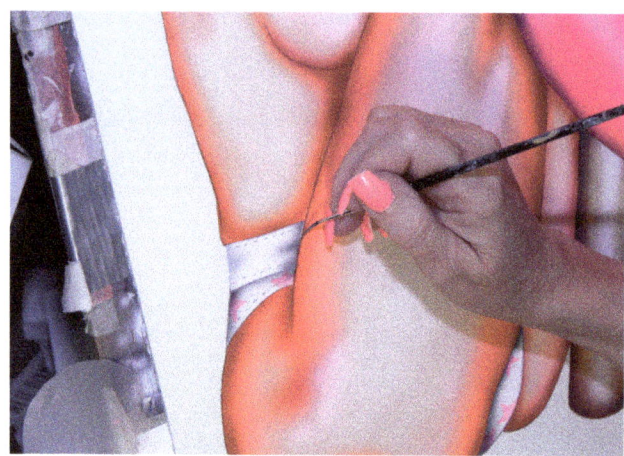

I now detail stitching in the panty waistline.

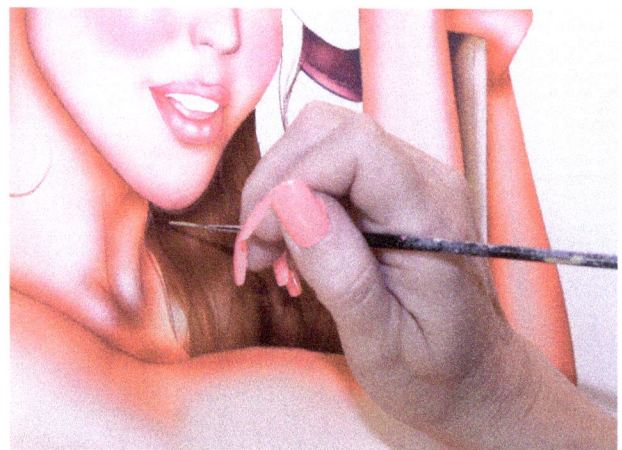

Using my fine brush and brown paint I add loose hair strands.

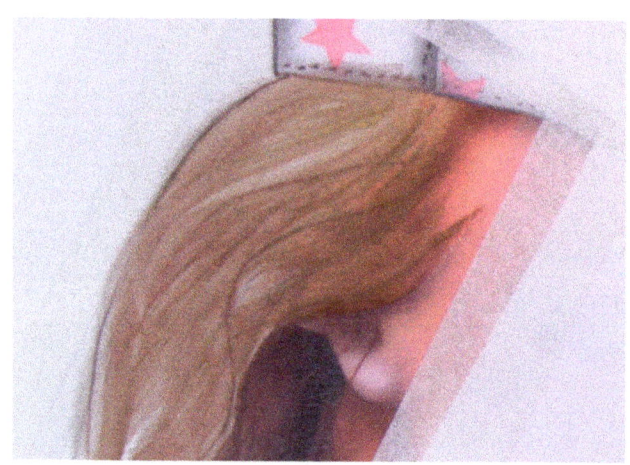

Close up of loose hair strands.

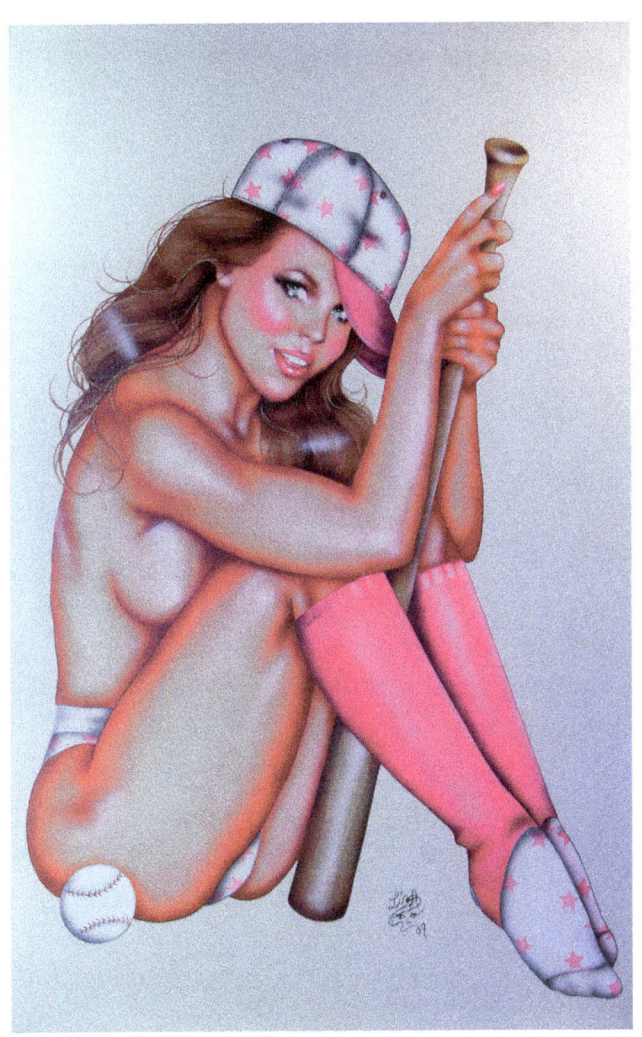

The last step - sign it. XOXO

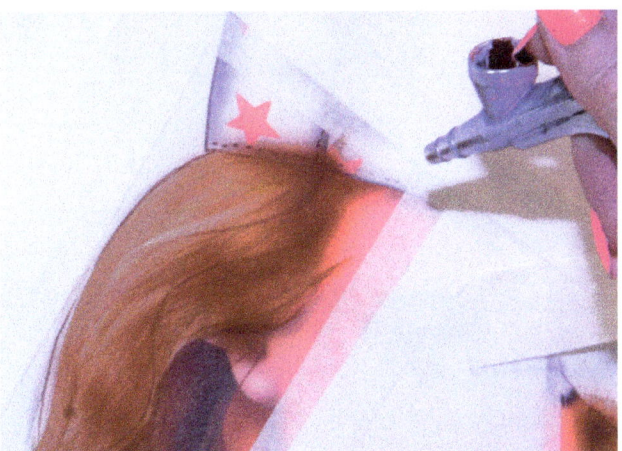

I blend the hair with a brown tone...

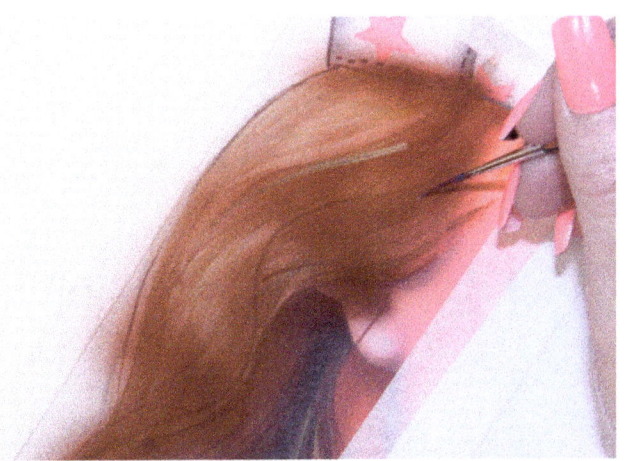

... and add loose strands in gold and brown.

Details make the difference: The eyes with their highlights, the wet-look lips, the hair with random strands in a lighter tone, even the stitching on the hat.

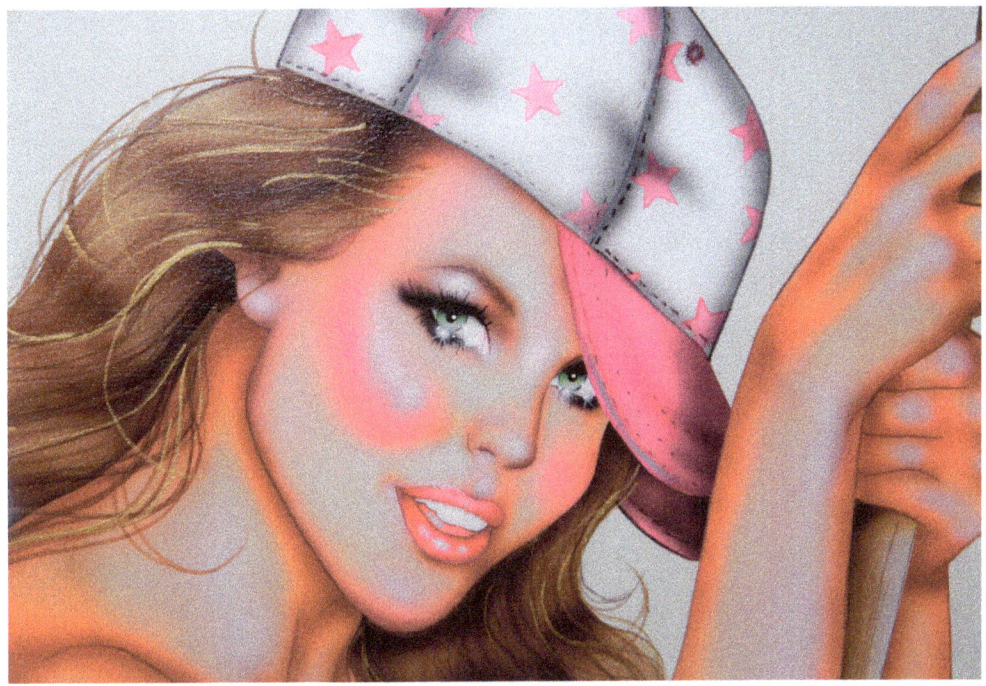

Elizabeth Austin Q&A

Give us a little background on you, how did you get started in art, and are pin-ups the main focus of the work you do?

I was always drawing; in fact I started to draw before I could write my name. When I was still pretty young I found my uncle's stash of magazines, that was my introduction to Vargas. Those images stayed in my brain since childhood.

In 2001 I finally decided to get an airbrush and give it a try, at that point I started studying Olivia and some others.

Who inspires you, who are some of the artists you look up to?

Olivia, Vargas and Petty I would say. I like the class, the subtleness, the beauty of the women, they're almost fantasy women. I also like Dru Blair for his photo-realism, his work is amazing.

Novice artists sometimes have trouble rendering believable skin tones, how do you achieve life-like skin tones?

A lot of mixing of colors, trial and error, always remember that there has to be some yellow in there somewhere. I start with yellow, with flesh and pink, all mixed together.

Another area where people have trouble is with faces, are there tricks or particular methods you use to create a good portrait?

I have always been focused on the face, it comes naturally to me. You have to focus on the eyes; they should follow you as you move around the room. If you have trouble with the balance of the face, you can hold it up to a mirror and then it's easy to see where you are off.

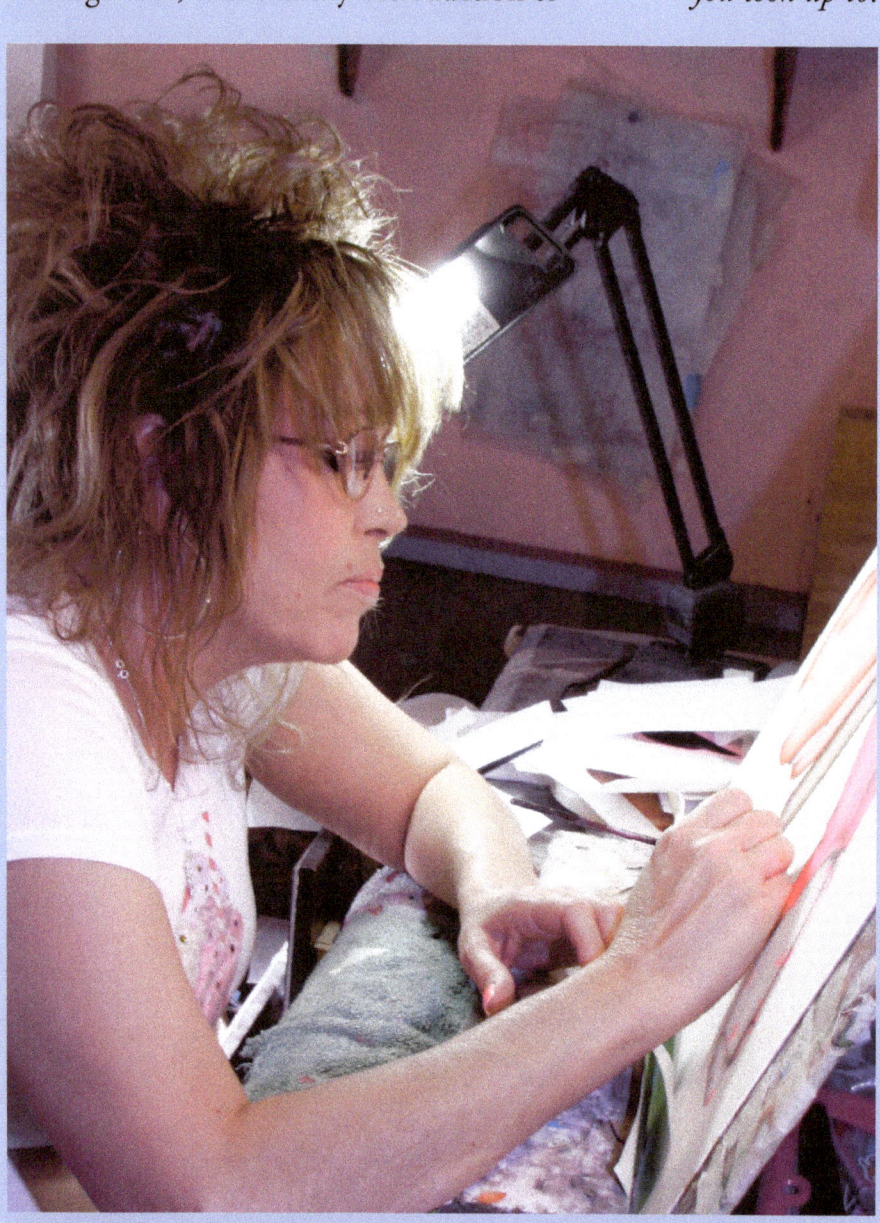

Another self-taught artist, Liz got her first taste of pin-ups when she discovered an uncle's stash of girlie magazines.

Elizabeth Austin Q&A

How about the equipment you use, which airbrush do you typically use and why? And what do you use for a compressor?

I like the Iwata hp-b, and a Delta compressor. I think all the compressors are good.

Which brand of paint do you use and why?

I use the Createx brand acrylic, it's the one I started with. I'm a creature of habit, I just stay with that paint.

How did you learn to mix paint to create unique colors?

Trial and error, also a lot of times you can find a good mentor, many artists are willing to share with other artists. I was missing the golden skin tones and it was Carlos Cartagena who told me I needed to have some yellow in the mix.

Do you use other media like hand brushes to add detail or achieve effects that are hard to do with an airbrush?

I have always used hand brushes, to add detail. I need them for eyelashes, outlining small details, and creating wild hair, The small brushes are good for hair.

If you do work with mod-els, how do you pick them and where do you find them?

A lot of models contact me. But their photos usually are not up to par.

What makes a good pin-up?

One that leaves something to the imagination. You want to see more but you are glad you can't, a pin up is a fantasy, it's what art is about.

If you were going to give ten words of advice to someone just starting out, what would that advice be?

Look at books, study the old masters, Petty, Vargas and Olivia, study, study, study. Books are the very best things. They don't even have to be how-to books, coffee table books are good too.

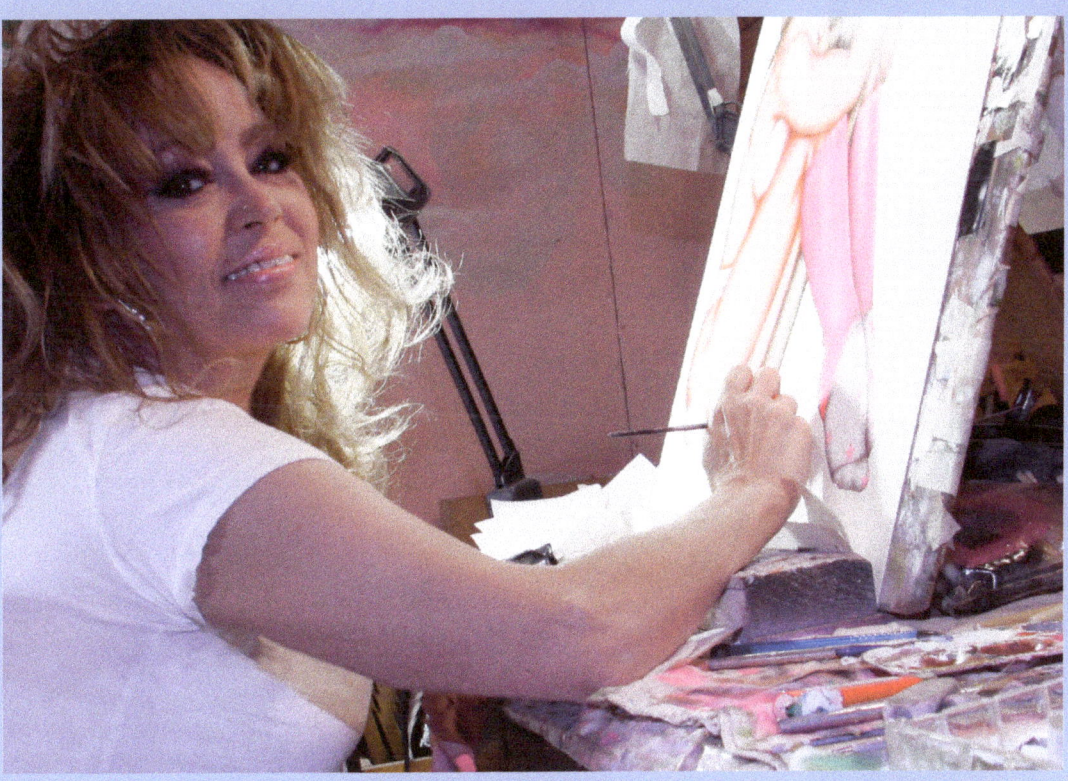

The one-time tattoo artist now spends her time doing pin-ups for a growing list of clients.

Find these Wolfgang titles on-line by title or ISBN

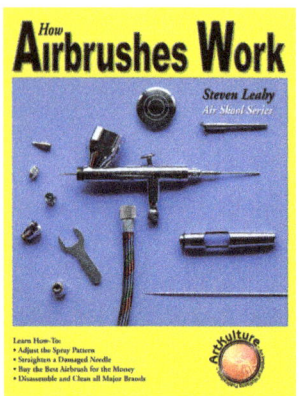

HOW AIRBRUSHES WORK

How Airbrushes Work is a comprehensive look at airbrush use, maintenance and repair. The book begins with a brief look at airbrush history, then moves to a discussion of the various airbrush types.

Too many first-time airbrush users have trouble because they don't know how to clean and maintain the airbrush. This new book from Wolfgang explains how to disassemble, clean and repair all the major brands. Even the best airbrush in the world isn't any good without a source of air. Steve discusses different compressor types and the advantages or disadvantages of each.

Two chapters explain airbrush painting basics - from types of paint to trigger control, and three basic strokes all painters need to know. Steve closes the book with a gallery of airbrush art, and an airbrush buyer's guide to help readers choose wisely when they buy their first, or their fifth, airbrush.

ISBN: 978-1-929133-71-0   144 Pages $24.95   Over 400 photos, B&W

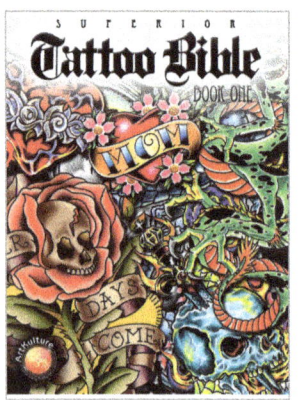

TATTOO BIBLE BOOK ONE

Whether you are preparing for your first tattoo or your twenty-seventh, you need artwork and designs that are just-right. Tattoo Bible, authored by Superior Tattoo, provides well over 500 pieces of unique flash art - flash never before compiled in one single book.

While most tattoo books available today concentrate on one specific genre, this book covers many different genres and the ideas are endless. This is not just a book to add to your collection - this is your collection. You can combine different pieces of art from within the book, or just take them as is. This book is for you and your imagination to do with as you wish.

ISBN: 978-1929133 84-0 $27.95   Over 500 photos, 100% color

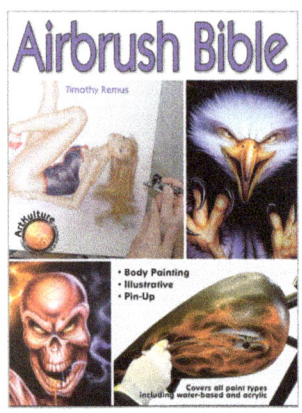

AIRBRUSH BIBLE

Airbrush Bible offers something for anyone interested in the art of airbrushing. Whether your goal is reality flames on a motorcycle tank, or a three-dimensional eagle in mid-pounce.

Airbrush Bible offers help spraying on various substrate and media. T-Shirt artists will find advice on the best paint to use, and how to give the image longevity. Anyone working with hot rods and motorcycles needs to know how much to over-reduce urethane-based paints. Hobby painters need to understand acrylic paints.

Each chapter is a one-on-one seminar that takes the reader from the first sketch to the finished product. In total, Airbrush Bible provides the reader with fourteen chapters, each one offering a complete sequence and an interview with the artist.

ISBN: 978-1-929133-86-4   176 Pages $29.95   Over 400 photos, 100% color

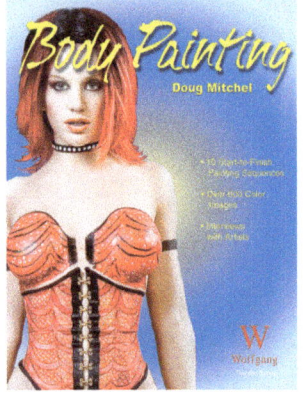

BODY PAINTING

Body Painting uses a wealth of photos to show just how the application of colorful paint can transform a child's face or a woman's body into another dimension. Each of ten chapters presents the start-to-finish painting project of one established artist.

The best teachers are the men and women who have already mastered a skill. Body Painting used interviews with the artists to explore their preference for tools, their favorite techniques and how they learned their skills.

The discussion of paint choices includes airbrushed body make up, textile acrylics, liquid latex and even markers from companies like Crayola. As pointed out in the captions and the interviews, each material has good points and bad, all are covered in Body Painting.

ISBN: 978-1-929133-66-6   144 Pages $27.95   Over 500 photos, 100% color

Wolfgang Publication Titles

For a current list visit our website at www.wolfpub.com

ILLUSTRATED HISTORY
Ultimate Triumph Collection	$49.95
American Police Motorcycles - Revised	$24.95

BIKER BASICS
Custom Motorcycle Fabrication	$27.95
Custom Bike Building Basics	$24.95
Custom Bike Building Advanced	$24.95
Sportster/Buell Engine Hop-Up Guide	$24.95
Sheet Metal Fabrication Basics	$24.95
How to Fix American T-Twin Motorcycles	$27.95

COMPOSITE GARAGE
Composite Materials Handbook #1	$27.95
Composite Materials Handbook #2	$27.95
Composite Materials Handbook #3	$27.95

HOT ROD BASICS
How to A/C Your Hot Rod	$24.95
So-Cal Speed Shop's How to Build Hot Rod Chassis	$24.95
Hot Rod Wiring	$27.95
How to Chop Tops	$24.95

CUSTOM BUILDER SERIES
H-D Sportster Hop-Up & Customizing Guide	$27.95
How to Build A Café Racer	$27.95
Advanced Custom Motorcycle Wiring - Revised	$27.95
How to Build an Old Skool Bobber Sec Ed	$27.95
How To Build The Ultimate V-Twin Motorcycle	$24.95
Advanced Custom Motorcycle Assembly & Fabrication	$27.95
How to Build a Cheap Chopper	$27.95

MOTORCYCLE RESTORATION SERIES
Triumph Restoration - Unit 650cc	$29.95
Triumph MC Restoration Pre-Unit	$29.95

SHEET METAL
Advanced Sheet Metal Fabrication	$27.95
Ultimate Sheet Metal Fabrication	$24.95
Sheet Metal Bible	$29.95

AIR SKOOL SKILLS
How To Draw Monsters	$27.95
Airbrush Bible	$29.95
How Airbrushes Work	$24.95

PAINT EXPERT
How To Airbrush, Pinstripe & Goldleaf	$27.95
Kosmoski's New Kustom Painting Secrets	$27.95
Pro Pinstripe Techniques	$27.95
Advanced Pinstripe Art	$27.95

TATTOO U Series
Advanced Tattoo Art - Revised	$27.95
Cultura Tattoo Sketchbook	$32.95
Tattoo Sketchbook by Jim Watson	$32.95
Tattoo Sketchbook by Nate Powers	$27.95
Into The Skin The Ultimate Tattoo Sourcebook (Includes companion DVD)	$34.95
American Tattoos	$27.95
Tattoo Bible Book One	$27.95
Tattoo Bible Book Two	$27.95
Tattoo Bible Book Three	$27.95
Tattoo Lettering Bible	$27.95

TRADE SCHOOL SERIES
Learning The English Wheel	$27.95

LIFESTYLE
Bean're — Motorcycle Nomad	$18.95
George The Painter	$18.95
The Colorful World of Tattoo Models	$34.95

GUIDE BOOKS
Honda Motorcycles - Enthusiast Guide	$27.95

Sources

Liz Austin
lizpinupart@machlink.com
www.elizabethspinupart.com
www.creativeimagelicensing.com

Steve Driscoll
stevedriscoll1@netzero.net
stevedriscollcustoms.com
Sabina Kelly - www.sabinakelley.com
& www.myspace.com/sabinakelley

Susan Heidi
Susan Heidi Art Studios
P.O. Box 115
Garrison, NY 10524
www.susanheidi.com
(845) 424-6016

Steven Leahy
www.stevenleahy.com
stevenleahy@comcast.net

Tom Nguyen
Tom Nguyen Art
2084 12th Ave. W.
Shakopee, MN 55379
www.TomNguyenArt.com
tom@tomnguyenart.com

Steve Nunez
Steve Nunez of NYC, Sponsored by Alsa Corp. Paint
www.stevenunez.com

Edward Reed
edward@edwardreed.com
www.edwardreed.com